MAN
OF WAR

Duff Hart-Davis has written and edited fifty books on a wide variety of subjects, including eight adventure novels and a number of biographies. He worked on the *Sunday Telegraph* as Literary Editor and features writer, reporting from many parts of the world, and from 1986 to 2001 he contributed the weekly *Country Matters* column on rural affairs to the *Independent*. Together with his wife Phyllida he now lives in a 17th-century farmhouse on the Cotswold escarpment.

Also available by Duff Hart-Davis

The War That Never Was

MAN OF WAR

DUFF HART-DAVIS

arrow books

Published by Arrow Books 2013
2 4 6 8 10 9 7 5 3 1

First published in Great Britain in 2012 by
Century
Random House, 20 Vauxhall Bridge Road,
London SW1V 2SA

www.randomhouse.co.uk

Addresses for companies within The Random House Group Limited can be
found at: www.randomhouse.co.uk/offices.htm

The Random House Group Limited Reg. No. 954009

A CIP catalogue record for this book
is available from the British Library

ISBN 9780099568667

The Random House Group Limited supports the Forest Stewardship Council®
(FSC®), the leading international forest-certification organisation. Our books
carrying the FSC label are printed on FSC®-certified paper. FSC is the only
forest-certification scheme supported by the leading environmental organisations,
including Greenpeace. Our paper procurement policy can be found at
www.randomhouse.co.uk/environment

Typeset by Palimpsest Book Production Limited, Falkirk, Stirlingshire
Printed and bound in Great Britain by
CPI Group (UK) Ltd, Croydon CR0 4YY

CONTENTS

Author's Note

*The subject of this book was christened George Hugh Jocelyn Evans,
and as a boy was called Hugh. Later he changed his name to Alan
Hugh Hillgarth, and for the rest of his life he was known as Alan.
I have called him Hugh for as long as the family did, and then
switched to Alan.*

For Jocelyn, Justin, Tristan and Nigella

Introduction

When my wife and I moved to Co. Tipperary early in 1978, we soon heard that a former naval officer called Alan Hillgarth had retired to a big white house called Illannanagh on the shore of Lough Derg. Locals spoke of him not exactly with awe, but with curiosity, as if there was some mystery about him: they could not quite make him out.

They knew he had a naval background, because he styled himself 'Captain', but they had no idea what ships he had sailed in or what campaigns he had fought. He had been – they thought – some kind of a spy. Rumour had it that he was a friend and confidant of the wartime Prime Minister Winston Churchill – but again, no one was sure of details. People felt he must have some connection with Spain, for he wore Spanish-style hats, and a long, black cloak lined with scarlet at the hunt ball, and he employed Spanish servants. Indeed, with his rather dark complexion and bushy black eyebrows, he might well *be* Spanish. But what he had done in Spain, nobody could tell. All people knew for certain was that he had a boat on the lake, that he walked around his modest estate a good deal, and that he loved trees: he had his staff plant hundreds, and he was often to be seen pruning them, always wearing a jacket and tie.

We never met Hillgarth, alas, for he died a few months after we had arrived in the neighbourhood. Over the years I continued to hear snippets of information about him, but it was only when I began to research his career that I realised what an extraordinary life he had led. All the rumours, it turned out, had some foundation, but many more facets of his existence had remained hidden.

He had indeed, mainly by chance, become a man of war. He had served in the Royal Navy, and he had been wounded in the disastrous Gallipoli campaign of 1915–16 when only sixteen. He had hunted for gold in the Andes. In the 1930s he was British Consul in Majorca during the Spanish Civil War, during which he saved hundreds of lives. He was also involved with espionage in various difficult environments, most notably in Madrid from 1939 to 1943, when he ran a network of secret agents and struggled to keep Spain out of the world war. He was indeed a friend and confidant of Churchill, with whom he corresponded during and after the war, and as Chief of British Naval Intelligence in the Far East he made a significant contribution to the ultimate victory over Japan in 1945.

One of Hillgarth's most attractive characteristics was his lack of conventional ambition. He never wanted to become an admiral or to command a fleet. What he *did* want was to do his duty whenever called upon, and in many fields he was conspicuously successful.

The reason for his obscurity is simple. Not only was he extremely modest, never boasting about his achievements, but he was also outstandingly patriotic and discreet, believing that naval and military secrets should never be disclosed, even in peacetime. Although frequently urged to write his memoirs, he declined to do so for fear that any release of classified information might be of advantage to potential enemies.

In a letter he once wrote, 'A lot of people know me, but I'm very much an enigma to most of them' – and so he remained, to the end of his days. It was my good fortune to make contact with his children, and, when they generously put their papers at my disposal, I saw that their father had lived a fascinating and much more important life than the world had yet suspected.

Duff Hart-Davis
Uley
Gloucestershire
March 2012

List Of Acronyms

ADM	Admiralty
C	Head of the Secret Intelligence Service
CBNIET	Chief of British Naval Intelligence, Eastern Theatre
CMG	Companion of St Michael and St George
COIS	Chief of Intelligence Staff
DNI	Director of Naval Intelligence
ENIGMA	German code cracked by the listening station at Bletchley Park
FO	Foreign Office
H/F D/F or HUFF-DUFF. High-frequency direction-finding	
HE	High explosive
HMG	His Majesty's Government
MI5	Government security service
MI6	Government intelligence service, operating overseas – same as SIS
NA	Naval Attaché
NID	Naval Intelligence Department
OBE	Order of the British Empire
PRO	Public Record Office (same as National Archives)
RIAS	Royal Institute of International Affairs
RIN	Royal Indian Navy
RM	Royal Marines
RN	Royal Navy
SEAC	South East Asia Command
SIS	Secret Intelligence Service – same as MI6
Snotty	A midshipman
SO, SO1, SO2	Early versions of
SOE	Special Operations Executive
WRNAS	Women's Royal Naval Australian Service
WRNS	Women's Royal Naval Service ('Wrens')

1

Mobilise!

'Dear Daddy,' wrote Hugh Evans to his father from the Royal Naval College at Dartmouth on 14 July 1914. 'I don't expect that you thought we might be mobilised. Well, we *are going to mobilise*, directly a telegram is received from the Admiralty.'

We had a long lecture from the skipper last night and have five hours to get on board the specials at Kingswear [railway station], if the telegram comes. We must have our chests and all our gear with us . . . Mind, all this is only precaution. If the telegram comes I go to Chatham and join my ship, the *Bacchante*. She's a very old cruiser flying an admiral's flag. I am the senior in our party of nine . . . We should have 1/- a day and would soon be midshipmen and perhaps go on landing parties or be present in some big naval battle.

Remember, daddy dear, this is all supposition and precaution.

Goodbye, daddy dear,

Remember, Your loving son, G.H.J. Evans.

P.S. I may go now.

I may go tonight.

I may go tomorrow.

I may not go at all.

P.P.S. Don't worry and don't let mother worry.

He went. Two weeks later he sent a telegram: MOBILISING CHATHAM NOW HUGH ADDRESS BACCHANTE. He was fifteen years and two months old, and had barely started what should have been a two-year training course at Dartmouth. But before his first term was over, along with 433 other boys much the same age he was suddenly catapulted into service by the imminent outbreak of the First World War.

His next letter home reported a frantic dash to Chatham, the naval dockyard on the River Medway in Kent:

> 2 August 1914 HMS *Bacchante*, Chatham
> Sunday Afternoon
> Dear Daddy
> At five minutes to four yesterday everybody was carrying on as usual when suddenly the word was given to mobilise and we all rushed off. We travelled all night and I slept on the rack. We arrived at Chatham barracks at 2.30 am and slept on the floor of the gym. This morning we joined our ships. I am in the *Bacchante* and the 3rd cruiser squadron. I expect we shall go out and convoy merchantmen in the Atlantic, or we might go into the Baltic ... Anyhow we get 2/6 a day war pay and a medal at the end. I'll write as often as I can. We are acting midshipmen and if the war lasts some time will be made snotties [midshipmen].

He had to cut the letter short because he was wanted in his gun turret 'to fuse lyddite shells'. Already he was 'second-in-command of the fore barbette. The lieutenant commander is in charge, but I do all [the] work except during battle. I expect I shall get some prize money.'

Bacchante was a veteran – a Cressy-class armoured cruiser laid down in 1899, 472 feet long, steam-powered, with four tall, vertical funnels amidships and a curved, underslung bow that protruded at the waterline, for ramming. Her main armament consisted of two 9.2-inch guns, one mounted fore and one aft, and twelve 6-inch. Her top speed was a paltry twenty-one knots.

Her skipper was Captain Algy Boyle, a younger son of the Earl of Shannon. Hugh never liked this bachelor and strict disciplinarian: he felt that Boyle had a down on him, and the other midshipmen were scared of the captain, although admitting that he was efficient and sometimes very kind. The crew included nineteen former policemen, one of whom was Leading Signalman Ryan, a tall, hefty fellow with a drooping moustache. Conversations with him always ended the same way. 'See this scar,' he would say, holding up a thumb. 'Bitten by Miss Sylvia Pankhurst, I was, while trying to arrest her.'

On 4 August 1914 – the day war was declared – *Bacchante* set out as part of Cruiser Force C, accompanied by her sister ships *Euryalus*, *Aboukir*, *Hogue* and *Cressy*, to patrol the area of the North Sea known as the Broad Fourteens. Four days later, back in Deal, the crew learnt that the scout cruiser *Amphion*, with which they had been working, had been sunk by a mine with the loss of 150 men, and that they themselves had steamed through the middle of a minefield. 'Our escape was miraculous,' wrote Able Seaman W. Chesterton in his diary, 'owing to the vastness of the field and [the fact] that our movements were restricted to that area.'

That same day, 8 August, Hugh thanked his mother for some things she had sent:

> The wristwatch is top hole. We are going somewhere (I can't say and don't quite know yet) and it is very likely that I shan't be able to write for some time ... I am awfully pleased with Uncle C's [field] glasses. They are topping, and it's awfully decent of him to lend them to me.

His next letter home bore no date – an unusual lapse for him – and struck an ominous note:

They read all letters going out, so I can't tell you where I am. Don't be surprised if I don't write for a month or so. If you hear that my ship has gone down, you'll know I've gone with it. The war may last for a month, or three, or six, or a year or even more. I don't know and can't guess.

The old cruisers were sailing north-east, and on 25 August Hugh had another chance to write when *Bacchante* put into port to refuel. The scent of battle had evidently sharpened his appetite for a fight – but by then the censors were at work, and some of his words had been heavily crossed out with a blue pencil:

We are now coaling at XXXXX and tomorrow will start XXXXX. We are going to be painted a light grey so that we shall be less discernible . . . We have been all over the shop, sometimes XXXXX sometimes XXXXX, some- times off XXXXX, once off XXXXX.
   Sometimes I can't realise that we are at war. It's all so peaceful . . . Yet, by God, if I don't have some chance of smashing a German I'll go mad. Are they *civilised?* Are they *men?* They are *barbarians, animals, worse than beasts, brutes, cowards, fiends!!* So it is here with every man jack aboard. We're all burning to cut the throats of the devils, and when we get at them, they won't like it.
   We have to keep watches at night – and two or three during the day . . . My station in night watches is the conning tower. I have to control and direct by megaphone the starboard twelve-pounders and two six-inch guns on the starboard side. I have to report where the shot falls

and correct the range and deflection so that the shots hit the target.

Three days later British and German warships clashed in the first battle of Heligoland Bight, the large bay on the north-east German coast. Cruiser Force C did not become involved in the strung-out engagement, merely acting as a screen, but Hugh got his first real taste of war when *Bacchante* took on casualties, and he was required to help the ship's doctor, Staff Surgeon Murray Levick, by throwing amputated limbs over the side. The experience does not seem to have disturbed him. 'We were in the manoeuvre but didn't fight,' he told his mother. 'We brought many wounded home to Chatham and some dead.'

There, on 22 September, dire news reached the crew over the wireless. Three of their sister ships – *Aboukir*, *Cressy* and *Hogue* – had been torpedoed and sunk in a murderous attack by a single U-boat, all within the space of a few minutes. More than 800 men had been rescued, but 1,459 had died, among them thirteen of Hugh's contemporaries, less than a month into their naval careers. Later it transpired that, because of exceptionally bad weather, the cruisers had been steaming at only ten knots, instead of the thirteen recommended, and that their captains had ignored the order to zigzag, because they thought there were no German submarines in the area. Hugh was shocked by the sight of the midshipmen who survived, coming back in a Dutch vessel. 'They were absolutely done . . . Several had spent *three hours* in the water. Most had fainted. Some had become delirious when pulled out.'

The disaster provoked an outcry in the newspapers. As one of Hugh's shipmates, Eric Bush, put it, 'A section of the British public could not understand how we boys could be of any use on board a ship in the grim business of war, and demanded our recall to the College.' Other people held different views. It was pointed out that one newly commissioned officer,

Midshipman Cazalet of the *Cressy*, using a whaler, had picked
up eighty-eight survivors, including the ship's captain, and the
Morning Post published a letter from 'The Mother of a
Dartmouth Cadet':

> If my son can best serve England by giving his life for
> her, I would not lift one finger to bring him home. If
> any act or word of mine should interfere with or take
> him from his grandest privilege, I could never look him
> in the face again.

In the middle of the summer term Winston Churchill, First
Lord of the Admiralty, had visited the College at Dartmouth,
where he inspected the cadets and seemed pleased with their
standard. Now he pitched into argument. Writing to the
Marquess of Crewe, Lord President of the Council, he declared:

> It wd. be a vy harsh measure to deprive these young boys
> of an experience wh they will always look back to, &
> from wh their professional value is sensibly increased. We
> have had piteous appeals from the parents of the Osborne
> cadets to allow their boys to go. I am assured they render
> useful services. It has always been the custom of the Navy;
> & for myself I cannot see much difference in the tragedy
> of a young life cut short at 16 or at 17.
>   I have satisfied myself that naval opinion supports the
> present Admiralty practice. I asked that it shd be carefully
> re-considered; but we were found united in keeping the
> lads at sea to take their chance.

Eric Bush was strongly on Churchill's side, and recorded
that 'we all prayed that we would not be sent back to the
College'. Hugh was equally undaunted, for life at sea had taken
a powerful grip of him.

Mother dear, do you realise that this war means that I will never go back to Dartmouth? Do you realise that in all probability I shall have several *years'* leave? That half the navy will be disbanded and the other half do very little work? That thousands of officers and men will chuck up the service and strike out for themselves?

I'll stick to it, for it's the breath of life to me. I couldn't live without the sea, and I love it. I used to think that there could be other professions better, brighter, happier, and even sometimes I have hated it. Several times I cursed myself for ever going down to the sea. Now I understand.

I have not set foot on dry ground for six and a half weeks . . . and how time has flown! Seven weeks gone like a day, and I scarcely feel it. Well, it's the sea that does it. When I feel the long, merry roll and heaving, jerky pitch of the old tub, I seem to roll and pitch with it, as though I were part of it and shared it. I love it.

By then he had got the measure of his fourteen- and fifteen-year-old colleagues, and his view of them was by no means indulgent:

The other chaps here aren't bad. *Dixon* you know through his mater. He's not bad. I don't like him very, very much, as he's rather a swine at times. Then *Bashall* is quite decent . . . although he's quite a swine sometimes. *Bush* is awfully decent and pure as anything. He's very small and I have always liked him. *Vereker*'s not bad, is the nephew of Jellicoe and Madden. He's no swine. Then there's *Barclay*. He's rather a bumptious ass, Canadian and thinks a lot of himself. Otherwise quite decent, and not a swine.

Mind, Daddy, I don't expect you to show this part about the other chaps to anyone but mother & Anne [Hamilton, a lifelong friend of the family]. Then *Tennant,*

J., is rather a prig and very rich . . . He's not bad and
not a swine. He's Asquith's nephew. His father is Under-
Secretary for war, and rather a fool, I believe. *Phipps* is
rather a fool . . .

Like the other acting midshipmen, Hugh had one primary
source of supply – a Mecca among emporia – in the form of
the naval outfitters Gieves. Even before boys gained admittance
to Osborne, the firm sent every potential cadet a telegram of
congratulations, by implication soliciting his custom; and Hugh,
succumbing to this overture, had opened an account at the
company's establishment in Chatham. He then had frequent
recourse to Gieves whenever he wanted clothes or other equipment. 'Please ask mother what she's done about my winter
underclothing,' he wrote, 'and write and tell me quick. Tell me
everything she's ordered at Gieves's for me. Don't order anything
more. I shall order what I want.' Later he called for

4 pairs of spare Gieves midshipman's patches
1 pair of sock suspenders
2 writing pads (thick paper with envelopes)
10 small buttons as on uniform waistcoats
25 large buttons as on uniform coats
One old badge if you can find one

You can get the buttons off my old uniform monkey
jackets, coat collars and waistcoats. I want them for white
uniforms, and it's hard to get buttons in XXXX.

He could not say where he was going; but white uniforms
obviously signified a hot climate: *Bacchante* was on her way
south, to Malta, Port Said and the nightmare of Gallipoli.

2

Early Days

Hugh was born in London on 7 June 1899, the second son of a leading London surgeon, Willmott Evans, who specialised in diseases of the skin and, at the age of forty, was widely known both as a practising doctor and as a man of exceptional erudition. An ardent bibliophile, author of a far-ranging survey of current practice, *Medical Science of Today*, and fluent enough in German to have translated Nobiling and Jankau's *Handbuch der Prophylaxe*, he was sufficiently versatile to have coached students in thirty different subjects. He was never one to suffer fools, and used to tell his children that when he explained something to them, it should be 'clear even to the meanest intellect'.

He is said to have spoken twelve languages, and his mild eccentricities included a passion for collecting; among the objects which cluttered his London house were a stuffed gorilla, prehistoric axe-heads and Roman water pipes dug up elsewhere in London. He seldom if ever asked patients to pay their bills, but devoted enormous energy to his work: his monumental study *Diseases of the Breast*, published in 1923, ran to 500 pages and was profusely – not to say revoltingly – illustrated with more than 100 hand-drawn and painted examples of cancers and other deformities.

Hugh's mother Frances was born in Canton on 17 May

1867, a daughter of the Revd George Piercy, a pioneer Methodist minister based in China. She once kept a diary describing a journey from England back to Canton, and she, too, had a distinguished career in medicine: from 1884 to 1893 she was at the London School of Medicine for Women, where she won, among other honours, a Gold Medal in *Materia Medica*, a Gold Medal in Anatomy, and Honours in Physiology. She then worked as a doctor in London, and held various posts, including those of Assistant Anaesthetist at the Royal Free Hospital and Demonstrator of Anatomy at her old school, before marrying Willmott in the summer of 1895.

As a child Hugh lived with his parents at their London home, 121 Harley Street, a large, tall house, where he had the company of his elder brother Evan, born in 1896, and his second brother, Arthur (known as Jim), born in 1902. A sister, Maureen (Molly), arrived in 1905, and another sister, Joyce (Jo), in 1907. Hugh was always the most mischievous and adventurous of the family: aged seven or eight he would take the lead weights off gas lamps and throw them in front of the horse-drawn carriages bringing patients for consultations in Harley Street. When he went to a pre-prep school called Greenhouse he soon acquired a reputation for toughness. A colleague remembered how he once climbed high into a giant laurel and amazed the company by sticking his arm out of the top.

One ineradicable memory from that time was his hatred of rice pudding: if ever he refused to eat his helping, he was sent up to his bedroom and ordered to stay there until he had finished it. Salvation seemed to have come one day when he spotted a loose floorboard: prising it up, he tipped the congealed mess into the space beneath – and all went well for a week or two, until a nauseating smell of rancid milk gave his secret repository away. When his father found out what had happened, he was furious – not with the boy but with the nanny – and directed that Hugh should never be given rice pudding again. In general, he was closer to his father than to his mother, with whom he had little rapport.

At about eleven Hugh and Jim both went to Mrs Egerton's Preparatory School, and one day when there was some bad behaviour during the boys' return from the sports field, the master threatened general punishment. Hugh owned up, but later told a friend that he had not been the culprit: he had taken the blame to save everyone else from retribution.

The tradition of service at sea was deeply embedded in the family, for seven earlier generations of Evanses had produced naval surgeons. So at the age of twelve Hugh moved on to Osborne College, the preparatory school for the Royal Navy on the Isle of Wight. A small, neat-looking boy, he was known from his dark hair and olive skin as 'the little dago', and in choosing a career he may well have been influenced by the log of his great-great-grandfather Evan Evans, who was appointed Second Surgeon's Mate aboard the *Niger*, a thirty-three-gun fifth-rate, or classic frigate, in June 1790.

Like his great-great-grandson, Evan had a lively pen and evidently enjoyed writing. As his ship prepared to leave Woolwich on 3 July 1790 he recorded: 'The guns and balls was taken in, with picks and poleaxes and various other dangerous weapons well invented to kill men', and on the 7th he went again to Woolwich 'to get Elix Nitr and Pulv Janob sent there from Apothecary Hall. Gave receipt for same.'

In September the *Niger* crossed the Channel as part of a small fleet sent to spy on the French ships in the harbour at Brest. On the night of the 29th she steered towards the port and at daylight laid-to.

The Comadore went in his own ship so near the Mouth of the Harbour as he could; so as to keep free from the Batteries. The French sent out a line of Battle ship and a Frigate towards the Comadore. At ten a.m. Comadore Englefield made signals for the *Niger* and the Cutter to make ready for Action. The *Niger* was ready to Engage in ten minutes after the drummer beat to Quarters; which was very well, considering it was the first time since the ship was Commissiond.

No action took place, as 'the French did not think proper to Insult us', but the English ships obtained valuable information, and sped back to Falmouth, where one of the officers went ashore to 'despatch Intelligence for Government'. Surgeon's Mate Evans was naturally interested in 'Accidents that happened on board the *Niger*', and reported details with admirable economy:

Wed 18 Aug. W. Allen, a fore Castle man . . . met with the following fatal Accident. He was standing close to the leading block of the top rope on the fore Castle, the Block gave way and gave him a violent blow on the Cheek bone; which caused a large contused wound to which we applied dry sutions, Bandege etc and I took him into Hazlar's Hospital directly, where he died delirious in two days after.

Mon Sepr. 27. Wm. Child, one of the Carpenters Crew, was at work in the Mison Top. He cut his thumb with the saw; in coming down to have it dressed, fainted and fell into the sea. He floated for some time, but before a Boat could go to his Assistance he came to, & not been able to swim, sunk.

Thur 25 Decr. 90. Wm. Westerfield, One of the Watchers, being in a state of Intoxication about Nine at Night and playing with Crowder the Lieutenant's Cook in the Galley, his foot slipd & he fell upon his Head & never spoke after. He died at One Next Morning, he remained in a state of Lithargy untill his death. This being Christ. Day & also his birthday, he was one & thirty years old.

The Royal Naval College at Osborne was housed in the former stables of Queen Victoria's palace, which, with its twin Italianate towers, stands in a commanding position on the hill above Osborne Bay. To boys of twelve it was a daunting place, and in 1912, when Hugh attended, life there was rigidly regimented. Accelerated by bugle calls or clashes on big brass gongs, the inmates sped from point to point at the double, risking immediate chastisement if any Cadet Captain saw them slow to a walk.

Thirty cadets lived in each dormitory, down one side of a long corridor, and at the foot of every bed stood a heavy sea chest, three feet square and two feet six inches high, containing its owner's possessions, with his name incised on a brass plate on the top. Across the corridor was the boys' living space, known as the gunroom. Each intake of cadets formed a term, named after some famous admiral: Hugh's term was Blake's. Jack Broome (who later rose to the rank of captain) was an exact contemporary of Hugh's, and remembered every detail of his time in that hectic forcing house:

Far too early for comfort, we awoke to the blast of a reveille bugle call. That meant out of bed and turn bedclothes back ... One gong which followed meant off pyjama tops, wash at our bedside basins, then, clad in towel only, stand by our sea-chest. When everyone was there, the next gong meant full-speed to the bathroom, into one end of the plunge baths (I suppose they were about ten feet square and five feet deep, full of tepid water), out the other end, find towel, back to sea-chest, dress and fall in for inspection alongside sea-chest, having made our beds. When all had fallen in . . . another gong signalled another stampede for Collingwood, the mess room . . .

After breakfast, Divisions – all candidates fallen in by Terms on the quarterdeck (the name given to the big hall) . . . The Chaplain read prayers, hymns were sung, and all cadets were marched away to their studies . . . This seemed to be the only time we marched. We doubled when we changed studies, we doubled up and down that long corridor when passing the gunroom of a senior team. Loitering past a senior gunroom was asking for trouble. Almost certainly you would be spotted, hauled into that gunroom, bent over a table and given at least three cuts on the bottom.

A sheet of menus headed 'Daily Routine of Dietary for Cadets' shows that the boys got plenty to eat, even if the food was monotonous. Every day there was porridge for breakfast, together with sausages and mashed potatoes on Sundays, cold ham on Mondays, and kippers, kedgeree or curried mutton on other days. Honey, marmalade and golden syrup came and went in rotation. For lunch there was some kind of meat – roast beef, roast chicken, Irish stew – usually with cabbage and potatoes, and various puddings, including 'Roley Poley'. For tea – boiled eggs, sardines, fresh fish or German sausage, besides bread and butter with various kinds of jam. Between these main repasts cadets were kept going by Ship's Biscuit and Cocoa at 6.45 a.m., Buns and Milk at 10.30–11.30 a.m., Biscuits and Milk at 4.30 p.m. and Biscuits at 8.30 p.m.

As for the education on offer: another former inmate, Stephen King-Hall, described it as 'monstrously mechanical . . . The humanities were hardly recognised. One of the results . . . was to produce a brand of naval officer incapable of expressing himself either in speech or on paper, and without any conception of the strategical and tactical problems of defence.' But this damning verdict referred to a period ten years earlier, and by the time Hugh reached Osborne, the curriculum had probably been modernised. In any case, he managed to escape the mental straitjacket that such a regime threatened. Far from being incapable of expressing himself, he clearly enjoyed writing, and sent home buoyant accounts of his doings:

On the 13th we went out to Alum Bay, Freshwater. It's a ripping place. Very lonely though. Had a sporting time. Went out to the cliff just above the Needles. 300 feet drop. Got some sporting photos. Love to all, 'H'

His most faithful correspondent was Dyddgu Hamilton, a lifelong friend of the family who had met his mother while they were both reading medicine at the Royal Holloway College – two of the first women to do so. A spinster, christened with an awkward Welsh name but always known as Anne, she lived with the Evanses in Harley Street. She was thirty years older than Hugh, and, although no blood relation, became a kind of benevolent aunt: she took him for long walks, wrote to him frequently, brought him out from school and saw him off when he joined the navy.

The description given in her passport was unflattering, but – to judge from a photograph – accurate: '*Height* 5′ 7″, *Forehead* Low, *Eyes* Brown, *Nose* Straight, *Mouth* Large, *Chin* Ordinary, *Complexion* Sallow, *Face* Long.' She may have looked like a governess, but she was highly intelligent, with wide interests, and clearly had some magic about her. A close friend of Elodie, the American wife of Hilaire Belloc, she did translating work for the author and corresponded with him extensively. She was fascinated by the literary world, and amassed a library of more than 5,000 volumes, many in French and many devoted to her special interest, natural history. She it was who got

Hugh reading, she who encouraged him to write. Throughout her life they remained very close: when he was in his twenties he wrote to her saying, 'I remember when I was a kid the thing I admired in you most was your unfailing cheerfulness.' Hugh's sister Maureen once remarked, 'Don't you like the way she can make her account of some very ordinary event sound like a terrific adventure? She does it when she reads aloud, too.'

Hugh's earliest surviving letters were scrawled in babyish capitals, but by the time he was twelve, at Osborne, both his handwriting and his descriptive powers had advanced tremendously:

23 March 1912   Saturday & Sunday

Dear Anne,
I never in my life saw worse weather at night, or rather heard it. The wind whistles through the trees and howls round the windows, which shake and bang as if a thousand devils were loose in the neighbourhood. Then crash, a door slams, and bang go the windows, bang, bang. Then someone snores. A chap near me talks and sings in his sleep. Another fellow groans, and then I laugh and can't get to sleep for some time. I don't mind though. It's awful fun.

Last Tuesday I felt awful. My throat hurt like 'Old Nick' . . . So of course I went to the sick-bay. The doctor looked, looked again and then whistled. I felt inclined to laugh, only it would have hurt me. So I said nothing and did nothing. Along came the Fleet Surgeon. He stared and stared, then announced that my right tonsil was colossal. I felt as if a thunderbolt had hit me on the nape of the neck, or, in plain words – I was knocked all of a heap . . . I was sent to the isolation hospital and had to gargol [*sic*] three times a day as well as having my throat swabbed and painted and wrapped up in cotton-wool.

One major excitement was an outing to the Spithead Review in the summer of 1913. For a few days the cadets were quartered in HMS *Bulwark*, a Formidable-class battleship laid down in 1899 and armed (to Hugh's great delight), with four twelve-inch guns. 'It's absolutely topping here,' he reported:

We arrived on board at 6.30 yesterday . . . As we were coming out the King arrived at Gosport and all the fleet saluted as we steamed down the double lines . . . There are no snotties [midshipmen] aboard. It's fine. It's top hole. The *'B'* is a sight better ship than we expected. Four twelves! Hearing the wireless at night is grand too. Last night the whole fleet had searchlight practice – 10 miles of it!! 10 by 4!!! We turned in at 10.30 and slept dead. I'd a long sight rather sleep in a hammock than a bed. They are canvas ones. I slept like a top and loved it.

In the morning we turned out leisurely and had a topping breakfast. Then there were Divisions and then Church, which was very interesting as it was celebrated on the quarter deck. The skipper took it, and we sat amongst the senior officers. We are treated exactly as midshipmen. Then after church the King came round and I saw him easily with a big telescope on the bridge of the Royal Yacht . . .

Tomorrow the King leads the fleet to sea and we fire 101 guns or something. Then we steam out to sea and, returning past the Royal Yacht, cheer him, ship after ship – over a hundred of 'em. Fine, eh! . . .

Goodbye, Anne dear, love to all, Hugh.

Throughout the spring of 1914 Hugh continued his chatty letters, asking Anne to send 'an old and patched pair of trousers and a coloured shirt' so that he could appear as a costermonger in a fancy-dress ball at the end of term. 'I expect Mother's got most of these things at home,' he wrote, and then added: 'Consult with her.' He had developed a passion for chocolate, but he seems to have become shy about being seen receiving any, and gave instructions that, if some was sent, it was to be hidden in the middle of the clothes. Anne in turn constantly encouraged him to press ahead with his writing.

In May 1914 he moved on to the Royal Naval College at Dartmouth for the start of a normal two-year course. But within weeks his future was drastically changed by the outbreak of the First World War, as he and his fellow-cadets were pitch-forked into fighting ships and sent off to battle. His letters to contemporaries have vanished; but several friends kept in touch, not least the irrepressibly cheerful and facetious Herbert Smart, who addressed him as 'My Worthy Snottie' or 'My beloved Snottie' and signed himself 'Your Old Pal Boozy Bertie'. To his chagrin, he was rejected by the Navy, and enlisted in the Army instead. 'After reams of correspondence,' he wrote in the autumn of 1914, 'the R.N.D. wept a few crocodile tears and said I was too young. That was in their eighth reply to me. My first letter had stated my age, so that anyone with ten per cent of the intelligence of a sea cow might have said so then and saved a few pounds worth of paper.'

Later he reported that he had enlisted as a private in the Artists' Rifles, then a popular unit for volunteers: 'I've been and gorn and done it, and you may now behold me a common-or-garden Tommy.' The Artists', he thought, offered 'a fairly quick road out to the Front and a good chance of a commission' – but for months he remained at home, moving around various camps in the south of England, until at last his wish was granted and he went out to join the British Expeditionary Force in France.

Some of Hugh's friends were just as bloodthirsty as he. 'We have met no German ships yet and are dying to meet one,' wrote Willie de Segundo from the battleship HMS *Albion* on the Cape of Good Hope station in December 1914.

We heard today that the *Scharnhorst* and *Gneisenau* and *Karlsruhe* have been interned in a Brazilan port. We are sorry for this as we wanted to have a smack at them. I expect we should be badly knocked up, but we could give her a big enough helping . . . We thought we were coming into action with two German cruisers once, but they turned out to be two neutral powers cruisers. We had cleared for action, sounded off 'action' and had cleared away all quarters when we discovered their flags. The 'Secure' was then sounded and everyone was fearfully disappointed . . . We have had two doses of heavy gun fire. The big guns do make a tremendous shine and a nasty blast of air.

Towards the end of 1914, as *Bacchante* moved around the Mediterranean, Hugh's own missives became ever more cryptic. 'Just a line to let you know I'm all right. I can't say where I am, but it's a topping place.' Then, three weeks later: 'We have been coaling since 5.30 am this morning till 4.0 pm this afternoon. We took in 1,100 tons of coal in 9½ hours. Not bad, eh, in an old cruiser like this? I had to turn out at 4.0 am, so am naturally a little tired.'

For members of the crew who liked writing and receiving letters, one advantage of the frequent need for coal was that it generally meant putting into port, where mail could be despatched and collected. But before the days of diesel engines, refuelling was a filthy and exhausting business, of which Stephen King-Hall left an excellent description:

In the holds of the collier were the gangs of fillers, who
... filled the 2 cwt bags, roped them together and hooked
them on to the sling from the derrick. Up went the hoist,
and down it came on the upper deck, where the barrow-
men, stripped to the waist, were waiting to rush each
sack, by carefully-worked-out routes, to the chutes down
which the coal poured into the bunkers, where the stokers,
dodging avalanches of black diamonds, trimmed the coal.
Everyone, including the parson, coaled ship . . . The
commotion went on for hours on end.

At one stage Hugh thought he might be home for Christmas,
but his hopes were dashed, for during the second half of
December *Bacchante* was still in the Med. On the 17th he sent
a photograph of himself going on leave at Gibraltar, and on
the 23rd the ship again put in to pick up the Christmas mails.
Hugh had 'a good many' cards, including two from the King
and Queen, who sent one to every officer and man in the
navy, and he described lavish celebrations:

I wasn't at church as I was snottie of the watch. After
church we all went in the wardroom (warrant officers,
gunroom and wardroom & the skipper) and drank the
King's health in bad champagne. At lunch we had soup,
fish, entrée, turkey, Xmas pudding, mince pies, and aspar-
agus as savoury. Not so bad, eh? Then fruit, cheese, wine
and coffee. The wine was port of an atrochious [*sic*] flavour.
Even the skipper said it was bad.
   We drank healths till everyone was tired of drinking.
(Don't worry, Daddy, the snotties only had two glasses, &
it was Xmas Day). There were crackers and chocolate.
Then the gunroom cleared out & we went round the
mess-deck wishing everyone the compliments of the
season and giving Xmas Boxes. I had to spend 15 bob

on this in cigarettes and tobacco for my turret crew and various acquaintances such as the gym instructor and my servant.

Bacchante did return to home waters in January 1915, and put in at Devonport. It is not clear whether or not Hugh managed to reach London, but in a hurried note to his father – sent from Plymouth, and undated except for 'Early morning' – he announced another imminent departure:

I have only about two minutes as I have to return on board at 7.45 am. We proceed to sea at about 8.30 am, or so I think. I am not sure where we are going. It may only be the usual patrol but on the other hand it might be something quite different.

3

Gallipoli

The Gallipoli campaign has gone down in history as one of
the great British military disasters. It was also a great gamble.
Had it come off, it might have changed the course of the First
World War and cut short the slaughter on the Western Front
in Europe. As it was, the ten-month conflict in 1915 and 1916,
which accomplished nothing, cost England and her allies the
French 44,000 dead and 96,000 wounded, while the losses of
the enemy, principally the Turks and Germans, were estimated
at 86,000 dead and 250,000 wounded. In due course Hugh
was swept into the eye of this horrible storm; but as *Bacchante*
steamed down to the Mediterranean in January 1915, escorting
a convoy, he and his fellow midshipmen could not be aware
that at the eastern end of the Aegean a catastrophe was brewing,
still less that they themselves would be caught up in it.

The Gallipoli peninsula is a forty-mile tongue of land
running down the north side of the Dardanelles, the channel
which separates Europe and Asia, linking the Aegean in the
west with the Sea of Marmara and, via the Bosphorus, with
the Black Sea in the east. In ancient times the strait was known
as the Hellespont, famous for the myth in which young Leander
swam across every night from the southern (Asian) side to visit
his lover, the priestess Hero, in her lighted tower at Sestos on
the northern (European) shore.

The British involvement in 1915 derived from a plan propounded by Churchill, who, at the age of forty, was already an experienced soldier and politician, with a reputation for adventurous and extravagant schemes. As an army officer he had served in India and the Sudan; as a war correspondent he had reported on the Boer War, during which he had been taken prisoner and escaped; and in politics he had been Home Secretary and President of the Board of Trade. Since 1911 he had been First Lord of the Admiralty, and now he reasoned that if a reliable supply route could be opened up to Russia (Britain's ally in the war against the Germans and the Ottoman Empire), it would relieve pressure on the Western Front in France and Belgium, where the Allies were bogged down in their confrontation with the invading German forces. Overland routes from Russia into Europe were blocked by Germany and Austria-Hungary, and sea routes were difficult if not impossible: the Sea of Okhotsk was thousands of miles away to the east and often ice-bound, as was the White Sea in the north, and the Baltic was effectively closed by the German Imperial Fleet.

The only other marine approach to Russia, via the Black Sea, was cut off by the fact that the Dardanelles were strongly defended by Turkish troops. If the Royal Navy could storm the strait (the theory went), they would quickly capture Constantinople, capital of the run-down Ottoman Empire. Such an attack would not only release the Russian navy, but would also knock Turkey – 'the sick man of Europe' – out of the war.

For the attack, the plan was to use obsolete battleships such as HMS *Ocean* and HMS *Goliath*, which lacked the firepower to take on the modern German Imperial Navy, but surely could blast their way past the Turkish forts along the shores of the Dardanelles. On 28 January, after many animated arguments about whether or not there should also be a simultaneous landing by the army, the War Council in London finally decided that the Navy alone should try to force a passage.

Hugh, knowing nothing of this, wrote cheerfully from the dockyard at Malta, where his ship had put in to coal:

1st February 1915

Dear Mother,

This is to let you know I'm alive & hope to remain so for some time to come, provided that I don't fall a victim to XXXXXX. But that's by the way . . . Please don't send any more warm garments . . . It's much too hot here . . . Well, it's quite likely I shall have to buy ducks soon. If we stay long, it'll run into a sun helmet etc. It's topping here now, but that doesn't signify much as you don't know where I am and can only guess. If at first you don't succeed, try, try again.

I remain, Your loving son, G.H.J. Evans

Bacchante's first task in the Mediterranean was to reinforce the British presence in Egypt against the threat of a Turkish attack – for although much weakened, the Ottoman Empire was still very large, and encompassed modern Syria, Lebanon, Israel, Palestine, Sinai, Iraq, Jordan and Saudi Arabia. Egypt, until recently a Turkish dominion, had become a British protectorate in 1914.

Bacchante arrived at Port Said on 9 February 1915 – and she was none too soon, for a week earlier the Turks had made a spirited attempt to invade across the Suez Canal. Having hauled some wheel-mounted, galvanised steel boats over the Sinai desert – in itself a phenomenal effort – they had crept up unobserved behind the high eastern bank of the canal at its narrowest point near Tussum, and the Punjabi soldiers holding that part of the British line opposite had not detected them until they began sliding their boats down to the water. The incursion was repelled, but some vicious fighting ensued, and the Turks lost 2,000 men.

In Port Said *Bacchante* embarked a Military Intelligence Officer, Major the Hon. Aubrey Herbert, who was fluent in Turkish and Arabic, to act as interpreter. He made a strong impression on the midshipmen with stories of how he had been through the Great Retreat in France, and told them 'a lot about Mons etc.' (where he had been wounded). The ship then went off along the Sinai coast to bombard the fort at El Arish, which the Turks had recently captured from the Egyptians.

As far as I could see through my glasses [Hugh told his father] it is a very small place, but it is very important, being on the great caravan route. There is, or rather was, a small but modern fort there. Several Turkish flags were visible, one on the new fort and one on the old fort and one in some trenches to the left. Worse luck for the Turks, most of the guns had been taken away to use with their army.

At 2.15 pm 'Action' was sounded off and we went to our guns. At 2.19 pm one of our 6″ guns fired the first shot. The range throughout the bombardment was about 7,000 [yards] = 3½ miles. The same gun fired another common shell and we altered course, bringing the port side to bear.

We knocked that old fort to pieces. I saw lots of men, looking like ants, running away to the left, disappearing behind the sand hills. More cleared out of the trenches and bunked. We knocked all three flags away and thoroughly reduced the fort. Fifty-six shots were fired altogether. At 3.12 p.m. we ceased firing and secured. The Turks were too frightened and we were too far off for them to offer any resistance worth mentioning. A rifle wouldn't carry, and all the guns they had were small and obsolete. At 4.0 p.m. we started back to Port Said at 10 knots. The next morning we entered harbour and coaled.

The next afternoon (13th) we proceeded to sea again and set a course for Joppa at 10 knots. We arrived off Joppa the next morning and proceeded up the coast, passing an American cruiser. We passed Haifa, Mt Carmel, Beirut and the mountains of the Lebanon. That night we passed Tyre and Sidon. Tripoli was passed next day. On 16th we arrived at Alexandretta [modern Iskenderun] and anchored in the bay.

The ship stayed on station for ten days, patrolling up and down the coast during daylight and lying at anchor off Alexandretta for the night. Throughout the hours of darkness crews remained at the guns, and searchlights were focused on the town. The importance of the place was that it controlled the only road along which guns could be towed back to Turkey: since the highway followed the shore for some distance, the Turkish army would have a dangerous line of retreat if a British warship was within range. The Turks were holding the neighbouring pass of Beilan and the hills behind. As Hugh told his father, 'The Beilan pass is the real key to the position. All the men who have led armies to conquer Asia have fought like demons to get that pass, Alexander the Great among them.'

Hugh sent his father a summary of the ten-day mission:

17th Took off two French refugees (priests).
18th Drove some Turks out of coves and trenches with 12-pounder common and 6″ lyddite shells. After lunch we opened fire on a railway bridge with one 6″ gun and the

after 9.2″ gun, smashing the bridge up. The railway also runs by the sea here. The range was about 4,000 yards.

19th Forenoon. Fired 20 common and seven shrapnel shells at guns on wagons drawn by oxen. Killed several men and smashed up guns.

Evening. Governor of town sent messenger in boat to parley.

20th Fired blanks at people trying to salvage guns.

21st Sent picket boat (armed) close in to reconnoitre.

22nd Fired eight 3-pdr and two 6″ shells at some Turks attempting to salvage guns. Fired ten 6″ shells at the telegraph posts, cutting the connection. They daren't snipe us, as they knew we would shell the town.

Perhaps to spare his parents' feelings, Hugh gave only that brief mention of the events of the 19th forenoon, and it was left to his shipmate Eric Bush to describe what happened in more detail:

The long-expected carts arrived crawling along the fore-shore, each drawn by a pair of bullocks. Captain Boyle hated the idea of firing at the defenceless drivers, so ordered a warning shot to be placed ahead of the convoy. The Turks immediately left their oxen and dived into a ditch, while their beasts went slowly forward, like automata. We now fired a second round, which injured the leading animal. Poor thing, how it bellowed and struggled.

The sight of it was too much for the driver, who emerged from the ditch, cut the bullock free and then, grasping the reins of its fellow, attempted to lead the procession. Again a warning shot was fired 'across his bows', but the driver went steadfastly on to what he must have known was certain death. In the end he was left lying by his oxen and their broken carts. We had given him every chance. If the admiration of our ship's company could reward a dead Anatolian for his courage, the reward was his. We loathed the whole thing.

For the time being a new threat to the Suez Canal drew *Bacchante* back to Port Said; but while she was busy with her intelligence gathering, momentous events had been taking place further north. A large Anglo-French fleet had assembled in the Aegean, based on the island of Lemnos, some forty miles off the Turkish coast, and at 0850, on the morning of 19 February, having steamed towards the mainland, Allied ships opened their offensive on the strait by bombarding the forts and gun positions along the shores on both sides. Optimistic naval commanders and politicians had predicted a quick breakthrough – but nothing of the sort occurred.

The initial targets were the four main forts at the entrance to the strait, two on the north (European) side on Cape Helles, and two on the Asian side at Kum Kale. To the chagrin of Vice Admiral Sackville Carden and his commanders, their long-range shells had little apparent effect: as soon as the heavy guns of *Queen Elizabeth* and *Inflexible* ceased firing, the defenders emerged from shelter and began to fire back.

That evening the weather broke, and for the next four days and nights a gale and heavy seas made accurate naval gunnery impossible; but when the attack was resumed on 25 February, the outer forts were silenced; two landing parties went ashore, one on either side of the strait, and blew up several guns, as well as a bridge. These minor successes again raised hopes of a rapid advance up the channel; but the Turks were full of fight, and their armoury included two particularly effective weapons: mobile howitzers and mines. The howitzers were hauled from place to place by teams of buffaloes, so that by the time the naval gunners thought they had pinpointed a firing position, and had begun to shell it, the howitzers had moved to a new site, from which they could rain down fire on any ship which ventured into range.

The mines proved even more deadly. Some four hundred had been moored in ten lines that reached across the strait from side to side, on a stretch beginning some twelve miles from the open sea, where the channel closed in towards the pinch-point known as The Narrows. The Allied minesweepers – unarmed North Sea trawlers – were hampered by their lack of power: a surface current was flowing east to west at two or three knots, and they could not sweep against it, so that they had to steam beyond their start-point, before turning to sweep downwards – and all the time they were being enfiladed by gunfire from both sides. Sweeping at night was not much safer, for they were quickly caught in the beams of searchlights.

On 16 March, with no progress made, Admiral Carden succumbed to nervous strain and was obliged to resign his command. He was replaced by Rear Admiral John de Robeck, who had already expressed doubts about the feasibility of silencing the Turkish defences; nevertheless on 18 March, urged on by Churchill from a safe distance of 3,000 miles, he launched a major attack with no fewer than eighteen battleships, British and French – three lines of four, and six more in support.

The result was catastrophic – mainly because the Allied commanders did not know that a small Turkish steamer, the *Nousret*, had laid a fresh line of twenty mines up- and down-stream almost in the entrance to the strait, above Eren Keui Bay. On the morning of the attack the invaders had some initial success in suppressing the Turkish guns, but then the French battleship *Bouvet* hit one of the new mines and sank within minutes, losing her entire crew of 630 men. At about 1600 HMS *Inflexible* also hit a mine. Thirty men and three officers were killed, but the battle cruiser stayed afloat; the remainder of the crew were taken off, and the ship eventually drifted ashore on the island of Tenedos, five miles off the coast.

The next victim was the battleship HMS *Irresistible*, which also struck a mine and wallowed out of control. De Robeck ordered HMS *Ocean* to take her in tow, but *Ocean* herself detonated a mine, which wrecked her steering gear, and at 7.30 p.m. she sank. Later *Irresistible* also went down – but almost all the crews of both ships were taken off by destroyers and saved. By then the Ottoman gunners were nearly out of ammunition, and so dispirited that they were on the point of abandoning their positions; but the British did not know this, and the order went out for the fleet to withdraw.

The loss of three major ships in a single day, and the disabling of three more, at last persuaded the British High Command that the navy alone could not force a passage. De Robeck was eager to try again, but in London the decision had already been taken to send in ground forces, which would knock out the mobile Ottoman batteries and allow the minesweepers to clear the channel without continuous harassment.

On 12 March the Secretary of State for War, the formidable Field Marshal Lord Kitchener, had sent for General Sir Ian Hamilton and appointed him to command a large expeditionary force destined for service in the Gallipoli campaign. Hamilton was an immensely experienced officer: twice recommended for the VC, holder of the DSO, he was (according to his nephew) 'a young sixty-two, wiry and vigorous', and the veteran of numerous campaigns. Since 1910 he had been Commander-in-Chief of British forces in the Mediterranean, so that he was a natural choice for the new post.

He set out from England at once: via Charing Cross, Dover and Calais, then by train to Marseilles, where the light cruiser *Phaeton* was under steam, awaiting him. He reached the eastern end of the Aegean just in time to be caught up in the final stages of the battle of 18 March. He was deeply moved by the spectacle of the crippled *Inflexible* creeping away, escorted by a bevy of destroyers, and *Phaeton* followed the wounded giant to safety at Tenedos. Next morning, after a rapid assessment of the situation, Hamilton telegraphed Kitchener to say that he was 'most reluctantly being driven to the conclusion' that the strait could not be forced by battleships, but that 'a deliberate and progressive military operation' was needed, 'carried out at full strength'.

Fortunately one large body of troops was already close at hand. The Australian and New Zealand Corps (Anzac) division, with a strength of some 30,000 men, commanded by Lieutenant General Sir William Birdwood, was already in Egypt, stationed near Cairo to protect the Suez Canal against Turkish attacks. Kitchener had long feared that Mehmet V, the Sultan of Turkey, would launch a jihad against the infidel British, and he had brought the Dominion soldiers to Egypt in December 1914 as a precaution. Now, by chance, they were within 500 miles of the Dardanelles, and would be able to reach the area within a couple of days. Designated to support them were the 29th Division (18,000-strong) and the Royal Naval Division (10,000), together with one French division (18,000) – a total of some 75,000 men. But these other units were widely scattered, and they took so long to reach the theatre of operations – nearly a month – that the Turks had ample time to strengthen their defences along the shores of the strait and on the bony ridges of the Gallipoli peninsula.

As the expeditionary force assembled, *Bacchante* was still becalmed in the Canal Zone, and Hugh was growing bored with his own lack of action: he was frustrated by censorship, and depressed (if not much disturbed) by the news from Gallipoli. 'It's rather bad luck in the Dardanelles, isn't it?' he wrote to his father on 21 March:

I expect we'll give 'em a jolly good licking soon, though, probably before you get this letter. We must expect to lose some ships during the bombardment, and three isn't very many. Besides, the *Ocean* and *Irresistible* aren't up to much either. I'm very glad it wasn't the *Albion* [in which Willie de Segundo was serving]. Send me the casualty lists when you get them, please. Only the *Bouvet* lost heavily. We may have a bit more fun soon, but I doubt it.

The locusts here are awful. Of course we don't get 'em so bad on board. They are just enough to be interesting. Yesterday ashore, however, they were the limit. Thick clouds of them rose under my horse's hoofs and they were like layers above our heads . . . My horse could go all right, but wouldn't stay. Evidently wanted feeding up . . . Altogether I'm sick of this hole and hope we'll clear out soon.

One consolation of *Bacchante*'s enforced wait was that her crew was able to exchange greetings with some of the Anzac force deployed on the banks of the canal, and formed a high opinion of them. Eric Bush saw that the behaviour of the soldiers from Down Under was rather coarse – they declined to salute officers and swore atrociously in the presence of superiors – but he admired their courage and determination, and decided that 'a finer set of men could hardly be found in any country'. Another asset was that they appeared to be natural seamen, and were very handy in boats – in contrast to a Senegalese contingent, whom Bush described as 'awkward as gollywogs'.

Not for another three weeks did *Bacchante* leave Egypt; then at last she was ordered north, and on 12 April she arrived at the Allies' main naval base at Moudros, the vast natural harbour on the island of Lemnos, as preparations went ahead to land the first ground forces. The bay, some two miles by three, looked like the flooded crater of an extinct volcano, ringed by

brown, treeless hills. One hazard of the harbour was that violent
south-west winds came blasting into it; yet, in spite of its
shortcomings, Moudros was a good anchorage, protected from
submarine attack by two small islands lying in its mouth, and
only thirty miles off the Turkish coast.

The Allied plan was that a 1,500-strong covering force of
Anzac troops should make a surprise landing before dawn near
Gaba Tepe, a headland some twelve miles north of Cape Helles,
and that later in the morning, after a naval bombardment had
softened up the defences, men of the 29th Division should
storm five beaches, designated Y, X, W, V and S, around the
southern tip of the peninsula. *Bacchante* was detailed to support
the northern assault.

The scent of battle evidently fired up the veteran Commander-
in-Chief, who gushed grotesquely inappropriate purple prose
in his diary. '*Nunc dimittis*, O Lord of Hosts,' he wrote:

> Not a man but knows he is making for the jaws of death
> . . . They are wild with joy, uplifted. Life spins superbly
> through their veins at the very moment they are seeking
> to sacrifice it for a cause. O Death, where is thy sting?
> O Grave, where is thy victory?

The Allied armada set out on the evening of 24–25 April. As
the force left harbour, Aubrey Herbert recorded, 'I have just seen
the most wonderful procession of ships I shall ever see.' The day
had been glorious, and as night fell the sky was bright and clear,
with a brilliant moon, due to set at 0256 a.m. *Bacchante*'s
midshipmen were in charge of the powered craft – the ship's
picket boat, pinnace, tugs and launches – which were to tow
the barges full of Anzac troops to the shore. For the sixteen-
year-olds, about to meet the enemy at close range for the first
time, apprehension was heightened by the fact that the time of
full darkness between moon-set and dawn at 0405 was

dangerously short. Hamilton was in the conning tower of HMS *Queen Elizabeth*, and with his classical education he must surely have had in mind the magical passage in Virgil's *Aeneid* which describes an uncannily similar scene supposed to have taken place 3,000 years earlier, as the Greeks set out from the island of Tenedos to accomplish the sack of Troy. Earlier they had sailed away from the mainland, leaving their great wooden horse on the shore and apparently abandoning their attempt to capture the city. The unsuspecting Trojans had hauled the monster inside the walls; and now at night the Greek ships came stealing back across the sea – *'tacitae per amica silentia lunae'* – through the friendly silence of the quiet moon – until the royal galley raised a beacon light, signalling the treacherous Sinon to release the warriors from the horse's belly. Out they poured, to throw open the city's gates to their comrades and put Troy to the flames.

Now, on another still and moonlit night, the Allied ships stole towards the coast. They too had a wooden horse, in the form of an old collier, the *River Clyde*, which was packed with 2,000 soldiers and had sally ports cut in her sides at lower deck level so that the men could burst out at speed when she was driven straight ashore on V Beach, at the peninsula's southernmost point.

Soon after the fleet had left harbour, the battleship HMS *Triumph* went ahead as a marker ship, her role being to stay five miles west of the Anzacs' landing point and then, at midnight, to show a light to seaward, to guide the rest of the squadron in. As the other ships approached the beacon, they slowed but did not anchor, for fear that the rattle of chains would alert the defenders on the coast. Their objective was a small beach just beyond the Gaba Tepe headland, and Eric Bush left a breathless account of the final approach:

The shore is now about two miles away. The moon has set, and it is one of the darkest nights I can remember.

The ships have left to take up their stations, and we are alone: twelve picket boats with their tows steaming in line-abreast, spearhead of the invasion.

It is not easy to keep station in the pitch dark, nor to prevent tell-tale sparks from coming out of the funnels. The line concertinas sometimes, then opens out again. The order 'tows are to be 150 yards apart', to give the soldiers the broad frontage they need for forming up, is proving impossible to carry out. I, for one, close in for fear of losing touch. Other tows are doing the same, reducing the frontage by one third, a serious matter.

Everyone knew that the beaches were defended with barbed wire entanglements, for *Bacchante*'s officers had seen them through binoculars on a reconnaissance cruise a few days earlier. Whether or not there was more barbed wire in the water, they could not tell; but it was certain that the Turks were well dug in along their trenches on the hills that rose behind the beaches.

For their final approach the powered vessels stopped their engines, and in the boats men lowered oars into position to row the last few yards. Suddenly the silence was pierced by a bugle call which raised the alarm on shore. Verey lights and star shells shot into the sky. Dawn was imminent, but it was still dark enough for the invaders to see flashes as small-arms fire broke out – and down on the invaders came a rain of bullets. As the crowded boats grounded, some men were killed or wounded when they stood up, preparing to go overboard; others, as they jumped, found themselves out of their depth and went under, dragged down by their heavy equipment.

In the tows of the 11th Battalion, which were to the north of the point and still had 200 yards of water to cross before they touched the beach, bullet after bullet was splintering the boats or thudding into their crowded freight. Every now and then a man slid to the bottom of the boat with a sharp moan or gurgling cry. One seaman was handing Captain Butler his satchel out of the boat when he fell back shot through the head.

Most of the men got ashore, with bullets striking sparks out of the shingle all round them; but, to their dismay and immediate confusion, they found that the terrain was not what they had been told to expect. They raced across a strip of sand and flung themselves down in the shelter of a low cliff at the edge of the beach, which was being raked by machine-gun fire; but beyond the little bank, instead of the wide open stretch predicted, they saw a scrub-covered hillside rising in front of them. At once it was clear they had landed in the wrong place. But their orders were to go forward and establish a bridgehead, whatever the opposition – so they fixed bayonets, and forward they went up the slope, to find themselves fighting for their lives among Turkish trenches. Later it became clear that the current had carried the landing force further north than intended, and that the men had come ashore on a very small beach which will forever be known as Anzac Cove.

The crews of the picket boats were not much safer than the soldiers on land. Having landed their first loads, they picked up their launches and steamed back out to the waiting ships to collect more human cargoes. *Bacchante*'s boat had received a direct hit from a shell: fortunately it had not exploded, but to Eric Bush the casualties lying in her launch were 'very distressing'. Worse still, when they reached one of the destroyers, fresh troops clambered down into the launch so fast that there was no time to remove the wounded, who had to endure at least one more voyage to the bullet-ridden shore before they had any hope of getting treatment.

The single hospital ship allocated to the Anzac landing steamed away at 0830 for Alexandria, already loaded to capacity.

A dressing station was set up in Anzac Cove, but the beach was full of wounded, some lying on stretchers, some sitting, all crowding under the low cliff, seeking shelter from the intermittent Turkish bombardment. As more and more transports came in, troops and stores were disembarked from one side of the boats while casualties were being lifted in on the other.

When General Birdwood, the Anzacs' stalwart commander, went ashore in the afternoon, he found the beach a confused mass of men, animals and stores, with bullets dropping all around; but after a brief reconnaissance up the hillside towards the fighting line established by the infantry, he concluded that the situation was in hand and returned to the flagship, the *Queen Elizabeth*. Three hours later, at 2000, an urgent message brought him back to land: this time he found his men utterly exhausted and demoralised, and, because he had no fresh troops available, he recommended immediate evacuation.

The crew of *Bacchante*'s picket boat were told, along with others, to pick up any small craft they could find and to stand by to ferry men back to the ships. They knew instinctively that if such a drastic step were taken, only a few would get away – and their fears were shared by Rear Admiral Thursby, who had helped plan the landings, and now told the Commander-in-Chief that it would take the best part of three days to get the mass of soldiers off the beach. The result was that Hamilton overrode Birdwood's recommendation and directed him to 'dig yourselves right in and stick it out'.

The reception given to the Anzacs was vicious, but it paled before the storm of fire that greeted the landings on V Beach, further south. No stealth there. At 0504, from a mile out to sea, *Albion* began a bombardment of the Turkish defences behind the beach, but as the sun rose it shone straight in the gunners' eyes, blinding their aim. When the barrage ceased,

silence reigned on shore. Then, at 0650, as the *River Clyde* –
the assault force's wooden horse, armed with Maxim machine
guns – was approaching the beach flanked by three tows of
boats, a single shot cracked out.

> Whether a prearranged signal or not, it was the immediate
> prelude to a shattering blast of Turkish small arms and
> automatic gun fire, soon to become a continuous roar.
> The placid water off the beach was hissing with bullets.
> The carnage and damage inflicted were appalling. In the
> leading boats most of the seamen and the soldiers were
> killed or wounded. Some boats were so riddled with
> bullets that they sank . . . In a few minutes nearly every
> man was a casualty . . . Those boats which still had some
> members of their crew unhurt did their best to return to
> the sweepers for a fresh load . . . The next flight to be
> landed had in many cases to climb on top of their dead
> comrades.

Everything went wrong. The *River Clyde* grounded further
out than had been hoped. The *Argyle*, a hopper brought along
to act as a link between parent ship and shore, also grounded
too far out, and two lighters were needed to fashion a makeshift gangway to the nearest rocks. The wooden horse gave up
its hidden cargo, but murderous small-arms fire mowed the
men down in their hundreds as they struggled to reach shelter.
    'In the first rush none got alive to land, and they repeated
these rushes all day,' wrote Josiah Wedgwood, who was aboard
the *River Clyde*.

> There was no room on the rocks; there was no room on
> the lighters and boats; they were so covered with dead
> and dying . . . All around the wounded cried for help and
> shelter against the bullets. Every man who landed that

night jumped on to the backs of dead men, to the most horrible accompaniment in the world.

At Morto Bay, designated S Beach, the landing went better, and casualties were far fewer; but at W Beach the Turkish defences were extremely strong, with entanglements of thick barbed wire sunk in the water and strung across the sand. Fighting raged from dawn, all day and through the night: heroes of the landing were the 1st Battalion, the Lancashire Fusiliers, who were later awarded six Victoria Crosses; but their losses were terrible. By the time the firing died down, the battalion had lost nine of its twenty-five officers and 632 of its 932 men. Of the eighty naval ratings who manned the cutters and lifeboats, sixty-three were killed or wounded.

At X Beach different tactics worked better. Led by HMS *Implacable*, the big ships came close inshore and continued to put down a stunning bombardment on the beach even as the boatloads of infantry were on their way. 'The blast of the guns of the *Implacable* over our heads as we went in was most unpleasant,' remembered Midshipman Hugh Tate, 'as were the bullets coming down all round like little wasps.' The battleship was so close that she made an irresistible target for the Turkish riflemen and machine-gunners; but because her bridge had been fortified with 800 sandbags before she left Portsmouth, she was immune to small-arms ammunition, and she drew a lot of fire away from the landing craft. The result was that infantry managed to climb a cliff with relatively few losses, but at the top fierce bayonet engagements ensued.

Y Beach, the southernmost landing point, was hardly a beach at all – a mere cleft in the cliff which the Turks had not defended because they thought it unassailable. When troops were put ashore at first light, they reached the shore and climbed the dry watercourse unopposed – but then their supporting battleship *Goliath* began to shell the summit, giving their presence away, and savage fighting broke out. Driving back the Turkish front line, the invaders gained the ridge, albeit with heavy losses – only to be undermined by confusing and contradictory orders from senior officers, who lost control of the battle. Historians have argued endlessly about who was to blame; but the result was that the surviving troops were withdrawn and the attack was abandoned.

In spite of this setback, and grievous losses all round, the Allies had established a foothold on the peninsula; and gradually, by dint of repeated naval bombardments, and infantry attacks which usually ended in bayonet charges, they forced their front lines forward. Aubrey Herbert described 'lines of men clinging like cockroaches under the cliffs'. Day after day, night after night, week after week and month after month, the bloody fighting continued. False reports of success found their way back to England. 'I suppose you know the wonderful rumours that we had, that you were through the Dardanelles,' wrote Herbert Smart from his home in Ealing. 'It was even posted up in Lloyds!'

Bacchante was frequently in action, bombarding the Turkish defences, every detail of her days and nights meticulously recorded in the ship's log. Thus on 'Saturday 1st day of May 1915', she 'Weighed [anchor] and proceeded as requisite'. During the day she opened fire on the coastal defences ten times, and in the evening tested her lifebuoys. Then: 'Hands to night action stations, burned searchlights as necessary on shores of Gaba Tepe ...Water distilled 54 tons, water expended 20 tons, fuel expended for all purposes 55 tons coal, fuel remaining 1,424 tons.' On 3 May the ship took on 1,608 lbs of fresh beef (where did it come from, and was it in joints or whole carcases?).

Onshore, the most ferocious Turkish attack of all began after the moon had set on the night of 19 May. At 3.30 a.m. the Allied sentries spotted dark figures creeping towards their trenches and opened fire, whereupon thousands of Turks leapt up and rushed forward screaming *'Allah! Allah!'* As Eric Bush recorded, 'the assailants came on so quickly that the Anzacs had only to fire point-blank to ensure that every shot told'. The battle raged for the rest of the night and all next morning; the assault was beaten off, and by the end of it the Turks had lost 5,000 men, 3,000 of whom lay dead in front of the trenches. The Anzac losses were fewer than 100 killed and 500 wounded.

That morning, 20 May, the weather turned hot, and the smell of bloating corpses rapidly became nauseating. A brief armistice was arranged so that the dead could be buried, and Aubrey Herbert went across to the Turkish side for a few hours to act as a hostage and interpreter. He had already held several unofficial parleys with the Turks, advancing into the forwardmost trench until only a few yards from the enemy, and then engaging them through a megaphone in their own language. Now a Turkish Red Crescent man gave him some antiseptic wool with scent on it, to hold against his face, and he described how bodies

filled acres of ground. One saw the result of machine-gun fire very clearly; entire companies annihilated – not wounded, but killed, their heads doubled under them with the impetus of their rush and both hands clasping their bayonets. It was as if God had breathed in their faces, as 'the Assyrian came down like a wolf on the fold'.

During that dreadful spring and summer *Bacchante* spent many more days on the firing stations off Gaba Tepe and Suvla Bay, ready to put down a bombardment whenever one was needed, either to precede an Allied advance or to repel a Turkish attack. Several times she withdrew 'due to proximity of heavy falling shell'. Pure chance dictated that she left her position on 24 May, and was replaced by the battleship HMS *Triumph*, just as a new menace was creeping into the arena.

Next day, a little after noon, the captain of *Triumph*'s escorting destroyer HMS *Chelmer* spotted a suspicious white streak in the water some 500 yards off the battleship's starboard beam – the wash of a submarine. *Triumph* opened fire at it, but too late. The submarine had dived, and a few moments later a tremendous explosion seemed to lift the whole battleship into the air as a torpedo struck her. Within seven minutes she capsized. By expert seamanship *Chelmer* managed to rescue 465 officers and men, but under its able captain, Lieutenant Commander Otto Hersing, the German submarine *U-21* slipped quietly away.

Even after all the death and destruction he had already seen, Hugh found the incident shocking. Writing on 31 May, a week before his sixteenth birthday, he told his mother:

The *Triumph* was struck at 12.25, turned turtle at 12.33 and sank at 12.50. About thirty-five men and two officers only were lost. The whole thing would be visible from the shore. All the time the vessel was sinking and the boats were picking up survivors, the Turks and Germans were firing on them. Shrapnel burst over us, and I should say that a fair percentage of the people who were killed were hit by shrapnel bullets while in the water. It was ghastly.

On the high ground above Anzac Cove and Suvla Bay the front line was now more than a mile inland. The coastal strip the Allies had captured became honeycombed not only with trenches, but also with tunnels and elaborately constructed dugouts in which life was relatively safe. In an unpublished short story Hugh later wrote a vivid description of the terrain:

These hills and dales were not regular by any means. They curved into a thousand corners, thus forming countless glens and gullies, little stretches of flat ground and many bits of hills. An easy country to defend, the very devil to attack!

These slopes formed a rabbit warren of holes and tunnellings in which the fighters lived. They called them 'dug-outs', 'bivvies', 'funk holes' – any name. There were no tents, or very few, so they used the kindly earth and fashioned houses that gave them shelter of a sort. Some were mere hollows in the ground with scraps of canvas or blankets stretched above. Others were more pretentious, boasting sandbags in their composition. A few had wooden beams and corrugated iron holding up the roof. At night there would come men to the engineers' store heaps and stealthily remove the wherewithal to build.

Although Hugh's main duty remained with the small boats, he spent a good deal of time ashore, for, whenever *Bacchante* went off for a few days on some other task, she left her picket boat behind, and the midshipman and crew slept in the naval beach party's lairs.

One of the picket boat's duties was to bury Indian dead at sea. A havildar (corporal) and two sepoys (privates) would bring the body down to the pier on a stretcher, tightly wrapped in a blanket and weighted with stones, with a priest in attendance. Half a mile out to sea, the engines were stopped, and after the priest had said prayers, one end of the stretcher was tipped up, so that the corpse slid into the water. The sea was so clear that the crew could watch the body twist and turn until it reached the bottom.

Concealing his own stoicism and courage, Hugh hardly ever complained in his letters home. But once, from Walker's Ridge Beach, he sent Anne a graphic account of the horrors of local life. He had dysentery and a bad cold, but was still carrying on, 'as we all have to do . . . The flies, gnats and flees [*sic*] are

hell. I jog along all right, working hard and watching for the
first signs of ptomaine poisoning from eating too much tinned
stuff.' He several times referred to the dangers of contaminated
tinned food, but ptomaine poisoning was generally thought to
have been caused by putrefaction.

A mule convoy is passing with stores to the depot . . .
Everything is hot and horrid. On the piers on the beach
crowds of men are sweating at work on various jobs, i.e.
loading and unloading stores. Away up the beach about
half a mile from me a picket boat is trying to tow off
some dead mules from the beach. I fancy I can smell
them from here.

Out in the bay a tow of launches is approaching a
hospital ship. More cases are waiting on the pier. Here is
a poor fellow in the last stages of enteric. There is another
with an arm and a leg gone. Yet they are so cheerful, so
patient. There is no groaning, no complaining, although
occasionally a curse is plainly audible. Here we have a
Maori with his head a mass of bandages; there is a Gurkha
in agony. His bowels are hanging out. Here is a case of
typhoid, there one of scarlet fever, there one of malaria.

If ever an exploit will live in the annals of war, surely
there is none more deserving than the taking of the
Dardanelles by the Allied forces in 1915. I have met many
men who have been through the Great Retreat, through
all the subsequent fighting until Ypres, and they said that
the fighting at the front was *eating cake* compared to the
war here. *Child's play*, they called it, and laughed. Here
we have hell unsweetened. There are no 48 [hour] spells
in the trenches, then rests in a nice base, with hot baths,
gorgeous food, clean beds, French peasants to wait on
you. Here there are no weekend leaves home, no rest, no
relaxation.

Out of 518 officers and men (28 officers) only 49 men and one officer remain on service! The remainder are killed, wounded, missing and sick. They have already been 4½ months in the trenches, and are likely to remain there till there are *none* left.

With love from your loving Hugh.

In June and July 'disembarkation parties' from *Bacchante* were sent to carry out various tasks on shore. On 2 July Hugh wrote again to his father:

Dear Daddy,

I'm just back from Gaba Tepe again after a week of beach and boat work. I used to live in a 'dug-out' ashore with another fellow, an awfully decent man and a thorough gentleman, who was in the New Zealand A.S.C. He is a Lance Sergeant and in charge of sanitary arrangements. His name is Cadogan & he's a distant relation of Lord Cadogan. And by George, he can cook some!

I have enclosed a plan of the 'dug-out' with dimensions. The roof was five feet thick, and although shells burst at XYZ and W (melinite 4.9″ Turkish shells), only one piece of shell came inside the inner 'room', and that didn't do any harm. It came in via the window. We were having tea at the time. It's no use saying it's as safe as houses because it is a jolly sight safer.

I must stop now so goodbye, Daddy Dear, lots of love to everyone at home.

From your loving son, Hugh

P.S. I forgot to tell I went up in the trenches where they call it 'Quinn's Post', and the Turks are only 15 yards away.

One not accustomed to it is nearly sickened by the smell of dead men, which lie between the two trenches – both New Zealanders and Turks. I was looking through a periscope and a Turk fired at it and knocked it out of my hands. The periscopic rifle is very interesting to fire with. I don't think I hit anyone, however – only a spade or two.

Death had become so ubiquitous that he did not commit to paper any account of his most traumatic moment ashore, when in a moment of crisis a filthy sergeant ran up to him, told him he was the most senior officer left alive in that sector and asked permission to launch an attack. Hugh gave it, and, as the sergeant went off, he grabbed a rifle which was lying on the beach. Seconds later an enormous Turk loomed up over the lip of the nearest trench, whereupon Hugh drove his bayonet into the man's diaphragm, skewering his first victim. Forty years later, he would recount this grisly incident to his children; but although he told the story with apparent relish, they sensed that it, and all the associated horrors of Gallipoli, had remained a burden to him throughout his life.

Meanwhile, in France, Herbert Smart was longing for precisely this kind of action. The slaughter and destruction of property around the front line had roused his ire against the Germans, and on 8 April 1916 he wrote to Hugh:

Having seen some of the villages the curs have left, I can pray for nothing better than to feel my bayonet go into one of them. One [village] I have been in you cannot see until you go up the old trenches. Then you come across two square feet of flooring and about the same amount of wall . . . all the trees cut down and the roads a mass of mine-craters. That is the Hun. Can you wonder if one longs to be across the frontier to teach the swine that frightfulness is a game that two can play?

At Gallipoli some relief from the heat and squalor of the trenches was provided by the sea. With the front line a mile or more inland, the beaches had become relatively safe. 'Hands to bathe' became a regular entry in the ships' logs, and men swam naked every day – except for the Indians, whose religion forbade them from baring all. Grooms, also naked, rode their horses in the sea, chancing stray bullets. Whenever the Turks began to strafe the shore with a big gun, the beach-master would blow his whistle, and everyone would strike out for land or scuttle into shelter under the piers – but a photograph in the archives of King's College London shows a row of soldiers sitting comfortably in the open with their rifles propped beside them, while a heavy Turkish gun known as Asiatic Annie is dropping shells into the water not far from shore. The caption explains, 'When Asiatic Annie has stopped firing, our men dive in and collect the fish'. Annie was by no means the only big gun known to the invaders by name: Fritz of Arkenoy was another, and Beachy Bill the most persistent of all.

In a buoyant letter to his mother, written on 19 July – perhaps in harbour at Moudros – Hugh described how he and three other snotties had gone over to the *Albion* for dinner and 'had a right good time', with the ship's company joining in a big sing-song. 'Quite the best night I've spent for a long time!' he reported, and afterwards, when they pulled back to the *Bacchante* in the whaler, the night 'was so topping and cool'.

In the midst of all the fighting he was finding time to read and think, and he asked to be sent books on Italian history, precisely specifying subject and period – 1580–1615, including 'habits, customs, dress, coinage, chief naval powers such as Venice, their fleets . . .'. From later scraps of evidence, it seems that he was already trying to write fiction, perhaps an historical novel.

On 6 August he was back off Gaba Tepe, where *Bacchante* was again bombarding the enemy trenches and gun positions. During the night and throughout all the next day she supported

the Anzac troops as they advanced on their left and drove the
Turks back. Some shells were aimed further north to help men
landing in, and close to, Suvla Bay. 'Sometimes we fired continuously for a long time, but it was all deliberate fire,' Hugh told
his father.

> The artillery officers on shore were 'spotting' for us. Several
> times enemy planes came over and dropped bombs – they
> may have been at us or other ships in the vicinity, as their
> aim may have been fairly bad or very good. Some of
> them came quite close to us. Our airmen chased them
> and we would fire at them with our anti-aerial guns. It
> was rather amusing.

Three weeks later he was ashore yet again, still with the
Anzac force on Walker's Ridge Beach. Scribbling in pencil, he
told his father that there was only himself, one other snottie
from another ship, one lieutenant and one gunner on the large
beach. 'I can give you no details, of course, as to what we do,'
he wrote, 'except that a great deal of it is embarkation of
wounded, so that I have a lot to do with the medical people.'

> Tell mother any grub is welcome, and I'm so glad to hear
> there's some more on the way. Lime-juice especially. Please
> excuse the bad writing, but I'm sitting in a very difficult
> place in a very sandy dug-out. This afternoon I'm free,
> so I'm going to bathe and then wander up to the firing
> line to have a smell at the Turks.

At the end of the month the grub reached him 'by a
circuitous route', and he sent his mother 'a thousand thanks . . .
The lime-juice was especially welcome, and the cakes also.'
With the letter he enclosed a sketch of his dugout, which was
seven feet wide and included two stretchers resting on low

boxes – 'very good beds they make. P.S. A d— sniper had the cheek to knock a tin out of my hand today.'

No record survives of his movements during September, but it seems to have been then that he was first wounded. He never wrote an account of what happened – though in later life he needed little encouragement to tell the story. One night as his picket boat was approaching the shore through the usual hail of rifle fire, a Turkish bullet seared through his scalp. He escaped with his life by almost literally a hair's breadth – if the round had been half or even quarter of an inch lower, he would have been dead. (Later in life he used to fascinate children by showing them the scar which ran through his hair towards the back of his head, from fore to aft.) Like all head wounds, this one bled a lot, but it was only skin-deep, and did not put him out of action for long.

A letter to his mother written on 8 October from Malta whither he was taken to recover, made no mention of being injured; but to his delight he discovered that his Uncle Charlie was living in a hotel on the island, and this proved an ideal refuge in which to recuperate. 'This place is a change after the last six months,' he told her. 'I saw Uncle Charlie yesterday, and by Jove, it was a relief to see a Home face again and to speak to one of the family. As I think that in about a month I shall go back to the Peninsula, I have given a rough list of things I should like sent . . . '

His requests included potted meat – 'one tin of grouse, one of partridge, one of pheasant', one of 'anchovy Lazonby', some potted prawns or shrimps, jam ('any amount') biscuits ('any amount') cakes – lawn tennis, chocolate cake with cream, Mrs Rodwell's cake, Louisa's rock cakes. In due course the Rodwell cake turned out 'awfully good', and some large slabs of chocolate reminded him of Osborne.

Anne Hamilton's letters were a powerful support. Early in October he told her he found them 'so cheering, so helpful, so remindful of home that I prize them very very highly'. He was glad to hear that Louis Belloc – son of Hilaire Belloc – had passed into the Royal Military Academy at Woolwich. 'Old Hilaire B. must be proud of him,' he wrote – and then suddenly: 'What is your opinion of Horatio Bottomley? I would rather not give mine, as it might shock some people.'

The hospitality offered by Uncle Charlie in his hotel was a huge comfort. One day Hugh wrote to Anne from his sitting room, with his host at the other side of the table, simultaneously composing a letter to his father. 'I cannot say how truly glad I am that such a providential meeting has occurred,' Hugh told her. With his letter he enclosed a recent photograph of the two of them, reporting that he was now five foot eight tall, 'if not more', and that he weighed nine stone eight pounds. 'But alas,' he wrote, 'my physical condition is bad. My muscles are out of practice and in sporting terms, "asleep" . . . As you have probably guessed already, I'm writing. The subject is north Italy, mostly round Verona, Venice, Lake di Guarda [sic] Milan and all Lombardy. I feel I never knew so much about any place before . . . The whole idea is *there*, or I should say *here*, tapping my cranium.

Now goodbye dear Anne. Lots of love from Hugh.

Suddenly his life took a new turn, signalled by a telegram stamped *SANSORIGINE* and sent home from Malta on 4 November:

AM TRANSFERRED DESTROYER WOLVERINE.

It turned out that *Wolverine*'s skipper, Lieutenant Commander Keyes, finding himself two officers short of complement, had asked around for spares, and Boyle, captain of *Bacchante*, had replied that he had 'two snotties capable enough that he did not mind parting with'. So, to his delight, Hugh and his fellow midshipman Douglas Dixon transferred to a much smaller ship, a Beagle-class torpedo-boat destroyer, with a complement of ninety-six, as opposed to *Bacchante*'s 750, and a top speed of twenty-seven knots.

News of Hugh's transfer provoked a swift riposte from Herbert Smart:

First you get on to the *Bacchante* and, well, we know what that means, and now you get on to the *Wolverine*, and, well, I went to the Natural History Museum this Monday and saw a nice little label

WOLVERINE

OR

GLUTTON

And knowing the love of those in high places for a vile bad joke, I cannot help thinking that there must be something in it. Still, it may be only a rumour.

At one point in his journal Aubrey Herbert remarked, 'The middies are the most splendid boys', and, in view of the hazardous part they played in the campaign, it seems astonishing that none of the nine midshipmen drafted to *Bacchante* from Blake term was killed at Gallipoli. Besides Hugh, one other, Tom Bashall, was wounded there, but the rest came through physically unscathed, transformed from boys into men by their ordeal.

Looking back a year or two later, Hugh wrote a moving valediction:

I see again the beach at Anzac with the dust and the piers.
I see the picket boats off shore, steaming with their tows.
I see the lines of dug-outs and the gullies and the hills.
And the men? I see them too. Burnt almost as brown as the sand, wearing the tattered remnants of their uniforms with a manly grace, stalwart, steadfast and true, I see them

still. Britons and Australians, New Zealanders and Indians, soldiers and sailors, they are all there. I see them quite as plainly now in the mirror of my memory as I saw them at Z beach in those glorious months.

Once I walked upon the beach at Anzac Cove and marvelled that mere men had ever landed there. After a while I grew to know the men who did this thing, and I marvelled no more.

Around the Med

By a stroke of good fortune Hugh had been released not only from a skipper he disliked (Boyle), but also – for the time being – from the hellish conflict at Gallipoli. His fellow midshipmen who stayed on *Bacchante* were still risking their lives every day and night, off and on the beaches at Anzac Cove and Suvla Bay, but *Wolverine* had gone to Malta for a refit, and she stayed there for three weeks. Thereafter she did frequently return to the peninsula to support the Anzac beach-head, but she also spent much time patrolling in the Aegean and Mediterranean. Hugh described her movements as 'strictly private and very uncertain.'

He joined her at Malta, and on 7 November he wrote to his father:

I hope you got my cable and rejoice with me in my good fortune. I am as happy as can be and as mad as a hatter. Uncle Charlie is still flourishing and laying himself out to give me a good time . . . My new skipper is a treasure. I shall take care not to lose him. The No 1 is a fine fellow too, and also the gunner and the artificer engineer. These, Dixon and myself compose the Wardroom.

In the dock at Malta hands were put to scraping the ship, cleaning the guns, painting the magazine and storerooms,

and drawing stores; and because his cabin was being redec-
orated Hugh was allowed to spend much time ashore, 'living
at the Savoy, Sliema', with time to worry about his possessions in England. He told his parents they should not expect
to see him 'for months and months'; also that he was sending
back an Egyptian fez and an axe-head which he had taken
from an old Turkish trench. One problem niggling him was
the future of his bicycle, a high-class model, bought for £8,
which was now standing idle at home. When his father
suggested that it should be given to his brother Evan, he
reacted sharply:

Of course I don't mind. What do you take me for? Let
him take the thing and smash it up if he likes. It's no
earthly good to me, and I shouldn't like him to be at
Woolwich with a shabby bike among a lot of decent ones,
when there was mine sitting at home. I don't suppose
I've ridden it more than fifteen miles altogether, and I
shall never ride a bike again. Of course I didn't bargain
for the war being so sudden when I paid £8 for the
article in question. But Evan can have it for a birthday
present in addition. It's no earthly use to me.

He was also annoyed about the fate of a large case of war
relics which he had assembled and despatched for home.
Most of the contents were what he described as 'of an innocent order – shells, fuses and so on'; but a few choice
specimens, which he had 'taken hours of trouble over securing
and keeping', were commandeered by his bugbear, Captain
Boyle, and then the whole lot was confiscated. When the
authorities demanded an explanation of how he had acquired
them, his new skipper stuck up for him and he escaped
censure; but he himself was furious, and wrote gloomily, 'I'm
afraid even the shells are collared.' Later he heard from Eric

Bush that most of his gear had been 'pinched out of the box' by Captain Boyle.

In Malta he pressed ahead with his writing. From several textbooks and grammars he was trying to learn Italian; but as his facilities for research were limited, he often turned to Anne for information, asking her in particular about Italian composers of the fourteenth and fifteenth centuries.

On 1 December *Wolverine* slipped anchor and set out for Moudros, which she reached in four days. Hugh and Dixon shared a cabin, and when at sea took turns to occupy the single bunk, while one of them spent the night on a couch in the wardroom. In a letter to Anne he cheerfully described his job of censoring the men's letters:

> Every letter – or nine out of ten – starts with 'I ope this finds you has it leafs me quiet in the pink and longin for a pint of ops' ('ops' meaning beer). One was like this: 'Oppin (hoping) has you are in the A 1 pink – has yours (yours truly) is at present dear ducky I ave a bad cold in my ead ands and feet'.
>
> No stops, of course. What is a cold in the ands?

'Truly life is not all monotony', he told his mother on 15 December, and he described how, in the two weeks since leaving Malta, *Wolverine* had been doing 'the most extraordinary things'.

> In two days I had seen three new towns (I mean new to me). We have fed on tinned grub and seen fresh meat and vegetables hanging in shops less than 100 yards away and been unable to get at them. We have passed through darkest night and come suddenly into a blaze of light, with shops and theatres. We have chased vessels and lost them among the islands and we have seen the workings

of a vast secret service. Oh, give me the Destroyer Navy, any day! There's nothing to beat it! Nothing! And what a school of seamanship!

Wolverine's log shows that she had been on patrol off Milo, in the entrance to the Gulf of Athens. By 13 December she was back at Moudros, and over the next two weeks, during the closing stages of the Gallipoli campaign, she frequently joined in the bombardment of the Turkish defences.

By then plans were being finalised for a phased withdrawal of the whole Allied force from the peninsula. After a visit to the theatre in November, Kitchener had at last concluded that evacuation was inevitable, and, as if to endorse his decision, a ferocious storm struck the Turkish coast on the nights of the 26th and 27th:

In the low flat ground of the Suvla plain the state of things was indescribable. Snow descended in a whirling blizzard. The surface of the pools and trenches froze. Men staggered down from the lines so numbed with cold that they could hardly hear or speak. Sentries left standing at their posts were found afterwards still watching from the parapet, rifle in hand, but frozen to death. The dead in IX Corps alone numbered over 200. From the Peninsula over 2,000 sick had to be removed. Many were frost bitten; many lost limbs; some lost their reason.

In spite of this devastating blow, the withdrawal was perfectly executed – a complete contrast to the shambles of the original landing. At Anzac and Suvla Bay elaborate steps were taken to conceal what was happening from the Turks; artillery fire was maintained until the last possible minute; soldiers constructed ingenious devices which would let off rifle and gunshots after they had departed; at night a destroyer kept a searchlight trained on the nearest Turkish lookout post, blinding its inhabitants.

Between storms, the weather remained miraculously calm. So good was the Allies' organisation that on the nights of 18 and 19 December almost 20,000 men of the Anzac force were embarked on the ships lying offshore without a single fatal casualty: only two men were slightly wounded. The second and final phase of the evacuation took place on the nights of 7 and 8 January 1916 – again a masterly operation. Yet a terrible residue had been left behind. Four hundred heavy draft horses – many of them prize-winners at English shows – had been shot, rather than let them fall into Turkish hands. Huge heaps of valuable equipment had been burnt, 1,600 vehicles had been abandoned, and at East Pier a fortnight's rations for 40,000 men had gone up in flames.

Wolverine's log shows that she was closely engaged during those last fraught days, helping to keep Turkish heads down:

19th December. Opened fire on Turkish beaches . . . 21st 6.5–6.20 Heavy Turkish attack. Opened fire on batteries . . . 27th Firing in short bursts, four 4″ rds . . . 7th Jan 1916 Heavy Turkish artillery attack on left flank. Fired 85 rds 4″ and 104 rds 12-pdr . . . 9th Sunk derelict steamer by gunfire of Gully Beach. Opened with shrapnel on advancing Turkish line.

It is a pity that, although *Wolverine*'s crew witnessed the evacuation at close quarters, Hugh did not describe it in his letters home. All he said on 8 January was, 'We did a great deal of strafing yesterday and expect to have a very busy night tonight. It's going to be rather a show. I expect you'll guess what I mean when you compare dates with a paper.' A busy night it was: during the hours of darkness, as the warships blazed away at the Turkish defences, the final 17,000 men were safely embarked.

Thereafter Hugh seems to have deliberately shut the ghast-
liness of Gallipoli out of his mind, writing home about his
mother's food parcels, and cheerful matters such as the
Christmas dinner (held in harbour at Moudros), during which
the company drank champagne and 'sat yarning and laughing
and shouting and drinking till I am on Boxing Day'.

He began the new year – 1916 – in fine fettle, reporting
that he was well and in good spirits, buoyed up by the fact
that *Wolverine* was due to return to England, and leave was in
prospect. On 1 February he reported that prize money was
going to be made equal to a year's pay – 'Very nice for some
people!' He reckoned that he himself would get only about
£32, 'as hard living money and extra allowances don't count'.
Then a change in the ship's programme plunged him into a
mood of cynical, almost suicidal gloom.

Call this war? I call my part of it hell. It's only just waiting
and fooling around. Why should the soldiers have all the
fighting? Of course I've done firing and been fired at,
but do I ever get in a bayonet charge or close hand-to-
hand work? Oh, I've seen it. I've even had more than a
taste of it at Anzac, dear old Walker's Ridge, Quinn's Port,
Lone Pine, Johnson's Gully, Death Valley, Brighton Beach,
Gaba Tepe Sand, old Number 3 port, Chocolate Hills,
Battleship Hill, the farmhouse, old Turkish camp, the fisherman's hut etc. I know them all and I've seen real fighting.
More, I know I could *fight*. Why keep me here, on a
waiting job? Who wants to murder Turks or Germans at
several thousand yards' range? Not I!

Oh, it's hard! And nothing to brake [*sic*] the monotony.
Always cruising, coaling, firing, searching and so on . . .
Small quarters, awful weather! Heaven – no, hell! Better
the mud and filth, better the trenches than this. Nothing
to show for it either. Oh! The times I spent at Anzac and

Walker's Ridge were the happiest in my life. I lived for
a week on one loaf and ¼ lb of ship's cocoa, solid. Was
I hungry? No! Did I mind? I'd do it again for a year and
be happy. I had dysentery – mildly. Did I care? Of course
it was awful while it lasted, but I'd have it again, for the
same reasons.

I love the sea, really, but I hate the Service sometimes.
I couldn't live long without the sea, sometimes, but the
Service makes me tired! Now I'm talking treason, so had
better stop. Oh what a life! Believe me or not as you like
– I've come to my senses since – but there *was* a time
when I would cheerfully have slipped over the side. D—
the war!

Oh mother dearest, goodbye till next time I write. I
feel better now, having relieved my feelings. Don't think
I shall ever be such a coward as to take my own life. I
have too great a sense of duty to God and you and Daddy
for that. I have something to keep me going. Something
to buoy me up. There's always hope . . . All the love in
the world from your own loving boy,

                                                    Hugh

Wolverine spent much of February at sea, then for eight days
in March docked in Alexandria. There Hugh's spirits revived,
and he enjoyed himself 'immensely'. He got himself a horse
and did a good deal of riding. Ashore with colleagues, he
sometimes became obstreperous, the young officers competing
to see how many policemen's helmets they could collect. Only
those actually removed from the heads of the owners counted,
and the record bag for an evening was seven; but the sport
came to an abrupt end when one constable suffered a sense
of humour failure and started firing his revolver into the air.
His central interest was his novel, with which he was making

good progress. 'I don't know what the finished article will be like, but I may finish by Midsummer.' All he told his parents about his naval life was that 'now and then we get a little excitement', and that he was becoming 'quite used to handling a rifle'. Then, in March, he let on that he had taken part 'in a wee bit of a show here', telling them that they could probably work out what it had been by comparing dates with the papers.

Far from sounding depressed, he was jubilant about his increased seniority. In *Bacchante* 'Captain B.' had 'had a down' on him, and he had been 'a great deal junior' to most of the other snotties, but now the order had been revised, and, aged sixteen and a half, he had become 'senior to Dixon and Co'. Also, he had gained four months' seniority, and dated as a snottie from 2 August 1914. His pay had increased as well: for serving on a destroyer he got two shillings a day extra, and he had recently managed to send home £4 5s., raising the total of his savings to £20. The money travelled via the Admiralty, which sent a notice to his parents, enabling them to collect the cash at a post office. 'I hope you are using my money as your own, as I don't want it,' he wrote, 'and after all it's only paying you back in a sort of way a little for what you've done for me.' In spite of this show of insouciance, he was sensitive about finance, and worried about the cost of the food parcels which his mother kept sending:

> Mother dear, if this is costing too much, just stop it, will you? Don't think I don't *love* to get them, but I wouldn't for all the world cause my only, darling mother more trouble than possible . . . I liked the biscuits awfully and the Rodwell cake. Never seem to get tired of that somehow. And 5 *lbs* of that topping chocolate! Oh, mother dear! And rusks & sweets & jam!! Oh, you dearest of all possible mothers!

A letter to Anne revealed a priggish streak in his nature, and a touch of pomposity which had never been evident before. It sounds as if he had had an embarrassing experience in the red-light district of Alexandria:

Do you remember a certain occasion some years ago, when you told me with confidence that in a few years – when about 20 or so – I would think women (particularly young and pretty ones) angels, and fall in and out of love every day? Well, whether you remember or not, you said so, and I reply that you were absolutely and irrevocally [sic] wrong. I have seen more in — and — in a short while than most men see in all their lives. I know more about the depths to which men and women – rakes and harlots – can descend than any other fellow of my age – 16 years & 10 months. Not one in 10,000 has seen what I have seen. Yet I have come out clean, untainted, sickened, thoroughly disgusted, furious against the weakness of human nature (the average), and hating the sight of young and pretty women. I know several nice girls, yet I avoid their company if possible, although I know them to be as good as they are made.

You will say that I'm not yet 17, but I reply that in a case like this age doesn't matter. It's experience and feelings that matter. So there you have it. What I may not have in years I have in experience and knowledge of these things. I am like 22–25 years old in this respect, and then only with people who travel round a lot. Most men have never even dreamt that such things exist as I have seen. Not two snotties in the Service have seen as much as I have, and they *usually* see and *take part* in these things . . . 'Truly the Devil hath an ingenious and inventive mind'.

Of course all this is strictly private. Don't tell anyone else or there'll be ructions.

Another letter reflected his unease about women in general. Someone had told him that after the war every man would be compelled to marry – 'at least, everyone of a decent age and respectably physically fit'. When *he* reached the age limit, he now wrote, 'no power on earth' would make him marry, unless he himself wanted to. 'That last is very unlikely indeed. So much so, in fact, that it is impossible – though I don't like that last word.' From someone who eventually married three times, this was not a very acute prediction.

For the time being, he was preoccupied with his novel, and, seeing himself a war veteran, he was chagrined by the discovery that as yet he lacked the literary skill to write a commercially viable book which drew on his own experiences. When he got a rejection from James B. Pinker, a literary agent with an office in Arundel Street, off the Strand in London, to whom he had submitted his manuscript, he was clearly annoyed as well as disappointed. To Anne, he claimed he was not surprised, but his injured pride showed through:

After all, what else could I expect? Has anyone ever appreciated a first or second book? I wouldn't mind betting he called it 'immature'. Then he says, 'Cut it down'! How? Where? Of course I *could* do that. There are some digressions, but on the whole I scarcely think it's worth the trouble . . . Stow it away somewhere. Let it rot . . . There are several ideas in my head, one especially suitable for the next venture. And I can write it anywhere.

Soon he had something far more serious to worry about. His last surviving letter of 1916, written to his mother on 21 March, ended 'I am well and happy . . . With lots of love to everyone from your loving boy, Hugh.' Then at 5.30 in the morning of 3 April *Wolverine*, still in the business of beating up coastal defences, entered Keugezi Bay, on the south-western corner of Turkey, between Marmaris and Fethiye. She was evidently not expecting trouble as she steamed across the bay and on into Ekinjek harbour, at its head – but her log tells the story:

> 6.20 Under heavy fire from trench ashore. 6.25 Midshipman G.H.J. Evans wounded. 6.27 proceeded out of harbour. 6.30 action stations. 6.45 re-entered harbour, bombarded trenches and houses.

It seems that Hugh had been standing at an exposed point on the ship when small-arms fire came crackling from the shore. The captain had just told him to get under cover when a heavy, long-range Turkish rifle bullet struck him in the thigh. The impact knocked him down a companionway, and somebody picked him up and carried him into the captain's cabin, where he became embarrassed because he was covering the bunk with blood. Someone must have staunched the flow efficiently, for he survived that night, and, next day, abeam of the island of Psara, *Wolverine* went alongside the hospital ship *Karapara* and discharged him into it.

Presumably he was taken first to Malta, and then invalided back to England – for if he had been laid up for long anywhere in the Mediterranean, he would surely have continued to write home, and some of his letters would have survived. Wherever he received treatment, the wound must have taken some time to heal, but it left him with no permanent disability and he never walked with a limp.

He next surfaces aboard HMS *Princess Royal*, a Lion-class battle cruiser which had sustained heavy damage the year before in the Battle of Jutland. In February 1918 he joined HMS *Lily*, a sloop built originally for minesweeping in 1915, but transferred to escort duty two years later. He caught up with her in Egypt, having travelled by train to Marseilles, which he reached in the record time of forty-seven hours from leaving Charing Cross. In Paris he and a colleague called Gordon had some difficulty with their luggage, which weighed 200 kilos; but 'after a little bluff and careful lying', during which Gordon drew himself up, flourishing his passport and announcing, '*Nous sommes les couriers diplomatiques!*', they muscled their way on to the *Marseilles Rapide*. On Christmas day they caught a P&O liner and reached Port Said on 3 January 1918, then lingered in Cairo until their ship came in.

The smallest vessel he had served on – only 250 feet long, with a complement of seventy-seven – *Lily* was one of the 'Cabbage class' or 'Herbaceous Borders', so-called because, from *Acacia* to *Veronica*, they were all named after flowers. One day at sea he told Anne:

> The ship is vibrating rather fiercely, so please forgive horrible scrawl. That's the worst of this class of ship – the terrible vibration. And they roll about 35 degrees a side, too, in comparative calm.

Now and then an armed party was put ashore to investigate an alleged dump of weapons. On one search, at Port Bardia in Libya, the posse discovered no arms or ammunition, but plenty of evidence of enemy activity: a number of fifty-gallon oil drums with German markings, mounted on neatly made beds at a convenient height for tipping the contents, and on the beach near the telegraph office a body gagged with its throat cut.

The ship's log shows that she spent much of her time escorting convoys, zigzagging ahead or astern of merchantmen to protect them from German submarines. This must have been tedious work, but also nerve-racking, for the convoys moved very slowly, at only six or seven knots, and were easy targets for U-boats – as on 27 May 1918:

0.27 am Action Stations sounded. RMT *Leasowe Castle* torpedoed. 0.35 am started picking up survivors. 1.29 am went alongside starboard side of *Leasowe Castle*. 2 am *Leasowe Castle* sunk. *Lily* proceeded at full speed full of survivors.

A week later, at 6 p.m. on 3 June, the SS *Nora* was torpedoed, whereupon *Lily* circled round and dropped depth charges on the assumed position of the submarine, but without result. On 7 June the log had a different kind of entry: somewhere between Alexandria and Bizerta 'Sub Lt. G. H. J. Evans lost convoy by neglect and was taken off watch-keeping during hours of darkness'. Beside this was written: 'Signed under protest: Jocelyn Evans' – the only time on record when he used the third of his Christian names.

Perhaps Hugh's mind had been on his latest story, for writing was now his main preoccupation, and through Anne he got to know her friend Edith Nesbit, the celebrated author of more than forty books for children, among them his own favourite, *The Railway Children*. Unworried by her strong Socialist leanings – she was a co-founder of the Fabian Society – he later went to see her at her home in London, and furnished her with details of foreign countries he had visited for her novels, especially one set in Syria.

At last he himself began to have some modest literary success. His agent, Pinker, failed to place at least three 'Anzac' short stories, which were perhaps too leisurely: although they were nicely turned, and vividly evoked the atmosphere on the shore at Gallipoli, they lacked the stirring action that would have brought them to life. Then in July 1918 the *Sketch* magazine accepted another of them, and published it under the by-line 'Sforza'. 'The Trawler' featured an irascible skipper trying to land stores for the Australian troops, hampered by the fall of Turkish shells and the bungling efforts of a half-witted boy signaller. The tone of the piece veered uncomfortably from jocular to menacing, but the story included some excellent turns of phrase: maddened by a particular outburst of stupidity from the boy, 'the Skipper consigned him to a hotter climate'.

Hugh next burst into print with 'The Submarines Which Never Returned', which appeared in the *Weekly Telegraph* on 20 July 1918. 'I had begun to despair of publishing anything more,' he wrote to Anne from *Lily* at sea, after Pinker had managed to sell his latest offering:

> Yet I hardly think this can be the beginning, even now. It wasn't much of a story, but it was quite different from the Anzac ones and the other early ones he [Pinker] has of mine. And the *Weekly Times* [sic] is *rather* a penny dreadful publication, isn't it? Sort of *Tit-Bits* style! However, I mustn't grumble. After all, a humble beginning is not to be sneezed at. A guinea a throw!

Billed as 'A Thrilling Story by Adrian Sforza', this melodramatic tale is set just before the Bolshevik revolution of 1917. Senior German naval officers go off in a flotilla of forty-six U-boats to capture the Russian revolutionary leaders who have gathered in Kronstadt, the seaport on the Gulf of Finland. 'The fate of the Fatherland may hang upon our venture,' their commander, Admiral Krauss, warns his team – and away they go, only for the whole strike force to wake up next morning to find their submarines immured in pack ice which has formed overnight. They head out on foot over the suddenly frozen sea towards the coast of Sweden. The cold overcomes them. Some of them die. The survivors resort to cannibalism – but in the end all perish. Krauss is the last to go. 'At sunset he died, and the snow covered him. Yet in Germany for many weeks they waited his return, while a revolution came to Russia unhindered.'

The multiple improbabilities of the story were to some extent masked by the author's vivid imagination, and by the device of bringing in submarines, which were then a relatively new menace in naval warfare. But even if the exercise was amateurish, at least it appeared in print.

In real life the news was sometimes as bad as in his fiction. On 16 October he wrote to Anne:

> I was very sorry to hear that Louis Belloc had made his last landfall. Or is there still a chance of him being a prisoner? Anyway, it's a good clean end, and I shan't grumble if I go that way too. But so young – so young! I sometimes think that this war will leave me friendless, having shorn me of everyone I ever liked. And half of them are gone already.

At the beginning of 1919 he was temporarily released from the Navy to go on a course at King's College, Cambridge. Before he left *Lily* he indented for a half-pay job on his return, on the grounds that he wanted to go to Switzerland for two months and then to France to learn French properly. He could not apply for the normal interpreter's leave, as he knew too little of the language to pass a preliminary exam, but he was encouraged to repeat his request when his university break was over.

King's has no record of his attendance, because students who joined for post-war courses did not matriculate – that is, enter the university formally – and they sat no exams, so that there is no account of what he studied; but his presence in Cambridge is confirmed by the survival of a few documents with the college shield embossed at the head of the writing paper. On 31 January 1919 the Honorary Secretary of the King's College Amalgamation Club sent a card inviting him to become a member (everyone joining the college was

thus invited), and in February he was elected a member of
the Walpole Society, which commemorates Sir Robert Walpole,
the first British Prime Minister. On Lady Day (25 March) he
went to a six-course dinner, at which the menu was signed
by fifteen friends, and on 9 May he wrote to Anne Hamilton
on headed paper.

Apart from these scraps of evidence, however, nothing
remains to document his stay at the university. His family
believe that his main subject was either English or history, in
both of which he already had a strong interest, and that the
course he took was one of those specially designed for officers
whose education had been broken off at fourteen or fifteen:
he may also have learnt some French. He does not seem to
have studied other languages, and after his return to the navy
he never took up the interpreters' course at which he had
been aiming earlier. He was up at King's for two terms, spring
and summer, and a nostalgic poem written while he was
there – but as though in old age – suggests that his mind
often strayed from East Anglia to his former environment:

The Book of Happy Memories

I sailed upon a moonlit sea,
And ghostly islands drifted by,
Flinging a fragrance back to me –
A memory.

A vineyard on a mountain side,
A hamlet in a sheltered bay,
An old, old road, washed by the tide,
Crumbling away . . .

The minaret, the silent street,
The painted houses by the sea,

The loungers in the mid-day heat
Come back to me.

I loved it then, I love it still –
The sunset Byron loved, the bay,
The fading light, the vines, the hill,
The dying day.

And there is stirred in me a thought
That comforts me in my old age.
The memories of youth are fraught
With happiness, writ page by page.

When in my chair I read that book,
How good the old adventures look!

September 1919 found him back in the Navy, temporarily aboard the battleship HMS *Barham*, a huge vessel of 30,000 tons armed with 15-inch guns, which had taken part in the Battle of Jutland. Off the Welsh coast, opposite Aberystwyth, on the way up to Scapa Flow, he was evidently in combative mood, reporting to Anne that she was 'a queer craft', and that he had created 'rather a sensation' two days after he arrived:

Till my predecessor left, you see, I lay low, and like Brer Rabbit said nuffin. Then I began to get busy, and the wretched midshipmen who'd thought me a bit of a fool got rather a shock. I had one arrested, and he was all but court-martialled. However, he got out of that because the Admiral knew his people – usual Service fashion – but he was heavily punished and so were several others.

You see, they were all slack as the devil and needed to be taught how to work, how to keep themselves clean, how to play the game and how to behave generally, as

well as to do what I told 'em to. Now things are OK,
and they've found I'm not the typical Naval Officer bully
they thought I was.

In the autumn of 1920 he took passage to Gibraltar, to rejoin
HMS *Ceres*, by then a member of the Third Light Cruiser
Squadron in the Mediterranean, and it was on board her that
he got his first taste of the Bolshevik revolution which had
convulsed Russia since 1917. He cannot have reached *Ceres*
until October, at the earliest, but by then she had spent a good
deal of time moving around the Black Sea. At the end of July
1920 she was at Sevastopol, the Russian naval base in the
Crimea, and she spent three weeks there before moving along
the coast to Yalta and thence, two days later, to Constantinople.
It is a great pity that her last surviving log goes no further than
the end of October 1920, so that her movements thereafter
cannot be reconstructed; but there is little doubt that Hugh
picked up his knowledge of revolutionary Russia from the ship's
visits to Black Sea ports during the last weeks of the year.

At that moment the civil war which followed the Bolshevik
uprising was at last coming to an end, as opposition to the
Communists finally crumbled in the south. After the Polish
army had surrendered on 20 October 1920, the White Russian
commanders, Generals Pyotr Wrangel and Anton Denikin, were
unable to hold out any longer, and on 29 October Wrangel
ordered the evacuation of all those who had been supporting
resistance to the Reds.

The presence of Royal Naval warships at Sevastopol fostered
apprehension about the intentions of the British government,
and a suspicion that Britain was planning to detach the Crimea
from Russia, or 'to secure its possession' to Wrangel. Yet this
was only a rumour, and in fact the ships were there to help
save the remnants of the White armies and transport them to
safety in Turkey.

Near the beginning of Hugh's novel *The Princess and the Perjurer* there is a description of a White Russian refugee ship arriving at Constantinople, so vivid as to make one certain that the author witnessed the scene himself. The ships were notoriously overcrowded; most of them carried little food or water, and the slowest needed five days to complete the voyage across the Black Sea. This passage is surely taken from life:

The ship was literally packed to her extreme limit – with human beings. There were so many people on board that hardly one had even room to turn round. Some stood, because they must; the rest sat, with their legs drawn under them, in hopeless heaps, or lay, careless of anything, upon and across one another. They were on every deck . . . I could see them huddled upon the ladders into the holds; they were on the bridge, even on the still-hot engine casing; in the outswung boats, in the lower rigging, in the tops.

There were soldiers, Cossacks, civilians, women and many children. There were wounded, too, and those stricken with disease, even those dead – all together, as they had been for several days, in the last stages of exhaustion, unprotected from the rain and from the cold, without sanitary arrangements of any sort, some of them nearly naked, none of them able to move. Those who looked at me had in their eyes a dull, glazed stare, devoid of any emotion . . . They were of every class, I knew. Refugees from the Crimea might be princes or peasants. You could seldom tell by looking at them, so begrimed were they by filth, so far sunk in despair.

Among the souvenirs which Hugh collected at the time were two issues of *Far Seas*, an occasional newspaper published in Constantinople by the 'U.S. Naval Detachment in Turkish

Waters'. No. 2, dated 27 November 1920, amply backed up his fictional description: during the past week American ships had transported 8,485 refugees, taking them off the dangerously overloaded escape vessels, feeding them, fumigating their clothes and moving them on to temporary camps. An editorial praised the cooperation of the various navies involved, and the 'never-failing chivalry of the sea' which had prevailed.

Hugh also kept physical evidence of a visit to the Crimea in the form of a few sheets of unused Russian stamps, which he picked up in an abandoned post office after the place had been sacked by rioters. The stamps – green for ten kopeks, red for fifteen, dark blue for seventy, and bearing the legend *EDINAYA ROSSIYA* (United Russia) had been issued in 1919 by the South Regional Government of General Denikin, and were still valid in 1920.

Later, *Ceres* was busy about the Mediterranean. When she called at Tunis in May 1921, Hugh told Anne that this was 'a semi-official visit to the authorities of the place' and meant 'a succession of shows of one sort or another'. But now he was more absorbed in his own writing than in naval affairs, reporting:

A book called *The Rebel* is now in the coloured man's hands & I am eagerly awaiting developments. No, I don't anticipate any trouble; my hopes are high. What a fall they'll have! I can't believe that anything's really to come my way at last.

'The coloured man' sounds like a reference to Pinker, the literary agent, who had sold two of Hugh's short stories to the *Sphere* magazine for eight guineas apiece, leading him to hope that his literary career was about to blossom: 'It's beginning to look like business at last.' His optimism proved premature: *The Rebel* went from publisher to publisher before sinking without trace, and for the moment his business remained with the

Royal Navy. A report dated July 1921 revealed that he had shown 'a particular interest in gunnery duties', and had carried out his work 'steadily and satisfactorily'. When he next wrote home, in September, *Ceres* was again in the Black Sea, 'lying in a little bay about twenty miles from Constantinople.'

Given his good looks, his intelligence, his far-flung travels and his questing spirit, he must have attracted girls whenever his ship put into some outpost of the British Empire. But he does not seem to have told his family that he was about to make a rather drastic career move. On 18 October 1921, in the registrar's office 'in the City and Garrison of Gibraltar', he married Violet Mary Tapper, described as a 'medical practitioner' – a nurse or doctor. He was twenty-two, and his home was given as 'HMS *Ceres*, Gibraltar Harbour'. She was twenty-seven, residing simply at 'Gibraltar', the daughter of a British colliery owner called Frank Burn, and already divorced from her first husband, an architect. History does not relate where she and Hugh lived during the short time they were together; but after a few weeks he went back to sea, and, when he returned to port, Violet had disappeared, never to enter his life again.

Where had he met her, and what did he know about her? He could tell – from her entry in the marriage register, if from nothing else – that she had been married before; but he could not have divined that she was a serial bolter, who would charge on through three more weddings before dying at the age of fifty-one.

Thinking back on the broadside against marriage which he had fired at Anne five years earlier, he surely felt embarrassed and humiliated – and perhaps it was this setback to his self-esteem that led to the only adverse report of his naval career, which he got in May 1922:

Not likely to go far. Chief defect an irritating and bad

manner with subordinates. Has carried out duties satisfactorily as far as ability goes. Category 3.

That assessment seems excessively harsh, especially as, in later
life, he was always particularly good with people junior to
himself. But the report also hinted at his tendency to ignore
orders if he thought they were misdirected, and no doubt it
increased his discontent with naval life in general. This burst
out in a letter to Anne written from *Ceres* in June 1922:

I'm so sorry they've rejected poor Peter Belloc for the
Navy. But perhaps he's had a fortunate escape, if he's
anything like his father. H. B. would not – *could* not –
have endured the stifling atmosphere of this glorified cabal.
Am I too abusive? After all, I have a lot to be grateful to
the Navy for – oh, a lot. But I have lost a lot, too, that,
in another place, I should have kept.

In August, when he wrote to Anne from Heriki on the
Izmir peninsula in the Sea of Marmora, his thoughts were
turning towards retirement from the Service and a career as
an author:

I once thought of an excellent plan – to take a small
house I know of in Sussex – a *minute* house – and live
there in absolute peace to write, with just you to talk
with, and then I thought of our 'flat' idea in town – that
would have been such a good scheme if I'd stayed at
home in England. I had hoped to be able to present you
with a copy of *The Rebel*, but no one has bitten yet.

He was placed on the Retired List on 26 September 1922,
and so his eight years of active service came to an end. If he
felt disillusioned, he was by no means alone, for many other

young men of his generation left the armed services prematurely. Unlike others, he had never been pressed into joining up by his family, but he seems to have realised that he lacked conventional ambition, and would never be a typical career officer. He had no craving to become an admiral – yet in later life he was always proud to have been in the Senior Service, and he derived enormous pleasure and benefit from the connections he had made while at sea.

5

On the Loose, 1922–8

His aim now was to become a writer, and over the next six years he travelled widely in search of backgrounds and subjects; he carried out journalistic assignments, produced articles and short stories, and had three novels published – and from the vivid descriptions which his writings contain one can infer that he spent time in Russia, Ireland, Morocco and America. But, as his surviving letters are few and far between, his movements are hard to pinpoint – as are his means of support. He had a pension from the Navy; but who else was paying him? Later in life he scarcely mentioned the following years to his children, and a veil of mystery still cloaks his activities, though occasional hints suggest that he was sometimes working in covert roles for the British government.

In 1922 he left the Navy as Lieutenant Hugh Evans, yet within two years, as an author, he was calling himself Alan Hillgarth. Not only that: he had begun writing his alternative name inside books as early as 1915.

Where this came from, nobody is now sure: there may have been some connection with the only place in England called Hillgarth – a village on the outskirts of Newcastle – and Alan believed that a rich widow called Hillgarth had come down from the north of England – perhaps from Cumberland – and married into the Evans family. Perhaps his research was set off by the fact that his father had told him this – and that he had another name which he did not always use: in *Who's Who* he appeared as Wilmott Henderson Evans, but in another work of reference he was Wilmott Henderson Hillgarth Evans. For whatever reason, when Alan's first published novel, *The Princess and the Perjurer*, came out in 1924, he styled himself Alan Hillgarth, and put that name on all his books thereafter.

At first he did not make any public announcement, but when he let the world know, he did so with some prominence. In the 1920s the front page of *The Times* carried nothing except advertisements, and of these easily the most celebrated were the personal announcements, collectively known as the Agony Column. Friday 3 September 1926 produced a typically varied selection of offers and *cris de coeur*: 'UNWANTED FALSE TEETH gratefully received for our Dental Aid Work' . . . 'LOST on Saturday last between the Playhouse Theatre and the Hotel Metropole a pair of HORN LORGNETTE GLASSES on a long gold chain'. Among these small fry appeared a more substantial item:

I, ALAN HUGH HILLGARTH EVANS, heretofore called and known by the name of GEORGE HUGH JOCELYN EVANS, of 121 Harley Street, in the County of London, Gentleman, Hereby give Public Notice that I hereby formally and absolutely renounce, relinquish and abandon the use of my said Christian names of George Jocelyn, and now assume and adopt and determine henceforth on all occasions whatsoever to use and subscribe the name of ALAN HUGH HILLGARTH EVANS instead of the said name of George Hugh Jocelyn Evans. Dated this 31st day of August, 1926. Signed ALAN HUGH HILLGARTH EVANS.

A brief note from the Admiralty told him, 'Your change of name has been noted'; but eighteen months later, in the *London*

Gazette of 24 February 1928, he made a further change, this time by Deed Poll, dropping the Evans and calling himself simply Alan Hugh Hillgarth. In a 'Change of Name' deed stamped at the Royal Courts of Justice he declared: 'I authorise and require all persons at all times to designate describe and address me and my children and issue by the adopted surname of Hillgarth.'

His travels, after he left the Navy in September 1922, are hard to plot with any precision – not least because he chose to keep his activities under wraps. Years later in a letter he wrote:

> A lot of people know me . . . but I'm very much an enigma to most of them and regarded with suspicion because I don't fit into any category. I'm not an ordinary naval officer . . . and I'm not a diplomat *de carrière*, and I'm always doing things my own way, and they can't make me fit in, and they hate it and dislike me in consequence . . . I'm a trouble-maker. I ride the storm. So I come in useful when times are unpleasant . . . and you have to act and be bold.

All that was true of his career in the 1920s. *The Princess and the Perjurer*, a first-person narrative, deploys an impressively detailed knowledge of south Russia and Bolshevik politics, but there is no record of a visit to Russia after he had become a civilian, and it seems most likely that he picked up his background information from brief visits to Black Sea ports while he was still serving in HMS *Ceres*.

Much of the novel is set inside Russia, and it is hard to believe that the author did not travel in the brave new world of Bolshevism, so vivid is his imagination. The first-person story is told by Paul Drage, British, but the son of a Russian mother and now a young officer in the Royal Naval Volunteer

Reserve, who is kidnapped at night in the middle of the Bosphorus and ends up in the hands of the Bolsheviks in Georgia, at a revolutionary control post on the coast, the Centrist headquarters, a 'distributing centre for Communist propaganda', where a long-range wireless is operating, and 'half the secrets of Bolshevist world-wide activity' are revealed to him.

So far, so good. The writing is taut, descriptions and back-grounds convincing. But then the story grows ever wilder, and the author seems to lose control. The narrator is taken to the port of Batoum, in the south-eastern corner of the Black Sea, meets a weird princess, then travels into the mountains of the interior. Somewhere up there is hidden the treasure of 'gold blocks' which once belonged to the Tsar.

A great deal of confused action ensues: threats of death and torture, sleigh rides, gun battles. When Paul tries to escape, the Princess shoots him with a pistol and smashes his shoulder. ('The Princess was on her knees beside me. "Oh, I've shot you!" she said faintly.') Rising above this unfriendly act, he falls in love with her, discovers that she already has the gold hoard in her possession and agrees to marry her.

For all its absurdities, the novel contains exciting sequences and vivid descriptions, and the story appears to be based on detailed research into Bolshevik habits and ideas – which raises tantalising questions about what the author did, where he went and under whose auspices he was operating.

Hard on the heels of *The Princess and the Perjurer* came *The Passionate Trail*, published by a different firm, Hutchinson – presumably because the author's original backers, Chapman & Dodd, had rejected the new offering. This time the setting is Egypt. In another first-person narrative, the young Harry Chester arrives in Port Said, having been jilted by his fiancée in England (was this an echo of the author's own marriage disaster?). At once he is gripped by a crafty old expatriate who assures him that a gigantic Pan-Islamic Moslem revival is about to sweep through Africa (echoes of John Buchan's *Greenmantle*).

Left on his own to fight a colossal ethnic movement, Harry is arrested, escapes, disguises himself as an Arab, is recaptured and becomes a prisoner of Alia, mysterious chieftainess of the Uled Ali tribes. As they head towards a tribal meeting in the desert, she slashes him across the face with her whip, then has him tied to her stirrup and drags him headlong over sand and rock until he is nearly dead – a startlingly masochistic passage. Although loathing her, he also worships her – especially when he discovers that she is not an Arab, but English. The book ends with a crowning improbability, when, in the middle of a gun battle and a sandstorm, he declares his everlasting love.

It was as if the author was prepared to risk any implausibility in order to use a background he knew well. He frequently dropped Arab words into the text, and described everyday scenes with easy informality. But close study of the text suggests that he could have picked up most of the detail during the frequent calls which his ships had made at Egyptian ports while he was serving, and that the passages about the interior are pure invention. As a novelist, his trouble was that he could not rein in his imagination: like a fiery horse, it kept running away with him. Nor could he refrain from bringing in impossibly exotic women, with whom his heroes inevitably fell in love.

Whatever he did in Russia and Egypt, he certainly visited Southern Ireland early in 1923. Family legend has it that he went there as one of the King's Messengers – the couriers who carry confidential government documents to British embassies and consulates around the world, often in briefcases chained to their wrists. Yet the truth was not as simple at that. The definitive account of the corps – *The History of the King's*

Messengers – shows that he was never a member: a few new men were chosen at selection boards held in January 1920 and September 1921, and again in September 1931, but his name does not feature in any of the lists.

There is another possibility. The history records that the Foreign Office also had a number of 'Acting King's Foreign Service Messengers', known as 'Diplomatic Couriers', who could be called upon when a regular member of the Corps was not available. Was he one of these? He certainly fitted two of the necessary criteria, being a British subject and having served in the armed forces of the Crown during the war. A third requirement – that candidates should be between thirty and forty – was sometimes waived by the Admiralty.

Alan was no ordinary messenger: he was also gathering intelligence about the revolutionary movements which were seeking to undermine not only the regime in Ireland, but the entire British Empire. A single, unused sheet of headed writing paper suggests that he visited Marlborough Barracks in Dublin, then the base of the King's Hussars; and in March 1923, as the civil war was stuttering to its bloody close, he produced a 1,000-word report entitled 'Bolshevism in Southern Ireland'. It may have been his knowledge of revolution in Russia which qualified him for this task, but there is no indication of what sources he used – whether he travelled the country, or merely got his information from contacts in Dublin.

In any case, his view of the Irish situation was uncompromising. The activities of the various Republican parties (he wrote) 'show that the object in view is twofold: (1) The establishment of a Workers' Republic in Ireland, and (2) The destruction of the British Empire.' The policy of the Irish Labour Party, he declared, was 'pure Bolshevism'.

The methods adopted by the revolutionary forces to achieve the desired ends are identical with those adopted

in Russia during the revolution there. These methods have
in the main taken the following forms –

(1) Destruction of private property.
(2) Appropriation of lands belonging to private owners,
     and
(3) Destruction of railway property throughout the
     country.

One appendix gave accounts of attacks on farms, and another
– a large map – displayed the sites of more than a thousand
instances of malicious damage done to the property of the
Great Southern and Western Railway during the second half
of 1922. On 10 April 1923, in a follow-up to his main report,
he made further trenchant observations:

No accurate idea of the present [political] position can
be gathered by what is stated in the Press. The Government
completely control the Press, which is used for propaganda
purposes . . . The abnormal drunkenness in the Army has
made a large section of it a terror to the local population.

After Ireland, Morocco. Again, uncertainty: Alan later told a
friend, Tom Burns, that he went there as military adviser to
the Spanish Foreign Legion, during its long-drawn out struggle
with the rebellious Rif tribes, which flared intermittently
between 1921 and 1926 as Spain tried to consolidate its grip
on that part of North Africa. No clue remains as to how he
secured this assignment; but an unpublished article shows that
he did travel the road from Tangier to Tetuan in May 1925,
and he gave a first-hand description of some of the measures
taken to control the tribesmen, among them the strategically
placed forts which the Spaniards had built along the route.
Morocco provided him with another exotic background for

a novel, *The War Maker*, which he completed in 1925. He called the story 'this tale of a man born 300 years too late', and prefaced it with an enigmatic statement, addressed to Admiral Sir William Hannam Henderson, a real and much-loved character known as 'Busy William' who had founded the *Naval Review* in 1912 and edited it until his death in 1931 at the age of eighty-five:

> Adventurer was once a noble appellation, borne proudly by men such as Raleigh and Drake. Unfortunately, like so many fine old words, it has now sunk to a poor use, being reserved for the better-dressed members of the criminal classes. This is so palpably a misnomer that it becomes in itself a crime.

It is hard to see what the author had in mind with this utterance. Did he see himself as a noble adventurer, and feel that, in creating a rough and ready central character, he had somehow devalued himself?

Yet another first-person narrative, the novel features a young Irishman called Shan McCarthy, who is offered £5,000 to mastermind an operation running guns to the Rif tribesmen in Morocco. There is some exciting action at the end, when a shipload of arms and ammunition for the Rifis at last comes into the African coast; but the chief interest of the novel now lies in the clues it holds about the author, for it is laced with quasi-autobiographical references – Wrangel in the Black Sea, the Troubles in Ireland, and a curiously prophetic look ahead to treasure-hunting in South America.

It also inadvertently hints at his own emotional insecurity. At the beginning the narrator is besotted with the Cannings' daughter, Mavis, who has blue eyes, golden hair, 'a face perfectly bewitching, and a figure it was a pleasure to watch'. But soon he becomes captivated by Señorita Antonia Roldán, niece of the Spanish general who interrogates him in gaol. The Señorita

at once affects him 'very strangely', and by the end of the book
he is longing to marry her. At one point he tells her:

> I'm a wanderer, a sort of stormy petrel, a war harbinger,
> a war maker, a soldier of fortune – in fact, an anachronism.
> I'm out of date, you know . . . I've been a soldier, a
> sailor, a cow-puncher, a smuggler, a politician, a pirate, a
> fireman, a miner, a dispatch rider, a policeman, a gambler,
> a seal hunter and a spy.

Most of this was fantasy. Yet the wealth of background detail,
together with unpublished articles, confirms that Alan travelled
in Morocco: he included vivid descriptions of Moorish towns
and people, among them the real-life revolutionary leader Abd
el-Krim, and it was apparently during (or for) this assignment
that he first learnt Spanish, a language of which he later obtained
complete mastery. The book's muscular action evokes memories of Bulldog Drummond, even if McCarthy lacks that amiable
bruiser's languid charm ('with a fall and a kick – an old trick
– I sent him clean over my head to land on his. He crumpled
up there. I think his neck was broken').

Some readers have supposed that the author fancied himself
in the roles of his central characters; but, years later, he wrote
in a letter: 'I have never identified myself with any character
in any of my books or ever tried to express my own notions
through the lips of men and women I created. I only used the
first person because it's easier in that sort of story.'

Before or after Morocco, Alan made a journey with four other
crew in a small motor yacht from Cannes on the French
Riviera to Almería in southern Spain. Once again, doubts linger
about the purpose of the expedition. Was it just a holiday jaunt,
or was the crew running weapons into Spain? The author made
the voyage sound innocent enough, describing it in a long,

apparently factual travelogue, running to seventy-nine typed pages, which lived up to its title, *The Last Cruise of the M.V. Constance*, by ending with a bang.

In the harbour at Almería only Cronyn, the cook and deckhand, was on board, and the narrator (Alan) was standing on the quay alongside the boat when a sudden explosion made him whip round, just in time to see a second explosion as the midship section of the boat went sky high in a burst of flame. The cathedral bells began to ring wildly as an alarm, and a huge crowd gathered on the quay, marshalled by soldiers and police. Excitement reached fever pitch when the considerable arsenal of ammunition and flares on board (allegedly for sporting purposes) began to detonate. By midnight the poor little *Constance* had been pretty well burnt out, and the fire was flickering out when she sank.

Some time in the mid-1920s Alan went to North America, and possibly to South America as well. From odd hints which he let fall later, his sister Maureen (to whom he was very close) gained the impression that this was another low-level, intelligence-gathering mission undertaken on behalf of the British government, which gave him the use of an ocean-going yacht, and told him to pose as a freelance, globe-trotting sailor so that he could assess the strength of foreign navies during apparently innocuous visits to their harbours. Was this why he applied for a Master's Certificate in June 1924, and was granted one at the end of July? Was the *Firefly*, of which he sent a postcard photograph from Cornwall on 30 July 1925, the yacht he sailed on a research voyage to South America? And was this service to the government the reason for his promotion to lieutenant commander (retired) in December 1927? There is now no means of answering these questions.

His cruise, which must have taken several months, apparently culminated in a stay at the Palm Beach Yacht Club in

Florida. He was certainly at Palm Beach for the annual regatta in 1926, held from 20 to 22 February, and may well have taken part in it. Large, elaborate souvenir programmes reveal a high-powered event. There were trophies for 151 Class hydroplanes, semi-speed cruisers, high-speed cruisers, Baby Gar runabouts, four-cylinder Dodge runabouts, eight-cylinder Dodge runabouts, free-for-all displacement boats, Express cruisers, Matthews cruisers, Elco cruisettes, and Sea Sled runabouts. Some of the races took place on the Lake Worth Course, and some on the Ocean Course, all set off by 'horse-race' starts, in which competitors manoeuvred to come up to the start line all at once.

The regatta programmes, packed with advertisements for banks, development companies, builders and purveyors of real estate, confirmed what was evident to any visitor – that Florida was in the throes of frenzied property development. 'Our clients have made MILLIONS through our office,' cried one realtor, offering 'Acreage, Everglade Lands, Grove Lands, Farm Lands, Subdivisions, Ocean Frontage' and much else. Another announcement boomed: 'Greater Palm Beach has tripled in population in five years! More than $30,000,000 in new buildings are now under construction. We see Greater Palm Beach as the world's most wonderful resort city.' Fascinated by this grossly vulgar commercialism, Alan later used it to good effect as the background for another novel, *What Price Paradise?*.

His stay at Palm Beach launched him into a new journalistic medium, and suddenly he became an acknowledged expert on powerboats and ocean-going yachts. In March 1926 the English journal *The Motor Boat* published an article on 'America's Great Winter Regatta', under the by-line 'Alan Hillgarth', which gave a spirited account of the races he had watched: 'In spite of criminally stupid interference by two big cruisers with more horse-power than their owners had horse-sense or common decency, the speeds recorded [by the 151 hydroplanes] were fairly high.' Also in March, the American glossy magazine *The Rudder* brought out his article on 'The British Yacht Racing Season' of 1925, on which he was billed as 'a British yachtsman who sails regularly on the big sloops which add so much to yachting in English waters'. The piece contained a mass of technical detail, and for once in his life the author indulged in a little showing off: 'Lastly, among these giants, consider *Westward*, which, to me, who have seen many schooners, is the finest racing craft afloat.'

His career as a nautical journalist blossomed with three more articles for *The Motor Boat* in March and April, and then, in July, a preview for *The Rudder* of the international race for the Duke of York's Trophy, to be held over a course of thirty-two sea miles up and down the Thames in London. In the same month a report on the race, which was won by one of the British teams, appeared in *The Motor Boat* under the by-line 'Alan Hillgarth-Evans'. (This was just before he made the first public announcement changing his name.) His piece included so much information that, even though it spread over five pages of the magazine, it had to be continued in the next issue. Again, it demonstrated a comfortable familiarity with technical detail and gave a blow-by-blow account of the races.

His visit to America also inspired a series of six long articles on whisky-running during Prohibition, which he sold to the *Daily Telegraph*. The pieces appeared anonymously, under a stack of headlines: 'The Modern Smuggler at Work, A Dangerous Enterprise, By One Who Has Tried It'. The author claimed to have spent 'a year at the business on sea and land', and described what he called 'a highly organised trade', whereby Scottish whisky leaving the distillery at four shillings a bottle finished up in a New York restaurant at fifty-five shillings a bottle. For the benefit of English readers unfamiliar with his subject, he set out some basic terms:

A *whisky ship* is a ship from a foreign country which sells wine and spirits off the American coast, outside the three-mile limit.

Smugglers are the men who run the whisky from the ship to shore in small boats.

Rum-runners are the men who run the whisky in motor cars from the shore to the warehouse or direct to the consumer.

High-jackers are pirates and highwaymen who waylay the smugglers and runners and seize their goods at the point of the revolver.

Moonshine is crude spirit made surreptitiously, and also covers adulterated or faked whisky.

A *blind pig* is a place where drinks are sold more or less secretly.

The articles were thoroughly entertaining, full as they were of exotic information, and also with warnings about the hazards of the trade, among them pirates disguised as US revenue officers, and 'foreign-made firewater in which wood alcohol, formaldehyde, creosote and other poisonous substances play a leading part' – and of which 'too free indulgence often means "flowers and the marble orchard," as the Americans say'.

He was back in England in time to volunteer for duty in the General Strike of May 1926, during which he acted for ten days as station master at Baker Street Underground station. In a letter written twenty years later he remarked that he had been in London 'by chance', and that he had been able to take the temporary job because 'the Admiralty didn't need' him at that moment. He may well have joined the strike-breakers out of sheer high spirits, like many of his well-to-do contemporaries; but what *else* was he doing, around that time, that the Admiralty sometimes had need of his services? Once more there is an implicit suggestion of some undercover role.

His next venture was into the theatre. Together with Marcel Godfrey, who had served in the Royal Marines, he wrote the script of *Little Miss Danger*, a 'Musical Play' with lyrics by Rowland Leigh and music by Dick Addinsell. The comedy featured the pretty niece of an admiral, and the trouble that sets in when the flag lieutenant with whom she is in love is ordered to the China station. From October to December the show toured extensively, playing in Preston, Southsea, Brighton, Sheffield, Leeds, Birmingham and Glasgow, in what (it had been hoped) was a run-up to a production in London. But the provincial reviews – some enthusiastic, some scathing – proved not quite buoyant enough to float it to the capital. One notice called it 'up-to-date, bright and humorous' and found that the story 'breathes Royal Navy from start to finish', but another damned it as 'a hotch-potch of stock farce ideas, with a sprinkling of repartee and topical remarks which only the most unsophisticated could mistake for wit and humour'.

Criticism did not worry him. He enjoyed writing wherever he was – but he never learnt to use a typewriter. In *Ceres*, working on the unpublished *The Rebel*, he must have scribbled away in odd corners; but he preferred to sit at a desk or table with a pen or pencil, composing in his clear, slightly italic hand, usually with few corrections, and then getting a professional typist to prepare the draft. At home in 121 Harley Street he would write on the dining-room table, a habit that never left him: towards the end of his life, in Ireland, he would still spend two or three hours every morning at his desk in the library.

At the beginning of 1927 he had a minor operation, from which he recovered quickly, but no record survives of where he went or what he did during the rest of the year. It is a safe bet that he spent a good deal of his time at his desk, for, although *What Price Paradise?* did not appear until 1929, he was abroad for most of 1928, and must have spent much of 1927 working on the novel. He also returned to the world of motor boating, contributing yet another account of the Duke of York's Trophy race to *The Rudder*, which appeared in October 1927, and in November and December two further articles on 'Motor Boating in England' and 'Motor Boating in Europe'. By then the American magazine was describing him as 'a leading figure in the sport' and 'an authority on the subject', who writes 'in his usual breezy style'. Had he continued in this vein, he might have become a colossus of the motor boating world; but, perhaps fortunately, early in 1928 he was distracted by the promise of a great new adventure.

6

Fools' Gold

Gold! Gold in barely imaginable quantities, hidden in a valley beneath the towering peaks of the Bolivian Andes. Gold said to be worth £12,000,000 (perhaps £400,000,000 at today's values). For Alan – a young writer with a taste for travel, short of money and in search of a subject for his next novel – the idea of a treasure hunt in wild country was irresistible. He had already used the lure of gold as an ingredient in *The Princess and the Perjurer*, so it is small wonder that he signed up for an expedition which went out from England in March 1928.

Rumours about a great hoard at Sacambaya had flickered around South America during much of the nineteenth century. A colossal amount of bullion, it was said, had been hidden by Jesuit priests living at the monastery of Plazuela, built at the confluence of two rivers. The buildings stood on a small area of flat ground beside the Khato, but the area in general was known by the name of the other stream, Sacambaya.

During the eighteenth century the Jesuits had steadily increased their wealth and influence in the Andes, chiefly through their exploitation of the area's gold and silver mines, and rumours that they were planning to set up an independent republic in the heart of South America apparently so alarmed King Charles V of Spain that in 1767 he ordered the expulsion of the entire order from the New World. The priests at Plazuela, knowing that it would be some time before they were physically evicted, were said to have put their remaining years to good use by burying their gold close to the monastery.

So the story went; but it was not until the early 1900s that a bull-necked, walrus-moustached English mining engineer, Cecil H. Prodgers, said to weigh twenty stone, brought the legend to life in Europe by himself going to the site and beginning excavations. He found nothing of value, yet the account of his peregrinations published in his book *Adventures in Bolivia* made the existence of the treasure seem irrefutable, and encouraged others to take up the hunt.

Prodgers was no ordinary traveller. An Old Etonian, he had dug diamonds in South Africa, fought in the Boer War, built railways and trained race-horses in Chile, where he also carried out research in the Andes for Kaiser Wilhelm of Germany. In 1903 he was engaged by the Challana & Tongo rubber company to find Indians who would work for the firm in the interior of Bolivia.

At forty-two he was a commanding figure, for he stood over six feet tall and weighed 285 lbs. Faced by the prospect of an arduous trek through the mountains, he became worried about his weight. By taking a cure at the 'famous springs of Jura, 9,000 feet up . . . a favourite resort of the Incas of Peru', near Cochabamba, he managed to shed thirty lbs, and, thus lightened, stormed off across country like one of the wild bulls which lived in the forests. He travelled mainly on foot, sometimes on a heavyweight mule, attended by his man Miguel and a few other Indian servants, who trusted him because he treated their rites and ceremonies with scrupulous respect. He crossed 17,000-foot passes, hacked his way through densely forested valleys and slept in huts or his own little tent. His narrative is packed with information and marvellously artless, skipping from subject to subject without a break:

At about five in the afternoon we put up for the night just outside a place called Machacamarca, not far from Lake Titicaca, paying the usual 2/- for the night for the use of a room with a mud bed and fireplace, and finding food, firewood and other necessaries ourselves. Fowls, potatoes, barley and fresh eggs can always be bought at these places. At this altitude it takes seven minutes to boil an egg, at 15,000 feet it takes even nine to ten minutes. I arranged to rent the accommodation here for two days and bought a double supply of barley for the mules, so that I should have a little time to walk along the shore of this magnificent lake and shoot a duck or two for a change.

On he went, buying food or shooting it along the way, fortified by Liebig's Extract – a black, molasses-like concentrate of meat – and copious drafts of gin and bitters. He loosed off fruitlessly with his rifle at the condors circling overhead, tried in vain to bag a man-eating jaguar, bathed regularly in ice-bound pools and panned the odd stream for gold. Although repeatedly warned that the Challana Indians would murder him if he entered their territory, he pressed on regardless to his target, the hill-top village of Paroma, and there made the agreement he had come to negotiate, whereby the local men agreed to work as rubber-pickers for the company. By the time he returned to the Bolivian capital La Paz, he reckoned he had walked 857 miles 'by the register of the speedometer' and ridden 210 miles on his outsized mule. After 'leading a fairly rough life', he had lost another ten pounds, 'which goes to show that a trip of this sort hurts nobody'.

So far, so good. Then, to his chagrin, he learnt that the rubber company wanted to back out of their agreement, so that his marathon trip seemed to have been in vain; but when he stopped again for a week at the Jura baths, he met Señorita

Corina San Román, daughter of the late General Miguel de
San Román, who had been elected President of Peru in 1862,
but died in office a few months later. Señorita Román showed
him a document in Spanish which gave particulars of an enormous cache of gold allegedly hidden by Jesuits in the eighteenth
century, and commissioned him to find it. The site, it said, was
on Caballo Cunco, a hill on the left bank of the River
Sacambaya, opposite the ruins of the monastery of Plazuela:

A steep hill all covered with dense forest, the top of which
is flat, with long grass growing . . . In the middle of the
grass, a large stone shaped like an egg, so big that it took
500 Indians to place it there. If you dig down underneath
this stone for five cordas [yards] you will find the roof of
a large cave, so big that it took 500 Indians two and a
half years to hollow out.

The roof is seventy cordas long and there are two
compartments and a long narrow passage leading from
the room on the east side to the main entrance 200 cordas
away. On reaching the door you must exercise great care
in opening. The door is a large iron one, and, inside to
the right, near the wall, you will find an image made of
pure gold, three feet high, the eyes of which are two large
diamonds. This image was placed here for the good of
mankind.

If you proceed along the passage you will find in the
first room thirty-seven large heaps of gold, and many gold
and silver ornaments and precious stones. On entering
the second room you will find in the right-hand corner
a large box clamped with three iron bars; inside this box
there are 90,000 Duros Reales in silver money and thirty-
seven big heaps of gold, of which the value has been
estimated at $60,000,000.

Great care must be taken on entering these rooms, as

enough strong poison to kill a regiment has been laid about. The walls of the two rooms have been strengthened by large blocks of granite; from the roof downwards the distance is five cordas more. The top of the roof is portioned off into three distinct esplanades, and the whole has been well covered over for a depth of five cordas with earth and stones. When you come to a place twenty feet high, with a wall so wide that two men can easily ride abreast, cross the river and you will find the church, monastery and other buildings.

Taking a copy of the document, and promising the Señorita that he would share any spoils he found, Prodgers set off for Sacambaya. During the next three years he made three short expeditions to the site. On the top of Caballo Cunco he found the big, egg-shaped stone exactly as described, and tackled it with characteristic delicacy, blowing it to pieces with dynamite. Then, wielding a crowbar himself, and urging on three Indian workers with shovels, he excavated what he felt sure was the cave described in the document, 'covered all over with stone, cut and shaped like bricks . . . very well and carefully done'. When, twelve feet down, he came on 'a yellow altar slab with flowers nicely engraved on it', he felt even more certain he was hot on the trail. On a later expedition, digging further down, he found a wall which he thought was man-made: having drilled a hole through it, he inserted a long bamboo stick, and, when he withdrew it, the end was coated with red oxide of mercury. This, he concluded, was the poison referred to in the document. Moreover, the air was filled with 'a very powerful smell . . . so strong that it made us all feel bad'. Yet these clues never led him to his quarry. Partly because he spent so much time hunting wild bulls and jaguars, he found no treasure of any kind, let alone any gold.

For whatever reason, the first book he wrote about his travels,

Adventures in Bolivia, was not published until 1922; but in 1920, with his health declining, he handed over all his information to another mining engineer, the Russian-born Swiss Dr Edgar Sanders, on condition that he would honour his original promise to the Señorita. A long list of the equipment Sanders should take with him included 'a good rifle . . . a big six-shooter . . . plenty of coca leaves for barter . . . fifty pounds of ship's biscuits . . . a vicuña wool mask and nightcap of same material . . . Liebig's extract . . . old port and old Madeira . . . a pith helmet . . . miner's helmet and dynamite . . . big carriage umbrella, and a thick horsehair rope to put round your tent to keep away snakes'.

Sanders, who was then living in England, was another man of unshakeable credulity. After two preliminary expeditions to Sacambaya in 1925 and 1926, he produced a substantial pamphlet announcing a third, declaring that 'there could not be the slightest doubt' that the San Román document had been handed down from somebody who had had first-hand information about the hiding place of the treasure. Every small discovery he made confirmed his certainty that the gold was still at Sacambaya, and intact.

Arriving there for the first time in 1925, he quickly decided that the huge stone blown up by Prodgers was not a cover for the chamber, but only a marker. On the other hand, a heap of very large rocks which he found among trees towards the bottom of the hill, close to the bank of the Khato, was 'undoubtedly made by the hand of man', and must be concealing and protecting the roof of the cave. He called this assembly of rocks 'the Square Stone Heap'.

When he returned to the site in 1926, he discovered a vertical shaft, solidly lined with stone, on the left bank of the Sacambaya, just before the confluence, at a point which he called 'the Fortress'. This shaft, he hoped, might well be the beginning of an entrance to the chambers. More exciting was the discovery of a tunnel going into the side of the mountain from the right bank of the Khato, which he believed was one of the secondary entrances: 'This is even more than a belief. In my own mind it is a certainty.' Like the vertical shaft, the tunnel had been filled in with earth and stones. Digging it out, he found 'a wooden board embedded in sheep's excrements'. On one side of it was nailed a primitive silver crucifix, which he took away. A few yards further in, he came up against a blocking wall of loose stones, among which he discovered the remains of a flimsy wooden casing. This fell apart at a touch, leaving in his hands 'a piece of parchment, well preserved,' on which was written in Spanish:

You who reach this place, withdraw. This spot is dedicated to God Almighty and the one who dares to enter a dolorous death awaits him in this world and eternal condemnation in the world he goes to. The riches that belong to God Our Master are not for humans.

More exhortations followed, ending with the sentence *En nomine Patris Filii et Spiritus Sancti. Amen'*. Sanders was so engrossed in deciphering the message that for some time he did not notice that his Indian helpers had become terrified. But because they refused to go on working, and the rainy season was approaching, he was forced to abandon operations for that year.

Back in England, he submitted the parchment to experts at the British Museum, who saw 'no reason to doubt' that it was 'perfectly genuine'. Further, he showed it to Professor Sir Edward Denison Ross, Director of the School of Oriental Studies at the University of London, 'one of the greatest living authorities on such manuscripts'. On 3 March 1927 Sir Denis obligingly scribbled him a note:

In my view this parchment containing the pious warning against touching the treasure is absolutely genuine. The parchment is roughly cut as one might expect, and the epigraphical characteristics are of the period.

This, to Sanders, was 'conclusive evidence that the tunnel was one of the entrances leading to the treasure chambers'. Further gleams lured him on. One fact he did not mention in his prospectus was that he had visited Charles Gladitz, a German scientist 'of undoubted reputation', owner of the New Process Company of Scotts Road, Southall, who was developing a unique method of locating metals. When Sanders showed him plates of photographs taken at Sacambaya, but did not tell him where the place was or why it interested him, Gladitz claimed that he could detect the existence of a large amount of gold beneath the Square Stone Heap, because rays given off by the metal had had some effect on the plates.

Even Sanders considered this diagnosis far-fetched. Nevertheless, fired up by all his evidence, he formed the Sacambaya Exploration Company Ltd, to 'excavate the treasure and transport it to La Paz, the capital of Bolivia'. Once there, the gold would be sold to the Bolivian State Bank, or to one of three firms which bought precious metals. One of these, in fact, had already offered to buy whatever gold he found at the 'very good price' of US $19 per fine ounce. He had the grace to admit that the venture was a speculative undertaking, but claimed that it offered 'every prospect of a successful conclusion and a very high return. If the entire treasure is found and secured, the profit for every £5 Ordinary Share will be £750. In other words, £100 will return £15,000, or at the rate of £150 for £1.'

The cost of the expedition, Sanders reckoned, would be £14,000, and when he published his company prospectus, some time in 1927, 'the directors and their friends' had already agreed to take up 2,000 Ordinary Shares. Other investors were also invited to subscribe. There were six directors (although only three went out with the expedition), and eighteen further members signed on.

Several of these were recruited by means of a letter dated 5 February 1928, sent out from 14 Jewry Chambers in the City of London, in which Sanders invited men to 'accompany the Sacambaya Exploration Company's Expedition which I will lead to Bolivia'. The conditions laid down were stringent. 'All the Members, Regular as well as Reserve, will have to do actual manual labour to any extent which the Leader of the Expedition may consider necessary . . . All Members must serve as armed guards while the treasure is being transported to safety . . . You undertake to remain with the Expedition until the Leader of the Expedition shall declare the enterprise abandoned or until the enterprise has been successful . . . '

There is no record of how Alan joined this band of optimists, nor of how much money he put into the venture. Most probably he answered one of Sanders' advertisements – and he hit it off so well with the leader that he soon became not only a director, but also the second-in-command. The rest of the volunteers were (in his own words) 'all men who had had a considerable experience of hard conditions, who had a pretty fair understanding of the work they would have to do, and the circumstances under which they would have to do it'. The team's doctor, P. B. P. Mellows – fortunately a man with a strong sense of humour – was commissioned by the daily newspaper the *Star* to act as a reporter and send back occasional articles on progress.

On 24 January 1928 the paper tried to give the expedition a fair wind by running banner headlines at the top of the front page – JESUIT TREASURE GUARDED BY DEATH THREAT . . . BRITISH EXPEDITION WITH MODERN MACHINERY STARTS ROMANTIC ENTERPRISE . . .

'SACAMBAYA' THE ALLURING. But even at this early stage the enterprise was threatened by farce. The reporter assigned to the story – clearly not Mellows – had become seriously confused: he said that it was Prodgers, rather than Sanders, who had found the crucifix and parchment, and wrote about Prodgers (who had been in his grave for five years) as though he were still alive.

Undaunted, the expedition sailed from Liverpool on 1 March aboard the Pacific Line RMS *Orcoma*, and on the way called at Bermuda, where an American mining engineer, Julius Nolte, joined the party. On 15 March the ship's captain, Commander A.W. Pearse, gave a seven-course dinner for members of the team. The menu included *Filets de Sole Sacambaya* and *Biscuit Glacé Inquisivi* (Inquisivi being another name for the same river), and the diners all signed their names in the space between cheerful slogans: *Audax fortuna juvat* (Fortune favours the brave) and *In omnia paratus* (Ready for anything).

Their confidence was no doubt increased by the fact that Sanders seemed to have made extremely thorough preparations. He had taken out a three-year lease for exploration from Jacinto Aguilar, owner of the land around Caballo Cunco, and he had left his local foreman, Juan Mandizabal (in whom, needless to say, he had 'entire confidence') to guard the site during the dry season of 1927. Moreover, his scout had reported to him regularly by letter and cable, so that he knew the spot was undisturbed.

In his 'Programme of work for 1928' Sanders had set out in some detail his plan to 'attack the Treasure from four points simultaneously', beginning with an assault on the tunnel. 'I do not think,' he had written, 'that there can be any doubt that at the termination of this tunnel the chambers will be found.' He had also persuaded himself that the Jesuits must have cut another tunnel through solid rock beneath the bed of the Khato, to give themselves direct access to chambers on the other side of the river. On a simple sketch map of the site he had marked the principal features and drawn dotted lines to 'show the directions in which the attacks will be made'. It would be advisable, he added, to launch all the assaults simultaneously, because the dry season would last only six or seven months, and, when the rains came, the rivers would rise so much that the site would become inaccessible.

Besides making detailed plans, Sanders had collected a formidable array of equipment. The largest items were two Morris six-wheel tractors, described by Alan as 'unusually handy vehicles in daily use by the Army, which had shown themselves capable of keeping up with cavalry on active manoeuvres across rather difficult country'. There were drills, cranes and hoists of many kinds, all powered by compressors. These used petrol, and were designed to work for hours on end: in choosing them, the directors had been impressed by a claim that four of their kind on a commercial job had run for nine months with only a single ten-minute stoppage. There were four pneumatic hoists, driven by the compressors, each guaranteed to lift 1,000 lbs direct. Four jackhammers (for drilling holes in rock) were complemented by one large stone-breaker, six pneumatic picks, two pneumatic spades and a drill-bit sharpener. All this equipment was made by the firm Ingersoll-Rand, and a specialist engineer from the firm, John Shotton, was on the team, ready to repair anything that broke down.

The six cranes could be transported by mule when dismantled. Two pumps supplied by Messrs Gwynne (one mounted on a trailer) were designed for 'hydraulicising' – that is, squirting water at high pressure to wash away loose material like earth or shale. The trailer-borne pump alone weighed half a ton. Lesser items included two motor winches, two electric light plants, forges, machine tools and wood-working tools of all kinds, crowbars, camping equipment of the strongest variety, mosquito nets, medical stores, cement, petrol, engine oil, and, of course, food. In all, the machinery and equipment weighed forty tons.

In his report written after the event Alan added: 'We were not such fools as to take an expedition into Bolivia without taking with us in addition to the machinery a certain supply of rifles and ammunition for protection against the often extremely unpleasant individuals with whom one is liable to come into contact in such places.' The armoury included twenty rifles, twenty pistols, three or four shotguns and two Thompson automatic rifles, together with a 'reasonable supply' of ammunition.

After going through the Panama Canal and heading south, the *Orcoma* docked at Arica, in Chile, on the last day of March. The mass of equipment and the weapons was cleared by Customs without fuss, and ten hours after landing the expedition was on its way eastwards towards La Paz in a specially ordered train. This was a necessity, because, as Alan remarked, the regular train ran once a week, and freight trains whenever they felt like it. In the 330-mile route to the Bolivian capital the track climbed from sea level to a 14,000-foot pass and on to the vast plateau between 12,000 and 13,000 feet known as the Altiplano. All ranks were afflicted to some degree by altitude sickness. Their discomfort was probably eased by the absolute ban on alcohol which Sanders had imposed, but still they suffered from headaches, drowsiness, shortage of breath and palpitations.

At Viacha, just short of La Paz, the train stopped for Sanders to make arrangements with the Foreign Ministry and the Ministry of the Interior for the expedition's material to be declared exempt from import duty, on condition that he left the machinery in the country when he departed. He would be allowed to sell it or give it away, but not to take it with him. Then the train turned south down the Antofagasta line, and deposited its cargo at Eucalyptus, the halt nearest to Sacambaya.

From there the going became ever more difficult. Alan disliked the landscape from the start, describing it in derogatory terms. First a rough road led across twenty miles of 'pretty poisonous, gradually rising desert'. Then it climbed through a succession of 'extremely unpleasant mountains' on to a higher plateau, rising again until it crossed the snow line at 17,000 feet, 'finally to descend in a series of perfectly horrible zigzags 5,000 feet into a nasty little valley, where the mining camp of Pongo is situated'.

Beyond Pongo a track of sorts wound down five miles to a primitive village called Quimé in the valley of the Khato. When the expedition arrived, men were working to widen the path, and in due course the expedition's lorries were able to traverse it. But beyond Quimé there was no road at all: although there had once been a mule trail, extra-heavy rains had washed most of it away, and there was no question of the lorries going down it to reach their destination. The six-wheeled monsters were useless: far from keeping up with charging cavalry, they could not go another yard.

The countryside in general as described by Alan consisted of

range upon range of mountains, separated by very deep valleys, following one upon another for many, many miles. In order to travel from one place to another one has to cross several of these valleys, in other words to climb perhaps four or five thousand feet in a few miles, then to descend into another deep valley and to climb again, and to repeat this performance several times.

Stuck at Quimé, the members of the expedition realised that their leader's planning was less perfect than it had seemed, and that, with the trucks grounded, a hideous approach march lay ahead of them. Five of them (including Alan), helped by twenty Indians, stripped the heavy equipment down into component parts. They engaged a train of mules specially chosen for their strength, and made up loads of between 200 and 300 lb. – but items such as some of the engines and the bed-plate of the circular saw weighed 500 or 600 lb. each, and only the sturdiest mules could carry them.

The track, where it still existed, had to be remade and strengthened. In many places a new path had to be cut, four or five feet wide, sometimes out of rock. In one twelve-mile stretch a river had to be crossed twenty-seven times. The descent from Inquisivi to the Rio Muracullini was so precipitous that in many places the compressors had to be lowered bodily with tackles, at one point 1,000 feet straight down. Tackles also had to be used for at least 150 ascents, many with a gradient steeper than one-in-two. Often corners were so sharp that loads had to be taken off the mules and carried round by hand. Alan's distaste for the whole environment may well have been exacerbated by the fact that he hated heights: for anyone suffering from vertigo, a worse scenario could scarcely be imagined.

Oxen were used wherever possible, but in one place they dragged a compressor over the edge of a cliff, and might have fallen 3,000 feet had not they, the compressor and three men been caught in the only tree on the cliff face thirty feet below. Tackles again came to the rescue, and hauled humans, animals and equipment back to the path, quite undamaged. Such were the problems of the forty-mile route that most mule trains took six days to cover it, and none completed it in less than three. Amazingly enough, the only item lost was one case containing 200 lb. of macaroni.

Photographs vividly illustrate the extreme difficulty of the approach to the target area: twenty men strung out in single file along a rope, struggling to haul one of the compressors up a stony track on its little four-wheeled carriage; the same team heaving on rope and pulley blocks to drag some other heavy item up a slope; mules sagging under the weight of enormous burdens; the track blocked by great slabs of fallen rock.

The site itself struck most members of the expedition as unpleasantly claustrophobic. They set out their tents on flat ground beside the Khato, and, although they were 7,000 feet above sea level, they were walled in by precipitous mountain faces: during the day the semi-tropical heat was suffocating, but the nights turned very cold (Prodgers had recorded that during his expeditions the temperature went from 22° below zero – 10°F – at night to 80°F at midday.) Soon most of the party were being tormented by what they called 'jiggers', very small fleas that lived in the sand and attacked their feet. Native labour proved difficult to recruit, because local people regarded Sacambaya with superstitious dread, and had to be heavily bribed before they would join the enterprise.

Alan must have increased his personal discomfort by habitually wearing a collar and tie – and he spared no term of abuse in damning his surroundings:

Sacambaya is a poisonous place – a dark, dirty valley, shut in by hills that rise almost immediately to a further 4,000 feet. It is either very dry or you are flooded out. It is generally very hot by day and pretty near freezing at night. It abounds in bugs, fleas, flies, ants, mosquitoes, sand-flies, rattlesnakes and other kinds of snakes. It is famous among Indians as a plague spot of malaria. There are also skunks.

In this insalubrious setting the gringo team made a careful survey of the ruins of Plazuela monastery, but then left it to concentrate on the key points beyond the rivers. At the place which Sanders had called the Fortress they found some graves and pieces of pottery, but no sign of treasure, so they turned their attention to the tunnel partially excavated two years earlier, and to the Square Stone Heap.

Work began as soon as the machinery was reassembled, much

of the hard labour being carried out by a gang of about forty Indians. The tunnel proved a grave disappointment. After clearing out falls from the roof, and black mud and debris washed in by the river, the diggers came to a dead end. Sanders was forced to conclude that the tunnel was either a deliberate blind or a repository for small objects of value, and had never been connected with the main treasure chambers.

Alan agreed that the Jesuits had probably made another tunnel through bedrock beneath the river, to give themselves easy and secret access to the far side; and, further, he came to believe that the treasure chambers had been cut out of rock 'between ninety and 100 feet into the hillside proper at the end of the tunnel'. All this, however, was pure speculation, not supported by any evidence.

The team's main effort was concentrated on the Square Stone Heap. As Alan remarked, it was 'fairly obvious that the Jesuits were not satisfied with the strength of their position, and chose to reinforce what I may call the roof of the chambers with a formation of boulders that, of course, in their time, would have defied any attempt at excavation'. The huge rocks on the surface were arranged in a rough rectangle, wedged up with stones, and the biggest was reckoned to weigh thirty or forty tons,

In tackling the ground beneath them, the explorers relied heavily on the diagnosis given by the German scientist Gladitz. His calculations had suggested that the gold was lying between 112 and 135 feet under the surface, and at ground level Sanders now took more photographs, which were immediately despatched to England, interpreted by Gladitz and returned to the scene. Later the team took aerial photographs with a camera suspended on a line slung right across the river from hill to hill.

Around the Square Stone Heap cranes were set up to hoist boulders out of the way. The compressors went into

action, driving the pneumatic drills and hoists for ten hours
a day, six days a week, week after week, until 37,000 tons
of rock and earth had been gouged out of a cavernous hole.
The deeper the excavations went, the more dangerous it
became: parts of the walls fell in, leaving unstable overhangs;
workmen had to be lowered on ropes and accidents became
frequent.

Mellows, the expedition doctor, was in his element, not only
dealing with sickness and injuries, but also writing admirably
clear, factual progress reports for the *Star*, which somehow
found their way back to London, together with excellent
photographs. He also had time to send home an article entitled
'Sacambayaitis' for the *St Bartholomew's Hospital Journal*, enlivened by more elaborate turns of phrase than he used for his
despatches to Fleet Street.

The article revealed that his stores had included 28,000
tablets of quinine bisulphate – 'Everybody, Gringos and Indians
alike, indulges in a daily prophylactic dose of 10 gr.' – as well
as 5,000 aspirin, 1,000 calomel, an army surplus operation set
and miles of bandage. 'All these,' he wrote, 'have justified their
inclusion and had full usage.'

The packing of such stores to stand a journey of some
9,000 miles by train, steamer, train, motor-tractor and
mule-back, including an unforeseen accidental descent of
some hundreds of feet down a precipice, resulting in the
demise of the animal carrying the cases, was fortunately
adequately attended to.

At our camp here in Sacambaya I have found even a
nodding acquaintance with the sciences of dentistry and
veterinary surgery to be a great asset. Such refinements
as the slaughtering of cows with a humane killer in the
form of a Mannlicher rifle, destroying lairs of Anopheles
[mosquitoes], and the ability to argue effectively with

Indians as to the respective merits of the treatment of
malaria by quinine or copious drafts of urine from a black
bullock – 'One with the slightest trace of white in its
coat is not the least bit of good' – come with practice,
of course.

Mellows was busy on the veterinary side, for abrasions suffered
by horses and mules quickly turned septic, and the animals were
much troubled by vampire bats, which alighted on their backs
and sank their incisor teeth into the gaps between vertebrae.
But it was naturally human patients who gave the doctor most
concern, and he performed several operations, one of them for
appendicitis, carried out on the mess table in an open-fronted
tent, at which Alan eagerly assisted (prompted, perhaps, by
thoughts of his naval-surgeon ancestors). Mellows was particularly anxious that none of the Indians in his charge should die,
for he knew that one loss of life would be attributed to the
malevolent spirits supposed to infest the valley, and would
precipitate the immediate departure of the entire workforce.

By the time he sent off his despatch to Bart's he had treated
gringos 600 times and Indians 700 times – which, he reckoned,
placed 'this rural retreat definitely in the category of ill-health
resorts'. He dealt with countless wounds caused by crane accidents, falling stones, dynamite explosions and 'too close an
acquaintance with cactus needles and thorns'. Even a slight
scratch became infected unless promptly treated with powerful
disinfectant. But his most persistent problem was chronic consti-
pation, brought on by the lack of fresh fruit and vegetables:
the Indians kept bringing eggs, for sale, and Alan later claimed
that he often ate eighteen or more in a day. The doctor
combated the consequent problem with 'a good range of
aperients and purges varying in propulsive powers from that
of 3ss Eno's to 3ij ol. ric'.

Although one Gringo accommodated on the first day of his costive state gr. ij cascara sagrada, on the second gr. iij pulv. rhei and on the third 3j. ol. ric. , followed that night by gr. vj. calomel and 3ij mag. sulph the next morning, even then he required an en. sap. to put a match to the gunpowder.

Not all the doctor's adventures were medical. One day, in his spare time, he was led 3,000 feet up on to the Altiplano by an Indian who had worked for Sanders on his earlier expeditions, and taken to a large fissure in the rock, with smooth walls only three feet apart. When he climbed up to a ledge on his right, he was startled to find a large heap of human skulls and bones. He counted 200 skeletons, and in the light of his torch saw more in a deep cul-de-sac on the other side of the cavern. Like all local Indians, his guide assured him these were the remains of the slaves who had buried the treasure and had then been massacred by the Jesuits to prevent them divulging the secret.

That encounter was disturbing enough; but a more noisome meeting occurred at two o'clock one morning, when he found Sanders hurling stones at a skunk and calling on him to get rid of it. As he approached with his acetylene lamp, the skunk let fly with its jet of stinking defensive fluid and caught him in the face. Luckily it missed his eyes, but the smell permeated the camp for days and was offensive 150 yards away.

Having decided there was nothing to be found at the Fortress site, one of the directors, Stratford Jolly, took a gang of Indians to investigate some old excavations near the summit of Caballo Cunco hill. Mellows went with him, and described a labyrinth of workings – hundreds of feet of tunnels and shafts, through which he crawled. These, the party concluded, were not treasure chambers, but the relics of an ancient gold mine which had been worked out, possibly by the Incas, or by the Jesuits.

Disappointed there, Jolly went off two miles downstream to the Abbot's Priory at Cutacutuni, where the ruins of an enormous Jesuit fort covered more than twenty-five acres on a plateau some fifty feet above river level. The stone walls were eight feet thick and fourteen high, with, halfway up on the inside, a parapet on which sentries used to stand.

Jolly planned to accelerate excavation by blasting water from one of the Gwynne hydraulicisers, and took the machine downriver on a raft made of empty petrol tins lashed to long poles. Unfortunately, as a team of twenty Indians tried to walk the contraption across the stream by wading, they stepped into a big pothole, and by clinging to the sides of the raft capsized it, sending the pump to the bottom in eight feet of water and three of mud. Although it was recovered, the submersion put its magneto out of action for some time.

Nothing was found at Cutacutuni beyond a few pots, some Indian, some of European manufacture; but the sheer size of the place confirmed Alan in his belief that the Jesuits had wielded huge power in the area, and led him to include a sharp passage in his report:

I have been told that there were never any Jesuits in the district. This is utter nonsense. The place is absolutely stiff with buildings that they left behind them, and you have only to talk to any Indian in or around the province of Ayopayo to hear story upon story about the Jesuits for whom his grandfathers and great-grandfathers worked as slaves. They [the Jesuits] never paid their Indian workers a penny, nor did they feed them. They had to feed themselves. They had to work nine months of the year for their masters, and for three months they were allowed to sow and gather their own crops.

Alan found the Indians, both Quechuas and Aymaras, 'intensely suspicious', and never happy unless they had white men alongside to protect them. As long as they were accompanied by a gringo, they would work long and hard, in burning sun; but they remained 'amazingly ignorant and childish'. When one of the other gringos went off to a nearby *finca*, or farmhouse, four or five hours' ride away, to get potatoes, he was irritated to notice a particular Indian always circling round in attempts to get behind him. In the end he demanded fiercely in Spanish to know what the fellow wanted, but because the Indian spoke only Quechua he had to ask the owner of the *finca*. It turned out that his shadow, believing that all white men had tails, wanted to see if this one kept his tail inside his trousers or in a special pocket.

With the other sites ruled out, work concentrated on excavating beneath the Square Stone Heap, and throughout August Mellows' reports remained optimistic. 'We are now removing 300 tons of material daily,' he cabled on the 23rd. 'The fact that we are working in a bedrock of shale is regarded as a very favourable sign, as we expect to find chambers there.' The American Julius Nolte annoyed everyone else by constantly walking about, prodding at the ground with a stick and gazing downwards so intently that people began to think him simple-minded.

Progress remained good in September, with the diggers working a seven-hour night shift, as well as all day; but then four days of heavy rain, unexpected in the dry season, caused an ominous rise in the level of the river. The deep pit began to flood, and from then on water was the main enemy.

At the end of October the monotony of the treasure-hunters' routine was enlivened by a minor rebellion. Against all orders Simon Quiraga, the Indian under-foreman, supplied some of the workmen with chicha, the local firewater, and all got roaring

drunk. Together with two of his gringo colleagues, armed with
revolvers and whips, Alan rounded up the revellers in a forest
glade, and in the melee Simon's shoulder was broken. After a
week under armed guard he was despatched to the prison at
Palka, some twenty leagues distant, but promptly escaped.

More torrential rain fell. The ground round the shaft turned
into a quagmire. The water in the pit rose higher. At first the
team thought they had broken into a subterranean stream –
and, of course, they attributed the alignment of this alleged
watercourse to the cunning of the Jesuits, who (they were
deluded enough to claim) must have deliberately diverted it
so as to deny all-comers access to their treasure.

The Cameron pump, which disgorged twenty-five gallons
per minute, was lowered into the pit, but after six hours the
water level had gone down only half an inch. Worse, when
the pump stopped, it returned to normal in a few minutes.
Next into the attack was the Gwynne hydrauliciser, repaired
and brought back from Cutacutini. It and the Cameron,
working in tandem, discharged 125 gallons a minute, but when
they were stopped after pumping for ten hours on end, the
water regained its original level in just over an hour.

As Sanders himself put it, he was 'now faced with a very
serious problem'. But he saw that the water seemed to be
coming from what he called 'the left hand end' of the pit, and
conceived the idea that it might be possible to build a dam to
keep it out. He therefore sent off to Oruro, several days' mule
journey away, for sandbags, which he proposed to fill with
mud. Then it began to rain, again.

Before the pumps could be hoisted out, a large portion
of one side of the cut fell in, burying the Cameron, and
the other sides, in spite of every possible effort on our
part, showed signs of falling in also. Owing to the rain,
our food supplies did not come through regularly, the

sand bags could not reach us for ten days, and many of our Indians expressed their wish to go to their homes.

Efforts to save the shaft became frantic. The men now worked in three shifts, including on Sundays. The heat and insect life were almost insufferable. The Cameron was recovered and restarted. A makeshift dam was fashioned from flattened petrol tins. As Sanders recorded, 'many of the white Members of the Expedition (notably Messrs Hillgarth and Shotton) had remained for hours on end working with the water above their waists'. For a while the dam seemed to be having the required effect. But then at last the team realised that water was coming in all round the shaft and under the dam. That could mean only one thing – that they were below the local water table.

This was the killer blow, and the directors finally had to accept defeat – for that season, anyway. Yet Sanders was still convinced of the treasure's existence, and of his proximity to it. 'We have every reason to believe that the treasure chambers are only between fifteen and thirty-five feet lower than we have reached,' he wrote in his final report on 12 November.

In view of the lateness of the season and the early and exceptionally heavy rains, the Directors on the spot decided, after considering the situation thoroughly, to store all the equipment, machinery etc, and to abandon operations for this year.

In his last despatch to the *Star*, Mellows hit an uncharacteristically doom-laden note:

At three in the morning the anxious faces peering down the shaft reflected our bitter realisation – the water had won, and the treasure will have to remain undisturbed for yet another year ... The disconsolate Indians, whose crops in the locality are ruined, attribute the heavy downfalls [of rain] to our disregard of the curse.

By then ridiculous rumours about the expedition had begun to circulate. As Alan reported:

We were supposed to be making false money, to be starting a special community with some fantastic religion of our own, to be agents of the Government of Paraguay for creating dissension in the centre of Bolivia, to be representatives of half a dozen different Bolivian political parties not actually in office, to be an armaments factory working for a well-known British firm.

Nothing, however, was more farcical than what followed. As other members of the expedition departed individually for home, Sanders was arrested on charges of having illegally imported an arsenal of weapons: he was said to have brought in several hundred rifles, between twenty-five and fifty machine guns, a million rounds of ammunition and 100 tons of poison gas, in preparation for a coup to topple the Bolivian government. It served him right, for, believing that officials were opening his mail, he had thrown out a lure in the form of a spoof letter to a chemicals manufacturing company in Bolivia, asking the firm to prepare a large amount of mustard gas – and, sure enough, the bait had been swallowed.

He was allowed to leave the country only after he had surrendered all the few weapons which the expedition had actually brought in, and having paid a heavy bribe; the Bolivians tried to impound all the machinery and equipment, but were frustrated by the intervention of the British Minister in La Paz, Mr R.C. Michell. In an interview with the *South Pacific Mail* Michell refuted suggestions that Sanders was a criminal, but called him 'a filibuster – a man who lives on his own sharp wits and other people's foolishness'.

Alan never returned to Sacambaya, but repercussions of the fiasco haunted him for years. The first Ordinary General Meeting of the Sacambaya Exploration Company Ltd was held at the Blackfriars Theatre in London on 23 April 1929. Because Sanders had been detained in Paris by what was described as 'a serious accident', it was Alan who took the chair. In his opening remarks he explained that he had flown to France the day before, 'and back in the afternoon', having spent three hours with the Managing Director, who was 'much better', but would not be able to travel for ten days or so.

There is no means of telling whether this injury was real or diplomatic; but in giving the shareholders an account of the expedition, Alan took an optimistic, not to say jaunty, line, which was scarcely justified by the events of the past year. He heaped lavish praise on the participants, Sanders especially, describing him as 'wonderful', and cracked up the equipment they had taken – with the exception of the drill-sharpener, which 'was a nuisance from the first day onwards; in fact I am kind to it when I only say that. It broke down forty times if once.'

Dr Sanders, he said, was 'very generously arranging to protect the Company's property in Bolivia at his own expense':

He asked me yesterday to tell you not to regard your share certificates as waste paper. Hang on to them. They may yet be very valuable. He asked me to say that, what-ever fresh arrangements are made, he hopes to provide the new capital himself.

Alan conceded that, 'in view of what happened', it had been considered inadvisable to mount another expedition during that year; but if the political situation in Bolivia seemed stable, plans would be made for a later attempt on the treasure.

> It is very early yet to say anything about this proposed expedition, but I should mention that the machinery required would not be so extensive as that for last year's expedition, and would consist mainly of a steel coffer dam, a pile driver, and certain other items specially designed to deal with the permanent water level.

On this note of cautious optimism the meeting closed. But the Directors' second annual report, signed by the Secretary and published eighteen months later, on 7 August 1930, told a different story. The hopes for a second expedition had not been realised, it said, 'as Dr Sanders finds himself unable to provide further capital'. The Directors therefore did not consider that the purpose of the Company could be realised, and proposed that the firm should be voluntarily wound up.

Six years later, in November 1936, the German bachelor Rob Gerstmann – one of Sanders' team – revisited the site and took many photographs. As he recounted in a letter to Bob Barnett (another expedition member), he found much of the machinery and equipment still in place, including the compressors, sunk to their axles in the earth. Also present was the watchman left by Sanders to keep an eye on the remains of the camp. 'That man is still dwelling there,' Barnett told Alan, 'I guess waiting the appearance of Dr Sanders to pay his wages. It is a foolish chap and a very optimistic one.'

Over the years that followed Sanders kept in touch with Alan: he sent good-natured letters from time to time; but in 1940 some dispute broke out over relics which Alan had put into store at Harrods, in London. These had been removed from Sanders' house at 14 Wetherby Gardens in March 1929, and included the silver crucifix which he said he had found on his first expedition, fifty-eight volumes of the *Universal Europa-Americana* encyclopaedia, box files, photographs, a diary, a folder and envelopes containing 'Sacambaya papers'. As time went by Alan became irritated at having to pay the storage costs and insurance premiums, modest as both were (£1 10s. every three months), and in April 1940, when he could not get Sanders to agree about disposing of the various items, he sought Counsel's opinion. This came in a letter from his solicitors, Hunt, Nicholson, Adams & Co., who advised him that since the items were in his possession, he had 'a possessary title valid against all the world except the true owner'.

Counsel suggested that he should write to Sanders and say he proposed to dispose of the goods. If no instructions were received within a reasonable time, he should sell them, reimburse himself for his expenses and pay surplus proceeds of sale into a deposit account – and then after six years he could do what he liked with the money.

A suitable letter was written and no reply was forthcoming. In 1943 Alan's solicitors sent Sanders a 'long and special letter . . . as advised by Counsel'. Again there was no answer, so the sale went ahead, raising £89, and the silver crucifix ended up in Alan's hands – though whether (as he claimed) Sanders had given it to him, or whether he had bought it, remains uncertain.

The two do not seem to have communicated again until 1948 – but then, in June, Sanders at last surfaced with a five-page, closely typed letter from Los Angeles. This made no mention of the sale. Rather, it described how he had taken up writing: he claimed he had had one novel published, but had lost out heavily by selling an earlier, unpublished manuscript to another author called Stewart Engstrand, who had rewritten it, changed the title and sold 265,000 copies, making himself $120,000.

Yet that little bit of bad luck was nothing compared with what followed. At the top of page four of his letter, Sanders had typed one short paragraph, preparing Alan for a thunderbolt of news:

Before you continue reading, get yourself a good, stiff drink, sit down solidly in a strong chair so that you do not fall over, and then – turn the page.

Page four began:

The Sacambaya treasure was lifted.

In 1938 an American crowd came down there, with caterpillar trucks and oodles of funny-looking equipment . . . These Americans did a lot of probing, test drilling and investigating. Then in 1939 they came back, with more equipment. They managed to build a plane landing and take-off strip on the bed of the Khato river, then three aeroplanes made their appearance, and all communications with the outside were by plane. They never had an accident.

After about a month's digging they found the chamber and started flying the loot to Antofagasta. In some three weeks they took away gold to the total value of over eight million dollars. Then the thing happened which we always feared would happen to us if we found the treasure and were not damn careful: on government orders a company of regular army soldiers descended on the Yanks. The Americans were chased out because they had no permission to dig, from anybody. All the equipment was confiscated, except one plane, and the army began removing what [treasure] was left. But the Americans had their eight million in safety . . .

When I left Chile for good last year, on my way back

to the States, I got off at Antofagasta and made a trip into
Bolivia, right up to Sacambaya . . . The entrance to the
cave is about thirty yards above the spot where we dug
our 'Big Hole', almost at the right-side rim of the Square
Stone Heap. Of course, last year [eight years after the
alleged American success] the cavern was in a very dilapidated condition, the entrance almost closed by debris and
vegetation, but one could still make out a lot of details.
The chamber must be about fifty by forty feet and has
several stone ledges around three walls . . .

Brother, did I have a sour taste in my mouth!!! And can
you guess who got up this American show? Julius Nolte!
That fellow who joined us in Bermuda, and who was such
an unmitigated fool, we thought. He lives now about a
hundred miles from here, near La Jolla. He built himself
the most tasteless huge mansion there, furnished with the
most tasteless things and knick-knacks I have ever seen.

And he, himself, has become a nasty antique son of a
bitch, as ugly and unpleasant as his abode, which, by the
way, he calls a 'castle'. I spent a whole day with him, and
he told me all the details of the affair.

All the gold and silver were [sic] in bars, each bar
weighing a little under forty pounds. There was many
times more silver, in weight, than gold, but they decided
not to bother with the silver at all. There were no jewels,
and no statues in any material. And, strangest thing of all,
there were no signs or objects which in any way could
be connected with Catholic religious ritual, or any ritual
. . . On the gold and silver bars there were no markings,
either. There was no iron door, the passage being merely
blocked up with large loose stones.

Nolte says the total value, at today's prices for gold and
silver, was estimated at over fifty million dollars. But they
only managed to get out what brought them a gross total

of 8,400,000 dollars ... Nolte's share was 1,500,000 dollars. I suggested that it would be only fair to give me a substantial present for having put him on to the thing. 'Like hell I'll give you anything!' was his answer, and he looked at me like a wildcat ready to spit.

Nolte says he found the signs leading to the entrance of the chamber when he was with us at Sacambaya. He decided not to tell us about it, but [to] come back at some later date with an outfit of his own. And this he did, in 1938 and 1939.

He says, every Sunday afternoon he roamed for hours over the Square Stone Heap, looking for signs, and one day he found them. I believe I still remember how we all laughed at him because of these 'walks' of his over the boulders, beating down the thicket with a stick ... Even you and I considered Nolte to be a little cracked in the head. Yeah! Who laughs last, laughs best!

Nolte says that if you or I had done the same thing, we would have found the spot, too. It was entirely too conspicuous to be missed. Also, he claims, he had invited me and you several times to go out with him on these strolls, to look for signs. I believe he did, and we both refused ...

I frankly admit that I am the one to blame for not having investigated the Square Stone Heap systematically, every square yard of it. But I, like yourself, was too much sold on that damned Charles Gladitz! Blast his soul, and my own stupidity!

And thus ends the story of the Sacambaya treasure. 'Crazy' Nolte is rich, while you and I are poor, at least I am, certainly. You may be quite well off, for all I know. Hell! Let's have another drink. Edgar.

How much of all that was fact, and how much fiction? Had Nolte really carried off $8 million worth of gold, or had he made his money in some other way, and cooked up his account in order to annoy Sanders? On the face of it his story rings true – but on closer examination certain elements seem suspect. First, his description of the treasure – plain, unmarked gold and silver bars – bore no relation to the account in the original document – thirty-seven heaps of gold, and many gold and silver ornaments, let alone a pure-gold image of the Madonna with blazing diamond eyes. Second, he made no mention of the large box clamped with iron bars, or of a passage and several different rooms. Third, it seems improbable that aeroplanes of 1930s vintage could have taken off heavily laden at 7,000 feet above sea level from the sandy beaches that line the banks of the river in the dry season. A fourth source of doubt is the fact that no mention of Nolte's alleged coup has been made by later explorers who went in search of the treasure, confident that it was still there.

It is clear that Sanders believed the Nolte version of the story, and was greatly annoyed by it. But what did *Alan* believe? It seems that he could never quite make up his mind, and for him Sacambaya retained its mystery. Later commentators have been sceptical, dismissing the whole story of the treasure as fictitious, and the alleged Jesuit parchment which started the hunt as an obvious fake, riddled with anachronistic expressions, including English idioms clumsily translated into Spanish. The original document has now disappeared, but the note by Professor Ross authenticating it remains in the possession of the Hillgarth family – as does the silver crucifix which Sanders claimed to have found on his first expedition.

One further enigma: in telling his children the story of the treasure hunt – which he always recounted with relish – Alan never mentioned Sanders' letter of 1948, or Nolte's alleged discovery of the gold. The family found the letter among their father's documents after his death.

Pastures New

The nine-month incarceration at Sacambaya was an endurance test for every member of the expedition; but Alan must have been under particular stress, for during all that time he was in love with a married woman with whom he had been having an affair. Perhaps she and Alan managed to exchange a few letters or cables, but they cannot have had any chance to speak to each other between March and November, and he must have been desperately anxious to know what the outcome of their long separation would be.

Once again he had fallen for a married woman older than himself (she was thirty-two to his twenty-nine). The Hon. Mary Hope-Morley — small, dark-haired, with lovely hands, and known in the family as 'M' — was the third daughter of the late Herbert Gardner, 1st Lord Burghclere, a prominent Liberal Member of Parliament and President of the Board of Agriculture, who had died in 1921.

He was a man of many accomplishments. In his youth he had been a celebrated cricketer and a skilled fly fisherman. He was addicted to amateur dramatics, well known as an actor, and the author of several comic plays which were produced in London theatres and country houses. When in London he often dined with the actor Henry Irving and Arthur Pinero, the dramatist and stage director, at the Beefsteak Club, where all members sit at a single long table. He also translated Virgil's pastoral poems, the Georgics, into English verse (not, it must be said, with any lasting resonance).

Mary's mother Winifred was the eldest daughter of the 4th Earl of Carnarvon, and a sister of the 5th Earl, who financed the expedition which discovered the tomb of Tutankhamen in 1922. She was a more serious author than her husband, with biographies of George Villiers, 2nd Duke of Buckingham, and James, 1st Duke of Ormonde, already to her name, and another life in preparation – that of Charles I's minister, Thomas Wentworth, 1st Earl of Strafford.

From her father Mary inherited an interest in politics, a lively sense of humour, and a genius for friendship, but she grew up in an autocratic atmosphere, and at fourteen or fifteen had to ask her mother's permission before she might read any new book, no matter how innocent. She never went to school, and so missed the chance to learn Latin, but was taught French and German so well by governesses that she became fluent in both languages, and also mastered Spanish.

Thanks to the wide intellectual interests of her parents, she grew up (in the words of her son Jocelyn) 'if not at the edge of the avant-garde, in a circle which included a number of the more interesting and cultivated figures of the time' – and she remained 'profoundly antagonistic to the unthinking Conservatism she encountered', both in her own circle and among the 'trousered Conservative ladies' she later encountered in Majorca. She was also athletic, and passionately fond of horses. 'I shall never recover,' she once told her mother, 'if you don't let me hunt.' A keen dancer, roller-skater and bicyclist, she longed to become a ballet dancer. At the age of fifteen she wrote, 'I have decided, when we are ruined, to be a skating instructress.'

In 1914, at the age of eighteen, she married the Hon. Geoffrey Hope-Morley, son of Lord Hollenden, in the Henry

VII Chapel of Westminster Abbey. He was a senior partner in the family textile firm I. & R. Morley, and lavished extravagant amounts of money and attention on his estate, Hall Place, at Leigh, near Tonbridge in Kent. He and Mary had two daughters, Joan and Elspeth, born in 1915 and 1917; but some time in the 1920s the couple separated, and Mary's marriage was formally dissolved in the Probate Divorce and Admiralty Division of the High Court of Justice on 3 December 1928, on the grounds of her adultery with Alan Hillgarth. If she had waited a few more weeks, she would have become Lady Hollenden, for Geoffrey succeeded to the title as second baron when his father died in February 1929. As it was, she was still the Hon. Mrs Hope-Morley when, aged thirty-two, she and Alan were married at the Chelsea register office on 2 January: three weeks later they solemnised their marriage at Holy Trinity Church, Hampstead, and they evidently wasted no time before adding to the family, for their son Jocelyn was born on 22 September that year.

Alan's sister Maureen claimed to have introduced them to each other, but it is clear that their association had not been easy, for they faced opposition from Mary's mother (though she later accepted the marriage). In any case, Alan had discussed his problems with Edgar Sanders during the expedition, and on 5 January 1929 Sanders wrote him an affectionate letter from Monte Carlo:

First of all, a Happy, Prosperous, Fat New Year to you and Mary. I hope that all your difficulties and troubles are over by now, and that you are able to look forward to a future of peace and bliss . . .

Now hurry up and come here quickly with Mary . . . My wife would very much like to meet you, as I have told her such a lot about your really bad character, your good-for-nothingness, and more things of that kind. It will

give both of us a real pleasure to see you in this part of
the world. So hurry up, and don't mind the bad things I
say about you. I also said a couple of good things.

Mary's good looks and high spirits were enhanced by another
substantial asset: when she was divorced, her former husband
gave her an allowance of £4,000 a year – at that time an
extremely handsome amount – which freed Alan from financial worries and presented him with the chance to do what
he really wanted – to write. This was wonderfully opportune,
for at the beginning of 1929, even after the publication of
three novels, he was still struggling to get his literary career
off the ground.

While he was away in South America his agents A.P. Watt
& Son (cables: Longevity, London) had had no luck placing
his latest book *What Price Paradise?*, set in America. One of the
firm's readers had pointed out that 'Miami Beach, the million-
aires' Boom City of Florida, dominates this novel and is really
the leading character . . . a paradise of swindlers . . . The book
opens extremely well – better, indeed than it finishes . . . The
writing is natural and unforced – at times, especially in the
narrative passages, reminiscent of John Buchan.' But by then
the book had been rejected by five publishers in England and
six in America.

In February 1929, when Alan and Mary were staying at
Cauldhame, near Dunblane in the Ochil Hills north of the
Firth of Forth, their hopes were briefly raised by a letter from
Arthur Barker, of the publishers William Heinemann, who
found the book 'lively and readable' and liked its 'sketch of
Florida', but felt 'there is something missing in the actual story
which has just missed the mark'. He asked if the author could
liven up the plot and strengthen the climax – but no: Alan
decided against working on the book any more.

Hard on the heels of this disappointment came a letter from

Buchan himself, who was then a director of the publishers Thomas Nelson & Sons. 'Indeed, I have not forgotten you,' he wrote on 7 February.

> I have read your novel *What Price Paradise?* with the greatest interest. I thought it a very remarkable story, and I wanted my firm to publish it; but my colleague was scared by the book. He thought the life a little too horrible and incredible . . . Will you give my love to Lady Burghclere? Indeed, I know the Ochils well. It is a beautiful countryside.

A week later Watt sent further depressing news: two more publishers 'have decided against us'. Next Constable turned the book down, making nine English rejections in all. Then at last came a breakthrough: Watt sent the book to Arthur Waugh, Managing Director of the publishers Chapman & Hall and father of the budding author Evelyn Waugh. Here Watt was exploiting a family connection, for young Waugh had married Mary's sister Evelyn Herbert in June the year before – hence their nicknames in the family circle, He-Evelyn and She-Evelyn – and Watt clearly hoped that the link would work in Alan's favour. His ruse came off. 'I shall be only too glad to read your manuscript and will give you my honest opinion, for what it is worth,' Arthur Waugh told Alan in a personal letter. 'I wonder if you would mind letting me know in the meanwhile something about the other books which Evelyn told me you had published.'

Waugh Senior finished reading the book 'with the same excited pleasure' which he had felt all through. The 'chief danger' of the story, he thought, was 'that there is so much America in it'. In spite of this reservation, he agreed to publish it. Alan and Mary were delighted – and their expectations were no doubt raised by the knowledge that Evelyn Waugh had scored an electrifying success with his first novel, *Decline and Fall*, published by his father's firm the previous autumn. Early in March further encouragement came from America. Ferris Greenslet, a partner in the Houghton Mifflin Company in Boston (and a friend of John Buchan), put in an offer, calling the book (not altogether flatteringly) 'a fine example of the "tired businessman's story" type, which not infrequently has a most excellent sale in the United States'.

In those days the publishing process moved at a gratifyingly brisk pace. On 9 March Waugh wrote: 'I am sending the manuscript to the printer today with every intention of getting published before the end of June . . . By the by, the title is being changed to CHANGE FOR HEAVEN.' This annoyed Alan considerably, but his irritation was soothed by Greenslet, who told Waugh: 'I had a most interesting interview with Commander Hillgarth, and am more than ever convinced that he is going to prove an important and successful author.' To Alan himself Greenslet wrote: 'We will certainly do all we can to try to make you a super-Oppenheim of the next generation.'

Flattery seems to have rendered Alan more amenable. When the Americans asked him to cut some of the detailed narrative about real-estate operations, he did so; but in England his attention to typographical exactitude and his habit of rewriting at the last minute were causing the publishers problems. He evidently apologised for being a nuisance, and Waugh, with his perfect manners and long experience of the trade, reassured him, going on to say that his son and daughter-in-law were back from their travels − a Mediterranean cruise during which She-Evelyn had been extremely ill − and that He-Evelyn had grown a moustache. 'When he was at Malta an officer said to him, "Scots Guards, I presume?" He certainly looks worthy of the service, though I must own I preferred him undecorated.'

With a last-minute switch of title, at the author's insistence, from *Change for Heaven* back to the original *What Price Paradise?*, the novel was published before the end of June. Alas for Alan's hopes! The publicity department of Chapman & Hall wrote to say that the subscription – advance orders – had been 'very disappointing'. Only 230 copies of the 7s. 6d. edition and 117 of the Total Colonial edition had been taken up. Nor did things improve after publication. Compared with Evelyn Waugh's *Decline and Fall*, which raced through 3,000 copies in its first three months, the performance of *What Price Paradise?* was pathetic. At the beginning of August Arthur Waugh, back from holiday, commiserated: 'It is . . . dreadfully disappointing about the sales . . . this summer has been almost a record for depression in the publishing trade.'

Even in bad times, Chapman & Hall's way of doing business was gentlemanly in the extreme. 'May we ask you, when you have examined the enclosed statement, kindly to return it in order that we may, as usual, file it here for reference', ran a letter accompanying the latest accounts; and then Alan's agent eased his financial anxieties with a charmingly relaxed note: 'Between ourselves, the income tax authorities have from time to time requested us to make a return of all payments made by us to our clients, but, so far, we have avoided doing so.' Not that much income tax would have been due, even if every penny of earnings had been declared. By the end of 1929 *What Price Paradise?* had earned £12 2s. 6d. in England and $77 (£15 16s. 10d.) in the United States. Greenslet wrote that it should have done better, but that 'it came out right on top of the financial cataclysm [the Wall Street crash] of last fall.'

Eighty years on, one can see why readers did not rush to buy the novel. As A.P. Watt said, it opened well, and the first sentence was a cracker: 'My father told me to go to hell, so I went to Florida.' The first-person narrator, Michael Henderson, a young Englishman, is soon swept into the highest reaches of Palm Beach society. He is urged to invest in real estate, which people are frenziedly snapping up, but is sidetracked by the beautiful Carol, with whom he falls in love.

The book carries a good, strong whiff of America under Prohibition; it also sharply reflects the author's disgust at the obsessive commercialism and abysmal architecture of Miami Beach: 'Already, before I was fairly ashore, I detested the place.' But the story moves at a very uneven pace, bogged down by long, inconsequential conversations. The romantic sequences were no doubt less embarrassing for 1920s readers than they are now, but today they are excruciating – as when Michael falls for Carol:

> In the exquisite terror of our new knowledge we abased ourselves. I worshipped her. I *knew*, but dared not believe that she could love me, or, alternatively, that it would last for her, that life would not snatch her away from me.

In the summer of 1929 it was surely Mary's generosity that enabled Alan to buy a beautiful, 150-foot, twin-masted Dutch schooner, to which he gave a name as graceful as its shape, *Blue Water*. Furnished with this spectacular new toy, he conceived the idea of going round the world, and determined to do it by wind power alone. Having decided that people were cheaper than machinery, he hired a crew of six or seven, including a captain and a cook, but declined to buy an engine, and sailed off towards the south. In the event his frugality proved expensive: other vessels, presuming because of her size that *Blue Water* had an engine, failed to give her priority as a sailing ship, with the result that she was twice dismasted, first off Dover and again off Gibraltar.

Once in the Mediterranean, Alan called at the Rif, where he had spent time a few years earlier. From there he continued eastwards; at one point, when his crew were about to mutiny, he quelled them by threatening them with his drawn swordstick. But he did not get very far, for when he reached the Balearic island of Majorca, off the east coast of Spain, he put into Palma, the principal port, and stopped, brought to a halt by alarm about the financial chaos which had hit world markets as Wall Street crashed, and by the feeling that Mary was suddenly less well off than she had been.

As she herself wrote, at that date Majorca seemed far away from England. Leaving London at Victoria Station, travellers who lacked their own yacht crossed the Channel, traversed Paris from one station to another, took another train, and in the morning raised the blinds of the *wagons-lits* to look out on olive groves and the Pyrenees.

Then the Frontier. Another train, for Spain had a different track to protect it from France. Of course enemies would only invade by train! And then the few hours along the Costa Brava, the first view of the Mediterranean, and of small enticing villages by the sea, and the arrival at Barcelona. The rather exhausting afternoon hours before the evening boat – a small, primitive steamer, called irreverently by the children 'Old Stinky', in which one chugged the 130 miles to the Island through the night.

The delights of Majorca were extolled by the poet and author Robert Graves, who went to live on the island in 1929, after what he called 'a painful domestic crisis' in England. Chief among its attractions were its climate ('better than any other in Europe') and its cheapness: Graves found he could exist there on a quarter of the income needed in England. He loved the fruit, the 'very sound heady wine' and the brandy at three pesetas a bottle, and he found the islanders 'excessively honest and friendly'.

Sharing his enthusiasm, the Hillgarths abandoned their idea of a round-the-world cruise and began to look for somewhere to live. At first they were nomadic, renting different houses and returning to England for some months when the Mediterranean weather became too hot. Young Jocelyn went with them, looked after by a nanny, and later by a governess. Then, in 1930, they came on a property which seized their imagination: a splendid old *finca*, called Son Torrella, near the village of Santa Maria, some twelve miles inland from Palma.

Standing out proud on low foothills against a background of densely forested mountains, the house handsomely dominated its surrounding olive groves and orchards of oranges, lemons and almonds. Mary herself described how its 'dignified façade of honey-coloured stone' seemed to bar the valley, 'as though guarding a secret hidden in the folds of the hills rising behind it'. The plain front was decorated by eight small iron balconies, and along the top storey, beneath the roof, open galleries flanked a central tower. Inside at ground level was a spacious patio with a sloping cobbled floor, a Florentine fountain and an arched colonnade running round all four sides. On the first floor another open, pillared gallery, known as the *claustra*, mirrored the storey below. The newcomers were surprised to find that when they walked out of one of the first-floor rooms at the back, they emerged at ground level once more, because the hill rose so steeply.

Alan and Mary were both smitten by the house, he the most. A farmer and his family were living on the lower level, but the *piano nobile* – the first floor – had not been occupied for at least 100 years. The mule stable was underground, within the house, down a flight of stone steps, with vertical slabs of stone separating the mangers, and to reach it the animals came in through the front door. There was no running water and no electricity, no glass in the windows (only wooden shutters), no fireplaces in the cavernous rooms. The internal walls, never plastered, were of rough stone. Nevertheless, both knew the place was for them. When Mary asked, 'How are we going to maintain it?' Alan, impulsive as ever, just said, 'Don't worry about anything like that. We must have it.'

They bought the house from an elderly Majorcan widow who was about to become a nun. Horrified to hear that her successors were Protestants, she had the private chapel stripped of everything, including the altar and a painting of the Magi – but Mary later had the altar restored.

The refurbishment of the house took two years; in went windows, shutters, piped water, lavatories, bathrooms, electricity, fireplaces and chimneys. Luckily, because of widespread unemployment, labour was very cheap – and the Hillgarths' financial worries were eased by a win on the local lottery, in which they had gone halves with a friendly barman in Palma. Mary's particular love was the new garden which she planned and planted with great imagination, using a mixture of northern and Mediterranean flowers, shrubs and trees. Long orders went out, both to specialist firms in England and to local suppliers, for *arboles frutales* – *albaricoqueros* (apricots), *castaños* (chestnuts), *cerezos* (cherries), *ciruelos* (plums) – for bulbs, acacias, buddleias, poinsettias, jacarandas, for many kinds of *rosales* (*hibridos de té*), and vegetable seeds galore, including lettuces, turnips, white cocktail onions, cucumbers, leeks, beetroot, carrots, and 300 plants of *esparragos*.

On top of all her other activities, Mary became one of the leading supporters of the Anglican church in Palma – and when it came to raising funds, she revealed a talent as a nimble versifier:

> Oh won't you
> Send a few
> Pesetas for a pew?
> And another
> Thirty-five will cover
> Cushions for the pew.

Oh won't you
Send a few
Cushions for the pew?

Then they say the choir
Want us to hire
Or to buy a
'n organ, & its weight,
Packing & the freight,
I can state,
Won't be much in view
Of the lovely mu-
Sic you'll listen to.

Send your free-
Will offerings to me
And you'll see
My monograph,
Mary Hillgarth.

As work on the house went on she and Alan gradually learnt
more of Son Torrella's long history. Ownership of a house on
the site could be traced back to the Christian conquest of the
island in the thirteenth century, when many people came from
the countryside near Girona, in Catalonia, the north-east corner
of mainland Spain. The property had always been highly valued,
because it commanded the district's main source of water – a
spring which rose at the head of the Coanegra valley and ran
down past the house, two and a half miles to Santa Maria,
with some of the flow carried by a small aqueduct.

Until 1670 the place belonged to members of the Torrella
family (*Son* means 'home of'), but then accumulated debts and
mortgages forced them to sell. The local government of Santa
Maria keenly wanted the water rights, but they were outbid

by Don Francisco Cotoner y Oleza, head of a powerful clan in the district. Having acquired the site, and more land round about, he started building, and for more than 250 years the house and farm belonged to the Cotoner family, who, through their ownership of the water supply, controlled the entire local economy.

Until the 1920s the estate was very extensive; then land was sold off, but the exterior of the dwelling remained little changed. In the words of Alan's son Jocelyn, the house still retains 'the happy Mediterranean combination of palace and farm achieved by the Romans and implanted by them in all the Latin lands, and nowhere more clearly than in Majorca'.

One of Son Torrella's most fascinating features was (and still is) the *tafona*, or olive press, powered by water from the Coanegra, which in earlier days had been used as a central depot by all the growers roundabout. Primitive but effective machinery was set up in a room – a barn, really – as big as a couple of squash courts, to which workers on the estate and local farmers would bring their crop in the autumn. Mule carts were driven on to an outside terrace and dropped their cargo through holes in its paved floor. Inside, the fruit was ground into pulp before being placed under four presses – immensely heavy stones, each fixed to one end of a great baulk of timber, thirty feet long and maybe fifteen inches in section. The mighty beams would be cranked up by vertical wooden worms or screws, with spiral threads cut in them, which were driven by the waterwheels outside; then each vast stone would be lowered on to sacks of pulp, so that the oil was forced out and ran off into vats. Latter-day experts calculated that twenty men would have been needed to run the mill when it was working at full stretch. By the time Alan arrived it had fallen into dereliction, and he was not much interested in it, but in due course Jocelyn had it restored with help from local government.

Bit by bit Alan and Mary furnished the house, buying most

pieces in Palma and bringing others out from England. One notable import was the portrait of Lady Chesterfield, M's great-great-grandmother, painted in about 1870, which came from Bretby, her family's house in Staffordshire. A very large picture, some ten feet high and six wide, it was shipped from England aboard the battle cruiser HMS *Hood*, and a group of petty officers came out to hang it. The house and its rooms were so large that they remained sparsely furnished and decorated, but this was what Alan preferred.

As usual, he was working on a novel – and once again the story sprang partly from his own experience, this time the disastrous gold-hunting expedition to Sacambaya. The Andes made a thrilling background, and, because he knew the scene so well, he brought the great, menacing mountains brilliantly to life as he told the story of a native boy of about eleven, Patricio, who runs away from his squalid home – a one-room hut with an earth floor – and travels on foot through the wilds with a *callaguaya*, or wandering witch doctor, who becomes his mentor.

Reaching civilisation, Patricio is adopted by a powerful Bolivian family, who send him to school and then to university, with the result that he becomes enmeshed in revolutionary politics. He is much troubled by doubts about his own paternity: is he a pure Quichua Indian, or was his father Spanish? He falls in love with a gringa girl, which gives the author a chance to make outspoken comments about race relations. The British diplomats in La Paz refer to him openly as 'that little dago'; white mining executives and their wives turn away from him at cocktail parties – but he rises easily above such naked racial insults.

The Black Mountain is easily the most accomplished of Alan's novels. He managed to convey Patricio's development, from illiterate peasant to articulate politician, with convincing insight, and the young man's conversations with Margaret, the daughter of a rich, white mining family, are in a different league from the stilted banalities of the earlier books.

The novel was published in England in July 1933, and in America nine months later, attracting respectful reviews on both sides of the Atlantic, among them an approving notice by Graham Greene. Yet once again real success eluded Alan: perhaps because the setting was so far away, and the subject so strange for English and American readers, sales were disappointingly modest. An American company bought film rights for $5,000, but the movie was never made. Alan later remarked that *The Black Mountain* was the only book he had written in which he had 'any pride in at all', and that he was 'frankly ashamed' of his earlier novels, which were 'juvenile' and spoilt by 'bad craftsmanship'.

When he arrived on Majorca he already spoke some Spanish, having perhaps learnt a smattering in Morocco; but now, though he retained a discernible foreign accent, he mastered the language completely. As one acquaintance put it, he spoke it 'not only fluently and idiomatically but with an accuracy which pleased and flattered his many influential Spanish friends'.

More than that, he found he had a powerful natural affinity for Spain. Not only did he like the people, the climate, the food, the wine: he also admired the country's history and traditions, and the courage of its inhabitants. So began a love affair which lasted all his life. His linguistic skill, combined with his convivial nature, enabled him to make friends not only among the numerous British expatriates living scattered about the island, but also with the locals round Son Torrella and the dignitaries in Palma, so that he quickly became a prominent figure in the community – not because of any social or political ambition on his part, but because of the interest he took in everything going on around him, his willingness to give help, and the common sense with which he settled disputes.

On 1 December 1932 the British government appointed him their Acting Vice Consul at Palma, and a fortnight later

confirmed him in that office, successor to Ivan Lake, who had
been appointed to the unsalaried post in 1924. At first the job
was a modest one, but work built up rapidly, and, becoming
annoyed by the personal expense to which he was being put,
Alan kept a detailed account of what it was costing him to
act as His Britannic Majesty's representative.

In a suburb of Palma he found a bare office. Except for the
safe and two old typewriters, the furnishings had belonged to
his predecessor, so he had to buy new ones. He also had to
engage staff to deal with the swiftly increasing volume of business: in the period 1 December 1932 to 31 March 1933 the
number of people calling at the office for advice or help aver-
aged thirty-two a day. When he took over, the office allowance
was £90 a year, which was supposed to cover everything – rent,
lighting, heating, telephone, staff salaries, cleaning and so on. In
fact it by no means met these essential costs – and on top of
them were what he called 'unavoidable expenses' such as transport and entertaining.

Transport was one major item. Son Torrella is eighteen
kilometres from Palma, which meant daily journeys amounting
to thirty-six kilometres, besides which he often had to drive
all over the island on consular business. 'Petrol is dear in Spain
and very bad,' he wrote in his account, 'and so are the roads.'
He estimated that fuel alone was costing him ninety pesetas
(about £2 5s.) a week – more than £100 a year, and more
than his entire allowance.

Transport, however, was nothing like as expensive as entertaining. This, Alan insisted, was 'practically impossible to avoid'.
In addition to the normal consular hospitality – 'people to
lunch, tea, dinner etc., whom I would never ask otherwise –
there is the entertaining due to visits of HM ships. In these
four months [December to March] there were many visits, at
one time involving seventy.'

Part of the trouble was that when he entertained, he liked

to do so in style – and one of his most successful parties was held at Son Torrella on 3 June 1935 in honour of King George V's seventieth birthday. Three hundred guests were invited, among them Don Juan Manent, the Civil Governor of the Province; and an enthusiastic English newspaper reported that 'Master Jocelyn Hillgarth, four and a half, dressed in a sailor's suit and carrying a small telescope, was introduced to Señor Manent, whom he saluted smartly'. The article went on to say: 'The word "palatial" is inadequate to describe Son Torrella: "castle-like" more closely describes the great finca.' Another English-language newspaper, sounding remarkably like the *Tatler*, was equally effusive:

> Seldom can there have been such a big party, so perfectly organised. If this is the way they do things, there can be nothing wrong with the British Navy . . . Almost the entire British Colony must have been present, and we noticed some lovely frocks among the ladies. Mrs Hugh Rose looked particularly effective in a beautiful frock of printed *crêpe de chine* over organdie, with a huge bow and lace gauntlets.

At 7 p.m. the National Anthem was sung, and Alan brought the reception to a climax by calling for a toast to the King. Standing on the balcony surrounding the patio, he first addressed, in perfect Spanish, the Civil Governor, who stood opposite him across the court. He then proposed the toast, after which champagne was drunk. The fiesta, which finished at about nine in the evening, was declared by a local Spanish paper to have been 'one of the most brilliant receptions organised by the Consular corps in Palma'. No wonder it strained Alan's budget, for it cost 5,500 pesetas – about £120. But he commemorated the occasion extravagantly by getting all his guests to sign their names – some more steadily than others

– in a large tome bound in gold-tooled red leather, with AHH embossed on the cover.

One person who did *not* go to the party was Robert Graves, who was living at Deyá, high above the sea on the north-west coast of the island, with his partner, the poet Laura Riding. 'Dear Hillgarth, and Mrs Hillgarth,' he had written,

> Many thanks for the invitation to the June 4th celebration and if I decline it, please understand that it is not for want of a strong personal feeling for H.M. the King as probably the best King we have had since Henry VIII, but because there are certain of his subjects whom I don't particularly want to meet and who will probably be there expressing their loyalty. Miss Riding is writing to much the same effect to you and I join her in hoping that one day you'll come here to Deyá & visit us.
>
> Yours very sincerely,
> Robert Graves

It was a year before that – in 1934 – that Graves had published the book which did most to establish his reputation – *I, Claudius*, a fictional, first-person account of the life of the Roman emperor. But he had already become notorious five years earlier with the publication (at thirty-four) of his unin-hibited autobiography, *Goodbye to All That*, which alienated many of his English friends, among them the poet Siegfried Sassoon, through its outspoken and sometimes cynical descrip-tions of slaughter in the First World War (Graves himself had been severely wounded in the Battle of the Somme). In 1929 he had abandoned his wife and children, and gone with the poet Laura Riding to live on Majorca, where he built himself the house at Deyá and ran a small publishing business, the Seizin Press.

He several times called on Alan for help, always referring in his letters to his mistress as 'Miss Riding' or 'Laura Riding' or 'L.R.', but never by her Christian name alone. When, at his behest, Alan wrote to some local functionary to help settle a dispute over a road, Graves replied:

> Very many thanks indeed for writing the letter . . . Every extra help in this business is welcome, and the personal letter is worth a thousand legal declarations in this country . . . If this letter reads a bit queerly it is from just coming away from seeing Charlie Chaplin, and laughing too much.

One interesting bird of passage was Winston Churchill, who came to the Mediterranean to paint in 1935. Churchill was then in his wilderness years, between major appointments, but beginning to warn of the danger posed by Hitler and pressing for the creation of a Ministry of Defence. He and his wife Clemmie had booked into the Hotel Formentor at Puerto Pollensa, on the north-eastern corner of the island; but after only one night Clemmie announced that they were leaving because the drains smelt so frightful. On their way back to Palma Alan invited the couple to lunch at Son Torrella, and the rapport instantly established between the two men over this one meal was so strong that it lasted for twenty years, to their mutual advantage. Alan already had a high regard for Churchill, and Churchill found in Alan a man of attractive intelligence and absolute integrity. During his brief visit he signed Alan's copy of *The River War*, his own account of the campaign in the Sudan, published in 1899; and then, as he was leaving and trying to be agreeable, asked five-year-old Jocelyn, 'What are you interested in? Roman history? Caesar and Cicero and all that?' To which the boy, who then had a slight speech impediment, replied, 'No – I'm interested in the tampaigns, Stipio and Sticily.' That was too much for Churchill, who got into the car groaning 'Take me away!' – whereupon the chauffeur drove him and Clemmie to Palma and the boat for Marrakesh.

Alan himself had a deep interest in history: he read widely, had an excellent memory and built up a fine library, which included many of Mary's books. The collection was further reinforced when his father Wilmott – by then seventy-five – decided to scale down his own library and wrote from his home in Kent:

My Dear Alan,
With regard to my offer of books – it was not due to any prospect of a speedy termination of my life, but I feel sure that it will save your mother much trouble when she *will* have to think what to do with them, be the time when it may. Many books indeed I have; I have never counted them, but they number some ten thousand, and there may be many more. I have always been omnivorous (with regard to books) and taken an interest in so many branches of knowledge . . . and as I rarely give away any . . . the number of books is large. If you come to England next year, you will be able to make your choice. I enclose a list of a few sets which I think you might consider worth having:

> Walter Scott's Life of Napoleon, 8 vols.
> Macaulay's History of England, 7 vols (from accession of James II). This belonged to my mother.
> Ben Jonson in 9 volumes.
> Edmund Spenser in 8 volumes.

Of course there are many, many others. Wait till you see them. A library is essential in your house.

In the intervals of answering expatriates' calls for assistance, and (as Jocelyn later put it) getting drunken British seamen out of Spanish jails, Alan was busy writing. Undaunted by the relative failure of *The Black Mountain*, he completed the draft of a new novel early in 1935. *Davy Jones* was set in and around the Royal Navy, and for an expert appraisal he sent the draft to his old shipmate Eric Bush, who returned a critique on 10 February. 'Taking the whole story as it stands, it is certainly "impossible,"' he wrote, before going into a lot of detail, 'but I don't think necessarily improbable.'

What did that ambiguous verdict mean? The story is agreeable enough, but based on a far-fetched idea: it carries echoes, in reverse, of Anthony Hope's *The Prisoner of Zenda*, in which a young Englishman, Rupert Rassendyll, is obliged to impersonate the King of Ruritania. Here 'David Jones', the son of a recently deposed north European monarch (the Tsar?), has been given sanctuary as a serving officer in the Royal Navy, but is required not to reveal that the arrangement has been made with the connivance of His Majesty's Government and the Admiralty.

One improbability piles on another, and the action in the book is perfunctory – one exciting rescue of a man fallen overboard, one dreadfully unrealistic encounter with pirates, and a great deal of padding in between. But the sailors' argot is admirably caught, and the narrative is packed to the gunwales with technical terms. The author clearly revelled in the chance to scatter these like shrapnel:

'Well, sir, it shouldn't have parted in that cat's paw.'
'He ought to have freshened the nip.'
'Certainly, sir. Or he ought to have put a leather Scotchman in it.'
'Wouldn't that have choked the luff?'
'Not with so worn a sheave, sir. Plenty of room in the swallow, passed taut and tacked with copper tacks.'

One gains the impression that Alan very much enjoyed plunging back into his old milieu, and being able to write without the need for research. But his agent had some difficulty placing the book: only at the beginning of November was Watt able to report that the publishers Ivor Nicholson & Watson had offered an advance of £50. 'Taking into consideration the sales of *The Black Mountain* etc,' the agent wrote, 'I think that this is an offer which we shall do well to accept.' Alan agreed, and a contract for the book was signed at the end of January 1936.

Meanwhile, the literary news from America was gloomy. By the beginning of February *The Black Mountain* had sold only 1,070 copies, in spite of energetic promotion and widespread reviews; the unsold copies had been remaindered and were being offered to the author at one shilling apiece. Then, in April, Knopf rejected *Davy Jones* with a withering dismissal:

This book is a romantic account of the British Navy, and it seems to us to have no appeal for Americans . . . I am quite certain this book would do his reputation hopeless injury.

The novel was published in England on 18 June at 7s. 6d., with a lurid jacket illustration which depicted the crew of a ship repelling cutlass-wielding pirates. According to William Hickey, the *Daily Express* gossip columnist, the author was dismayed when he saw it, having written 'a perfectly serious novel', and by the publishers' first breathless blurb, which had to be toned down. In the end this read: 'While intensely exciting, this book is something more, for it presents the true Navy, lower deck and quarter deck, in spirit and tradition, as no one has contrived to do since the time of Captain Marryat.'

Even if the publishers over-reached themselves, it was shrewd of them to invite comparison with Frederick Marryat, the

nineteenth-century sailor who tried to run away to sea, joined
the Navy as a midshipman and later had huge success with
his sea stories, principally *Mr Midshipman Easy*. The famous
name gave reviewers an easy yardstick against which to measure
their opinions.

Alan was up against stiff opposition, for in the same month
Elinor Glyn, then seventy-one but still notorious for her
remarks about sinning on tiger skins, published her autobiography *Romantic Adventure*. Another literary distraction was the
death on 14 June of the immensely prolific author G. K.
Chesterton, which focused critics' attention on his new collection of essays, *As I Was Saying*.

Realising that he needed support, Alan for once sought a
favour from Robert Graves, sending him a copy of *Davy Jones*,
and asking if he would review it. Back came a prompt answer:

> Glad to hear from you and many thanks for *Davy Jones*.
> L.R. and I have a rule about not giving propaganda
> opinions about books: it seems to us unethical – like self-
> advertising. Lawyers and doctors and soldiers, probably
> also sailors, have analogous scruples.
>
> But what I can do and shall do with great pleasure is
> to try to get the job of reviewing the book for the
> *Observer*: which is ethical enough and carries more weight.
> It will be a critical review, making the Marryat connexion,
> and leading the public to buy the book by a judicious
> parade of its points . . . I have dipped into it and it reads
> like good clean stuff: all I ask for, nowadays.

A letter to the *Observer* evoked a 'nice "Yes of course"', so
Graves wrote an appraisal and sent it off, warning Alan that 'It
doesn't read like a log-rolling review, but I think will sell a
few copies'. The piece duly appeared in the newspaper on 28
June and occupied an impressive amount of space under a

two-column heading 'The Naval Officer'. It began with an encouraging statement: 'An interesting and cleanly-written account in fictional form of the life of a naval officer today', and called the novel 'a sort of centenary tribute to *Mr Midshipman Easy*'; but the rest of the piece consisted mainly of comparisons between the two, with long quotations from each, and no further praise or recommendation. Nevertheless, a notice from such a celebrated writer must have done something for sales.

Another distinguished literary expatriate who sought Alan's help was that giant of Irish poetry and drama W.B. Yeats, who had arrived in Majorca in 1934. In his youth he had been pale and lanky, but now, at sixty-nine, rejuvenated by his recent vasectomy (then known as the Steinach operation), he cut a fine figure. Sir William Rothenstein, Principal of the Royal College of Art, saw him as 'brown-skinned under his white hair, his dark eyes aslant, broad-shouldered and ample of form.'

Yeats came to the island to work with Shri Swami Purohit, the Hindu monk, poet and teacher who soon became a close friend. Having written an introduction to his autobiography, *An Indian Monk*, published in 1932, Yeats helped him with the marathon task of translating into English the *Upanishads* – philosophical texts of the Hindu religion. The first ten or twelve are known as the *Principal Upanishads*, among them the *Bhagavad Gita* – Song of God – a 700-verse dialogue between Lord Krishna and Arjuna, the great warrior and archer. As the Swami grappled with his mighty task, Yeats became so fascinated that he planned to accompany him on a journey to India and complete the job there; but in the end he abandoned the idea and continued the work in Majorca.

Exactly what role Alan played in the process is not easy to determine; but letters show that he earned the Swami's warm gratitude. 'My dear Commander Hillgarth,' the monk wrote from Casa Pastor at San Augustín, Yeats's home near Palma, in May 1936:

> I hear from Mrs Yeats that you have written to me; perhaps the post-office has not found it convenient to deliver your letter.
>
> I got the almonds from the Consulate. Are they for planting? There were no instructions inside. Please let me know.
>
> I am leaving tomorrow in the afternoon. Thank you very much for your kindness. I am staying with Dr Yeats. Please write to me c/o Thomas Cook, Bombay.
>
>   God bless you all, Swami.

A month later he wrote again, still at San Augustín: 'God bless you and yours is the prayer of an humble monk, Swami.'

At least once the monk stayed at Son Torrella, which Yeats described as 'a medieval villa furnished with exquisite taste', and with his many fads he proved an exacting guest: one day Yeats summoned Alan privily to swat a mosquito, knowing that the Swami would sustain a fearful shock if he witnessed the insect's murder. Tiresome though Yeats could be, with his hypochondria and constant changes of focus, Alan became fond of him and offered to help pay for the Swami's return to India – whereupon Yeats wrote: 'Dear Commander Hillgarth . . . You have been so extraordinary [sic] kind that I would not lay any further burden upon you. Yrs W.B Yeats'

A still more tiresome participant in Yeats's tangled affairs was the actress and poet Margot Ruddock, whose habit was to go about chanting her own verses in a low contralto voice. In 1934, when she was twenty-seven, her life was already in disarray: she had abandoned her first husband and daughter, and married a second husband, the actor Raymond Lovell, by whom she had a six-month-old baby. When she conceived the idea of establishing a poets' theatre in London, she sought Yeats's help; and he, admiring her beautiful voice and her eyes (which he called 'generous'), shared her enthusiasm and began an affair.

In 1936 Margot followed him to Majorca and appeared at San Augustín, but after only a few hours she vanished, causing him acute anxiety. As she herself recounted later, she found her way to Barcelona, on the coast of the mainland, and wandered through the streets, half out of her mind, before falling through a roof and cracking a knee.

Hearing that something awful had happened, Yeats hastened to Barcelona, and there – as he told Alan in an agonised letter – he found Margot in distress.

May 27

Dear Hillgarth,

My wife and I have been in Barcelona to help . . . send an English poetess home. She is a friend of mine of some years' standing, & her husband and brother gave my name. She was here for a few hours, went to Barcelona, was out of her mind and window alas, falling through a roof, hiding with a broken knee-cap in the hold of a ship and most of the time singing her own poems and her own tunes. She is a beautiful tragic creature with some genius.

Yours W.B. Yeats

Margot was taken back to England, where in 1937 she published *The Lemon Tree*, a collection of poems which included an account of her 'Adventure'. She also worked with Yeats on his broadcasts, sometimes singing his poems; but she came to a miserable end: committed to a mental institution, she died in 1951 at the age of forty-four. Her 'Adventure' found a melancholy echo in Yeats's poem *The Crazed Girl*:

No matter what disaster occurred
She stood in desperate music wound,
Wound, wound, and she made in her triumph
Where the bales and the baskets lay
No common intelligible sound
But sang 'O sea-starved, hungry sea.'

In June 1936, while Yeats was still enmeshed in Margot's problems, Alan went to England on leave, and took six-year-old Jocelyn to watch the ceremony of Trooping the Colour on Horse Guards Parade – a magnificent spectacle, in which sixty-seven officers and 1,738 other ranks took part, with Edward VIII himself riding at the head of the King's Guard. 'Saw it from garden of 10 Downing Street,' Alan wrote on the thick card of the souvenir programme – but there is no record of why the Prime Minister, Stanley Baldwin, had invited him.

8

Saving Lives

To their family and friends it seemed that for Alan and Mary the years 1932 to 1936 were a halcyon era, short but golden. Both were writing; she was busy with her garden, and he (in a relaxed way) with consular affairs. In their splendid house they were looked after by servants, entertained lavishly and became popular figures on the island. Jocelyn (three in 1932) was with them, plus nanny, who had been with the family for years and became a great figure in the house – though she could not speak Spanish. Mary's daughters, Joan and Elspeth, now in their teens, came out from England to stay. Alan was disappointed that Mary could not have any more children, for he would have liked her to bear another son. He was also anxious about his marriage: as he himself revealed many years later, doubts had set in at the start, but for the time being he suppressed them, and on the surface all appeared well.

Then, in the second half of 1936, their lives were abruptly changed by the outbreak of the Spanish Civil War, which thrust Alan into a huge humanitarian mission and landed a heavy weight of responsibility on his shoulders. Fond as he was of Spain and its inhabitants, he held a clear view of their foibles, and in one of the secret memoranda which he began sending to the Foreign Office he wrote:

Generally speaking, the Spaniard fears the German, he hates the Italian, he hates the French even more, and he does not like but would tolerate the British if he were quite certain that we were strong enough to win a war with Germany. Really, he loathes all foreigners and is so extremely individual that he loathes most of his fellow countrymen as well.

Never was this more true than in the summer of 1936. Since the resignation and departure of the dictator General Primo de Rivera in 1930, and the equally bloodless abdication of King Alfonso XIII in 1931, the political structure in Spain had been progressively fragmenting as numerous factions squared up for a major confrontation, with more than twenty political parties and labour unions represented in Parliament. In the words of Hugh Thomas, the history of Spain during the two-and-a-half years leading up to the autumn of 1936 'was marked by a steady decline into chaos, violence, murder and, finally, war.'

The population was split between two ideologies. On one side were the Nationalists, right-wing Falangists (the 'Whites'), who soon united under Generalissimo Francisco Franco and were backed by both Hitler and Mussolini. On the other side was the elected Republican government (the 'Reds'), which attracted left-wing support from many quarters, not least the Soviet Union and Mexico, but also from more than 30,000 individual volunteers of the International Brigades, among them George Orwell and Ernest Hemingway.

The war erupted on 17 July 1936, when Nationalist generals led an army coup in an attempt to depose the recently elected Popular Front government. At the outset of hostilities Spain was physically divided in two, with the south-eastern half of the country, including Madrid, in Republican hands, and the north-western half (with the important exception of the Basque

Country, along the north coast) Nationalist. Of the Balearic islands, Minorca was Republican, but Ibiza and Majorca declared for the Nationalists. In Alan's own words, Majorca was 'completely in the hands of the Right'.

As Robert Graves remarked, none of the Majorcans (or Minorquins, as he often called them) thought that the revolution would affect them, since 'the most recent fighting in the island had taken place around 1450'. But in fact they were in for a shock.

First Ibiza, lying fewer than fifty miles to the south-west, was invaded on 8 August by a Republican force which rapidly took control of the island. As the Reds set about burning churches and murdering clergymen (killing twenty-one out of about fifty), left-wing supporters emerged from the caves and forests in which they had been hiding, and right-wing sympathisers disappeared into the countryside

On Majorca, expatriate residents were strongly advised to leave. More than 200 Britons, over 100 Germans, 80 French and 49 Americans had already sailed to Marseilles aboard the battle-cruiser HMS *Repulse*, many along with their dogs and cats, which were housed in kennels on the boat deck. Of the British subjects remaining, those who agreed to go were swiftly evacuated in the destroyer HMS *Grenville*: all their possessions, except what they could carry, were stacked in the Anglican church at Palma, which was filled to the roof. As the long-term expatriate Charles Elwell recorded, the church 'was filled to overflowing not with the faithful but with their furniture'.

Among the evacuees was Robert Graves, who received a note telling him that *Grenville* would sail that afternoon, 'probably your last chance of leaving Spain in safety. Luggage limited to one hold-all.' Having hastily packed his manuscripts and some clothes, he left home within an hour in a taxi which Alan had provided. He had no time to deposit anything in the church – but it turned out that there was no need for him to

have done so. When he returned to the island after ten years'
wandering, 'he found his house and garden untouched, and he
was greeted by his village friends with as many tears of welcome
as they had shed on his departure'.

Through his numerous contacts Alan had seen what was
coming. He had been on holiday in England, and early in
August, leaving the family in London, he returned to Palma
aboard the destroyer HMS *Gipsy* and at once began sending
secret reports to the Foreign Office. Without any official invitation, he suddenly became an agent of HMG.

As the crisis developed, he reported more and more
frequently, describing Majorca's preparations to resist attack,
'which is expected at any moment'. The defence arrangements
were amateurish, to say the least: they consisted of 'a very
sharp lookout at all points, a trench system on all low-lying
coasts, stiffened by nests of machine-guns and improvised
batteries, and backed by a strategic disposition of troops and
a mobile armament of howitzers on lorries'. A camouflaged
covered way had been made by building a second wall parallel
with an existing structure and roofing the space between with
branches of trees and other vegetation.

One of Alan's problems was the hard core of expatriates
who were determined to stay put. In another secret message,
dated 15 August, he reported: 'British Nationals remaining total
eighty-eight repetition eighty-eight. Of these, three Consulate,
seven indispensable, twelve sick, remainder at present refuse to
leave.' He had been round all the local authorities warning
them of the danger, and had arranged three gathering points
for British subjects in the event of an emergency. Now he told
the Foreign Office: 'Attack on Majorca imminent.'

Sure enough: at first light on 16 August a force of one
Republican battleship, two destroyers, three submarines and a
hospital ship, supported by tugs and lighters, appeared off the
east coast opposite the fishing village of Porto Cristo. After a

bombardment from the sea, a mixed expeditionary force of 2,500 men from Catalonia and Valencia landed at dawn. Ferocious house-to-house fighting ensued, and 300 of the invaders were killed. 'No prisoners were taken,' Alan reported (though he later amended this to say that six or a dozen had been spared 'in return for information'). Having captured the town, the Catalans pressed on into the hinterland, establishing a semicircular enclave some four kilometres deep. Then, however, they hesitated, as if unsure what to do next, and devoted themselves to smashing up churches and statues.

There were few Nationalist troops on the island, as most of them had gone to Barcelona to support the revolution there; but those who had remained in Majorca took advantage of the invaders' vacillation to rally themselves for a counter-attack. HMS *Kempenfelt* and *Valorous*, meanwhile, were evacuating refugees to St Jean de Luz on the Atlantic coast of France.

On 20 August Alan reported: 'The attack upon the island . . . has definitely failed, and the invaders still ashore are being reduced at a rate that will mean their annihilation by the 22nd unless help is forthcoming.' He added that no foreigner's person or property had been in any way molested, and that the island was 'orderly and peaceful in so far as it is not affected by attempts at invasion or bombing'. Four days later he told London:

A very large number of arrests of known Left sympathisers have been carried out, and at least fifteen Communists have been shot every night, but this cannot last long as there are not many left to shoot.

To the islanders' aid came an Italian fighter squadron and three bombers, led by Arconovaldo Bonaccorsi, a red-bearded Fascist who styled himself the Conte Rossi and took command of Majorca's defences. After meeting him, Alan described him as 'certainly a tough adventurer, sent by Mussolini', and within a few days he became alarmed by the rapid build-up of Italian forces on the island. Rossi, assuming command of the defences, roared about in a red Bugatti, accompanied by an armed Falange chaplain. Italian ships began to arrive at Palma, unloading anti-aircraft guns. Three large monoplane bombers flew over the city and landed at San Juan aerodrome. From there air-raids began to be launched against Ibiza and targets on the mainland, and night-flying started, with the runway illuminated by the headlamps of 200 cars. The Italian naval mail plane opened a new schedule, arriving and leaving every two or three days. Alan warned the Foreign Office:

> I am being driven to the conclusion that Italy has some private intentions of her own in connection with the Balearic islands. The conversation and attitude of Italian naval officers have begun to display it . . . Sooner than be conquered by Catalan Communists, Majorca will appeal to Italy for a protectorate. Both the Civil Governor and the Fascists have admitted this in one of their many excited and unguarded comments.

On 3 September the Nationalists launched a counter-attack in the east, and the Republicans ran for their ships: some made good their escape, but many were killed on the beaches, and most of those taken prisoner were shot. The last of the invaders were driven off on 4 September, after a nocturnal battle – but their rout did not deter Barcelona radio from announcing that 'the heroic Catalan columns' had returned from Majorca 'after a magnificent action. Not a single man suffered from the effects of the embarkation, for Captain Bayo, with unique tactical skill, succeeded in carrying it out, thanks to the morale and discipline of our invincible militiamen.'

On 6 September thousands of people celebrated Majorca's

escape at an open-air mass in Palma. Aircraft flew overhead, and afterwards, during a march past, scores of Catalan flags were dragged through the dust. At the head of the first Fascist contingent rode Rossi, dressed entirely in black, except for a white cross at the neck, drawing special applause from the crowd. Alan reported that although local Fascists regarded the count with respect, they disliked him heartily, not least because he personally ordered the execution of prisoners, including women. He told London that Rossi was 'trying to make himself a local Mussolini', and hoping to engineer a coup which would lead to the seizure of the island by Italy.

> Under his forceful guidance . . . the placid Majorcans have been jolted out of their usual lazy form of life. Troops, fascists, ballila, baby Carlists in red caps, women and girl fascists are all busy drilling every evening, the children and babies with wooden rifles.

Mercedes Bonsoms, an old friend of the Hillgarths who had lived on the island and whom Alan had helped, spoke for many when she wrote from Italy:

> What anxious days you have had whilst the Reds had taken possession of part of the coast! Thank God they were almost annihilated . . . It is such a ghastly war – not the fighting, which is magnificent and makes one proud, but cruelty, the destruction of beauty and artistic treasure makes one so miserable. What will remain of Spain?

Mercedes did not exaggerate. Appalling struggles were taking place on the mainland, not least in and around the Simancas barracks at Gijón, on the north coast of Asturias, where 180 Nationalists held out for weeks during July and August against an army of Republican miners. Even when the attackers brought the two sons of the defending commander, a fanatical colonel called Antonio Pinilla, to demand that he surrender, he refused, and the young men were shot. In the end he sent a message to the Nationalist warships offshore saying, 'Defence is impossible . . . fire on us.' The demand was obeyed, and the last defenders of the Simancas barracks died in the flames.

As the war gathered momentum on the mainland, hot-headed young men in other countries began flocking to join the Republican side – a development not at all to the liking of Alan's colleague Norman King, the Consul in Barcelona, who considered that the Spaniards were, for the most part, 'still a race of bloodthirsty savages, with a thin veneer of civilisation in times of peace'. He deplored the fact that British volunteers were leaving England for Barcelona to join the government forces, and reported in a telegram to the Admiralty:

> I consider it most unfortunate that these people have obtained travel facilities to come and swell the rabble of bloodthirsty anarchists . . . I have ordered all British subjects out of this district, and beg to decline any responsibility for people who enter without permission.

Once Gijón had fallen, the Nationalists could concentrate their fleet in the Mediterranean, and they decided to use Majorca as the principal base for a blockade of the only Spanish coast remaining in Republican hands. On 10 September a delegation of twenty-eight more Italians arrived and were put up at the Grand Hotel, where (Alan reported) they messed together as if in barracks, and gave 'vent to concerted shouts in honour of the Duce, especially just before sitting down to meals'.

> At 0800 every day they fall in in the hotel lounge for inspection, and the place rings with words of command

. . . The martial arrogance of this behaviour in a leading
hotel is offensive to many Spaniards. It is evident that an
increasing number of Mallorquins, of all conditions, view
this Italian bombast with dislike and the future with doubt
. . . They are beginning to wonder if it will be easy to
get rid of the Italians when it is all over.

A rumour went round that the Italians were planning to
requisition Son Torrella and make it their headquarters. Had
they done so, the house might well have been destroyed – for,
standing out prominently in the foothills, it would have made
a splendid target for marauding Republican bombers. Fortunately,
the idea was never carried through.

In the middle of September Alan got wind of the fact that
the Italians were planning to attack Ibiza, which had been in
Republican hands for only five weeks. As usual, his information was accurate, and he witnessed the departure of a small
invasion force from Palma on the night of the 19th:

Immediately it was dark, the *Ciudad de Palma* was painted
black . . . At 2330, still wet and with all her lights burning,
she left with 300 picked Falangists, one company of the
Foreign Legion of Majorca and a heavy machine-gun
battery, making a total of 650 men. The Marques de Zayas,
the Fascist leader, commanded, assisted by Count Rossi.
At daylight on the 20th the *Ciudad de Palma* entered Ibiza
port, and the town was occupied without opposition.

This walkover had been facilitated by earlier brutalities. Heavy
bombing by Italian aircraft had driven the principal Red elements
from the island, but before they left they had killed nearly 100
White sympathisers in the prison by machine-gunning them
and throwing hand grenades into the cells. They had also pillaged
every church and bank, and some private houses. By the time

the Fascists arrived, there were only twelve Reds left. 'Of these,' Alan reported, 'four have been shot, and the rest will be.'

In London the Italian takeover of Majorca was evaluated by a Chiefs of Staff sub-committee, which minuted that, although the island was 450 miles east of Gibraltar, 'occupation of it would give Italy a base for naval and air operations 250 miles closer to Gibraltar than anything which she possesses at the present time. The menace to our control of the straits and to Gibraltar itself would thus be increased . . . It is essential that Gibraltar should continue to be available to us as a secure naval base.' The committee's recommendation was that HMG should press for a pact of non-interference in Spain, embracing France, Russia, Portugal, Germany, Italy and the United Kingdom.

This pact, duly signed, put Alan in a difficult position, for HMG's decision to maintain a non-interventionist stance meant that, in the middle of a ferociously fought conflict, he had to do the same – and the refusal of the British to become involved in the conflict soon made them unpopular on the island. As he himself later reported, 'The Majorcans could not understand why we did not take sides with them.' At one point he was threatened by a visitor carrying a gun, who insisted that he make the United Kingdom come in on the Nationalist side.

He himself had always been politically neutral, and in a kind of wry commentary on his own irresolution he cut out and kept a poem printed in an American journal:

Lament for a Wavering Viewpoint

I want to be a Tory
And with the Tories stand,
Elect and bound for glory
With a proud, congenial band.
Or in the Leftist hallways

I gladly would abide,
But from my youth I always
Could see the Other Side . . .

Ah, snug lie those that slumber
Beneath Conviction's roof.
Their floors are sturdy lumber,
Their windows weatherproof.
But I sleep cold forever,
And cold sleep all my kind,
For I was born to shiver
In the draft from an open mind.

His acute dislike of Communism made him naturally incline towards the Nationalists – and fate had landed him in a hotbed of Nationalism. Yet, at the same time, he detested Fascism, and was alarmed by the rise of Hitler in Germany. Nearer home, he was disgusted by the barbarities being committed by either side, and thought the Whites no less reprehensible than the Reds. Yet he too had to walk the tightrope of non-intervention.

All through the autumn and early winter of 1936 the Axis build-up on Majorca continued. German soldiers began to supplement the Italian airmen, and in mid-August the German destroyer *Leopard* put into Palma to disembark four anti-aircraft guns and a large quantity of ammunition. Italian ships bringing further war stores constantly came and went. The number of Italian aircraft based on the island rose to more than forty.

The bombers, flown by the unit known as the *Falchi delle Balean* (Balearic Falcons), were mostly three-engined Savoia-Marchetti SM 79s, which had just come into production. Made mainly of metal but with wooden wings, these were excellent aircraft, fast for their day, with a cruising speed of around 200 mph and an endurance of more than four hours. This meant that targets such as Valencia, Cartagena and Barcelona, not much over 100 miles away on the east coast of the mainland, were easily within range of Palma, even when the aircraft set out fully loaded with five 550-lb. bombs or a dozen 110-pounders and a crew of six. By October 1937 a raid on one or more of the Republican-held ports was being launched every day; in November, when twelve of the Savoias were moved to a base on the mainland, the Italian ground crews followed by sea, disguised as commercial travellers.

In a private letter written after the war Alan remarked that the Italian airmen 'were not conspicuous for their courage'. Once, when a big Republican bombardment was expected (but never happened), all the Italian air force personnel, including the general commanding, took refuge in the tunnels under Bellver Castle (the medieval fortress some two miles out of Palma) 'and had to be almost forcibly ejected by the Spaniards'. Another time, after Italian aircraft had mistakenly (and futilely) attacked the destroyer HMS *Gallant* off Valencia, a Spanish pilot remarked to Alan that although he, personally, never dropped a bomb from more than 500 metres, the Italians never dropped one from fewer than 3,000 metres.

One of their officers particularly distinguished himself when a German Zeppelin passed over Majorca on its way to South America. A number of fighters went up to form an escort of honour, but one pilot, *not* ordered to take off, nevertheless did so, imagining that enemy aircraft were approaching. Sighting the Zeppelin, he opened fire on it with his machine gun and expended 600 rounds, all of which missed the target because it was too far away. It is hardly surprising that some of Alan's messages to the Foreign Office took on a cynical note:

In my last memorandum I reported that three planes bombed Alicante on 20th October. This should be qualified to read: 'On 20 October three bombing planes went to the westward with a full load of bombs and returned

4½ hours later without their bombs. They claimed to have bombed Alicante.'

Fuelled by the bombers' apparent success, Count Rossi's propaganda speeches grew more and more bombastic: 'It is necessary for the peace of the world that the Balearics should remain under Italian influence . . . Spain and Italy are united with ties of unbreakable fraternity, and we shall dominate the Mediterranean. The Mediterranean is ours.'

When Franco's brother Don Ramón Franco arrived to take command of the air forces of the Balearic Islands, the Italians admitted that Palma was to become a naval base for a blockade of ports on the Spanish coast. On a memorandum in London someone noted: 'Majorca is fast becoming an important insurgent centre', and a visiting rear admiral feared that Rossi might be going to 'use his influence to effect a coup and try to proclaim an Italian protectorate'.

If the Reds are successful on the mainland . . . a very dangerous position will ensue. It is most improbable that the Majorcans would ever tolerate domination by a Red Spain. They would naturally turn to some power for protection, and in the present conditions this power would certainly be Italy.

When the Commander-in-Chief, Mediterranean, decided that it was no longer necessary to station a large naval vessel at Palma, and to withdraw the battleship HMS *Valiant*, Alan reacted vigorously, saying that the intermittent presence of a British warship was the most effective deterrent to Italian activity, and that a cruiser was better in this respect than a destroyer, 'on account of its added appearance of power'.

In December he reported that there was still plenty of food on the island, but that many things had become unobtainable.

Cooking oil, coffee and pepper had vanished; sugar, rice and butter were difficult to find, and there was no white flour to be had. Medicines were short, 'and in fact all goods normally imported are at an end.'

News of events on the mainland reached Majorca rapidly by wireless broadcasts, and in March 1937 the defeat of the Italian army at Guadalajara, after its abortive attempt to encircle the Republican stronghold in Madrid, did serious damage to Italian prestige on the island. The Republicans' victory – their biggest of the war – was never mentioned publicly, but it inflicted a severe loss of face, and to counter-balance it anti-British propaganda was stepped up. 'Press articles extolling Italian might and stressing Italy's common heritage with Spain have also shown a marked revival,' Alan noted.

Barely a month later, on the afternoon of 26 April, the air-raids on the town of Guernica, in the Basque Country, carried out by German and Italian aircraft at the behest of Franco, sent waves of shock round the civilised world. No mention of it survives in Alan's messages, but news of the attack spread quickly, and he must have been appalled by this, the first deliberate bombing of innocent civilians. Estimates of casualties vary wildly, from 800 to 3,000, but the raids destroyed most of the town's buildings and brought about its surrender. The horror of the massacre was caught for ever in the angularities of Picasso's huge and infinitely disturbing canvas, *Guernica*, which now hangs in the National Museum in Madrid.

On Majorca things changed slightly for the better when the Civil Governor, Don Mateo Torres, who was himself a Fascist, helped the Military Governor get rid of Rossi, whom, in Alan's words, 'he had grown to loathe'. Both governors had recently shown themselves 'particularly friendly' to Alan and the Royal Navy, and he felt that there was no longer any danger of the Italians trying to gain further control of the island.

They already had control enough for their purposes, and by

the spring of 1937 Majorca had become their main airbase, from which they launched raid after raid on the Republican-held cities along the mainland coast – Valencia, Tarragona, Castellón and Port Bou, just south of the border with France. Cant seaplanes also made many reconnaissance sorties in search of enemy warships or merchant vessels heading for Valencian government ports.

Retaliation was inevitable. On 24 May ten bombers from Valencia dropped about eighty bombs on and around Palma, killing fourteen people and wounding fifty-six. 'The military result was nothing,' Alan reported, 'but this sudden attack, after so long a rest and on the morning after a feast day, frightened the people a good deal.' Fighter aircraft did not take off in defence until twenty minutes after the alarm had sounded, almost certainly because the pilots were 'in a stupor after a night of revelry'. In another attack a week later ten civilians were killed and thirty-two wounded, and one plane, a twin-engined Potez, was shot down. Fear of a night attack led to a complete blackout, which was apparently effective, for although Republican aircraft made occasional nocturnal sorties, no bombs were dropped after dark.

In many ways Majorca was fortunate, in that it lay well clear of the main theatre of war. On the mainland Alan's consular colleagues were reporting dreadful atrocities – pitched battles lasting for weeks, massacres, prisoners shot out of hand, betrayal within families; but after the initial invasion and reprisals the Majorcans escaped most of the slaughter.

Even so, Alan estimated that in the first year of the war between 850 and 900 people were killed on the island, a quarter of them murdered 'for private reasons' in the early stages of the conflict. The executions carried out by the Fascists were done mainly at night, when victims were dragged from their houses, driven into the countryside and shot dead at some out-of-the-way spot. Their bodies were left beside the road, and when they were discovered in the morning no questions were asked. Alan never found evidence that any woman or child had been killed, apart from five women serving in the Catalan militia at Porto Cristo, who had been shot by order of Count Rossi. Nor had he been able to 'discover a single case of mutilation, torture or rape, or any other method of murder other than by shooting.'

During the first months of the war Alan had thought it prudent to live in Palma, so he and Mary (who had also come back to the island by destroyer) first put up in hotels, then rented a house, returning to Son Torrella at weekends. Once things had settled, they moved back to the *finca*, and Alan persuaded the Spanish army to install a telephone – the first beyond the village of Santa Maria – so that, even though the line was not secure, he could keep in touch with the town and with the British fleet. He himself moved freely about the island, checking on the welfare of the remaining expatriates, and, when asked by the Foreign Office if he needed extra protection, he replied that he did not. This was an optimistic assessment, for he was threatened by Falangists, and took enormous risks. As Jocelyn wrote later,

If it had been generally known that my father and mother had saved the lives of the former Mayor of Palma – a moderate Republican, but all Republicans were considered guilty by the Nationalists – and of his wife by smuggling them on board a British destroyer in the harbour, their position in the island would have become intolerable.

It seemed that the whole island had been poisoned by the outbreak of hostilities. At Vespers one Sunday the priest at Son Rapiña, near Palma, declared: 'All the Reds must be killed, down to the children, so that they cannot grow and have the vices of their parents' – whereupon some of the congregation cried out *'Viva España! Arriba España! Abajo Inglaterra! Abajo Francia! Viva Italia! Viva Alemania!'* But, as Alan reported, many of the people were disgusted. Mary herself wrote, 'There is something corroding about civil war. It breeds such a mass of suspicion and distrust that one wonders whether people here will ever be the same again.'

As time went on, Alan manoeuvred so adroitly, walking the tightrope between the two sides, that he won the admiration of the Spanish authorities, and he established a good working relationship with Vice Admiral Francisco Moreno Fernández, Commander-in-Chief of Nationalist forces in the Balearic Islands. Alan described him as short, spare and active, with a mild temperament: 'Indeed, a casual observer might be tempted to think him too mild for an admiral and to rate him, while not exactly insignificant, as lacking in that quality of command essential to his position.' But, Alan added, Moreno's manner was deceptive: 'He is never worried, and is a natural leader.' At first the admiral proved a valuable contact, but then seemed to deteriorate. 'He has changed a great deal,' wrote Alan later in the war. 'Frequent disappointments and a stupid wife have made him sour, distrustful and sometimes unjust, besides being uncertain of himself. As the war dragged on, it became increasingly difficult to get him to see reason.'

On the British side, Alan's own reputation became ever higher. The captain of a visiting ship, the destroyer HMS *Hostile*, declared of the Vice Consul:

He has been of the very greatest assistance to me. As far as one can judge in a short time, he appears to carry out his duties with outstanding ability; he is *persona grata* with all the leading Spaniards who administer the island, and is treated by them with friendliness and respect.

What he needed was a better office and more staff, to deal with repeated emergencies, and in March 1937 he got permission from the Foreign Office to move into a larger building, normally the palace of a Majorcan noble. At first he himself had to pay the difference in rent, and to finance the rewiring, repositioning of telephone points and so on; but at least he had more secure premises, and also a place of business that gratified his modest taste for theatre: it suited him that visitors should gain admittance to his own sanctum via a series of smaller anterooms.

In April 1937, when HMG recognised his work with the award of the OBE, many friends wrote to congratulate him. One was Robert Graves, languishing in exile, who said: 'You must be getting a bit tired of it by now ... I suppose this war will end sometime.' Another plaudit (and protest) came from Rear Admiral Sir James Somerville, then Commander of the Mediterranean destroyer flotillas, who had helped protect Majorca, and now wrote from HMS *Galatea*:

I was *most* disappointed to see that you had been awarded an OBE for all your good work at Palma. So far we have only had the naval list, so I don't know whether any other consular awards have been made. I think not, in which case the OBE may refer only to work done for the Navy, and I think the CMG [Companion of the Order of St Michael and St George] will arrive in due course. When you think of the way CMGs are awarded for 'peace' services, it seems monstrous that those who have been doing such important and exacting work as you have been doing for the last year should not be properly recognised.

For month after month Alan continued to report the activities of the occupying Italians and Germans, the coming and going

of ships, the bombing sorties launched against targets on the
mainland by the Italian air force, and the occasional Republican
air-raid on Palma. His secret memoranda to the Foreign Office
often included details that could be picked up only by unobtru-
sive but close observation on the ground – for instance, that the
bombs at the Pollensa Bay submarine base were in broken wooden
cases lying in the open, and that torpedoes were stored in the
village garage. The German airmen at Pollensa, he noted, were
very popular among the local inhabitants, who called them *negrillos*
(niggers) because they were almost all blond.

That little touch of humour was uncharacteristic. Alan's
reports were models of clarity, and perfectly grammatical, but
they hardly ever included anything amusing. This seems strange,
because his family remember him as full of jokes, practical
jokes especially. At home he was always making everyone laugh
– Spaniards, particularly – and he had quite a lavatorial sense
of humour. Yet he never *wrote* jokes or risqué stories. He seems
almost to have had a dual personality: serious and professional
at work, far more expansive off duty.

By the summer of 1937, after a year of war, a certain weari-
ness was creeping into his bulletins. 'As the months go by with
no sign of the end,' he wrote, 'discontent grows.'

> It is not directed against the existing regime; it has no
> affinity with Communism or socialism; it is just that the
> Mallorquin peasants and middle class, as a whole, are
> getting thoroughly fed up. But I do not expect this disgust
> to find expression in revolt. There is neither the leadership
> nor the means nor the inclination to revolt.

The number of British subjects on the island had built up
again to 137, as forty-seven of those evacuated on naval vessels
the year before had returned to their homes. But, Alan reported,
largely owing to Italian propaganda and an 'amazing output of

lies . . . Great Britain is now more unpopular here than she
has ever been since we were last at war with Spain'.

By the end of 1937 there were more than 400 Italian airmen
on the island, wearing the khaki uniform of the legionary air
force. They were becoming more and more heartily disliked,
Alan reported, because they were both boastful and stingy.
Their least attractive attribute was that 'half of them have
venereal disease, and have not scrupled to pass it on . . . This
has affected not only the brothels . . . but has contaminated
many of the daughters of the staidest middle class.'

Even more outspoken comments came in a memorandum
of 21 March 1938. Having said that by then the number of
Italians on the island had reached 500, he let fly:

Italians are undisciplined, cowardly and ineffective. They
will not attack the military objectives ordered because
they fear AA fire. When directed to attack a port such as
Barcelona, they bomb the city instead, utterly contrary to
instructions. For this reason all bombing of large ports
has had to be suspended again. Of the three attacks ordered
on Cartagena, only one was delivered. On the other two
occasions the bombs were dropped out at sea.

Italian General here is obstructive and unnecessary . . .
Admiral Moreno has now requested his removal and the
early replacement here of all the Italians by Spaniards . . .
The Italians have made themselves hated, though it is not
politic to say so publicly . . . The four destroyers brought
from Italy are worn out and a swindle . . . Admiral Moreno
was most emphatic that no Italian designs on these islands
need be feared except in the event of a general war, and
would in any case be resisted.

Whenever a British warship came in, Alan escorted the
captain to meet the island's Civil Governor, Don Mateo Torres,

and he was always on hand to act as a skilled interpreter. One minor but difficult problem was that of refugees swimming out to warships anchored in the bay in the hope of gaining asylum. What was the captain to do with such people when they were dragged aboard? He knew that if he took them back ashore, they would be shot. Equally, if it became known that he had removed them from the island, he would set off a serious diplomatic row. One naval officer, who decided not to inform the authorities that he had fished an exhausted Spaniard out of the water, and proposed to take him to Gibraltar, gave his reasons:

1. It was almost certain the man had escaped unseen.
2. Four French warships were anchored nearer the shore than *Aberdeen*, there being no reason why it should not be presumed he had swum to one of them.
3. He was not an offender against the common law.
4. It would probably cause unnecessary friction with the local authorities.

Through his strong naval connections Alan himself rescued several men in acute danger. His private efforts naturally found no mention in official despatches, but they certainly saved lives, among them that of Fernando Morenes y Carvajal, el Conde del Asalto, who had been captured by the Reds during the fighting in Tarragona, and was held on the prison ship *Uruguay*, anchored in the habour at Barcelona. Learning that he was about to be shot, Alan went across in a British vessel, sent him a message telling him to shave off his moustache and slipped him out dressed as a Royal Naval officer – a highly illegal operation. After the war the count remained a close family friend of the Hillgarths, and his sister-in-law Pilín became Nigella's godmother.

For Alan one of the most traumatic incidents of the war was the sinking of the Spanish heavy cruiser *Baleares*. He knew the ship, for she had several times come into Palma while he was there, and he may even have seen her when she went out of the bay for the last time on 5 March 1938 accompanied by another heavy cruiser, a light cruiser and three destroyers, escorting a convoy. That night the destroyers returned to base, but the cruisers held their course and quite by chance met a Republican squadron coming in the opposite direction off Cape Palos, near Cartagena. After inconclusive exchanges of fire at about 5,000 yards, three Republican destroyers closed in and launched a total of twelve torpedoes. Two of these hit *Baleares* and detonated her forward magazine, with terrible results.

Thirty years later Alan described the aftermath in an article for *The Times* which finely illustrated two fundamental elements in his character: pride in the courage and skill of Royal Naval officers, and admiration of their Spanish counterparts. His taut sentences simmered with barely contained emotion.

One afternoon in March 1938 I stood on the quay at Palma, Majorca, among a group of silent Spanish officers, as Captain Rhoderick McGrigor berthed his ship. H.M.S. *Kempenfelt* was bringing in their dead. Not British dead but Spanish, men who had died on board after rescue from fire and from the sea, and from the sea on fire. The living, more than 300 of them, he had transferred to Spanish vessels he met on his way, but the dead he brought in himself. This was the last scene in the sinking of the *Baleares*.

The Nationalist flagship, with a complement of over 1,000 officers and men, she had left Palma the day before to cover a convoy bound for Cadiz. The night was dark, with heavy cloud, though no sea worth mentioning. At about midnight, without sighting her adversary, she was torpedoed under the bridge by a Republican destroyer. The result was instant disaster.

Those 10,000-ton cruisers, though magnificent vessels, were a designer's compromise and very vulnerable. Magazines exploded, the superstructure collapsed, the forepart of the ship filled and dipped and the midship section burst into uncontrollable flames. Admiral Vierna, his captain, all the senior officers and two-thirds of the ship's company perished in a matter of minutes, though the afterpart remained, stopped, a wreck, surrounded by burning oil fuel.

Every boat had gone, the convoy and the rest of the covering force had continued on their course, as they had to, and what was left of the ship might sink at any minute. In these extreme circumstances the survivors showed a discipline and courage worthy of Spanish naval traditions. While fire parties tried to prevent the conflagration amidships from spreading aft – the only task left to do – the remainder were mustered on the sloping quarterdeck by two young lieutenants and so endured, without hope but without vestige of panic.

McGrigor told me that this indomitable spirit made a great impression on him. For they were like that when he found them two hours later. On patrol in company with another of his destroyers, *Boreas* . . . he saw the glare and steered for it. The problem of rescue presented great difficulties. He could not go alongside because of burning oil and wreckage; nor could any boat reach *Baleares*. Patently, too, there was not much time. But, a truly great seaman, McGrigor divined at once what had to be done and did it without hesitation.

Only at the stern itself was there no wreckage and less oil, so very skilfully he manoeuvred his ship till he had got *Kempenfelt*'s bow under the cruiser's high counter between the two propellers, which of course were out of the water and liable to crush the destroyer's bow plates.

There he kept her – not an easy thing to do – while the Spaniards came down on to the forecastle in rapid but ordered sequence, as their officers directed. The task was not completed when *Baleares* sank, suddenly, with a great gush of suction, and he only just got clear. But he had been waiting for it, from one moment to another.

This may not sound much, but in its own way it was as fine a piece of seamanship as any in any annals. There followed a search of the area for more survivors, with all the destroyer's boats down. Some exhausted Spaniards were kept up by British sailors who went into the oil after them . . .

What McGrigor and his destroyers did that night has never been forgotten by the Spanish Navy. After the Civil War was over, the Spanish Government wanted to give him the Cross of Naval Merit and to distribute other decorations among his officers and men, but it was not considered that they could be allowed to accept. The rescue had taken place during a civil war in which we were strictly neutral. That fact led to a confusion between the political and the humanitarian aspects of the matter, and the idea had to be abandoned. But the Spanish Navy has never forgotten.

What the article did not say was that when *Kempenfelt* came into Palma, some of the ill-natured Spaniards present were delighted, thinking that her flags at half-mast signified British deaths; and an absurd rumour went round that it was a ship of the Royal Navy which had torpedoed *Baleares*. Nevertheless, two of the rescued officers professed their extreme gratitude to Alan for the rest of their lives, and, more than twenty years later, another of the survivors, Captain Emilio Serra y de Armas, wrote to the Editor of *The Times* praising the 'gallant behaviour and true comradeship' of Sub-Lieutenant Brian Anson of the

Kempenfelt. Anson had been 'in a very difficult situation, as the boat he was commanding had capsized because she had picked up too many survivors', but he had held Emilio in the water for a long time, 'with evident danger to himself, besides saving many others'.

Through all the horrors of the war, Alan never gave up trying to save Majorcan lives. In the winter of 1936 he attempted to broker an exchange of hostages between the two sides, and in particular to arrange the release of prisoners held by the Republicans on board the SS *Uruguay*, the prison ship anchored in the harbour at Barcelona. The men included Manuel Goded, son of General Goded (one of the instigators of the Nationalist uprising, who had already been murdered), and Antonio Espina, a former Civil Governor of Majorca. Alan believed that if the exchange succeeded, it would help restore British prestige and emphasise the neutrality of her position; but when he went to Barcelona in December, he found that the Popular Court would not sanction any swap 'for fear of violent reaction by the anarchists'. His intervention did bear fruit in the end: Manuel Goded was exchanged for a Republican prisoner in 1937, but Espina was kept in prison, leaving his wife in distress in Palma, where Mary helped look after her.

In June 1938 there were still forty prisoners under sentence of death in Palma, among them eight men from Soller, on the north-west coast of the island. One of them was a former mayor of the town, whose only crime was to belong to a left-wing party. When Alan pointed out that if he were executed, the sole result would be an increase of retaliatory murders in Barcelona, the man was eventually spared.

In July 1938 Alan managed to escape for some leave in England, but his time there was cut short by the arrival of a large new wave of Italian aircraft on Majorca, which were obviously causing a problem. He asked the Foreign Office to tell his deputy on the island, George Saward, not to speak to Admiral Moreno about the influx, as 'the question was one which he would greatly prefer to deal with himself'. He therefore hurried back to Palma, whence he despatched a cryptic Secret and Immediate telegram:

> Has seen Admiral Moreno. Foreign Office instructions carried out. Reception was satisfactory. It will probably be reported to General Franco, but that cannot be prevented and does not matter.

Meanwhile, Minorca, lying some 100 miles south-west of Majorca, and dominated by the Republicans, had been reduced to a wretched state by the savagery of the war. Alan had visited the island in September 1937, taking passage in HMS *Hostile*, and had found the capital, Port Mahon, deplorably rundown: the naval base derelict, the inside of the cathedral wrecked, the people so hungry that in the harbour boats circled the warship picking up scraps of bread thrown overboard. Now, at the beginning of 1939, the idea that the whole island might change sides was secretly brought to his notice by the Conde de San Luis, who believed that Minorca might switch its allegiance if those wishing to leave were given a chance to do so.

In January 1939 the matter came to a crisis. Through his scouts Alan learnt that the Nationalist government had ordered a destructive bombardment of Port Mahon, and that this was to be the precursor of an invasion by ground troops. Of course the Italian air force officers on Majorca were enthusiastically in favour of attacking a defenceless target within easy range.

On 25 January Alan cabled the Foreign Office to say that San Luis had asked if a British warship could ferry him to Minorca, to negotiate the surrender of the island. The reaction in London was characteristically obstructive and lacking in urgency. 'There are considerable objections to this proposal,' said one minute. 'We have no idea whether the Spanish Government would welcome our cooperating with General Franco for the surrender of Minorca . . . The approach to Commander Hillgarth may be purely a bluff and the Nationalists may not really be in a position to carry out an effective air bombardment.' The Foreign Office tried to pass the buck to the Admiralty. The Admiralty said it was a matter for the Foreign Office. The French also had to be consulted. The British Ambassador in Paris, Sir Eric Phipps, replied that the French 'gave us a free hand, to do what we like'. Still the Foreign Office objected, telling Alan:

> Proposal would in practice mean that Commander of British destroyer would act as intermediary between the Nationalist authorities in Majorca and the Republican authorities in Minorca . . . This is a role which we are not prepared to undertake.

Knowing that the Republicans had committed appalling atrocities on the mainland, Alan was by no means predisposed in their favour; but he also knew that the projected raids on the island would cause a terrible number of casualties, and he urgently repeated his request to London. This time permission was granted – *provided* San Luis secured Franco's agreement beforehand. This the count did, by flying to Burgos on the 26th. On the 31st Alan sent London another cable saying that San Luis had returned after an interview with Franco, who was an old friend, and had obtained approval and full power to negotiate. 'General Franco is determined to secure Minorca at once.'

Even then, on 1 February, some sluggard in the Foreign Office penned another procrastinating minute: 'I would suggest that in the first instance we should ask Mr Hillgarth whether the whole of this plan has collapsed.' Far from it: the cruiser HMS *Devonshire* was detailed to take the count to Port Mahon

and to act as the platform for a meeting with the authorities
there. It was strictly stipulated that no member of the ship's
company was to take any part in the negotiations, and Alan
himself was forbidden to leave Palma. Another telegram from
London emphasised that

> Every action should be avoided which might give any
> impression that HMG were taking part in, or responsibility
> for, these negotiations. Their share is entirely confined to
> providing transport.

Devonshire sailed with the count on 4 February. At Port
Mahon negotiations were held on board and on the 8th had
nearly reached a conclusion when Italian bombers from Majorca
suddenly came droning overhead and dropped six bombs on
the fort and cliffs half a mile from the ship. In an agitated
wireless message sent at 1400 the ship's captain, P.C. Muirhead-
Gould, told Alan that he had 'protested most strongly against
this violation of terms agreed upon', but that he could not
withdraw for the moment 'as there are emissaries ashore whose
lives are in danger'. In another message, at 1810, after six more
air-raids during the afternoon, including two on the town, he
reported that as a protest he had temporarily pulled out to a
position off the coast, and that San Luis had told Franco by
telegraph that he was resigning his task, which had been
'rendered impossible'. The attacks had killed more than a
hundred people. Then things swung back the other way. In yet
another message, at 2127, the captain told Alan:

> In spite of abominable bombardment . . . local authorities
> have established order and are still prepared to surrender
> tomorrow Thursday . . . Have returned to Port Mahon
> in order to embark refugees whose safety has been guar-
> anteed.

The loading of refugees began next morning; but the authorities in the town had made a dangerous mistake in releasing all the prisoners from the gaol on the promise that they would behave themselves. On the contrary: within two hours they had got their hands on liquor and weapons, and began shooting the very men who had let them out. This caused panic and a rush for the harbour, where tugs and small boats swarmed alongside *Devonshire* and people started jumping into the water in their desperation to get aboard, so that it became impossible for the crew to tell who had passes for boarding and who had not. Eventually the cruiser sailed for Marseilles with about 450 passengers.

At the same time several military units, led by junior officers, declared for the Nationalists, and the island was occupied without any major fighting. Mass murder had been averted by a matter of hours: as Alan later discovered, before *Devonshire* arrived, Red extremists had already arrested hundreds of their enemies and prepared lists for execution.

It is impossible to know how many people would have been killed if the bombardment and invasion had taken place, but the death toll, from indiscriminate bombing, fighting and straight murder would inevitably have been very large. Alan himself reckoned that 20,000 people might have died. He pointed out that it was quite untrue to suggest (as a few people did) that the captain of *Devonshire* persuaded the Republican commander to surrender. Since he could not speak Spanish, Muirhead-Gould took no part in the talks. All he did was offer the Republican representative the chance of discussing possible terms with the Nationalist envoy on board a neutral vessel, and after a few minutes' thought the Republican accepted. There was no suggestion of mediation.

In Palma Alan lodged a protest about the air-raids with Moreno. The problem (the admiral told him) had been disobedience of orders. In an official letter expressing regret, he said that the Italian pilots had acted 'outside their instruction' and that they had been duly punished. 'I am the first to regret this incident, which I hope will never be repeated.' He admitted confidentially that it was the air force brigadier in Palma who gave the order, but, as Alan told the Foreign Office, 'this cannot be quoted'. On the other hand, one positive advantage of the incident was that Moreno asked Franco to remove all the Italian airmen from Majorca.

In London repercussions of the evacuation rumbled on. Questions were asked in the House of Commons, and answered by the Prime Minister, Neville Chamberlain. On 15 February the Spanish Embassy, angered by the fact that their Ambassador had not been consulted, delivered a formal protest to the Foreign Office. On the 20th Franco's representative in London, the Duke of Alba, called on Sir George Mounsey, Assistant Under-Secretary, to convey to HMG an expression of gratitude from the Generalissimo and the Burgos government for the help afforded by the Royal Navy. Franco, the Duke added, 'hoped he would some day be permitted to recompense the officers of HMS *Devonshire* in recognition of the services rendered to him'. On the 25th, after a mere ten days of inter-departmental consultation, the Foreign Office concocted an emollient reply to the Spanish Embassy's protest. His Majesty's Government, it said, had done nothing but provide a means of communication. HMG 'must have felt themselves severely to blame if they had neglected any means of preventing such useless bloodshed'.

As usual, Alan played down his own role in the proceedings; but his intervention was his single most important act during the whole war, and must have saved more lives than all the rest put together. It was his friendship with San Luis, his total command of Spanish, his steady nerve, his ability to comman-deer a British warship, and his reputation as a diplomat with Spain's best interests at heart, that made Minorca's peaceful transfer of loyalty possible: by averting the threat of a Nationalist invasion, he had prevented hundreds of deaths and wholesale destruction of property. For this he was remembered on the island with intense gratitude for the rest of his life, and for more than twenty years after his death.

Even he, however, had not been able to save Minorca from desecration. On 3 March 1939, nearly a month after the evacuation, he went there on an official visit, taking passage in HMS *Impulsive*. His reception was cordial, and no restrictions were placed on his movements. 'There are definitely no Germans or Italians in island except two Italian airmen who were prisoners now convalescing,' he reported. 'No warships or seaplanes in Mahon. Dry dock badly damaged. Submarine dock slightly damaged. No aircraft on aerodrome which is in bad condition . . . So far only six prisoners shot, all proved assassins.'

It was left to *Impulsive*'s captain to record that the main church in Mahon was in a deplorable state. A ramp had been built up the steps so that lorries could be driven through the main door. Inside were two broken-down trucks, covered with debris from the roof, which had been blown in by a bomb. All the altars, statues and religious pictures had been smashed or torn to pieces; every tile had been removed from the floor, leaving bare earth. The crypt had been used as a *refugio* and also as a public lavatory.

On Majorca, on 13 June, in drenching rain, 286 Italian officers and men embarked at Palma in the Italian liner *Duilio* to return to Italy. They were officially the last of all the air legionaries to leave, and they were seen off in a grand ceremony. As Alan reported, 'Spanish and Italian bands, with Spanish and Italian medals, Spanish and Italian speeches all emphasised the indissoluble band between the two sister nations.'

Eight days earlier a party of Italian legionaries, accompanied by some ratings from the Italian destroyer *Procione*, had come into collision with seamen from the Spanish fleet. When the police interfered, the Italians produced revolvers. One policeman was killed and a Spanish passer-by seriously injured. The affray was not mentioned in the newspapers, and the murderers, who evaded arrest, were smuggled on board the weekly steamer for Genoa; but, in Alan's words, 'there was no Spaniard here who was not thinking of it when he saw the last of the main body eight days later'.

On the mainland the bloody struggle was drawing to its close as Republican resistance crumbled. In December the Nationalists had launched a huge invasion of Catalonia, and in two months they captured Tarragona (on 15 January) Barcelona (on the 26th) and Gerona on 2 February. On 28 March Madrid at last fell to them, and next day Valencia capitulated, after a two-year siege. On 1 April Franco proclaimed victory.

In June, with the war over, but with another worse conflict threatening, Alan gave an account of Italian and German war materials remaining on the island, and summed up his views in a long memorandum to the Foreign Office:

In Majorca, which is in a sense un-Spanish and yet very much part of Spain, these things [inter-Service rivalries] are seen as it were in miniature, since everybody comes here, and here, in Spain and yet not in it, in a small but important island, in a concentrated society and a peculiar atmosphere made even more peculiar by the war, they spill out their bile and their hopes and their doubts and their secrets.

At the moment everybody, of every class, is concerned about the chances of a European war . . . Last September they were frightened of a war because of the effect it would have on their own civil war. Now they are worried because they believe that a European war would force them into

In his captain's uniform, Alan cut a formidable figure.
'I'm a trouble-maker,' he said. 'I ride the storm.'

Great-great-grandfather Evan Evans, surgeon's mate aboard the 33-gun fifth-rate *Niger*, also wielded a lively pen.

Hugh's father Willmott Evans, a distinguished and erudite surgeon, had a stuffed gorilla in his house in Harley Street.

Hugh Evans at 15, smart in his midshipman's uniform, little knowing that his ship was about to head for Gallipoli.

Dyddgu Hamilton, known as Anne, was Hugh's most faithful correspondent throughout his life.

Second from the right in the front row of his tutor set at Osborne College, Hugh was known from his dark complexion as 'the little dago'.

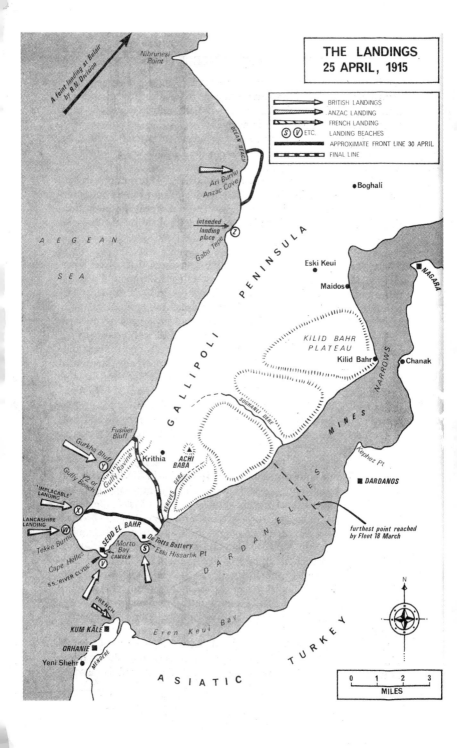

THE LANDINGS
25 APRIL, 1915

BRITISH LANDINGS
ANZAC LANDING
FRENCH LANDING
S V ETC.   LANDING BEACHES
APPROXIMATE FRONT LINE 30 APRIL
FINAL LINE

A feint landing at Bulair by R.N. Division

Nibrunesi Point

OCEAN BEACH

Ari Burnu
Anzac Cove

• Boghali

intended landing place

Gaba Tepe

A E G E A N

S E A

G A L L I P O L I   P E N I N S U L A

Eski Keui •

Maidos •

NAGARA

KILID BAHR
PLATEAU

Kilid Bahr •

• Chanak

SOGHANLI DERE

M I N E S

N A R R O W S

Fusilier Bluff

Gurkha Bluff

Y2 or Gully Beach

Gully Ravine

Krithia •

ACHI BABA

KEREVES DERE

Kephez Pt

■ DARDANOS

'IMPLACABLE' LANDING

LANCASHIRE LANDING

Tekke Burnu

SEDD EL BAHR

Morto Bay

Du Totts Battery
Eski Hissarlik Pt

furthest point reached by Fleet 18 March

Cape Helles

CAMBER

S.S. 'RIVER CLYDE'

D A R D A N E L L E S

Eren Keui Bay

N

KUM KĂLE ■

ORHANIE ■

Yeni Shehr •

MENDERE

FRENCH

A S I A T I C

T U R K E Y

0   1   2   3
MILES

Hugh's first ship, HMS *Bacchante*, was a veteran armoured cruiser, powered by coal, with a crew of 750.

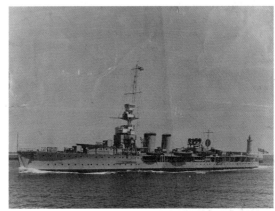

It was while serving on HMS *Wolverine*, a torpedo boat destroyer, that Hugh was twice wounded, aged 16.

Hugh and a colleague recovering from wounds in the hospital at Malta, in the summer of 1916.

Mary Hillgarth, Alan's second wife, known in the family as 'M', whom he married in 1929.

THE PRINCESS
AND THE PERJURER
ALAN HILLGARTH

Blood and thunder: the jacket of Alan's first novel, set partly in Russia and published in 1924.

The silver crucifix found by Edgar Sanders in the tunnel at Sacambaya during his 1926 expedition.

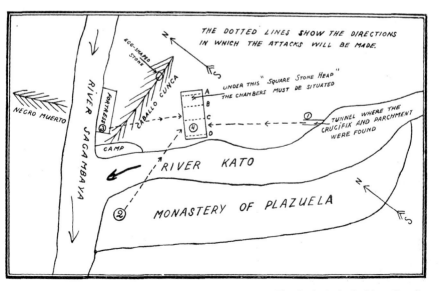

THE DOTTED LINES SHOW THE DIRECTIONS IN WHICH THE ATTACKS WILL BE MADE.

UNDER THIS "SQUARE STONE HEAP" THE CHAMBERS MUST BE SITUATED

TUNNEL WHERE THE CRUCIFIX AND PARCHMENT WERE FOUND

NEGRO MUERTO

RIVER SAGAMBAYA

EGG-SHAPED STONE

FORTRESS

CABALLO CUNCA

CAMP

RIVER KATO

MONASTERY OF PLAZUELA

Edgar Sanders's sketch of the treasure site at Sacambaya, in the Bolivian Andes.

A relatively cheerful moment: Alan in cowboy mode with
one of the expedition's horses.

active participation on the side of the Axis, a thing they do not want but believe they could not avoid . . .

They agree that General Franco wished to be neutral in 1938 and may well wish to be neutral in 1939, but they believe he cannot maintain neutrality. When asked why, they cannot explain . . . The fact is that Germany has impressed them so much that they believe she is invincible.

Throughout the civil war Alan kept up his meticulous record of the financial damage he personally had suffered. He described the cost of helping British subjects in trouble as 'appalling', and another major expense continued to be entertaining – although he admitted that most of this was for the officers of HM ships, one or two of which were nearly always present, but not on official visits – 'therefore most of it could have been avoided!' He cultivated the naval visitors partly because many of them were friends, but also because the ships offered secure communications and the only safe means of travel between Majorca and the mainland: his own naval record and his status on the island ensured that he could always get a lift.

At the end of a twenty-five page memorandum, in which he set out to demonstrate what it had cost him to be, first, Vice Consul and, later, Consul at Palma, he summed things up:

It shows what I have paid that I would not have paid if I had not had this job for the last six and a half years . . . The indirect (really direct) consequence of the Spanish Civil War on my finances had been severe, in so much as it has ruined all my arrangements and obliged me to maintain a rented establishment in England for most of my family for two-and-a-half years. If I had been a sala-ried consul, I could not complain. If I had been a private individual, I should have no cause to complain, because

I should have shut up my house here and lived with my family in England. If there had been no war, my family would have been here.

He estimated that the cost to him of representing Great Britain as Vice Consul and Consul had been £3,483 3s. 0. – over £100,000 in today's values. It is no longer clear how much of this he recouped in compensation from the Foreign Office, but there is no doubt that the war cost him dear, both financially and in the usurpation of his own working time, as well as in separation from his family.

After the civil war had ended Admiral Pound, Commander-in-Chief Mediterranean station, recommended that Alan should be promoted to commander on the Retired List in recognition of his work during the past three years – but the Admiralty rejected his suggestion on the grounds that he had not put in enough service on the Active List.

By the autumn of 1939 a major European war seemed both inevitable and imminent. All the same, Alan went ahead with a holiday and rented two apartments in the Château de Châtel in the commune of Usinans, in the Haute Savoie, for the months of July and August.

9

Naval Attaché

One of Alan's most fortunate contacts during the civil war was with Captain (later Admiral) John Godfrey, who twice put into Palma in command of the battle cruiser *Repulse*. During his first visit, in July 1936, when he called to evacuate British subjects, the two men did not meet, as Alan was away on leave; but when *Repulse* came to Majorca again in the spring of 1938 they hit it off immediately, not least because they had both served at Gallipoli.

Godfrey's mission was to make contact with John Leche, who had recently been appointed chargé d'affaires in the British Legation at Caldetas, on the mainland a few miles north of Barcelona, and there was a risk that his ship would be caught up in one of the Italian air-raids on the coast. Alan, through his contact with the Spanish Captain-General in Majorca, arranged that the Italians would refrain from bombing the area during the *Repulse*'s visit – which Godfrey reckoned 'a remarkable achievement in practical diplomacy'. So impressed was he with Alan's intelligence, integrity and knowledge of Spain that after he had become Director of Naval Intelligence he arranged for him to be posted as Assistant Naval Attaché in Madrid in August 1939, and for the post to be upgraded.

Godfrey, with his challenging, bright blue eyes and explosive temper, was not an easy man to work for. The author Patrick

Beesly, who served under him for three years in the Naval
Intelligence Division, based in Room 39 at the Admiralty,
described him thus:

> Ambitious, extremely able, physically and mentally resil-
> ient, he was shy and suffered from an inferiority complex;
> liberal minded, forward looking, and capable of many acts
> of personal kindness and thoughtfulness, he was also ruth-
> less and sometimes selfish; inspiring general admiration,
> much loyalty and often affection, he could equally arouse
> antagonism, jealousy, even dislike; a charming host and a
> good listener, he did not suffer fools gladly and made little
> attempt to conceal his contempt for colleagues of lesser
> mental calibre.

Alan was perfectly at ease in dealing with Godfrey. Not only
did he like him: he also respected him, and remained a close
friend for the rest of Godfrey's life. The admiral rated Alan
'rather a super-attaché', and encouraged him, during his visits
to London, to report direct to the Prime Minister and to 'C'
(Sir Stewart Menzies, Head of the Secret Intelligence Service).
Godfrey considered Alan 'an A 1 source of intelligence in
Spain', and saw that he was the only member of the Madrid
Embassy staff who knew the country thoroughly and had
numerous contacts in high places, naval, political and social.

Shortly before the outbreak of war in 1939 Alan was recalled
to the Navy's Active List and arrived in Madrid to find the
city still scarred by the violence of the civil war, especially in
the outskirts, where many buildings were no more than heaps
of rubble, shops were boarded up, trees reduced to skeletons,
the streets pockmarked with craters, and donkey carts outnum-
bered cars. 'The situation here is very bad,' wrote the diplomat
David Eccles in November. 'The poor people are starving, eggs
eightpence each, no meat, no olive oil, and some days not

enough bread.' Groups of pro-Fascist Falange youths paraded up and down chanting *'Gibraltar Español! Gibraltar Español!'* in their attempts to stir up bad feeling against the Allies. Meanwhile Franco's regime was still taking revenge on its opponents: at least a hundred political prisoners were being executed every month. Another diplomat recalled how during the civil war Spain had become an 'isolated and remote world of grim and terrible fanaticism', and how much of the same atmosphere 'was still hanging over Spanish life'.

The city was alive with spies of every European nationality, and awash with noxious propaganda, as Axis officials, journalists and others sought to provoke anti-British agitation and create the impression that Britain was on the brink of defeat. In the German Embassy alone more than half the 400-strong staff belonged to the Abwehr – the military intelligence organisation responsible for espionage and counter-espionage – which had maybe 1,500 agents at large in the country.

During the civil war Hitler had supplied Franco liberally with arms, and now, in this febrile atmosphere, the Caudillo was again siding openly with Germany, flattered by bombastic overtures from the Führer. 'I consider, as you yourself do,' (Hitler told him) 'that the destiny of history has united you with myself and with the Duce in an indissoluble way.' The paramount task of the British Embassy was thus to persuade Franco to remain neutral and to keep Spain out of the war – on the one hand to stop Spain inviting the German armies in, and on the other to prevent Germany invading Spain. Had the Axis powers captured the Iberian peninsula, including Gibraltar, and cut off access to the Mediterranean, the result would have been catastrophic for the Allies.

Alan faced a daunting task. The British Ambassador, Sir Maurice Peterson, had not cared for Madrid, preferring to reside in France. No British naval attaché had lived in Madrid since 1923. For the sixteen years before 1939 the attachés accredited to Spain had also stayed in France, and as Alan wrote, 'Although they visited Spain from time to time and made useful reports, they had no knowledge of the place or people and no influence whatever.'

The Embassy building was a large, four-storey house dating from 1905, handsome in vaguely French fashion, with a spacious garden behind, at 16 Calle Fernando el Santo, which runs at right angles off the city's main thoroughfare, the Paseo de la Castellana. In the absence of the previous Ambassador the interior had been partially dismantled, and needed extensive restoration.

Alan was put at a further disadvantage by the fact that, because of a recent policy change, he arrived as assistant to the Naval Attaché in Lisbon. This man visited Madrid once during the summer of 1939, but was too busy ever to come again after the war had started. His absence, as Alan remarked, did not matter much – except that 'the Spaniards felt even more irritated at being considered subordinate to Portugal than they had when in the same minor position *vis-à-vis* France'. They were therefore pleased when, in January 1940, his own appointment was changed to that of Naval Attaché, and his subservience to the man in Lisbon came to an end. As he later recorded, he had not realised the potential strength of his position in Spain, but he had to 'build it up from the bottom'.

Fortunately he himself possessed most of the requirements he considered essential for someone in his position. The first was 'an intense interest in his job and in Spain', and this presupposed a natural sympathy for Spain and Spaniards. 'Without that,' he wrote, 'he will be useless, however good he may be in other respects. With it, he has already half the victory.' He admitted that there were still some officers who believed that 'all Dagoes begin at Dover', but anyone who felt that would be 'bowled out by the Spaniards in five minutes'.

His second requirement was 'tact, patience and determination combined', the third, 'a generally wide knowledge of one's profession', the fourth, diplomatic discretion, and the fifth – surely of fundamental importance – 'a knowledge of Spanish'. It was here that Alan scored most heavily, for his Spanish was so perfect as to delight native listeners, and gave him an immediate advantage over expatriates less gifted linguistically.

As further essentials he listed 'an unquarrelsome disposition', common sense and the possession of private means. As for 'minor requirements' – he wrote that 'a knowledge of French is very useful', and that 'a presentable wife, who is prepared to learn Spanish and to show the Spaniards that she likes them, is very useful indeed'. He assumed that the Naval Attaché would be 'of sober habits', but added 'he will be at a definite disadvantage if he is a teetotaller'. Being naturally convivial himself, Alan 'cultivated his contacts like an expert forester planting trees, propagating and nourishing them, metaphorically and literally, with large and lavish dinners'.

What he failed to mention was that, because the Foreign Office would not allow him to employ the extra staff he needed, he imported his step daughters Joan and Elspeth Hope-Morley (then twenty-one and nineteen) to work as secretaries. Mary brought them out from London, and the family lived not in the Embassy, but in a succession of spacious flats, looked after by a butler, Rafael Cortes, his wife Maria, and an outstandingly skilful cook, Pedro, all of whom had worked for them at Son Torrella.

One wartime colleague remembered Alan as 'a handsome, dark man with a delightful outgoing personality. His brain was quick and incisive, and he had the gift, so important in the Intelligence game, of being able to put together the jigsaw when many of the pieces were missing. Above and beyond that, he was almost intuitive in spotting any pieces which had been forged.' The colleague might have mentioned another substantial asset: Alan never gave away his thoughts by facial expressions: he had the useful knack of being able to maintain a non-committal appearance or, when appropriate, to smile, no matter what was going on in his mind. Another associate remembered him as the *'éminence grise'* of the Chancery, with 'quarter-deck manners and a conspiratorial style of talking out of the side of his mouth'.

He himself acknowledged that, ideally, a naval attaché should never become personally engaged in covert intelligence work, and that his own standing, as well as that of his assistants, depended entirely on their being seen to be above reproach. But in Madrid in 1940 he found that he constantly had to break the rule and take an active part in information gathering, as well as in counter-espionage. At the start of the war SIS (MI6) had been very weak in Spain, and with the collapse of France he had to take what he called 'extemporised measures' to create 'a sort of substitute SIS' on his own: 'When SIS proper was rebuilt, I retained what I had created gradually, however relinquishing sections as their usefulness faded.' The first official SIS head of station was Leonard Hamilton Stokes, whom he found quite difficult.

Without much help at first, Alan began to recruit agents – mostly through his outstanding right-hand man, the Assistant Naval Attaché, Lieutenant Commander Salvador Augustus Gómez-Beare, known to all as 'Don'. Anglo-Spanish, born in Gibraltar, with a dark complexion and southern accent, Don blended easily into any Spanish background without drawing attention to himself, and yet remained (as Alan put it) 'essentially English', with perfect English manners. He was a man of exceptional charm and ability, with the remarkable record of having held a commission in all three British armed services. He had joined the army in 1914, and survived two years of trench warfare as an infantryman before transferring to the Royal Flying Corps (and later the Royal Air Force) as a fighter pilot, resigning a permanent commission only because of injuries. During the Spanish Civil War he had worked for military intelligence in the Nationalist army, and in 1939 was co-opted into the Royal Naval Volunteer Reserve, with the rank of lieutenant commander, on condition that he shaved off his handlebar moustache.

Travelling all over the country, he was at home in every level of Spanish life, from the underworld and the docks to the highest reaches of society in Madrid. No wonder Alan described him as 'invaluable . . . His loyalty and discretion are unequalled, and the Spaniards, particularly the Spanish Navy, love him.' He and Alan knew that they were liable to be followed and watched wherever they went, but they had followers of their own shadowing the followers, and observers keeping eyes on the watchers.

Soon, through the covert assistance of one officer in the Spanish Security Service, who set up a special section to monitor German spies, Alan knew many details of the opposition, including the identity of every important Abwehr operator. When the Spaniard offered him a complete list of names, he managed to buy it, having obtained authorisation from 'C' (Sir Stewart Menzies) to spend a considerable sum.

A much cheaper, but still effective, weapon in the intelligence battle was gossip. 'Rumours, for the purpose of cover plans or for pure propaganda . . . are extremely easy to spread in Spain,' Alan wrote. 'The country lives on word-of-mouth stories . . . A casual word in a club or café is often enough. The Naval Attaché should select among his acquaintance those who are the most inveterate gossips.' With this advice came a waspish qualification: 'Most of the people who move regularly in Society and are to be found at all diplomatic functions are, however, of small value to a Naval Attaché, or, indeed, to anybody.'

His most powerful contact throughout his time in Madrid was the man often described as 'the last pirate of the Mediterranean'. Juan March Ordinas, reputed to be the richest person in Spain, was physically unattractive but financially inspired. Born in poverty at Santa Margarita in Majorca – over the hills from Son Torrella – he was almost sixty when the Second World War broke out. Short, frail, bald, pale-faced, with thick spectacles and a bent, crooked walk which seemed to match his character, he was usually preceded by heavyweight bodyguards who created an atmosphere of menace; and in negotiation his nerve, patience, guile and readiness to deploy colossal bribes carried all before him. Many people considered him an out-and-out criminal, and Alan himself once described him as 'the most unscrupulous and the richest man in Spain, besides one of the cleverest'. His nominees, Alan added, conduct business. 'He never does anything openly himself.'

March had certainly made enemies as well as millions. His first fortune came from smuggling North African tobacco into Spain, and in the 1920s he was granted a State monopoly, which brought him millions more. During the Republic he was imprisoned but later released; it was he who financed the flight of the de Havilland Dragon Rapide which brought Franco from the Canary Islands to Spanish Morocco in July 1936, at the start of the military rebellion which began the civil war. Then he began to provide Franco with immense sums of money made from deals in oil and property, besides presenting Mussolini with a dozen bombers.

Alan was introduced to March in September 1939 by Sir Maurice Peterson, the Ambassador at the time, who instructed him to keep in touch with the entrepreneur throughout the war – which he did. March soon approached Alan with a grandiose project, suggesting that he himself should buy all fifty-nine German ships laid up in Spanish ports, twenty-one of them in Vigo. His idea was that the Germans would be paid in a series of instalments, all in pesetas, deposited in Spanish banks in blocked credits, and that the money would remain there earning 5 per cent annual interest until the end of the war. Spain would have the use of the money, and Britain the use of the ships.

In September 1939 Alan sent March to London, ostensibly travelling on business for his own import-export firm, but really to put the idea of the ships to Godfrey. Speaking through an interpreter, March said he wanted to place his services entirely at the disposal of the Admiralty. He claimed to have control of the oil supplies in Tenerife, Morocco and the Canary Islands, and was arranging to take control of practically the entire oil supply in Spain. He was prepared to cut off supplies of fuel to German submarines, and would share intelligence with the Naval Attaché in Madrid.

Godfrey was impressed by his strange visitor. So was Churchill, who on the morning of the visit wrote Godfrey a note ending 'I should like to see Señor Marche [sic] this afternoon at five o'clock if possible.' For some reason the meeting did not take place, but Churchill added:

> This man is most important, and may be able to render the greatest service in bringing about friendly relations with Spain. The fact that during the last War when Spain was neutral, and somewhat pro-German, he made money by devious means in no way affects his value to us at the present time or his reputation as a Spanish patriot. He risked everything for General Franco at the outset of the struggle against Bolshevism in Spain, and financed the Rebel Government to the extent of his whole private fortune. I have no doubt that he hates the Nazi as much as the Bolsheviks both being equally inimical to capital.

Back in Spain, March told Alan that the idea about buying the ships was his own, that he now represented the Spanish government in the matter, that a Cabinet meeting had been much in favour and that Franco approved of the project.

Reporting to London, Alan said he regarded the scheme as 'feasible, and possibly very useful to Great Britain'. One drawback, he warned, was that the Germans might end up getting the money; and another was the character of Señor March:

> It would be a mistake to trust him an inch. But as long as that is kept in mind and every possibility provided against, it need not in itself prevent the scheme going through.
>
> The advantages of his organisation . . . are, that it is entirely Spanish, that it is entirely in his hands, that I deal with no one but himself, that it costs us nothing, that he is perfectly ruthless when necessary. He has already had two German agents shot in Ibiza, though I did not ask him to do so and knew nothing about it till afterwards.

In spite of his reservations, Alan did come to trust March, believing that he could keep him under control when dealing with him. What was more, Churchill — influenced by Alan — was also prepared to give March a chance. In a note of 10 November 1939 he wrote, 'On the whole I am inclined to favour the transaction proposed', and when disparaging remarks by Sir Andrew Duncan, Chairman of the British Iron and Steel Federation, were passed on in a memorandum, the First Lord added some crisp annotations in his habitual, tiny red squiggles (here rendered in brackets). Sir Andrew said he had known of Juan March in the last war and had heard a good deal of him since. 'He was pro-German [*why shd he not be?* scribbled Churchill] and later pro-Nazi [*why not?*] and a clever [√], self-seeking [√] rogue. He would certainly double-cross us if he could. He made a lot of money [*why not?*] and money-making is his main interest [*quite untrue — he was ready to sacrifice everything for Franco*].'

In the end Churchill's intuition proved correct, and March came through the war as a staunch friend of Britain. The more Alan saw of him, the more he valued him, and he later wrote:

> He was to my personal knowledge not only a very clever man but a scrupulously honourable one. He always carried out his undertakings and always stood by those who trusted him. He was also a patriotic Spaniard who detested Hitler and all he stood for, believing that he was a menace to Spain and to the world in general.

Godfrey, also, was in favour of the ship-buying project, for he believed that the sale would encourage March to install spies and bribe the harbour and customs officials at Vigo and the other ports in Spain's north-west, thus making it impossible for German submarines to call there, as Alan reported they had done in February. During and after the war rumours persisted that U-boats had also refuelled there, but Alan was adamant that they had not. In 1950, replying to a question from an American researcher, he wrote:

> You can take it as definite that no German submarine refuelled at Vigo during World War II . . . Refuelling submarines needs a lot of preparation, and Spanish precautions, perhaps fortified by representations on behalf of my American colleagues and myself, effectively stultified German hopes in that direction.
>
> There was, indeed, no question of Spain *allowing* German submarines to refuel in Spanish ports surreptitiously. In spite of her difficult position, with German troops on her frontier, and many German sympathisers in the country, Spain did not wish to allow anything of the kind. The only question was whether it could be done without Spanish connivance. Well, it wasn't.

On 18 March 1940 Alan was granted the acting rank of captain – and by then his network of agents was doing good work, particularly on the west coast. Never exposing himself, but keeping in cover behind the code-name 'Armada', and working through intermediaries, he and Don Gómez-Beare enlisted the services of dockworkers, stevedores, policemen, taxi-drivers, shopkeepers and others in a covert campaign to prevent small Spanish vessels servicing German submarines. Night watchers maintained surveillance on the movements of Nazi ships; other agents were hot on the trail of 'auxiliary schooners or similar craft' bought or hired by German spies for the purpose of privily supplying U-boats with food, water, oil and changes of personnel.

For some time (Alan told Godfrey in March) he had been receiving information about a Spanish vessel called *Carmelita*, bought in Barcelona by a German agent posing as a Chilean, who was planning to fit her with special tanks for refuelling submarines. 'By a roundabout route' he arranged for three men to join her as master, mate and engineer, but they were put off again and again. 'The three men do not know of me,' he added, 'but will keep in touch with agents ashore.'

Don had to be careful when moving around the country, for all attachés were required to tell their respective Ministries whenever they proposed to travel to a Service establishment or a naval base outside the environs of Madrid, and local authorities were told to report whether or not they had been where they claimed. No doubt German spies were doing the same. At a very difficult time, Alan reckoned that Don's 'resource, courage and ingenuity were invaluable.'

One outstanding recruit to the Allied cause was the slim young Spaniard called Juan Pujol García. Born in Barcelona, son of a Basque mother, he was bearded and, at thirty-one, already balding, 'with a high forehead, a face of ascetic, almost El Grecoish angularity, and eyes which impressed you with the burning sincerity of the man behind them'. During the war he never divulged his proper name, and not until many years later was his real identity revealed.

In 1941, disgusted by the excesses of the Nazi regime, he first offered his services to the British, hoping to pass them confidential information which would help the Allied cause; but when he walked into the Embassy in Madrid, he was shunted from one secretary or official to another before being sent away. He then turned to the Germans, with the idea of damaging the Nazi cause by feeding the regime false information, and after some cautious preliminary meetings he was taken on by the Abwehr, who supplied him with codes and invisible ink, sent him (as they thought) via Portugal to England, to report to them from there, and assigned him the code-name Arabel.

Pretending to have joined a textile firm in Lancashire, but in fact living at Cascais, in Portugal, he began composing fictitious reports about conditions and events in England. The despatches, he claimed, were being brought to Portugal by a friendly airline pilot and placed in a safe-deposit box, thus explaining the lack of any postmark. Since the first few were based on information extracted from a Baedeker's travel guide, a railway timetable and a large map of England, they included nothing of the slightest use to the Abwehr – yet they fooled the Germans, and in particular they fooled the dandyish Major Karl-Erich Kühlenthal, head of the Abwehr's espionage section in Madrid.

Kühlenthal was not an attractive fellow. Of slender build, about 5 foot 10 inches tall, he was described by a fellow German as having 'Face: round, cat-like. Complexion: yellow. Appearance: nervous, uncertain. Peculiarity: shifty eyes.' Since he had a Jewish mother, he had been unable to join the Wehrmacht, but had become a protégé of Admiral Wilhelm Canaris, head of the Abwehr, who took him to Spain and gave him a special rank. On the telephone Kühlenthal called himself 'Carlos', but to the network of spies whom he ran he was known as 'Felipe', and to ordinary Spanish citizens as 'Don Pablo'. He was morbidly secretive, and kept moving his *Treffpunkte*, or meeting points, to different rooms around Madrid.

In Portugal his new protégé Arabel began to lose his nerve when he realised that, with his severely limited knowledge of England, his credibility would soon be destroyed. He therefore approached the American Embassy in Lisbon, and through the Naval Attaché there was put in touch with the American Naval Attaché in Madrid, Lieutenant M. W. Williams, a good friend of Alan's.

Thus the British learnt of the shadowy operator in Cascais, and when they heard that he had usefully directed German submarines towards a non-existent Allied convoy in the Atlantic, allegedly bound for Malta, Alan sent Don Gómez-Beare to meet him in Portugal. Invited to carry on his good work from England, he proceeded to do just that. Yet even now uncertainty cloaks his movements: according to Alan's own account, he and Don smuggled Pujol out through Gibraltar and organised his onward passage aboard HMS *London*, which was escorting a convoy to Britain. Pujol himself, in his autobiography published more than forty years later, told a different story. He agreed that he was taken to Gibraltar on a British ship, but said nothing about any further voyage. Rather, he claimed that he was flown to England in a military plane and landed at Plymouth.

In any case, an exceptionally talented case officer, Tomás Harris (known as 'Tommy'), half Spanish, half English, and at home in both languages, took him in hand and gave him the cover-name Garbo. So successful was the fictitious build-up which the pair concocted that in time the Germans came to believe that Garbo had recruited a network of twenty-six sub-agents, including a sex-starved spinster in the War Cabinet

Office. As the distinguished war historian Michael Howard remarked, 'The reader should bear in mind that none of these people actually existed.' The two ringleaders of the deception proved phenomenally industrious: between them they wrote 315 letters, averaging 2,000 words apiece, with their apparently important information conveyed in invisible ink beneath harm-less covering texts. So comprehensively did they deceive the Germans about Allied plans for the invasion of Europe that, come D-Day in June 1944, their reports had the invaluable effect of drawing major enemy forces away from the Normandy beaches which were the real point of attack.

For Alan, caught up in a maelstrom of trickery, deceit and danger, it must have been depressing to get gloomy reports from members of his family; his father had died in 1938, and further sad news came in March 1940, when he learnt that his mother had died peacefully after a short illness at her home in Kent, aged seventy-two. He had seen her in December, and she had written her last letter to him in January, during a freeze-up in England, rather eccentrically offering to send out a pair of ice-skates. Now, in a long and loving letter his sister Joy (still calling him 'Hugh'), gave details of her burial:

> We had the funeral on March 11 and Mother was buried with Father. My vicar came over to take it. It was a lovely sunny spring day and the wreaths of spring flowers were beautiful. We got wreaths from the five of us [children] and they all went on the coffin. Yours and Mary's and Jocelyn's was yellow tulips, white narcissi and lilies. There were seventeen wreaths altogether from various relations and friends. I think Mother must have liked her funeral.

Joy went on to discuss the financial situation. The house and its contents might be sold, and the proceeds divided among the family – but the amounts of money involved now seem pathetically small. The house had been valued at £600. There was a bank overdraft of £15, and some outstanding bills amounted to £8. There was also a £15 invoice for a new boiler which had just been installed. But on the credit side some Southern Railway shares were worth £60, and the rates for the current quarter (£12 4s. 3d.) had already been paid.

Joy was much exercised about the immediate future. She did not think that the property could be sold for the time being – so what should she do about the house and its contents? What about their mother's papers and clothes? What about the garden? (A gardener had been coming for one day a week and charged 9s. (45p). She was worried about her sister Molly, the doctor, who was working 'terribly hard, seeing 150 patients a day'. A greater anxiety was that England might at any minute be invaded by the Germans. But her immediate concern was about money. With all the family under pressure, she asked Alan if he would pay the rates on the house for the time being – which he did.

A little of his sadness came out in a letter to Anne Hamilton, lamenting his mother's death. 'Now you are all there is left of my childhood,' he wrote. 'Please write to me now and then . . . I haven't seen you for four years. I've been living in an atmosphere of war and hatred. But you know how I love you. Please write to me. My dearest love to you. Hugh.'

Early in June 1940, a month after Churchill had become Prime Minister, Alan flew to London with another of his ambitious clandestine plans. His idea, hatched with Juan March, was to rally anti-German forces in Spain and put pressure on Franco to remain neutral by secretly bribing senior Spanish army officers who might be able to influence him. Churchill was immediately enthusiastic, as were the Chancellor of the Exchequer and Anthony Eden, the Foreign Secretary. It was left to March to

devise a scheme which obliterated any sign of British involvement and made it appear that the proposal had originated in
Spain, 'financed by Spanish banks and businesses in order to
spare the country the horrors of another war'.

Ten million dollars were paid into the Swiss Banking
Corporation in New York, but the Foreign Office and the
Treasury repeatedly raised objections to the scheme, fearing
that word of it would leak out. The result was that most of
the money remained frozen for months, and a Treasury official
reported that 'our friends [i.e. the bribeable Spanish generals]
were greatly perturbed and suspicious that we were conniving
at baulking them of their reward'.

The tentacles of Alan's network had spread all over Spain
and Portugal by the time a new Ambassador, Sir Samuel Hoare,
arrived in Madrid on 1 June 1940. Hoare's career had been
exceptionally varied: a senior Conservative politician, he had
fought in the First World War and gone to Russia on an intelligence mission, as well as to Italy, where he had met Mussolini.
He had been Secretary of State for Air during the 1920s,
Secretary of State for India in 1931, Foreign Secretary from
1935 to 1937 and Home Secretary from 1937 to 1939 – yet
it was as Foreign Secretary that he had been humiliated by
the failure of the pact over Abyssinia which he tried to forge
with the French Prime Minister Pierre Laval. He was also
discredited because of his unswerving loyalty to the arch-
appeaser Neville Chamberlain, and in 1940 many politicians
thought that Churchill was sending him to Spain to get him
out of the way. 'S. Hoare now to go to Madrid!' noted Sir
Alexander Cadogan, Permanent Head of the Foreign Office,
in his diary on 12 May, lacing his sentences with derisive
exclamation marks. 'I suppose they want him out of the
country!' A week later he told a colleague, not entirely in jest,
that there were 'lots of Germans and Italians in Madrid, and
therefore a good chance of S.H. being murdered.'

Hoare reached Spain in an exceedingly nervous state – so much so that he did not wish the aircraft in which he had arrived to return to Britain, in case he felt he had to make a run for it. He had taken the precaution of bringing with him an automatic pistol, on which he had had some training in England, but he imagined that he was 'surrounded by German agents and gunmen who would stick at nothing, and that he might well be kidnapped.

Later a large house was found for him within walking distance of the Embassy, but for the first few weeks he and his wife, Lady Maud, stayed at the Ritz Hotel, which had recently been restored after use as a military hospital during the civil war: its white and gold décor looked pristine, but was slightly tarnished by the fact that the building was infested by Abwehr agents.

From these uncomfortable surroundings Hoare fired off one alarmist letter after another. To Lord Beaverbrook: 'If I had known of the difficulties of this place, I would never have come here.' To his close friend and ally Neville Chamberlain: 'You told me the other day in Downing Street that you thought I was very courageous in undertaking this job. After a week in Madrid I would say that it was more than courageous, it was foolhardy.' To Lord Halifax: 'You cannot imagine how isolated I feel here.' To Lord Halifax again: 'I wonder which of us two is the more bewildered, you in the middle of things or I in my almost complete isolation.'

To gain his bearings, Hoare must have relied heavily on the Military Attaché, Brigadier Bill Torr, and on Alan. One day after his arrival, Alan wrote him a sharply worded memorandum on the state of the Embassy, which (he said) for the past eight months had been behaving 'exactly as if the war were a distant matter':

In accordance with Your Excellency's instructions, I am frankly expressing my view of the present position. The

British Embassy in Spain, as a whole, has until recently
refused to take into practical account the fact that we are
at war . . . In effect, the Embassy Your Excellency has
come to command is defeatist. [I recommend] a drastic
reorganisation of the Embassy Staff, and of the work and
of the premises . . .

The leisurely methods of peacetime diplomacy are
useless in the present situation . . . All members of the
staff, including the typists, should be encouraged to believe
in our ultimate invincibility . . . The Special Branch here
is not allowed to be efficient. This I cannot report to Your
Excellency in writing. If I may I will do so personally. . .
The Cipher Staff work very hard but are quite uncontrolled.
Like Spanish housemaids, they are always in a gang or not
available at all.

Hoare took these remarks to heart, and after only ten days
in Madrid he told Churchill privately, 'I have a really excellent
Naval Attaché in your friend Hillgarth. I am finding Hillgarth
a great prop. Our minds work quickly and closely together.'
In 1941 he wrote to Cadogan, recommending Alan for recognition in the Birthday Honours and saying, 'Hillgarth has been
a key man here and any success we have had has been a good
deal due to him.' But later, all he could find to say about him
in his memoir *Ambassador on Special Mission* was that he had
been 'the embodiment of drive', 'a veritable sleuth on the track
of enemy submarines in Spanish waters', and the producer of
'valuable contacts that effectively helped at critical moments'
– three lukewarm lines in a book of 300 pages. Alan was more
generous: although he could never bring himself to *like* Hoare,
he admired the way the Ambassador buckled down to his task,
and defended him stoutly against criticism from the Foreign
Office.

When Hoare arrived in Spain, British fortunes were at a

low ebb. The evacuation from Dunkirk was completed on 3 June 1940, and a German invasion of England was expected at any minute. At the end of the month the fall of France sharply increased pressure on the Embassy and made the new Ambassador even more agitated – so much so that on the 27th he wrote to Churchill:

> Dear Winston, You can imagine the state of nerves in which Spain and Madrid find themselves after the German arrival on the Pyrenees. I try to keep an appearance of calm but it is not always easy in face of a completely germanised press and many germanised departments of State. I still think, however, that it is worth trying to keep some influence here . . . Supposing we can keep Spain out of the war even for a comparatively short time, it is worth the attempt. I am only saying that I have never found myself before in such a baffling maze or in the presence of so many enemies who are determined that I shall not get out of it.

Alan took a far more robust view of the situation, and on the same day told Churchill, 'Things are going quite well here really . . . Our new Ambassador has done wonders. I am not a professional diplomat, so I can, perhaps, be allowed to say that at this moment Sir Samuel Hoare is doing better than any diplomat I know could do.' Between them they played an important role in persuading London not to enforce a stringent economic blockade, which might have pushed Spain over the edge into active partnership with Germany.

Alan liked the way Hoare treated his staff as a team:

> He was never too occupied or too bored to listen . . . and he was always prepared to back his staff up. He encouraged a vigorous policy. He wanted results. That I

had occasional differences of opinion with him was inevitable, but they counted as nothing when compared to the successful work of several years.

One of the brightest of the bright young men recruited by the DNI to work in Room 39 was Lieutenant Ian Fleming of the Royal Naval Volunteer Reserve. As Personal Assistant to Godfrey, he was based in London, but travelled widely and like Alan had many arrows in his quiver. In August 1940 the DNI charged him with the task of laying the foundations for Operation GOLDEN EYE, a plan hatched by the NID to prepare for a campaign of sabotage in Spain and to maintain contact with London if the Nazis invaded the Iberian peninsula.

After flying to Lisbon and on to Madrid, Fleming stayed with the Hillgarths, and then went on by road with Alan to Gibraltar, taking Mary with them to make the party look more domestic, and flying the White Ensign from the radio aerial. Mary found Fleming amusing, but her opinion of his efficiency as a secret agent was undermined when he left his wallet behind on the table in a restaurant.

The travellers' main task was to establish an office for GOLDEN EYE, but they also met Colonel William 'Wild Bill' Donovan, Roosevelt's chief of intelligence, who was on a fact-finding tour, and briefed him on the absolute necessity of keeping Spain neutral. Next Fleming went on to Tangier to create a fall-back facility, in case the Rock was overrun, as it almost certainly would be if the Germans swamped Spain. Then, as he reported to Godfrey, in order to get back to England as quickly as possible, he found it necessary to charter a special plane from Tangier to Lisbon at a cost of £110.

Having returned to London, Fleming sent Alan a Secret and Personal letter, thanking him and Mary for their hospitality and letting him know 'how much I appreciated being "under your wing" and how much my education gained'. He declared himself greatly impressed by what he had seen of Alan's organisation, and by the 'wonderful work' that he and his staff were doing, 'not only along your own lines but in imparting a little balance to that rather hysterical Embassy. It is lucky that we have such a team in our last European stronghold, and results have already shown the great contribution you are all making towards winning the war.'

At that stage of the conflict Spain was in greater danger than even Alan realised, for none of his agents had picked up any trace of Operation FELIX, whereby Franco would grant Hitler transit rights for the Wehrmacht to drive down through the country to attack Gibraltar and so close the straits to Britain. The Führer had long believed that the capture of Gibraltar would be the first step in his conquest of Spain, and that such a move would forestall any plans the British might have for occupying the Canaries. Fortunately, when the two leaders met at Hendaye in November, Franco sought to impose so many conditions on the operation that Hitler became exasperated and abandoned the whole project, deciding instead to bring forward another scheme which he had plotting for some time – Operation BARBAROSSA, the invasion of Soviet Russia. Some historians believe that this change of mind cost Hitler the war.

In September 1940, as the Battle of Britain raged, Alan sent Churchill a long and forthright analysis of the political situation in Spain, claiming that things were going 'better here than they appear to be. The Germans are getting desperate and the Spaniards obstinate. Our wonderful fight is impressing them':

General Franco has lost almost all his prestige. He is regarded, by everybody, as being asleep and under the thumb of his brother-in-law, [Ramón] Serrano Suñer, the Minister of the Interior. The country is not really governed at all . . . Peculation and bribery are worse than at any

time in the past century. Yet no one wants a return to
the republic, which also failed because it could not govern
... Some kind of a military dictatorship, with or without
a king, of the mild form remembered as that of Primo
de Rivera, appeals to most Spaniards as the best solution.

The memorandum went on to say that the one stable
element in the country was the army. All the principal posts
in government were held by members of the Falange party,
of whom 40 per cent were 'professional log-rollers of no
particular political affiliation'. Fifty per cent of the remainder
were ex-Communists or ex-Anarchists. Only 10 per cent were
honest. In the middle of this chaos, the army stood out as the
one hope of the State. What would happen if the Germans
decided to invade?

Spain's Army is ill-equipped and nothing like mobilised.
Her Air Force is rotten. An unadvertised attack along main
roads by motorised divisions would soon overcome resistance. I calculate that the first German vehicles could reach
Gibraltar in six or eight days, without heavy forces, of
course. But ... it would be necessary to occupy the whole
country, a singularly difficult, mountainous country, and
the Spaniards are a singularly tough, cruel, stiff-necked
people. Twenty divisions could not hold down the whole
of Spain. If the Spaniards had help from abroad, thirty
divisions would not be enough.

The Spanish generals, Alan wrote, were contemptuous of
the French collapse, and felt sure the British would step in if
Spain were attacked:

That is not to say that any of the generals, or, indeed,
many of the Spanish people are pro-British, for they are

not. They dislike us heartily. But they are anti-Falange and anti-German, and as Germany's enemy we should, in their reckoning, hasten to their help if they had to fight Germany.

Churchill found this analysis so valuable that he circulated it to his colleagues in the War Cabinet; and in January 1941, during one of Alan's visits to London, summoned him to attend a meeting of the Defence Committee, at which the Chiefs of Staff were present.

Preoccupied though he was by affairs in Spain, Alan was also keeping watch in other directions. Late on the afternoon of 10 September 1940 he was visited at his flat by the French Naval Attaché – a good friend – who told him that a squadron of three cruisers and three destroyers had left Toulon, the port on the south coast of France between Marseilles and Nice. Alan went straight to the Embassy and sent off a signal marked 'Immediate' to the Admiralty, repeated to the Flag Officer, Gibraltar, warning that the ships were heading for the Atlantic.

To his chagrin, he found out too late that he had not been told about Operation MENACE, the Allied plan to capture the harbour at Dakar, on the West African coast, in which Vichy warships had been sheltering. Because his signal was slow to reach its destination, the French squadron from Toulon outran pursuing Royal Naval vessels, and two of the cruisers reinforced the defences at Dakar to such an effect that the Franco-British attack was beaten off on 23–25 September.

Blame for the failure to stop the reinforcements passing through the Strait of Gibraltar was laid on Admiral Dudley North, commander of the North Atlantic station, for his 'unforgiveable lack of initiative'; but Alan always felt that this was grossly unfair. If he himself had known about MENACE, he would have made his signal not only 'Most Immediate' (the highest classification) but also 'Personal for First Sea Lord', so that Churchill would have seen it at once. Later, in response to an inquiry from the American naval historian Arthur Marder, Alan wrote: 'I feel very strongly that in circumstances like those ruling at that juncture, and with such a vital project in contemplation, it was foolish not to warn me to watch for some French naval movement of the kind, *and to tell me about Operation MENACE.*'

Signals from Madrid were generally sent by cipher telegrams, which were secure, and although many messages arrived mutilated, Alan did not believe that the mistakes were ever deliberate. What he knew for sure was that copies of the Embassy's telegrams were passed to the Germans – 'but that did not help them much'. The most tiresome feature was delay, which was often deliberate and exasperating, with a message taking as many as six days to reach London from Madrid.

If Germany did invade Spain, GOLDEN EYE's sabotage would be carried out by agents of the newly created H Section of Special Operations Executive (SOE, known first as SO2), which was formed as a separate entity from SIS. Both Hoare and his fellow Ambassador in Portugal were strongly opposed to the idea of irregular operations, because they feared that if SOE agents were captured, or made contact with Communists, they would inadvertently precipitate revolution in Spain. Nevertheless, SO2 wanted Alan to carry on, maintaining that he was 'in every way the best person suited to their activities', as he was not only *persona grata* with the Spanish government, but also had 'unique knowledge of the political situation'.

Alan himself welcomed the idea – and, what was more, he took charge of it. In the course of a visit to London he saw Hugh Dalton, the Minister of Economic Warfare, who was head of SOE. 'Hillgarth has recently returned to this country,' Dalton told the Prime Minister on 7 January 1941. 'We have,

I am glad to say, established the closest relations with him and he has consented to supervise the whole of our activities in Spain.'

The vulnerability of Gibraltar worried Alan greatly, and in a secret memorandum of January 1941 he detailed 'Preparatory Measures' to be taken against the event of a German invasion. 'I should be kept informed of every hint at a German attempt or a new German plan, so that I can tip off the Spaniards,' he wrote. He called for the immediate establishment of a military mission in Gibraltar, with the stores, vehicles and equipment for a whole brigade, 'so that only the men will have to follow'. He also asked for three Spanish-speaking naval officers to act as interpreters, 'to be sent out by air to join me when the balloon goes up'. Further, he demanded that 100,000 tons of wheat should be made available immediately, and that Spain should be offered two squadrons of fighters and credits to buy them: 'A secret understanding can be reached on this subject.' To make his own position clear, he added: 'The Minister in charge of SOE has agreed that all activities by SO1 or SO2 in the Iberian peninsula should be subject to my control, though not my direction.'

Godfrey was apprehensive about Alan's connection with SOE, fearing that it might lead to his star attaché being compromised, with the result that he would have to be withdrawn from Madrid. A draft memorandum to Hoare acknowledged that 'The DNI would regard this as disastrous, owing to the importance of the other work which Captain Hillgarth is now performing.' On 3 April 1941 Godfrey wrote to the Chiefs of Staff:

My own contention is that at the present juncture Intelligence is of primary importance and that, therefore, steps should be taken to ensure that the SIS is given precedence in regard to its requirement now and in the future . . . The SIS should be put in full and detailed possession of all present and future plans and projects of SO2, and they should have the right of veto in principle and in detail on these projects.

Alan pointed out that SOE had 'a natural desire' to operate in the Iberian peninsula, and he managed to persuade Hoare that agents could do important work preparing for a possible German invasion, 'provided they were rigidly controlled'. After some discussions, he reported,

A compromise was reached by which SOE were allowed to operate in the peninsula in a precautionary way only, and I was chosen to control them. That is to say, they could initiate nothing without my approval, and the progress of what had been approved had to be fully disclosed to me every day.

On the whole this worked very well, but it was an unenviable task for the controller. I was continually berated by the Ambassador – and by the Foreign Office whenever I went to London – for allowing anything at all, while the chiefs of SOE on the other side were continually at me to allow more. Meanwhile the DNI was always fearful that I would slip from controlling into directing and get involved and compromised. So I was under fire from three sides.

Later in the spring of 1941, when a German invasion seemed imminent, Alan made another quick visit to Gibraltar, to check on the readiness of the mission which he had helped plan. He was dismayed to find that when or if the mission moved to Spain, Brigadier Torr, the Military Attaché, would command it, that the Air Attaché, Wing Commander Dixon, would be head of the air side, but that he himself would be superseded.

In an uncharacteristically petulant, handwritten letter to Godfrey he protested:

> I am not quite clear what I'm to be or do – either just a lackey to the Ambassador and separated from the Mission, or a sort of glorified interpreter . . . Please take me away out of it to another job where I can be some use . . . If I'm not to be the head of the Naval Mission, please get me out of the country altogether and let me be useful elsewhere.

In the event, after an intervention by Godfrey, he was designated Chief British Naval Liaison Officer and given the dormant rank of Commodore, First Class. Although no invasion came about, in 1942 steps were taken to put the mission into a state of operational readiness, and Alan was provided with equipment, stores, a portable wireless transmitter and two cars, in case the staff suddenly had to take to the road. One of the vehicles was a Humber Super Snipe with huge tyres, and Alan hated it from the start. 'It was never any good,' he wrote later. 'One of my Assistant Naval Attachés smashed it up, and on one unpleasant occasion the steering broke at 40 mph and nearly killed your humble servant. It looks awful and is awful. When every other service attaché, of every nation, has a decent, modern, good-looking car, it would be both criminal and stupid to expect the British Naval Attaché to show himself in that sort of thing.'

He nearly lost his own staff car one day when it was parked in the street outside the Embassy. On the morning of 24 June 1941 – two days after Germany had invaded Russia – Serrano Suñer, who particularly hated the British, made a fiery speech from the balcony of the Falange headquarters, inciting a crowd to violence; when the mob moved on, its members were eager to attack someone or something, and since there was no

Russian Embassy, the British Embassy was their natural target. They took up station at either end of Fernando el Santo, and there followed what Hoare described as 'a carefully organised riot'.

A wagon arrived full of stones, for missiles, along with German vehicles equipped with 'cinema cameras'. The mob's principal aim was to set fire to the Embassy's cars, but since nobody in the crowd could lay hands on a match, this plan was frustrated, and the rioters were reduced to pelting the cars and the Embassy itself with the stones thoughtfully provided. Mary and her daughters watched from an upper floor as the cars were badly damaged, and windows in the building were broken; but the attack was repelled by the Embassy's regular guards, reinforced by sixteen escaped prisoners awaiting repatriation (there were often more than twenty in the building). The police, having held off for more than half an hour, eventually moved in to clear the crowd, but made no arrests.

In his memoirs Hoare gave the impression that he was present during the riot; but in fact he was not, and as the Minister, Arthur Yencken, was also away, the officer in charge was Alan. The scene that ensued would have gone down well in a comic-opera production.

Hoare returned, demanded a meeting with Serrano Suñer, and in due course was granted one, at his official residence. Alan himself described what happened:

The Ambassador was accompanied, as he had warned that he would be, by his diplomatic secretaries and by his three service attachés. Serrano Suñer said [later, in an article] 'accompanied by all his military attachés with arms.' This gives a deliberately false impression. The only arms were our swords, which are part of the uniform on an official occasion.

Sir Samuel declined to be seated, and made his protest

standing, with dignity but calmly. When he had finished, Serrrano Suñer answered, expressing regret and promising inquiry, but without any evident sign of the horror that the occasion demanded. The Ambassador then said that he did not expect such an incident in a civilised country like Spain, and we left.

Like Hoare, who drove all over the country cheering up British expatriate communities, Alan travelled about a good deal, visiting the outlying Consuls, who were always starved of information. At home in Madrid he and Mary entertained stylishly, maintaining the pretence of normal diplomatic life. Perhaps in order to sustain his own morale, he filed away newspaper articles denigrating the Nazis and their allies – notably two whole columns in *The Times* listing Hitler's lies and *volte-faces* – and he stored up the sarcastic aphorisms of the day:

1. Never have so many owed so much to so few. CHURCHILL
2. Never have so few stolen so much from so many. HITLER
3. Never have so many run away from so few. MUSSOLINI
4. Never have so few run after so many. METAXAS
5. Never have so many obtained so much at the risk of so little. STALIN
6. Never have so many eaten so little. FRANCO
7. Never have so many suffered so much through the fault of so few. PÉTAIN
8. Never have so many earned so much at the expense of so few. ROOSEVELT

Meanwhile Godfrey's lively assistant Ian Fleming, irritated by the delay over Juan March's ship deal, drew attention to the entrepreneur's financial frailties. Before the war he had taken out a loan of £1 million from Kleinwort's, but on the outbreak of hostilities the bank had called it, putting him in a difficult situation. Barings then took the loan over, with the concurrence (and possibly at the instigation of) the Treasury – so that HMG was already to some extent involved. A hint that the loan might be called again, Fleming wrote, 'would certainly bring March to his senses . . . Once we have ensured a firm grip of March through his pocket, I suggest we should get him over here to see the First [Sea] Lord. I would be in favour of delivering ourselves into March's hands to a large extent . . . I think we should quickly get this matter out of the docket stage and see if it will walk, otherwise let it die. It is already half throttled with paper.'

With the project dragging on, Godfrey suggested to Churchill that they should lure March over on some business pretext, 'spiced with hints of larger fish to be fried', and asked the Prime Minister if he would be willing to see him. 'I feel sure that a private talk between you and him would be the best way of obtaining his allegiance, which would be of value in many ways,' he wrote. 'If we do not obtain it, Germany probably will.' The interview never came off, but the matter was eventually settled when, as a result of Fleming's remarks, secret British funds were released to buy the ships.

The scheme to bribe Spanish generals was still becalmed, but Alan was pleased with initial indications, and a handwritten letter to Churchill dated 21 June 1940 had suggested that some money had already changed hands:

Commander Furse [the Assistant Naval Attaché, who had been sent to London] will explain what the Ambassador could not telegraph. As the idea was originally mine, I feel you would want me to tell you myself that it is practical and is already showing results. It should save us many lives and a great deal of trouble, besides making so

much trouble for our enemies that it may well help to
the breaking of them.

Hoare agreed with this estimate, and so did Dalton, who,
in his diary noted that in Spain 'the cavalry of St George have
been charging . . . hence Attaché H.'s concern for J.M.'s tinplate'
– a cryptic reminder that gold sovereigns, which bear an image
of St George slaying the dragon, had been let loose in Spain,
causing Attaché Hillgarth anxiety that Juan March's money was
being well spent.

According to Alan, 'many millions of dollars' had been made
available, and thirteen million of them, 'originally ours', had
been paid over into the Swiss Bank in New York. 'It is now
essential in the interest of the State that ten million should be
unblocked,' he wrote. 'The American Government should tell
the Swiss Bank merely that ten million are unblocked, without
stating what ten million or why . . . If the President has power
to order the unblocking without explanation, it would be far
quicker – and speed is important.'

Churchill grew impatient with the dithering, and on 25
September 1941 sent the Foreign Secretary and the Chancellor
of the Exchequer a crisp note saying,

Can't you give them something on account? We must
not lose them now after all we have sent – and gained.
Vital strategic issues depend on Spain keeping out or
resisting. Hillgarth is pretty good.

In due course the British Treasury released the $10 million,
which was deposited by a roundabout route in banks in
Argentina and New York. It took time for March to make
his arrangements, and details of what happened to the money
remain unclear, but it seems that half was paid out in regular
instalments of cash, and the remainder held in blocked

accounts. Among the beneficiaries, apparently, were General Antonio Aranda Mata, Commander of the Spanish War College, who was said to have received $2 million, and General Luiz Orgaz y Yaldi, the Captain-General of Catalonia and a fervent monarchist. Aranda was certainly one of Alan's principal contacts – but how much effect the money had, it is impossible to say.

Another complication for Alan was that both his stepdaughters had married early emissaries of SOE: Elspeth had married David Muirhead, and Joan had become the wife of David Babington Smith. The men were nominally members of the Madrid Embassy staff, but in fact members of the sabotage organisation.

Two distinct plans had been set in train for the event of a German invasion. In one, Operation SPRINKLER, SOE operators would reinforce the Spanish army if it resisted the Nazis. In the other, Operation SCONCE, agents would blow up bridges and other targets, and infiltrate any unit that collaborated with the enemy. Two squads of SCONCEs, each of sixteen Spaniards, had been in training at Arisaig, in the Scottish Highlands, since December 1940, learning to organise communications, lay explosive charges and so on. Their instructors were enthusiastic about their recruits' potential, but their reports made the training sound amateurish, and reminiscent of the farcical scenes in Evelyn Waugh's *Sword of Honour* trilogy: 'They all ride bikes. I got six personally trained in motor cycling before the machine broke down and stopped our progress on the third day. There is no car: we practise on the tractor.' On the other hand, a note by one Professor Patterson could easily have been written by Alan himself: 'The most striking thing about the Spanish troops is their pride in being members of the British army, and also their gratitude for the work that has been done in this country on their behalf.'

*

A particularly valuable clandestine associate in Madrid was Eduardo Martínez Alonso, the tall, good-looking surgeon and physician to the British Embassy, whom Alan recruited early in the war after Churchill had urged him to establish an escape route for Allied servicemen on the run. Eduardo had a natural affinity with the British, since he had grown up in Liverpool, where his father had been the Uruguayan Consul General. During the civil war he had had a lively time, to say the least, at one stage being thrown into prison for attending wounded Republican soldiers, before being appointed Surgeon-Captain in Franco's army.

He and Alan became the closest of friends, trusting each other absolutely, each seeing in the other a man prepared to take risks for a humanitarian cause. Since Eduardo – known to the British as Agent 055 – had a flat near the Embassy, and often treated British patients in his surgery, his meetings with Alan aroused no suspicion among the Gestapo, and it seemed natural enough to German spies or anyone else that they would get together for a drink at the Embassy tea room-cum-bar on a corner of Madrid's main thoroughfare, the Paseo de la Castellana (the name of the bar was confusing, as it had nothing to do with any official Embassy). The establishment was owned and run by Margarita Taylor, an Irish woman who lived in a flat above the bar and attracted many members of the city's fashionable set with her high-spirited elegance. She and Alan became good friends, and kept in touch for a long time after the war.

It was only forty years later, when Eduardo's daughter Patricia came across her father's diary, that the world learnt what he and Alan had been discussing as they lingered over their cakes or cocktails. In fact they were making plans for the rescue of escapers, and Eduardo suggested that men on the run could be channelled through La Portela, his family home at Vigo, in Galicia. If they could reach that safe haven, local fishermen would row them out at night to a British ship standing by in the estuary. This system proved effective, and when further exhortations came from Churchill to save Jews as well Poles, the flow of fugitives increased to a torrent.

Refugees from France poured over the Pyrenees, and those arrested by the Spanish police were interned in the concentration camp at Miranda de Ebro, near Burgos, three hours by car north-east of Madrid. The camp – a rectangular compound surrounded by stone walls and barbed wire, containing lines of two-storey, whitewashed huts – was out in an open plain about one kilometre north of the town, burning hot in summer and freezing in winter. The accommodation was overcrowded, and rations were meagre, but the British Embassy sent up regular lorry-loads of supplementary food for its own subjects, and put pressure on the authorities to release into their custody those Britons who were so seriously ill as to be in danger of losing their lives.

Since Eduardo was active in the Red Cross, he could easily diagnose imaginary noxious diseases, falsify medical records and certify that some of the camp's inmates would be at death's door if not given prompt treatment. Soon Red Cross ambulances and Embassy vehicles were ferrying these alleged casualties to Madrid, where Margarita hid them in her rooms above the bar until they had been equipped with false papers. Then, dressed in new clothes which she had procured for them, they would come downstairs and pass between tables occupied by undercover German agents, before, at the exit on to the street, she would see them off with effusive goodbyes, as if they were old friends. Next they would be driven south-east to Gibraltar or north-west to Galicia, usually in the boots of diplomatic cars, and posted back to freedom.

With the help of one taxi driver, Manuel Rios, and families who gave shelter in safe houses along the way, the escape route functioned well; from 1939 until the end of 1941 an average

of ten people a week were smuggled down it; then in December
Alan got wind that the Gestapo were closing in on Eduardo
and started making arrangements for him to leave the country.

The doctor was engaged to be married, and his nerve held
long enough for him to go through with the wedding in
Madrid on 3 January 1942. David Babington Smith then drove
him and his wife to Lisbon; they crossed the border into
Portugal without difficulty, but had to wait eighteen days before
Embassy staff could secure first-class priority and put them on
a plane for Bristol, where they arrived, minus most of their
belongings, on 2 February. For the time being Eduardo was
paid a monthly stipend of £20, tax-free, by the Foreign Office
in recognition of his courage and effectiveness, and later he
got a job at Queen Mary's Hospital, Roehampton. After the
war he was able to return to Madrid, and he and Alan remained
lifelong friends.

Another useful ally in Madrid was the British journalist Tom
Burns, who had gone out to Spain in the spring of 1940 as a
member of the Ministry of Information, and was then appointed
Press Attaché at the British Embassy. He and Alan had some
background in common: through his first job with the
publishers Sheed & Ward Tom had met Hilaire Belloc; later he
had roistered in London with Evelyn Waugh, and in 1929 met
Graham Greene. A good-looking, friendly young man, he was,
like Don Gómez-Beare, an excellent mixer; besides, he spoke
Spanish well, having visited the country twice before: the first
time, he walked in over the Pyrenees, guided only by a hopelessly misleading plan which Belloc had drawn for him. As a
journalist during the war he could frequent Madrid's seedier
clubs, bars and restaurants without exciting suspicion, and in
such places he picked up many a snatch of gossip that made
useful grist for the Naval Attaché's intelligence mill.

Careful though he was about passing on unreliable information, Alan occasionally made mistakes, and for once he

overreached himself in the summer of 1941, when he and Bill Torr picked up rumours that within the next three weeks Franco would be toppled by a junta of leading generals. On 17 July the Caudillo had made an outrageous speech, caustically criticising Britain and America, and apparently aligning Spain firmly with the Axis powers – and it was this that precipitated talk of a coup. This 'absurd speech', Alan told Churchill on 12 August 1941, 'has cost him his last scrap of prestige . . . He thought the Russian war would be over in two weeks, and our friends believe their chance has come.' The 'friends' included Generals Aranda and Ortaz – but for once their information was faulty. Franco easily rode out the storm, and in London Cadogan no doubt felt some satisfaction at having earlier denounced Alan in his diary as 'rather a charlatan'. (Since Cadogan had described Hoare as a 'dirty little dog', the insult may be considered relatively slight.)

Alan made few personal enemies – on the side of the Allies, at any rate – but one was Kim Philby, who worked as a spy for the Soviet Union right through from his time at Cambridge in the 1930s until his defection to Moscow in 1963. He had spent most of the civil war in Spain as the correspondent of *The Times* accredited to Franco's forces, but also surreptitiously reporting to Moscow, and in the summer of 1940 he was recruited into the SIS, which he joined as a member of the Iberian section in London.

In his self-serving (though crisply written) little memoir *My Silent War*, published after his defection to Moscow, Philby claimed that Alan had chosen the pseudonym Armada to feed his 'illusions of grandeur'. In the margin of his copy of the book, beside this fatuous invention Alan wrote 'Rot'. Philby also claimed that Alan had been given 'a very large sum' to buy details of the leading Abwehr officers in Spain, and that the information he sent back about them was 'distressingly short'. Against this paragraph Alan wrote 'Pure invention', and then opposite another sentence, lower down, 'Ditto'. Almost certainly it was the Naval Attaché's access to Churchill , 'C' and Godfrey that irritated the treacherous Philby so much.

Alan, in fact, robustly defended his habit of communicating directly with the Prime Minister, the head of the SIS and the DNI. He pointed out that as Naval Attaché he was responsible for keeping both the DNI and his Ambassador informed, and that there was no clash in this dual loyalty. Further, he believed he had the duty 'to write personally to the DNI on occasion . . . The personal touch between the D.N.I and his service attachés is, in my view, of paramount importance. Without it one never gets the best results.'

Deeply involved though he was in high-level political manoeuvring, Alan was occasionally called upon to perform some service well outside his normal remit − as when he helped kidnap a French recruit to MI6 known as Paul Lewis Claire who had given away secrets to the Vichy naval attaché in Madrid. Alan helped his SIS colleague Hamilton Stokes lure Claire to the British Embassy, where they drugged him with morphia and loaded him into a car bound overnight for Gibraltar. The idea was that on arrival he was to be arrested, charged with treason and deported − but the plan misfired. Early in the morning SIS agent 51000 sent a message saying that 'the consignment' had arrived 'completely destroyed owing to over-attention in transit. . . Salvage being quietly disposed of tonight . . . damage regretted, but I submit it is for the best.' It transpired that Claire had come round during the journey and made so much noise that his captors had hit him on the head with a revolver and accidentally silenced him for ever.

Less violent, but more ridiculous, was an incident in October 1941, when Alan had to extract Lieutenant Colonel Dudley Wrangel Clarke from a Spanish gaol. Clarke, a lifelong bachelor with 'a face like a sort of merry-eyed potato', was no ordinary officer, and had had an exceptionally varied military career, which included special missions to Africa and Norway. Rescuing prisoners had long been one of Alan's skills, but this case was different, for Clarke, when arrested in a main street in Madrid, had been in drag, and the Spanish police had photographed him wearing a flowery print dress, a necklace, elbow-length black gloves, high heels and a white cloche hat, sitting on a chair with his legs neatly crossed in one shot, standing by the chair in another. Since he was the head of 'A Force', the secret deception unit based in Cairo, and since he was supposed to be in Egypt at the time, his detention caused some surprise, both to the Spanish and to the British Embassy.

He claimed he had been taking the feminine garments to a lady in Gibraltar and had tried them on for a prank; but, as the Embassy pointed out, this hardly squared with the fact that the dress and shoes fitted him. Alan, knowing Clarke's eccentricity – including his habit of never accepting a table in a restaurant unless he had his back to the wall – made the most of the event by sending photographs of the colonel, in drag and in a civilian suit, to Churchill's personal assistant Charles Thompson, accompanied by a deadpan note: 'Herewith some photographs of Mr Dudley Wrangel Clarke as he was when arrested and after he had been allowed to change. I promised them to the Prime Minister, and thought you might like to see them too.'

For Alan to make a joke in a message to London was something of a departure; but a much greater departure from normal hit him on 6 November 1941, when he was struck by a thunderbolt which nearly blew him overboard.

Enter Jean

Professional matters often took Alan from Madrid to Lisbon, a short flight or a ten-hour drive to the south-west; and on the evening of 6 November 1941 he was dining at Estoril, the seaside resort along the coast from the Portuguese capital, when he happened to glance down the long table and saw in its polished mahogany surface the reflection of a pretty young woman on the other side. As he looked up, his eyes met hers – and that fateful flash of contact changed both their lives.

Jean Cobb was twenty-seven and came from Sheffield, where her father, Frank, had founded a factory making fine silverware. The business had flourished, and the family lived comfortably in Newlyn, a spacious house with six bedrooms in Ranmoor, the fashionable part of the city, where they were looked after by a cook, several servants and old Renton the gardener, Jean's favourite, 'with his apple cheeks, his eyes very bright and his hands the colour of earth and hard as leather'. Her father – whenever he could get enough petrol – drove a Bentley and fished in Scotland. Jean was devoted to her parents, and along with her sisters, Sheila and Mavis, and her brother, Ian, made up a happy family, among whom she was known as 'Bunts' or 'Bunty'.

A spirited girl, to say the least, dark-haired and immediately attractive, she had a rather round, mobile, mischievous face and remarkable brown eyes. Among her many accomplishments she painted and wrote poetry; but she had never taken kindly to discipline and had been expelled from five or six different schools before finishing at Westonbirt, the colossal Victorian pile in Gloucestershire. There she made a strong impression on the headmistress, Margaret Popham, who wrote to her mother in June 1934 asking if she might stay on for an extra year so that she could go to Oxford or Cambridge: 'I am very much struck with both her ability and character. She is one of the nicest girls I've known for a long time. She is totally unselfish, clever and sensible. I think it would make all the difference to her whole life to have a University education.'

In the event she did not go to university, but spent time profitably staying with families and learning languages in France and Germany. Her sojourn in Hamburg during the summer of 1936 included a trip to Berlin and a visit to the Olympic Games – 'which', she reminded her parents in a letter, 'are famous, you know'.

In November 1939 she travelled to Bulawayo in Southern Rhodesia, on behalf of the British Social Hygiene Council (forerunner of the World Health Organisation) to write a report on the living conditions of the colony's Coloured people (those of mixed race), towards whom she proved commendably sympathetic. Having stayed for six months, and visited 168 houses in the municipal area of the city, she concluded:

Many of the unfavourable opinions so often heard about the Coloured people are inaccurate and not founded on facts. The Coloured people are cheerful, intelligent and full of talent . . . They are courteous, respectful and hospitable, and their manners and behaviour in their own houses are exceptionally good. There is a naturalness and candour about them which is unusually refreshing.

Meanwhile in Europe her brother Ian, to whom she was very close, had joined the Argyll & Sutherland Highlanders, and when he was captured at Dunkirk in June 1940 she felt she must do something for the war effort, and for him; she then discovered that another Ian, husband of her friend Louise Campbell, had also been captured, so she volunteered to work with Louise, who was in Lisbon, running Mrs Ian Campbell's British Prisoners of War Parcels Depot, an outpost of the Red Cross.

Alan's existence often seemed to be ruled by the power of chance. Pure chance had put him in the intake of boys at Dartmouth who were swept into action at Gallipoli in 1915. By chance Wall Street had crashed in October 1929 just as he reached Majorca, cutting short his circumnavigation of the globe, grounding him on the island and giving him a new life there. By chance he had met and impressed John Godfrey in 1938 when the admiral came into Palma during the Spanish Civil War – the meeting which led to his appointment as Naval Attaché in Madrid. And now some divine chance had positioned him face to face with the love of his life. It seems very strange that a middle-aged man with such steely self-control and such wide experience of life should have fallen headlong for a girl fifteen years his junior – but so he did. He and Jean were like two magnets, drawn irresistibly to each other, immediately enchanted.

Opportunities for meeting were severely limited, but they started writing to each other at once – and so began an extraordinary correspondence, astonishing alike in its intensity and its endurance. Over the next five years they exchanged more than 1,000 letters. Cautious at first, but increasingly outspoken, their messages of love flew to and fro between Portugal and Spain, and then to the Far East and back, two, three or four a week in each direction. None of them was short: missives of eight, ten, twelve, eighteen sides became commonplace. Alan wrote with pen and ink in his elegant italic hand, and Jean's letters matched his for neatness: her script was more upright, but she wrote with amazing fluency, never changing a word or making a blot.

Much of Alan's news was trivial, and, although he never mentioned his secret work, he sometimes became slightly indiscreet. 'Sam [Hoare] considers the Lisbon embassy a lot of idiots, and so do I,' he wrote in February 1942. 'The embassy spends half its time imagining slights and suspecting everyone else of treachery.' More often he was pouring out endearments: 'Riding this morning – another heavenly day – I kept feeling you were riding beside me and looking round to smile at you.' At the start Jean, for her part, was very correct, as if scarcely daring to admit that her heart and mind were in turmoil. She was still in the process of seeing off an earlier suitor called Charles, but in February she summed up the courage to tell Alan, 'I'm going to marry *you* – not Charles or anyone else.'

Alan, suddenly convinced that Jean would be his ideal partner, could not conceal the fact from Mary. He took her to meet Jean, and she, with her sweet nature, was glad that he had done so. 'It is awful – everything,' she wrote afterwards, 'but you know I feel that.' Mary inevitably became distraught, fell ill and returned to England for the time being, leaving Alan to carry on his dangerous work and to conceal from his colleagues the fact that he was caught in emotional cross-fire.

Jean's employer, Louise, known to her staff as 'Mrs Ian', had become very fond of her and valued her highly as an assistant. Jean was frequently in her house, and helped look after her five-year-old son, 'Little Ian', once describing to Alan how they romped on the floor in the evening: 'We played wolves in a very noisy game in which Boomph, the dog, is supposed to join, only we always have to pretend he's dead because he *will* go to sleep in the middle.' After a while Louise put pressure

on her to end the affair, and with no mean courage she agreed
to do so. On 30 March 1942 she wrote from Casa Verde, the
pension in which she was staying:

A week ago tonight I had dinner by myself on the terrace
. . . and I was thinking about Mary and about us. I told
you that I would listen to my own heart, and suddenly
that night I saw everything so clearly and so really. We
can't do this, Alan – it's all mistaken and wrong. I made
up my mind to write and tell you.

Somehow I feel that my having made up my mind that
we shall never see each other again will be a relief to you.
You too must have felt that the agony of causing so much
sorrow was unbearable . . . I hope with all my heart that
soon everything will be as it was before we met at Estremoz,
and that this won't leave too deep a scar . . . I'm so deeply
sorry about it all, but it won't help to talk any more about
my feelings or to wonder about yours.

Bless you, Alan. I shall always have the very gentlest
thoughts about you, and about Mary, who is dear and lovely.
Something that must have been so real and fine can't be
broken, and I shall pray that it will all be made right again.

Jean.

Such was the impact of this rejection that it forced Alan to
admit that he had misgivings about his relationship with Mary
even before they were married in 1929. He could suppress his
innermost feelings no longer. In an immense, twenty-five-page
letter, begun on Good Friday 1942, he poured out his heart:

I cannot pretend any longer . . . Joan and Elspeth and
everyone else, including Mary, who is most concerned,
have a conception of the past fourteen years that is not

true, largely through my fault. To go back, then, to what never existed as they see it, is not possible. More, to go back to what did exist is now equally impossible.

I say this quite calmly, even cold-bloodedly, because I can't tell you anything that isn't absolutely true . . . I must go on to repeat – at the risk of hurting you – you whom I regard as above the angels and therefore very human and easily hurt – that whatever you decide you cannot alter the fact that I love you with my whole heart and mind, body and soul . . . Yes, I have, like you, felt the agony of causing so much sorrow, but I have not felt it unbearable, because there was no way of altering it. That you decide not to see me again cannot alter that.

I confess, the vista of days and years without your presence or without your voice or without even casual news of you is torment. My spirit is frightened, because, as you know, I must go on. I must write my unwritten book. I must do my work in this war and after it.

Please do one thing for me, in the full knowledge that I shan't bother you. Don't marry anyone just to shut still one more door. Marry if you really, honestly love someone. Not for any other reason . . . You once called me your captain and once your knight. I shall always try to be both, with all my heart and soul, just as I love you, my dearest, my dearest.

Your Alan.

He intended this to be his last letter to Jean, but he left it open overnight and then began writing again at the bottom of the last page, promising he would do all he could to make Mary happy 'in the limited way that is now possible'. He said he would accept Jean's decision – 'now. Forever, I will not.' But then on Easter Day he started yet again:

Mary arrived, by air, with Elspeth, yesterday. She was
apparently afraid I should be furious or hate her or something, which was silly but natural. She is very weak but
a little stronger and her mind is clearer than it has been
for some time . . . She says she likes you and would have
liked you for a friend.

Mary had suggested to Mrs Ian that she and Alan were
already more or less separated. This annoyed him. 'It was not
a marriage as Mary now describes it,' he told Jean, 'even from
her view. And much less from mine.' He went on to say that
even if Jean would not marry him, he would have to ask Mary
for a divorce.

I have been — weakly but humanly — thinking of myself
and of what I have lost, the only real rest I have ever known
— for to be with you was that — and the only perfect
companionship, that sense of complete confidence and trust,
and now I can't touch your hand, which to me was life.

God bless you. There is a God. You have shown a proof
of his existence in your character and just by being alive.
He will take care of you. He will guard and protect you
from evil in all its forms, from wicked men, from fear,
from lack of faith, from loss of hope, from danger to the
body, to the mind and to the soul.

I love you, Jean, my sweetheart, my darling Jean.

Your Alan.

A cynic might well remark that to blame one's unhappiness
on the failure of one's marriage, or the deficiencies of one's
wife, is the oldest and lamest of excuses. Yet one of Alan's most
conspicuous qualities was his honesty: throughout his life he
never told lies — except to discomfit the enemy — and there

seems no reason to doubt that in this vital matter he was telling the truth.

In any case, his broadside had its desired effect. Jean changed her mind, and the lovers resumed their correspondence in ever more ardent terms. In their letters they never descended to anything carnal or coarse or lascivious: rather, they wrote about what they had been doing, about books, about places they had visited, but above all about their longing for each other. Pressure of work usually forced Alan to write late at night: he often had to go to official dinners or gave parties of his own, entertaining officers and diplomats, and the Spanish habit of starting to eat at 10 p.m. or later meant that he did not reach his flat, or the cottage outside the city which he rented for the summer, until after midnight. Then, declaring himself too exhausted to start a letter, he would reel off eight or ten pages of endearments, which grew more and more extravagant – as on 22 May 1942:

I *worship* you, but all of you, and I give you everything of myself, the breath of my body and the whisper of my soul. It is perhaps in that absolute giving and receiving, that complete unity, that twinship, that our strength lies . . . Only you are truth and reality to me.

Alan was already under heavy pressure from his work, and the affair enormously increased the stress of his existence. When he began to suffer abdominal pains, his doctor suspected a recrudescence of an ulcer which had troubled him in Majorca. One activity which helped preserve his health and sanity was riding. He would set off at dawn to hire one of the horses from a stable in the Royal Park outside Madrid, and he found that the exercise and fresh air made the 'troubles and hates and horrors of the city and the war just fade away'. The terrain was not ideal, for many civil war trenches were still open, and unexploded shells and grenades lay about, so that he could not 'just go gaily blinding along up any old hill and down any old dale'. All the same, he told Jean, 'you get some good gallops and some nice stiff climbs and lots of trotting'. Jean, who had ridden in the early mornings in Rhodesia, echoed his enthusiasm: 'Something in that combination of animal, air, aloneness and movement is *very* good for one's nerves.'

His work in the Embassy was never less than harassing, and he told Jean that, although he loathed rows and fights, he had gained a reputation for being combative – no doubt from his insistence that things should be done as efficiently as possible. 'There's always some new trouble,' he wrote one day. 'The Minister (who is Chargé now) is very tiresome and hangs round my neck.' Another night he reported:

> The Germans are trying everything they can to embroil Spain with us. Every little incident is magnified, and incidents are created. Some disgruntled [Spanish] generals have been approached by Germany to try and manoeuvre Spain into war against us. Everyone began believing fantastic things . . . and certain measures had to be taken which have kept me on the jump for the last four days.

His domestic situation was becoming insufferable, and towards the end of September 1942 he persuaded Mary to go back to England, at any rate for the time being. 'It'll be better for her and for everyone,' he told Jean. 'I have tried steadily to take all the blame, to resent nothing and to help where I could.' That same day (without having heard this latest news) Jean covered fourteen pages with protestations of love, and told him she felt she had been reborn: 'Since our last meeting it has been as though I had come into the lightness of the world like a calf, or any animal that can run and dance and leap for joy.'

War work went on inexorably. For months Alan and his team had been reporting on the build-up of German and Spanish observation posts on both sides of the Strait of Gibraltar, and in particular on the construction of a sophisticated, infrared tracking system for nocturnal surveillance, known by the code-name BODDEN. Churchill became so alarmed by these developments that he proposed Commando raids to take out the detection stations, but the Chiefs of Staff feared that any such action might drive Spain into the arms of the Axis, and decided against armed intervention. Hoare was instructed to confront Franco with the evidence, which he did on 23 May. The Caudillo promised an urgent inquiry, and three days later Admiral Moreno admitted to Alan that the Germans had presented the Spanish air force and army with a complete radar installation.

BODDEN and the other listening posts were closed down – only just in time: had they still been operating later in 1942, they would certainly have detected the build-up to Operation TORCH, the Allied landings along the coast of North Africa, which began on 8 November. As it was, through a combination of absolute secrecy about the operation itself, and deceptive radio messages which decoyed German attention elsewhere, the Allied warships transporting troop convoys from Atlantic to Mediterranean reached their dropping-off points undetected.

As battle raged along the North African coast, Alan was grappling with the problem of the *Olterra*, a 5,000-ton tanker which had been scuttled in Gibraltar harbour early in the war but in November 1940 had been refloated and towed within the breakwater of Algeciras Bay, less than ten miles away across the gulf. There Italian naval personnel had covertly built a concealed compartment in the forepeak from which manned torpedoes, known as *maiali* (pigs), could be launched from below the waterline. The first attack, in December 1942, was foiled by Gibraltar's underwater defences, and three Italian *nuotatori* (frogmen) were killed, but others, in April and July 1943, inflicted severe damage on merchant ships at Gibraltar.

Suspicion fell on the *Olterra*, and, after a protest from Alan, Admiral Moreno had the ship thoroughly searched. Nothing was found; but later, when Italy had fallen out of the war, Alan discovered from an Italian diplomat in Madrid that the launch compartment did exist, but that it had escaped detection because there was no access to it from inboard. He then insisted that the ship be towed to Cadiz, where engineers finally cut open its secret.

Another persistent annoyance was that German ships were carrying off large quantities of iron ore and wolfram (or tungsten) ore – the ultra-hard metal used for gun barrels, shell-casings and aircraft parts. In an attempt to block this trade the Allies, through the British Embassy, began making pre-emptive purchases of wolfram from Spain and Portugal; but a crisis blew up when the Anglo-South American Bank, from which the Embassy had been drawing funds, suddenly ran out of pesetas. Confronted by the need to find a solution within twenty-four hours, Hoare told Alan to go and see Juan March. The financier promptly put on his hat and accompanied Alan to the bank, where he opened a new account and lodged in it enough millions to avert disaster.

Alan's relationship with John Godfrey had always been easy; and so, in September 1942, he was both shocked and disappointed when the admiral was suddenly dismissed from his post as DNI, apparently for no reason other than that his brusque manner had annoyed a number of senior officers. Alan had no option but to continue working with his successor, Commodore (later Rear Admiral) Edmund Rushbrooke (known to some subordinates as Rush Admiral Rearbrooke), and he got on perfectly well with the new incumbent, but the relationship was never so warm.

By then Alan and Don had agents in every Spanish port. 'JOSEF is of Russian origin and uncertain nationality,' one of their signals reported.

His earlier history is shrouded in mystery and contradic-
tions . . . PLATO is a Greek who has been in touch with
the German Secret Service organisation in Lisbon on two
separate trips . . . FIREMAN was born of Belgian parents
in Russia and has a very cosmopolitan background . . .
EDITH is an Englishman, 2nd radio officer on the SS
Empire Tern.

Whenever Alan got wind of imminent German activity, some of Don's agents were sent to the port to persuade the local police, dock watchmen and stevedores to collaborate – their cover story being that they were acting on behalf of Spanish shipping interests anxious to forestall an incident. 'Often money had to be distributed,' Alan remembered, 'but not a great deal considering the importance of the matter. It undoubt-edly increased the enemy's difficulties and led to the abandon-ment of several attempts.'

Private worries kept invading his professional life. For the past few months he had been doing what he could to help Louise and Jean with their Red Cross work, contributing money and arranging for books and cans of beer to be sent to the prison camps, supplementing the food – sardines, tunny fish, corned beef, chocolate, cheese and honey – that the inmates most craved. Then he heard that Ian Campbell and 230 of his fellow prisoners were being kept in handcuffs for twelve hours a day as a reprisal for alleged ill treatment of Germans in the Red Sea, and that their toothbrushes, razors, knives, forks and all the clothes but what they were wearing had been confiscated. This news made him exceedingly angry and – if it were possible – increased his hatred of the Nazis.

Every kind of scheme was being devised to outwit the enemy. In December 1942, when the last aircraft carrier in the Indian Ocean, HMS *Illustrious*, was about to be withdrawn because of urgent need elsewhere, Sir James Somerville, the Commander-in-Chief, appealed for help. The Admiralty responded with Operation BIJOU, an exercise which apparently reinforced him with a second carrier, HMS *Indefatigable*. This ship existed only as a phantom; but reports – some of them Alan's – coupled with deceptive radio traffic, not only concealed the return of the *Illustrious* from India, but sketched the eastward progress of a companion. In the words of the historian Sir Michael Howard, 'The voyage [to the East] of the *Indefatigable* was projected to the enemy entirely by radio traffic put out by the appropriate commands *en route* until she notionally reached Simonstown, where she came under Somerville's command.' The Germans and Japanese, swallowing the invention whole, believed that two British carriers were at large in the Indian Ocean, and the ghostly *Indefatigable*, as evanescent as the *Flying Dutchman*, put in a good year's imaginary service in the Far East before she was 'brought back' in time to link up seamlessly with the creation of her real self. (Commissioned in May 1944, the battleship saw service with the Home Fleet and launched attacks on the *Tirpitz* in July and August that year, before joining the Eastern Fleet in November.)

January 1943 began cheerfully for Alan with the news that he had been appointed a Companion of the Most Distinguished Order of St Michael and St George – a CMG to add to his OBE. Soon after that he was delighted to hear that Jocelyn had made an admirable start at Eton.

On the outbreak of the civil war in 1936 Jocelyn had been left in England, in the charge of the beloved old amah (or nanny) who had also looked after his mother. For the next three years he had been taught by a governess, and then in

1939 he had gone to St Piran's, the preparatory school high on a hill above the Thames at Maidenhead. He always regarded this as a rather dim establishment: nevertheless, he learnt enough there to gain a place at Eton. His first half (term) at public school was a short one, with no trials (exams) at the end of it, but the masters who taught him were so impressed that he was given a double remove – that is, moved up two divisions (classes) instead of one. In a warm letter his house master added that he had shown 'a simple and natural cordiality and charm'. Naturally this pleased Alan, who was extremely fond of the boy, even though he had seen so little of him; but now he was faced with the awful problem of breaking the news that he intended to leave his mother. On the grounds that it was better to wait until Jocelyn was older, he did nothing for the time being.

In February he wrote to Jean about one of his periodic excursions from Madrid. Together with a chauffeur and a colleague from the Embassy, he drove northwards over the Guadarrama range to Burgos, and after lunch there went on to the prison camp at Miranda, from which the inmates were at last being dispersed. He reached the village of Albiz by moonlight, and was entertained by the Count of Albiz with whisky and cheese. On, then, to Bilbao, on the north coast, where at 10 p.m. he dined in a restaurant with the Consul, who was so eager for information that he kept his visitor talking until 4 a.m. – and in the end Alan got away only because he walked out. On Sunday he had lunch in a beach restaurant and went – as he put it – 'to call on some people on business'. Then he proceeded along the coast to Santander, went through the town and stayed another night in a primitive village. On the way back to Madrid over the mountains he picked some primroses for the wife of the Ambassador, Lady Maud.

Described to Jean in such innocent terms, the trip sounded like a holiday jaunt; but in fact it was one of Alan's agent-finding

and agent-briefing missions. Hints of how deviously he was
operating emerge from Most Secret messages to Rushbrooke,
headed 'Dear DNI' in his own hand, in February and March
1943. After those visits to Bilbao and Santander, he advocated
aggressive action against Axis shipping round the Spanish coast,
both from seaward and from the shore, and on 18 February he
wrote:

> It is time to pass from the defensive to the offensive. It
> is time to get tough . . . The war has now reached a stage
> when a considered campaign against Axis maritime activ-
> ities in Spanish ports and in waters adjacent to the Spanish
> coast can be staged without much risk to Anglo-Spanish
> relations. It is recognised that the maintenance of
> Spanish neutrality is still the ruling factor in our policy
> . . . and that any serious incident between Spain and the
> Allies could only be of benefit to our enemies, but it is
> no longer necessary for us to put up with all that we
> have had to endure hitherto.

The land-based operation might, he wrote, by carried out
by himself, 'or, more probably, through people engaged by me
in the most careful way in the world'. All such operations, he
told Rushbrooke,

> would be better left to me, <u>without your official knowledge
> and certainly without the knowledge of the Ambassador.</u>
> I say this in no spirit of disloyalty to Sir Samuel Hoare,
> but it is far better that he should be able to deny all
> knowledge of it honestly, and you the same. If anything
> went wrong, which is not likely . . . I could always be
> dismissed and officially sacrificed. In any case, I am happy
> to stand the rub, particularly as I feel so strongly that the
> situation now warrants action of this kind.

The only help I may want from outside is a few special requirements in the shape of bombs. It is part of my submission that I may be able to ask for these, and get them quietly, from Gibraltar, without any questions being asked . . . We now really can do things in this country.

On 5 March he reported: 'I have found – not directly – a good man prepared to stick a limpet bomb on one of the larger German ore ships at Bilbao while waiting in the outer anchorage.' He proposed that the operation should be carried out 'on a dark night with rain' by one of the small fishing boats that went out after sundown. The price had not yet been settled, but it would probably be 5,000 pesetas in advance, and another 5,000 if the attack succeeded. 'Of course,' he added, 'the limpet will be set to go off after the ship has left.' His problem was to procure a suitable bomb, containing about 30 lb. of high explosive, and he asked Rushbrooke if he could 'find out quietly' what was available in Gibraltar. 'I believe SOE has all these bombs,' he added, 'but I do not like to ask SOE any questions myself from here.' At the end of the note he added: 'If the man were caught, he would not be able to give me away, though that is the least important thing. The most important is that the Foreign Office should not be informed. After all, the ship will not sink in the harbour.'

To his chagrin, the Admiralty turned his proposals down flat. A memorandum from the DNI conceded that 'it would indeed be attractive to proceed to a campaign of irregular activity in Spain', but pointed out that the Chiefs of Staff had recently vetoed any increase in sabotage in the Iberian peninsula. Besides, the Admiralty would not accept 'at any price' the possibility of him being recalled from Spain: the importance of his duties in Spain was 'likely to increase very markedly in the near future', and it was 'essential that the office of Naval Attaché and Assistant Naval Attaché throughout the world should remain uncontaminated. I realise that you and your staff have shown that you are quite able to take care of yourselves, but nevertheless at the present time I am not prepared to take a chance of anything going wrong.'

This was a disappointing response; but, although Alan did not yet know it, the team at the NID were putting the final touches to a far more ambitious and important operation, in which (as that last message had hinted) his particular expertise would play a critical part.

Making Mincemeat

The story of Operation MINCEMEAT, one of the greatest and most successful deception exercises of the entire Second World War, has been admirably told, in fascinating detail, by Ben Macintyre in his book of that name, and only an outline of the preparations for it need be given here. The plan was to slip the Germans documents which showed that the Allies' next major landings and assault during the summer of 1943 would take place in Greece, rather than in Sicily, which was the real objective, and so decoy German forces away from the target area.

The idea came initially from Charles Cholmondeley, an eccentric young RAF officer seconded to MI5, and the plan was hatched by him and the Hon. Ewen Montagu, a brilliant lawyer whom Godfrey had recruited into the NID, where he soon had his own top-secret Section 17M. The aim of MINCEMEAT was to float faked documents ashore on the coast of Spain, in a briefcase attached to a dead body, apparently the victim of an air crash.

Immense care was taken to make every detail seem authentic. The body found for the enterprise – that of a Welsh tramp called Glyndwr Michael, who had died in London from eating rat poison – was equipped with a new identity, becoming Major William Martin of the Royal Marines, and furnished with a new past, including a fictitious girlfriend who had recently become his fiancée. The documents he was to carry were refined again and again. The most important – a letter from General Sir Archibald Nye, Vice Chief of the Imperial General Staff, to General Sir Harold Alexander in Tunis, hinting that any apparent threat to Sicily would be merely a feint – was drafted and redrafted by one hand after another, but never seemed perfectly authentic. The final version was written by Nye himself: beginning 'My Dear Alex' and ending 'Best of luck, Yours ever, Archie Nye', it struck exactly the right note throughout, not too formal, not too familiar, as it purported to reveal what the Allies had in mind. As a final precaution, a fair and barely visible eyelash was hidden in the fold of the document.

It is not clear when Alan was first warned about the operation; but he certainly knew about it by late March 1943, when Don Gómez-Beare was summoned to London for a briefing, to make sure (as Montagu put it) 'that there would be no foreseeable danger of things going wrong' in Spain. On Don's advice it was decided that the body would be dropped off near Huelva, the fishing port in the Gulf of Cadiz on the south-west corner of Spain, 'as it is there that the Germans are at their strongest *vis-à-vis* the Spanish police and the chances are regarded as very high that anything that washes ashore there will be made available to the Germans'.

From radio intercepts and Alan's reports Montagu knew that one of the Abwehr's most reliable spies, the gaunt and emaciated Adolf Clauss, kept watch on that coast from his farm at La Rabida, bribing Spanish port officials and running a network of agents with such zeal and efficiency that no ship could move in or out, no floating body be retrieved, without his knowledge.

Don flew back to Madrid via Gibraltar with instructions to contact 'the necessary consuls on the coast', and in particular to make sure that Francis Haselden, Vice Consul at Huelva, knew exactly what to do if a body was washed up on his beat. If or when a corpse came ashore, Haselden was to telephone Gómez-Beare in Madrid and report the news; Don would then ask him to arrange burial, while he himself sent word to London. A day or two later, when a signal from London might plausibly have reached him, Don would ring Haselden again to ask if anything had been washed ashore with the body; he would then say that he could not talk any more on the phone, but would himself come down to Huelva – thus feigning ignorance of the corpse's provenance but hinting at its importance. Everything was arranged in the knowledge that the telephones in the Madrid embassy were bugged by the Germans, and that Clauss probably had an agent in the Huelva Consulate.

On 19 April the body – which had been kept refrigerated for three months – was driven from London to Scotland in a specially built, air-tight cylinder packed with dry ice, and loaded on to the submarine HMS *Seraph*, which sailed out into the Clyde from Holy Loch that afternoon. Ten days later, at 0400 hours on 30 April 1943, as the dawn sky was starting to lighten, she surfaced a mile off the Spanish coast, and Major Martin – by now badly decomposed and stinking – was taken from his outsized cigar tube and dropped into the sea on his last, short voyage, with his briefcase clipped to his belt. At 0733 *Seraph* sent out a Most Secret cipher message: 'Operation Mincemeat completed. Request onward route.'

The bait was found by a fisherman later that morning, but because the ferry across the estuary was not operating, it did not reach Huelva till next day, 1 May. Meanwhile, in Madrid and London British intelligence officers were waiting for news with increasing anxiety. Not until 0500 on 2 May was Alan able to send DNI a signal: 'Consul Huelva reports body ashore. No details yet.' Later that day he followed up with a *faux-naif* message which he marked 'Confidential' but which he knew the Germans would read:

Huelva reports body identified as Major W Martin RM card number 148228 has been washed ashore at Huelva. Death due to drowning probably 8 to 10 days ago. Spanish Naval Authorities have possession of papers found. Consul at Huelva has arranged for funeral today.

For the architects of the operation, one immediate worry was that the putrefaction of the body might have gone too far – that a post-mortem would arouse suspicion because immersion in seawater could hardly have reduced the corpse to its present state – and in fact when the local pathologist began his examination at Huelva, the abdomen exploded at his first incision. Luckily he did not bother to dissect the lungs, to determine whether they were full of seawater, but concluded that death had been due to drowning eight or ten days earlier.

There came a dangerous moment when a Spanish lieutenant offered to hand Martin's briefcase over to Haselden, who, reacting swiftly, managed to decline it, on the grounds that the Spaniard's superiors would want to examine the contents. Had Haselden not rejected it, the whole scheme would have been in jeopardy, for if the papers had come straight into British hands it would have been exceedingly difficult to arrange for the Germans to see them.

At 2030 that evening Haselden cabled Gómez-Beare in Madrid: 'Body is identified as Major W. Martin R.M. identity card 148228 dated 2nd Feb. 1943 Cardiff. Naval judge has taken possession of all papers. Death due to drowning probably 8 to 10 days at sea. I am having funeral Sunday noon.'

The funeral took place, in baking heat, at noon on 2 May 1943. A crowd of Spanish officials and military personnel, bolstered by a few locals, escorted the wooden coffin to Huelva's cemetery, where it was safely buried. Among the onlookers was the gaunt master spy Adolf Clauss – and observing the scene unnoticed, from a discreet distance, was Don Gómez-Beare.

Next day – 3 May – Alan confirmed to London by cipher that the body was that of Martin, and that the Spanish Naval Authorities had all the papers, which 'will have to go to Madrid'. On the fourth Montagu concocted a personal message which he knew would suggest to the Germans that the NID was seriously alarmed:

Some of papers Major Martin had in his possession are of great importance and secrecy. Make formal demand for all papers and notify me by personal signal immediately of addressees of any official letters recovered. Such letters should be returned addressed to Commodore Rushbrooke, Personal, by fastest safe route and should not repetition not be opened or tampered with in any way. If no official letters are recovered make searching but discreet inquiries at Huelva and Madrid to find whether they were washed ashore and if so what has happened to them.

In another message, this time in Alan's secret personal cipher, Montagu told him to carry out the instructions just sent, 'as this is necessary cover, but lack of success is desirable'. On 6 May Alan told the DNI that he had made the demand as instructed. Later that day, in a Most Secret signal sent by 'Special Route', Montagu told him:

Normally you would be getting frantic messages asking you to get the secret documents at once, and to hurry the Spaniards. You must adjust your actions to achieve desired results and maintain normal appearances.

The British were certain that by now Clauss would be doing his best to get a look at the documents. How to persuade the Spanish to let the Germans see them? Alan's answer was first

to spread rumours about the importance of the papers, and
then to send a verbal message to the Minister of Marine, his
old acquaintance from civil war days, Admiral Moreno, who,
in 1935, had struck him as 'a man of character, quiet but
determined and very able'. Now, however, the admiral had
drifted rather too close to the German Embassy for comfort,
and was in frequent contact with the German Ambassador.
Alan was confident that Moreno would get hold of the documents and hand them over, but also that he would arrange for
the Germans to see them first. As a back-up, he arranged for
his most reliable informer, a man known only as Agent Andros,
to monitor what was taking place.

On the 7th, giving the impression that some checks had
been made in London, the DNI told Alan: 'Secret papers probably in black briefcase. Earliest possible information required
whether this came ashore.' If it had landed (the message
continued) it should be recovered at once; and if it had not
yet been found, 'care should be taken that it does not get into
undesirable hands if it comes ashore later'.

On the 8th Alan summed up the situation in a cable intended
as much for the Germans as for the DNI. He confirmed that
the Vice Consul at Huelva had seen the body, that a post-
mortem had been carried out, that the verdict was drowning
several days previously, that the body had been buried, and that
the funeral had been attended by representative military and
naval officers. The dead man's effects were:

(1) Pocket book containing private letters.
(2) Identity disc.
(3) Identity papers.
(4) Medal and crucifix.
(5) Black leather document case locked and straight [*sic*]
     attached to strap.

'Sacambaya is a poisonous place,' wrote Alan, 'a dark, dirty valley, shut in by hills that rise to a further 4,000 feet.'

The Big Hole, at the bottom of which Sanders was convinced he would find the buried gold.

Images clockwise from left:

1. Only man-power could haul one of the compressors across the river to the excavation site.

2. In primitive conditions, Alan (foreground) lent an expert hand as Dr Mellows operated for appendicitis.

3. Wearing (as usual) collar and tie, Alan sits with fellow explorers at the entrance to the tunnel discovered by Sanders.

Skulls alleged to be those of Indians who buried the Sacambaya gold, murdered to prevent them divulging its whereabouts.

At 24, Jean Cobb was 15 years younger than Alan when they met in Portugal in November 1941.

Jean (centre, holding white paper) in Louise Campbell's Red Cross depot in Lisbon, sorting parcels for prisoners of war.

Son Torrella, the grand *finca* on Majorca, bought and refurbished by Alan and Mary in the early 1930s.

Images clockwise from left:

1. With Don Gómez-Beare (centre), his Assistant Naval Attaché and right-hand man in Madrid.

2. The British Consul: Alan at his desk in Palma, Majorca, during the 1930s.

3. Admiral John Godfrey, Director of Naval Intelligence, with whom Alan formed a close partnership.

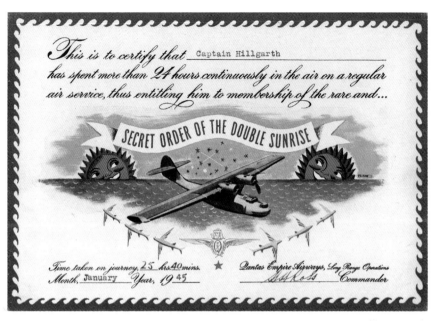

This is to certify that **Captain Hillgarth**
has spent more than *24 hours continuously in the air on a regular air service, thus entitling him to membership of the rare and...*

SECRET ORDER OF THE DOUBLE SUNRISE

Time taken on journey, 25 hrs 40 mins. ★ Qantas Empire Airways, Long Range Operations
Month, January Year, 19 45 A.A. Ross Commander

Marathon flights across the Pacific and Indian Oceans gave Alan plenty of time to write to Jean.

Qantas
EMPIRE
AIRWAYS

Vol. 11   OCTOBER, 1945   No. 10

A GAZETTE
PUBLISHED
MONTHLY BY
QANTAS
EMPIRE
AIRWAYS

Alan in Australia with Clare Blanshard, his personal assistant, to whom Ian Fleming took a strong fancy.

Alan and Jean in later life: they remained devoted to each other.

GREECE

CATHEDRAL

OLD CHURCH

THE PORT

SOUVENIR · SANTORINI ·

OLD CHURCH   THE VOLCANO   THE STEPS

On tour in the Aegean after a return visit to Gallipoli in the company of Eric Bush.

Illannanagh, on the shore of Lough Derg in Co. Tipperary, bought by Alan and Jean in 1946.

IN GRATITUDE AND APPRECIATION OF ALAN HILLGARTH,

BRITISH CONSUL IN MAJORCA, FOR HIS HUMANITARIAN

AID TO THE PEOPLE OF MINORCA AT THE END OF

THE SPANISH CIVIL WAR, FEBRUARY 1939.

A GROUP OF MINORCANS

JULY, 2000

More than 20 years after Alan's death, a plaque was presented to the church at Terryglass by grateful Minorcans

Alan never liked being photographed, but in 1977, a year before he died, his son Tristan sneaked up on him and took this shot.

By lifting flap envelope could be seen inside . . . Vice Consul was informed all effects must be sent to [Spanish] C-in-C Cadiz (who is unfortunately pro-German). In due course they will reach the Ministry of Marine and be handed to me. Official procedure is always slow. Vice Consul had no repetition no chance of obtaining posses-sion of case. I am trying everything possible but fear too much display of interest or suggestion of urgency will only increase official curiosity which is already aroused.

Maintaining its show of anxiety, the DNI told Alan it was 'most important' that letters from the black bag should be sent back by the quickest route and not tested or tampered with in any way, as 'secret checks' had been arranged in England to see whether they had been opened illicitly.

As the MINCEMEAT team expected, the Germans were doing their utmost to obtain a sight of the documents, which had escaped them at Huelva and then again at Cadiz. When, on Moreno's orders, the briefcase was taken to Madrid, its contents were at last violated by Lieutenant Colonel Ramón Pardo Suárez, a staff officer in regular contact with the Germans, who arranged for experts to open the letters.

This they did with the greatest skill. The envelopes had been stuck down with gum, but this had washed off in the sea, and only oval wax seals held the flaps in place. By squeezing the top and bottom of each envelope together, the investigators could make the lower half gape open. 'Inserting a thin metal double prong with a blunt metal hook into the gap, the Spanish spies snagged the bottom edge of the letter, wound the still-damp paper tightly around the probe into a cylindrical shape, and then pulled it out through the hole.' When each of the sheets was opened up, no one noticed a tiny eyelash drop out of the fold – but apart from that lapse, the Spaniards performed their task brilliantly.

The letters, dried out, were taken to Wilhelm Leissner, head of the Abwehr station in Spain, who promptly had them photographed. The originals were then infiltrated back into the envelopes by the same method, and given a soaking in saltwater. Such was the apparent importance of the information the documents contained that the cat-faced Major Kühlenthal was immediately despatched by air to Berlin, taking with him what seemed to be red-hot news. Unfortunately for the German High Command, their high regard for him was entirely unfounded: they believed he had been producing a flow of valuable information about troop movements and dispositions in England, and now his apparent omniscience lent credibility to the MINCEMEAT documents. In fact for months he had been comprehensively duped by Garbo and all the other notional agents in his organisation.

For the time being London did not know what had happened to Major Martin's belongings; but on 12 May 1943, in an open message Alan reported to the DNI that the Chief of the Spanish Naval Staff had handed over 'all effects and papers including black brief case (open with key in lock) containing official documents'. Many of the documents were 'much damaged by sea water' but many were still legible.

> While not tampering with them in any way I can see somebody else has. Envelopes have been opened. Among others there appear letters addressed General Eisenhower and Alexander and Admiral Cunningham. These look as if drier than other papers. Everything will be sent as instructed. I regret it was not possible to recover case intact.

A fuller Personal message to the DNI, in cipher, confirmed details:

A. [Spanish] Chief of Naval Staff has just given me personally all effects and black bag containing papers. Minister of Marine is away.

B. Bag was open with key in lock. He volunteered remark, 'They're all there.'

C. While expressing gratitude, I showed both relief and concern. Neither secretary nor I showed any wish discuss matter further.
Everything leaving by bag May 14th (earliest possible).

D. I have of course observed instructions in your Tel 874 May 10th but it is obvious contents of bag have been examined though some of documents appear to be stuck together by sea water.

E. From his manner it was obvious Chief Naval Staff knew something contents. While I do not believe he will divulge his knowledge to enemy it is clear number of other people are in secret and it is to say the least extremely probable that it has been communicated to enemy.

F. In any case notes or copies have certainly been made and if you concur I will ask 23000 [an agent] to discover through his channels whether Germans have got them, as he can do if they get to Combined General Staff (which they almost all certainly will.) Is there anything further that I can do?

That same day – 12 May – an Enigma intercept at Bletchley Park brought the first sign that the Germans had swallowed the bait: a message sent out by General Alfred Jodl, Chief of Hitler's Operations Staff, quoting 'a source which may be regarded as being absolutely reliable'. Not only did it say that 'an enemy landing on a large scale is projected in the near

future in both the East and West Mediterranean'; it also outlined
an attack on Greece in exactly the terms given in the faked
letter from General Nye. Montagu and his colleagues were
elated, literally jumping up and down.

Not yet knowing of the intercept, Alan packed up Martin's
letters and effects, addressed them to the DNI personally and
put them into one of the Embassy's diplomatic bags, which
left Madrid on 14 May. When the vital consignment failed to
show in London, anxiety quickly mounted. 'Bag not yet arrived.
Urgent that letters should be received earliest possible',
signalled Montagu in secret cipher. '1. Was bag sent by air or
sea? 2. Was the rubber dinghy washed up? 3. Evidence that
operation successful but vital that no suspicion should be
aroused.'

The items had been packed in a small, sealed bag, Alan
answered in cipher. 'Your paragraph two. No repetition no.
Your paragraph three every precaution has been and is being
taken to ensure this.'

On 15 May, at a diplomatic cocktail party in Madrid, Alan
met Moreno who himself brought up the subject of the papers,
claiming that when he was in Valencia, and heard that the
documents had reached Madrid, he had given the Chief of
Naval Staff orders to hand them over at once. 'I asked him
why he had gone to so much trouble,' Alan reported, 'and he
replied my request had indicated importance of documents
and he was anxious no one should have unauthorised look at
them, which "might be a serious matter".'

The admiral had given himself away. When Alan first asked
him, through a third party, to return the papers, he had *not*
said that the papers were secret or important. Now Alan told
London, 'He obviously did not know the exact terms of my
request, which was verbal and could never alone have led him
to say what he did. It can be taken as a certainty that Spanish
Govt. know contents of documents. I am not so certain they

have [reached] enemy. Yet they were more than a week in Huelva and Cadiz.'

There was huge relief in London when the package containing Martin's effects at last arrived at the Admiralty on 21 May. The letters were immediately taken to the Special Examiners (Censorship) for minute analysis. The seals were found not to have changed in any way, but the tell tale eyelash was missing from each envelope, and microscopic examination revealed that one letter had been unfolded when dry and refolded when wet, so that the creases were fractionally different from the original. A final confirmation of skulduggery came from the fact that, when drawn out of its envelope, the still damp, folded letter began to curl up, demonstrating how it had been extracted in the first place.

The DNI now had proof that the letters had been opened and read – but still it was essential to maintain the fiction that all was well, and instructions were drafted for Alan to renew his contact with Moreno:

Inform Minister of Marine as soon as possible that sealed envelopes have been tested by experts and there was no trace of opening or tampering before they reached care of Spanish Navy and that you are instructed to express our deep appreciation for the efficiency and promptitude with which the Spanish Navy took charge of all documents before any evilly disposed person could get at them. You should say that you may tell him in confidence that one of the letters was of the greatest importance and secrecy and the appreciation expressed at this token of friendship is most sincere.

That message was designed to be read by the Germans; but another, in secret cipher, told Alan that although the letters *had* been opened, he should put it about that the British were

confident that no one in Spain had read them. On 21 May a
further message from the DNI suggested that, 'unless unusual',
a medium-priced tombstone should be erected on Major
Martin's grave with the inscription

> Born 29th March 1907 died 24 repetition 24 April 1943
> beloved son of John Glyndwyr repetition Glyndwyr
> Martin and the late Antonia Martin of Cardiff, Wales.
> Dulce et decorum est pro patria mori. RIP.

A note at the end added: 'Order for this tombstone should
be given at once.' Montagu had spelled 'Glyndwr' wrong, but
no one noticed, and the second Y was incised on the stone.
Two days later the DNI instructed Alan that 'a reasonable
reward of not more than £25' should be given to the person
who handed the papers to the safe custody of the Naval
Authorities. 'It is left to your judgment whether this should
be done by you through Naval Authorities or by Consul Huelva
direct.' Alan replied with a Most Secret message: 'Please send
me ordinary cipher signal saying that relations would like this
stone put up and telling me to get on with it if cost not
excessive.' DNI came back with an open answer: 'Relatives
wish erection of tombstone with inscription . . . Also arrange
for wreath to be placed on grave now, with card "From Father
and Pam".'

On 4 June 1943 all the other elements of the deception
were reinforced by an announcement in *The Times*, recording
the death of Martin on active service. Alongside was a news
story reporting the death of the well-known actor Leslie
Howard, whose aircraft had been shot down into the sea by
German fighters on a flight from Lisbon to England. (One
theory was that Abwehr agents had mistaken Howard's manager,
Alfred Chenhalls, for Churchill, whom he resembled, and
believed that the Prime Minister was on the plane.) In any

case, camouflaged by more significant news, the alleged demise
of Martin aroused no interest among the British public.

Alan had given a party for Howard a few weeks earlier, and
now he wrote angrily to Jean: 'So Leslie Howard has gone . . .
It's a filthy trick of the Huns, attacking commercial aircraft . . .
If I'd gone back when Mary & Jocelyn wanted me to, I might
have been in that plane. The whole thing has aroused a storm
of indignation among the Spaniards . . . so his death has done
his murderers more harm than anything he did while living.'

The ends of the MINCEMEAT deception still needed
tidying up, and on 9 June Alan dictated a letter a to 'John G.
Martin Esq.,' care of the Admiralty, which he hoped Kühlenthal
would read:

Sir, In accordance with instructions from the Admiralty,
I have now arranged for a gravestone for your son's grave.
It will be a simple white marble slab with the inscription
which you sent me through the Admiralty, and the cost
will be 900 pesetas. The grave itself cost 500 pesetas, and,
as I think you know, it is in a Roman Catholic cemetery.

A wreath with a card on it, with the message you asked
for, has been laid on the grave. The flowers came from
the garden of an English mining company in Huelva.

I have taken the liberty of thanking the Vice Consul
Huelva on your behalf for all he has done.

May I express my deep sympathy with you and your
son's fiancée in your great sorrow.

I am, Sir, your obedient servant, Alan Hillgarth.

Shedding more crocodile tears for German consumption,
Montagu told Alan that he had been asked by Martin's family
to say how much they appreciated the prompt return of the
dead man's effects. 'Few though these were, as Major Martin

was an only son, and just engaged to be married, they will be greatly treasured.' This message confirmed that the briefcase and letters were safely back in England – and Alan quickly carried out a request from Martin's father, that he should take and send a photograph of the grave.

Reverberations of the great deception rumbled on. On 20 June 1943 Alan told Montagu that one of his most valuable contacts, a high official in the Spanish intelligence service, had become very excited about the documents found on the body at Huelva, and had given him a detailed report on the Spanish findings. This Alan forwarded to Montagu in London, and he in turn passed it on to Lieutenant Colonel John Bevan, the Controller of Deception, with a warning note:

The official, of course, knows nothing whatsoever about Operation MINCEMEAT, and is still under the impression that Captain Hillgarth's interest was from the normal security aspect. The portions omitted from the report have been taken out for the sake of brevity and security . . . The source [of the document] is one of very considerable value to 'C' (although worked by Captain Hillgarth), and the number of names used would give away the source. I hope that for this reason you will take the utmost care of the attached copy, as it in itself would be highly compromising to this very valuable source.

On the bottom of his memorandum Montagu wrote by hand: 'In view of the description of the source, could you please burn this letter' – and beneath that another hand scrawled: 'Attached copy burnt, 25/6/43.'

By then the Germans had not only swallowed the bait: they had also reacted vigorously to it. One of the few people to suspect a hoax was Hitler, but after initial doubts he persuaded himself that the documents were genuine, and he began to remove units from Sicily to strengthen his forces in the Allies' supposed targets, Crete, mainland Greece and Sardinia. The result was that when Operation HUSKY was launched on the night of 9–10 July 1943, the conquest of Sicily – though still a tough and costly operation – proceeded more swiftly than would otherwise have been possible and hastened the Allied advance up the Italian mainland. Operation MINCEMEAT had scored a resounding success.

In Madrid, throughout the weeks of high tension, Alan had kept closely in touch with Jean. In the middle of April he had written to her complaining that 'The atmosphere of this place is really rather awful. There's a sort of nervous tension about the Embassy as soon as I set foot in it', and then on the 27th: 'This place is like a voracious animal. It is always trying to swallow me.' Never mind the intricacies of MINCEMEAT, which of course he did not mention: his most acute personal worry was that Mary might return to Spain, which 'would mean even more open war than at present . . . I'll have to think out exactly how I would deal with it.'

On 3 May 1943 – with the deception manoeuvres at a critical point – he went out riding early but had a fall when his mare Fresa (Strawberry) refused at a ditch, leaving him shaken but luckily unhurt. Next morning he rang Jean in Estremoz and for once got a clear line. Their talk provoked a sixteen-page letter in which she recalled how she had once got 'extreme pleasure' in disquieting members of the Bulawayo Rotary Club with her liberal views about half-castes. 'Smooth, righteous, respected men they were,' she wrote, 'the wretches.' On 6 May she wrote again, anxious about the row that Mary's re-entry to Madrid might cause: 'I think she must believe that you are still caught up in madness and that to come here to you now would anger you enough to make you overthrow everything.'

On 7 May 1943 MINCEMEAT exchanges gave Alan what

he described to Jean only as 'a heavy day's work'. When this finished at 8.15, he went and had a drink, collected a friend from England, took him out to dinner at 10 p.m., returned him to the Ritz Hotel at 1 a.m., stayed talking till nearly 2 a.m., 'then came back here and just had to write to you'.

The success of Operation TORCH, the Allied landings in North Africa, which began in November 1942 and ended with the surrender of the Nazi-Fascist forces in Tunisia in May 1943, removed much of the threat to the Mediterranean. The fact that the enemy no longer had any realistic chance of closing the Strait of Gibraltar meant that the Iberian peninsula lost some of its strategic importance, and the role of the Naval Attaché in Madrid became correspondingly less crucial. When Admiral Sir James Somerville, Commander-in-Chief, Eastern Fleet, asked the DNI if it would be possible to release Alan 'in the fairly near future for an important intelligence appointment in his Command in the Far East', Rushbrooke relayed the request to Hoare, but said he thought it wise that Alan should stay where he was for a few more months, until the situation in the Iberian peninsula had become more settled:

> I realise that the idea of replacing your Naval Attaché at this stage of the war may strike you as regrettable, but I should like to emphasise that the post I have in view for him is also a very important one, and his selection as a possible candidate is a great compliment to him personally.

The new post was that of Chief of British Naval Intelligence Eastern Theatre – an enormous responsibility. Although pleased by Alan's promotion, Jean was appalled by the idea of him being sent so far away: 'I must and will overcome my horror of being separated from you by sea and by land.' Her one compensation was that the news had suddenly become much more cheerful, and it seemed possible that the war would end sooner than she had feared. After initial setbacks, the Allied assault in Sicily had gone well, and Italy was so severely threatened that on 25 July 1943 Mussolini was dismissed from his command and arrested. Alan heard the news while dining with Hoare, and one of his last messages to Churchill from Spain declared that 'Sicily has impressed everyone and delighted most. Mussolini's resignation and what it presages has stunned opponents. The bombing of Rome went down almost as well as the bombs.' To Jean he wrote: 'It isn't the end, though the end is much nearer. For us, ourselves, my darling, it is the opening of the skies.'

During that summer, with its stifling heat, Hoare became unsettled by the apparent hostility of the Foreign Office, but Alan stood by him manfully. In a Secret and Personal letter to Churchill of 28 July 1943 he warned the Prime Minister that the Ambassador was 'not so well content and full of fight' as he had been before. Hoare, he said, was wondering whether 'H.M. Government really want him to stay on in Spain'. Alan himself had noticed how the FO seemed to 'look askance' at what Hoare was doing, and contrived to give the impression that British policy in Spain was *his* policy.

> While every man of sense knows that ambassadors imple-
> ment policy, but do not form it, there are too many people
> without sense, and my Ambassador finds himself pilloried
> as a Fascist and as hand in glove with Franco, whom, in
> fact, he abominates . . . Probably it is none of my business
> to make suggestions, but I have made so many about
> Spain in the past three years that I feel sure you will not
> mind one more.

Alan felt that 'the Foreign Office was hiding behind Hoare's pre-war reputation as an appeaser, in order to pursue a complaisant line towards Franco' – and his protest stirred Churchill, who on 6 August sent him a line, addressing him as 'My Dear Hillgarth' and thanking him for his letter, which he passed to the Foreign Secretary, Anthony Eden, with a note:

> This absolutely private letter written me by Captain Hillgarth, of whom I think very highly, should have your attention. I want Sam to stay on in Spain for I do not see any other work for him at the present time . . . He has done very well in Spain and I am impressed by the way in which he evidently commands the admiration of a man like Hillgarth who has seen his work so long at close quarters and is an extremely independent person, wealthy, well-married, retired from the Navy before the war and largely resident in Spain or Majorca. I should be quite willing to submit his [Sam's] name for a Civil G.C.B if you think it would help.

Eden stalled, saying that he thought any award should await the end of Hoare's term; and he claimed that there was 'no truth in the suggestion' that the Ambassador was not fully supported by the Foreign Office. On the other hand, he admitted that his minions were 'sometimes irritated by the Ambassador's habit of dressing up bogeys and then complimenting himself on their demolition'.

In the middle of August 1943, with his time in Madrid running out, Alan took a Spanish naval officer, a great friend, out to dinner, and was not altogether pleased by what he heard:

> He told me what a lot of Spaniards think of me. They think I'm Machiavelli. I knew it before, of some of them, but I suppose when you're going you may expect to hear more true opinions. Sad reflection. I'm supposed, in certain circles, to be I don't know what, and to have arranged

everything here for a long time. Without giving me any credit for loving the country and the people. But I don't mind. It's always complimentary to know that people are afraid of you. As they seem to be. But already I've met a lot of genuine regret at my leaving.

When he left Madrid in October, many favourable comments sent him on his way. Godfrey – now put out to grass as flag officer commanding the Royal Indian Navy – gave him a ringing endorsement. In his time as Naval Attaché, the admiral wrote, Alan had 'conducted himself very greatly to my satisfaction. Of outstanding ability he has done exceptional work at a most difficult time in Anglo-Spanish relations. An officer of great initiative and determination.'

In London Alan stayed at the Army & Navy Club or the Savile, and spent most of the next few weeks learning about his new role. One day he went to Eton and took Jocelyn out to lunch: together they watched boys playing the Field Game, which to Alan 'looked remarkably like a cross between rugger and socker' [sic]. He was glad to find that Jocelyn was doing well academically and becoming more independent – but still he could not tell him his awful secret. He knew that sooner or later, Mary would break the bad news to their son – and when she did, Jocelyn felt bitterly estranged from his father, refusing to see or speak to him.

Had Alan's naval colleagues known what was going on in his heart and in his head, they would have been astonished. Not only was this highly efficient and apparently straightforward naval attaché secretly in love, and learning as fast as he could about the Far East: he was also nursing a strange idea for a new novel. All his books had been to some extent fantastical extensions of his own experience – but this one was something more mysterious.

A sketch he made on four sheets of the heavy foolscap paper used for Admiralty minutes, with NOTHING TO BE WRITTEN IN THIS MARGIN printed vertically up the left-hand column, gives a fascinating glimpse of his imagination at work. The narrator of the story was to be John Wingram, aged thirty, 'on holiday after an illness consequent on a muddled love affair that led to a scandal and the death of his mother'. The opening sentences immediately suggested Spain and a feeling of desolation:

> I have been walking for several days through a pleasant mountain country, avoiding towns and keeping to the comparatively deserted uplands. One evening, tired and perhaps a little lost . . . I come down through terraced olive groves into a lightless valley that drops gently between dark slopes thick with trees.

After nightfall the traveller reaches an old-fashioned farm-house, where he is reluctantly taken in as a lodger. The place has a strange atmosphere – 'something odd, breathless, brooding'. He is given supper and shown to a bedroom, but before he goes to sleep he looks out of the window and sees a fairy dancing 'in a space between the hills'.

The narrator sketches the local characters: the old farmer (unnamed), the farmer's wife, Mathilde, the carter, Marín, 'the girl', Marida, 'twenty-two or so, dark and beautiful, in love with Marín'. But the creature who really grips the storyteller's imagination is the fairy:

> Grand-daughter of the farmer, by their only daughter, who died. No one knows who the husband was. She disappeared in the mountains for a year and came back one night only to give birth and die.
>
> Not a midget. Not a dwarf. Ten inches high. Perfect in

feature and in figure. Dark blue eyes and hair of red gold, and flowing curls. Prefers night to day. Frightened of some animals but friends with those she knows. Will ride on the dog. Unhappy with the cat but has an understanding.

Can sing in a strange tongue – a voice like thistledown, drifting with the wind, light as a flute but clear as a deep-toned bell. In speaking, minute volume but quite clear and one soon forgets the tiny nature of the voice. Full of wonder and strange sayings. Has a sense of companionship beyond human knowledge . . . Age seventeen. Sometimes imperious. Always slightly mocking except when melancholy. Will say strange things . . . Likes Marín and depends on him but teases him. He is desperately in love with her.

Are there elements of Jean in this curiously precise and vivid sketch? One cannot tell; but Alan was haunted by his vision of the fairy for many years, and mentioned it to friends in Ireland during the 1970s.

His story seems to have progressed no farther – and in view of his schedule, that is hardly surprising. On 7 November he went down to Chequers for discussions with Churchill, and then spent four days in what he discreetly called 'a naval establishment in the country', learning his new trade. Back in London, a bad reaction to inoculations for paratyphoid and tetanus depressed him, and led him to exclaim, 'I am appalled by the difficulties of my new job'. He was wounded by reports that people had been telling 'rotten stories' about him, but responded vigorously in a letter to Jean, who was still in Lisbon: 'I just don't care. I have done my duty as well as I was able, and no more can any man do. I have never allowed my private feeling to interfere with my duty.'

Jean had become his rock and the hiding place of all his innermost thoughts. 'When I hear you I feel strengthened and re-armed,' he wrote, 'girded with faith and drawn forward with the promise of fairyland.' Her feelings were much the same: 'I cling to you here in this unreal world, and always will no matter where I am, for you are everything.' It was a cruel stroke of fate that, with their emotions at such a pitch, duty should send him to the far side of the earth, to carry on fighting a war that seemed to have no end.

Far East

Alan left England on 14 December 1943, on the first of the marathon journeys which occupied much of his next two years. He flew prodigious distances, almost always in slow, primitive military aircraft, often unheated, with tiresomely frequent stops for refuelling. Wherever he went, his rank and position made him a Very Important Passenger, and sometimes he was able to commandeer a small plane of his own; but normally he was as prone as any other traveller to maddening delays, when engines failed and had to be repaired or monsoon storms forced pilots to turn back. In all he reckoned he covered more than 200,000 miles and he crossed the Indian Ocean six times.

One compensation for many hundred hours of boredom and discomfort in the air was the chance the flights gave him to write to Jean – and write he did, one impassioned letter after another, scribbling page after page with a pencil on any paper he could procure, his script always wonderfully legible in spite of the aircraft's unpredictable movements. Jean, too, wrote indefatigably, and both correspondents numbered their letters, so that the recipient could tell if any had gone astray. The system worked fairly well, but was often disrupted by the vagaries of the wartime postal service, when letters went missing or landed out of sequence. Often four or five arrived simultaneously, with information contained in the earlier ones already superseded. All, except those that went by Diplomatic Bag, were liable to be opened and read by the censors.

Alan's first journey – out to Delhi – was typically staccato. A two-hour hop took him from England to Gibraltar, but there he was held up by a twenty-four-hour delay. On the third day he flew low over the North African desert, where he saw hundreds of smashed tanks and lorries lying in the sand. After another hold-up he crossed the Suez Canal at dawn and thought the Sinai desert looked 'somehow terrible', partly because he imagined the Israelites wandering for forty years in that arid terrain, and 'wondered which mountain Moses had climbed to receive the Commandments from Our Lord'.

Coming into Delhi at last, after a seven-day trip, he saw the city's great buildings from the air and touched down in the Indian capital on the afternoon of 21 December, to find that he had been billeted not (as he had feared) in a tent, but in the Viceroy's palatial house, with a bedroom and bathroom all his own. He had also been allotted a bearer, Nizam, 'a nice gentle creature, very efficient and good and by no means a fool' – but, 'owing to an idiot in Gibraltar', most of his gear had been sent back to England, and he had to go out and buy sheets, towels, pillowcases and a lamp.

His first impression of the city was of 'a beautiful nightmare', all pink buildings and white cupolas. 'We British seem to be superimposed on India, not to belong to it at all,' he told Jean. 'Yet because we do belong to it, in the sense of running it, the whole thing is a contradiction and therefore unreal.' Much more earthly were the jackals, which he heard howling whenever he came home at night.

He was under no illusions about the difficulties of his job as Chief of Intelligence Staff (COIS), under Admiral Sir James Somerville, and reporting ultimately to the Supreme Commander, South East Asia Command, Lord Louis Mountbatten. He got on well with Somerville, whom he had met in Ibiza in 1936, and later in life he told his children that his main task in the Far East had been to keep the peace between the British and the Americans. This was said only half in jest, for when he arrived in theatre relations between the two were edgy, to say the least.

Until then the United States Navy had fought a lone and bloody maritime war against the Japanese in the Pacific, and American officers – perhaps not appreciating how fully committed the British were to the battle against the U-boats in the Atlantic – resented the fact that the Royal Navy had not come earlier to the aid of the US Pacific Fleet. Now they were eager to finish off Japan on their own, and reluctant for the British to gain kudos by joining in at the last minute. Some Americans cynically claimed that SEAC stood for 'Save England's Asian Colonies'.

It was the surprise Japanese attack on Pearl Harbor in Hawaii on 7 December 1941 that had brought the Americans into the war. Stung into action, they had set about reconstructing their shattered battle fleet with phenomenal energy, and during the next two years they built up their Pacific Fleet to a strength never equalled in naval history. Because the distances involved were so huge, they also put together a very large Fleet Train of transport vessels that supplied the combat units. As Alan himself put it, 'every single thing needed, every round of ammunition, every gallon of fuel and every pound of food, every article of equipment, everything, had to be brought over thousands and thousands of miles of sea'.

Britain, in contrast, was poorly represented in the East. Stretched to its limits in the Atlantic, the Royal Navy could spare no modern warships for the defence of the Indian Ocean; and after the Japanese had attacked Ceylon (now Sri Lanka) in January 1942, hoping (but failing) to achieve a second Pearl Harbor in the bases at Colombo and Trincomalee, the elderly ships of the British Eastern Fleet had withdrawn to the east coast of Africa, where they remained for nearly two years.

The Americans lost no time in starting to counter-attack in the Pacific. In the great battle of Midway, fought between aircraft-carrier forces at the north-western end of the Hawaian islands, from 4 to 7 June 1942, they beat off Japanese attempts to take over their base on the atoll, not least because intelligence sources had intercepted the enemy's communications and discovered their plan of attack. From that moment the Americans began to master the powerful Japanese navy, with its hundreds of carrier-based fighters – but more than two years of ferocious battles passed, and thousands of American lives were lost, before the British were in a position to add to their allies' strike power.

When Churchill offered to send a Royal Naval detachment to the Pacific in the autumn of 1943, Admiral Ernest King, the American Commander-in-Chief, was at first anything but enthusiastic. Whether he simply disliked the British (as some people thought), or whether he doubted the ability of the Royal Navy to adapt its ships and operations to the vast distances of the Pacific, he later became more appreciative, and preparations to send a British fleet to the Far East were begun early in 1944.

Thus Alan arrived in Delhi at a time of intensive planning activity. The main British naval base was being constructed in Sydney, and huge stocks of stores and equipment were being shipped to Australia. The Torres Strait, between Australia and New Guinea, was being dredged to allow the passage of battleships. Alan's own task was to devise an intelligence network, scattered across thousands of miles of ocean, which would eavesdrop on Japanese communications and by deceptive radio traffic obfuscate the position of British and American naval forces, create phantom units which did not exist, decoy the enemy away from real targets and lure them to fruitless rendezvous by adumbrating manoeuvres which were not going to happen.

He had already discerned that if the working of intelligence against the Japanese was to be effective he must have an autonomous organisation, free from the Admiralty's preoccupation with the Atlantic and the Mediterranean. With Churchill's backing, he had acquired the necessary authority to develop British naval intelligence in the Eastern Theatre, and to build cooperation with American and Australian intelligence bodies.

At first he operated from Delhi, where Mountbatten still had his headquarters. He acquired a bicycle, on which he rode to and from his office, keeping his own timetable. 'As long as I produce the goods, I don't have to bother about my own hours,' he told Jean. 'As a result, perhaps, I'm seldom on time but always last to leave . . . I have to break rules, or I should go mad. I *can't* conform to sameness, whether of civilian custom or service requirements.' His whole policy, he said (perhaps with a touch of exaggeration), was 'to decentralise as much as possible and to do as little actual work as possible. If you don't do exactly that, in a complex job like mine, you either become a nervous wreck sooner or later or you drop dead from overwork.' To help ward off either of those fates he had taken the precaution of importing his own supply of sherry and brandy 'for dinner parties'.

On a tour of the city he admired the Red Fort – the mighty seventeenth-century palace of the Mughal emperor Shah Jahan – and reflected that the British governance of India had always been a bluff. 'But is it bluff if a few of you are really leaders and really ready to sacrifice yourselves for what you believe in? Nowadays the idea of Empire is *démodé*. We fight not for our country, but for ill-defined international ideals.'

Early in 1944 he moved his base to Colombo, the capital of Ceylon, on the south-western corner of the island, where he arrived for the first time early in February. His office faced the ocean, and all he could see, sitting at his desk, was the water. In the stifling heat and saturating humidity he soon got used to spending the day in white shirt, shorts and stockings, 'like a white boy scout'; but within a week he went down with dengue fever and spent several days in bed with a temperature of 102.5°. Although he recovered quickly, he was left feeling lonely and despondent. For the time being his work was dull, because Europe was still the centre of action. 'I long to come and take you away,' he told Jean, 'but not here. We don't belong here in the tropics. Europe is more our home.' Then a day at Nuwara Eliya, 1,500 feet above sea level in Ceylon's central mountains, made him feel 'ten times better and stronger'. Apart from the drop in temperature which the height created, he loved the 'green meadows and lakes like Scottish tarns and little but wild waterfalls and great tree-covered mountains of impressive but very friendly majesty'.

This was the setting that beguiled Mountbatten, who shifted his headquarters from Delhi to Colombo at the same time – a move that necessitated several aircraft and four special trains – and established an enormous hutted camp of almost 10,000 staff at Kandy. This he considered 'probably the most beautiful spot in the world' – as well he might, living himself in the King's Pavilion, far above the privations of those condemned to work on the coast.

The hub of Alan's empire was HMS Anderson, an establishment so deeply secret that even Mountbatten knew almost nothing about it, except that it produced vital information about enemy ships, their positions and their movements. (In 1977 he asked Alan for details of Anderson, on behalf of the historian Arthur Marder, who was collecting information about the war in the Far East. 'I know Anderson had a tremendously high reputation,' Mountbatten wrote, 'but, of course, what you did was so secret that practically nobody spoke about it and I can find no records.')

In spite of its name, Anderson was no ship, but a radio station next to the golf course about ten miles out of Colombo, once semi-derelict but now refurbished. The staff included signals officers, cryptanalysts, interpreters, telegraphists and WRNS personnel, who intercepted and analysed Japanese radio traffic coming in from the Pacific and Indian Oceans and passed relevant information on to the Code and Cypher School at Bletchley Park. All the station's documents were marked 'To be destroyed by fire if superseded'.

In 1942 decrypts from Anderson had given advance warning of plans for the Japanese attack on Colombo, enabling the British to limit damage by strengthening the defences and getting the fleet to sea. For safety, the facility was then moved to Kilindini, on the coast of Kenya, but returned to Colombo late in 1943, and over the next two years became the control centre for an immensely wide scatter of D/F (direction-finding) stations, from Durban and Mauritius in the west to the South China Sea and the Strait of Malacca in the east, taking in the whole of the Indian Ocean and reaching as far to the south-east as Cocos Keeling, an atoll in the Cocos Islands half way from Colombo to Perth in Western Australia. All these out-stations were manned round the clock, seven days a week.

Anderson was spaciously laid out on a level, open site surrounded by jungle. Dozens of single-storey huts with shallow verandahs lined the roads, with beds of shrubs softening their rectangular shapes. Some of the buildings had tiled roofs, but most were clad in rattan, which was cooler. The all-important direction-finding hut stood alone, bristling with aerials, in a clear, round space 200 yards in diameter, with no other struc-tures near it.

The main reception area had some 100 receiver bays which monitored the medium-frequency bands most used by the Japanese. Each bay was manned by one or two operators, who were allotted a single Japanese radio channel to monitor: their

job was to record all signals, and to alert their superiors if they
detected transmissions from an enemy vessel. The bulk of their
work was in H/F D/F – high-frequency direction-finding,
commonly known as 'Huff-Duff' – and analysis of radio traffic,
aimed at locating Japanese ships of all kinds from their signals,
so that British or American aircraft, submarines and surface
craft could be guided towards them and given a better chance
of intercepting them. As the war went on, more and more
destroyers were equipped with direction-finding parties and
Huff-Duff antennae, which enabled them to pick up telltale
signals at a range of fifty miles.

Anderson was able to decipher Purple, the code used by
the Japanese for diplomatic messages, which the Americans had
broken in 1940, and the station also received Ultra decrypts
from Bletchley Park; but its principal strength was its ability
to read the 'fingerprints' of individual Japanese ships' transmissions:

> Individual operators, of course, had their own recognisable
> styles of using their keypad, and signal intelligence had
> earlier perfected the art of reading individuals' transmis-
> sions. But W/T transmitters also left their own tell-tale
> evidence, so that even though operators came and went,
> W/T equipment remained.

The difficulties of direction-finding in such a huge area are
well illustrated by entries in Anderson's daily records. Many
call-signs were known for sure: U SU 7, for instance, was the
collective sign for the Japanese 4th Fleet, and KE SO3 the
Yokohama flying-boat squadron. But there was much uncertainty: 'Ships marked + are those most frequently heard,
undoubtedly destroyers . . . Others may be junior destroyers
or armed auxiliaries.' 'Call-signs underlined are considered to
have a fair degree of reliability, while the rest are considered

tentative suggestions.' 'HA N4 has the appearance of being a fixed station . . . This would be on PARACE VELA (Douglas Reef).' Another entry: 'U-boat A in Japan, fitting new battery. ST off Sydney, torpedoed ship on 24th. WE probably in Japan, due to complete repairs, docking and alterations in January.'

There was always a chance that the listeners were being hoodwinked:

> The exceptionally heavy activity on 8/9 and 9/9 inter-cepted at Bimlipatam is of interest, as it adds weight to the inference made last month that this unit may use dummy aircraft call-signs for deception at the same time as it is carrying out operational patrols.

Alan's spirits rose as he flew down to Australia for the first time, and then across the continent from Perth – a comfortable journey in a peacetime-style airliner, with meals and drinks on board and a stewardess ('called an air hostess'). But even this luxurious conveyance had to refuel three times – at Kalgoorlie, Forrest and Ceduna – on its way from Perth to Adelaide. Going on to Brisbane, Melbourne and Canberra, Alan quickly became fascinated by Australia – 'a most sympa-thetic and interesting country'. At Brisbane he swam in the Pacific – his first sea bathe since 1941 – and played with the three sons of his host (an admiral) in the shallows. A shark was reported, but it turned out to be a penguin. The boys, aged nine, seven and five, were adorable, he reported, 'but nothing to what your sons will be – and daughters. *Our* sons and daughters.'

Work frequently took him back from Colombo to Delhi for short periods, and the 1,600-mile flight north could normally be accomplished in a day, but sometimes during the monsoon season it took three: as Alan remarked, 'aircraft do have to admit defeat now and then'. As in Madrid, to his staff he seemed enigmatic and slightly alarming. On the one hand, if someone had personal problems, he showed great kindness, but on the other, he could be ruthless in the Navy's interest. As Charles Sheppard, one of his senior intelligence officers, remembered, 'On arrival he was always rushed to the C-in-C Eastern Fleet as someone with the latest news on the highest direction of the war, who had had a private meal with Churchill just before leaving.'

His people saw him as a trouble-shooter who could always get things done – recruit extra officers, change the organisation – in a way that no one else could manage. They saw, also, that he had a powerful imagination, coupled with a certain ruthlessness and determination to achieve what he thought right for the Navy – and this sometimes caused ructions in the NID. When things were going well, he would exclaim '*Bueno! Bueno!* – Good! Good!' and in due course 'Bueno' became his nickname, faintly mocking but also affectionate.

He was well aware of his own reputation, and did nothing to soften it. 'A lot of people know me,' he once told Jean,

but I'm very much an enigma to most of them and regarded with suspicion because I don't fit into any category. I'm not an ordinary naval officer . . . and I'm not a diplomat *de carrière*, and I'm always doing things my own way, and they can't make me fit in, and they hate it and dislike me in consequence . . . I'm a trouble-maker. I ride the storm. So I come in useful when times are unpleasant . . . and you have to act and be bold. But as soon as that's over, I'm just a nuisance . . . and I'm happier in the shadow than in the limelight.

This last remark was particularly apt: he liked to make things happen without being in the forefront of the action. To achieve his ends, he recruited staff from a wide variety of sources – the

Royal Air Force, the Royal New Zealand Air Force, the Indian
Navy and the Dutch Navy, among others – and he would
sometimes deliberately startle them by making outrageous
remarks, which they never forgot. To his secretary, Captain Bill
Michell: 'I regard you, Michell, as a shyster lawyer employed
by a gang of crooks to keep them out of trouble!' Again: 'We
are getting ten new sub-lieutenants this week. We will send
them to New Guinea. Some of them will get fever, and some
will die, but it will be good experience.'

Commander John Parker, who worked closely with him in
Colombo and Australia, found that he 'always appeared to be
surrounded by an air of mystery which I am sure he encouraged'.

He was a four-ring Captain, Royal Navy [equivalent to
a full colonel in the army], and a contemporary of most
of the senior officers in the Fleet – so apart from the
friends in high places at home he had considerable built-
in influence. Unlike the other regular R.N. and R.M.
officers in intelligence, he did not have the compulsive
itch to get back to sea which they had to protect their
careers.

His predecessor as Chief of Intelligence Staff, East Indies,
had been shunted into the position of a figurehead in
Delhi, while the power remained with his Deputy in
Colombo. It had been hoped by the shunters that he
would remain in that harmless position, but he had come
out to do a job, and he intended to do it. He soon took
full charge of the organisation.

As usual, he gave the people round him no inkling of his
innermost thoughts, which were directed 5,000 miles westwards. Already he was considering names for the children he
and Jean were going to have, and he seems to have become

convinced that the first would be a girl, whom he would call
Nigella – 'an Elizabethan name'. Once on a slip of paper
headed 'The Australia Hotel, Sydney' he pencilled a list of
twelve names: as usual, Nigella was the front-runner, followed
by Clorinda, with Adrian, Sebastian, Francis and a string of
others bringing up the rear.

In March 1944 Jean at last decided to leave Lisbon and go
back to England, partly so that, face to face, she could tell her
parents about Alan, whom she had never mentioned in her
letters home. She was reluctant to leave Louise, who was still
inundated with Red Cross work, but she had done a long stint
– three years – and her employer was immensely grateful. 'Her
unselfishness, loyalty and consideration in everything have never
ceased to amaze me,' Louise told her mother. 'I would like to
end this letter by saying once more of what real assistance your
daughter has been and how much everyone who meets her
loves her.'

At home again in Sheffield, Jean found her father's Bentley
sitting in the garage, grounded by lack of petrol, alongside her
brother Ian's Rover. She was not much interested in cars, but
the sight made her reminisce about a Standard Swallow which
she had once owned – 'black, long and low . . . with a definite
personality'.

Although not in the least snobbish, she had been brought
up to certain standards, and she was pained to find that the
household now had 'almost no servants'. Renton, the ancient
gardener, was still doing a wonderful job, but 'Cook, poor old
thing, was too old, and the other maids were young and had
to be taken away to the factories, and Mummie – quite rightly
– won't have people in the house unless they are the kind of
servants she likes'. Jean herself was totally undomesticated, and
could hardly boil an egg.

She wanted to find a job, but in the past three years she
had lost a lot of weight – a whole stone: the 'old doctor' told

her she was far too thin, and must rest for three months before taking on any work. For a while she obediently stayed at home, but during the summer she went south to see other members of her family.

As Alan anxiously followed the progress of the war in Europe, he was encouraged by news of the D-Day landings early in June 1944, but then became worried by reports of Hitler's new weapons, the V-1 flying bombs, which began to rain down on south-east England in the middle of the month. He told Jean to stay away from London – a prohibition which, of course, she ignored.

'The trains are crowded beyond belief and hundreds of people are literally left on the platform,' she reported, but after a struggle she managed to reach London, stayed a night at Brown's Hotel and went on to Basingstoke, where she found her 'small Wren sister' Mavis. Next she stayed a night with her other sister, Sheila, by then a sergeant in the Women's Auxiliary Air Force, at her camp near Aylesbury. But all her most intense thoughts were directed eastwards, and at home again she spread out the heavy volumes of the *Encyclopaedia Britannica* so that she could try to work out from occasional hints where Alan might be. 'Are we mad, dear love, to love one another so and hope one day to be together always, surrounded as we are by difficulties?' she asked. 'If we are, how do we become sane?'

Alan was not much enjoying Colombo. 'I'm with the Eastern Fleet now, fighting the Japanese,' he told Anne Hamilton. 'Very interesting, especially as they are such loathsome animals. But I don't care for the tropics much.' In spite of the heat and humidity, he was riding out again in the mornings, having imported, at fearful expense, a fifteen-hand chestnut cob called Timmy, 'reliable but full of energy'. The horse had cost £30, but the bill for its transport from Delhi had been £57 – 'a bit of a facer'.

In September 1944 he returned briefly to England for

high-level briefings, and also for an examination at the Middlesex Hospital, which revealed, by means of a barium meal, that 'the duodenal cap [of the stomach] was deformed by scarring, and an ulcer was present on the posterior wall'. This was tiresome news; but no operation was prescribed. The summit of his stay must have been his reunion with Jean, and the next highest point his first meeting with her parents, which turned out an all-round success. On 19 September he wrote to her mother from Claridge's:

> You have given me more pleasure and shown me more kindness than I can hope to tell you . . . Both you and her father have been wonderful to me . . . Everything I told you about Jean and myself is true. She matters to me more than anything else in this world.

All too soon he was off again, westwards for once, heading for America at the start of another hectic schedule. In Washington he was impressed by the White House and the Lincoln and Jefferson memorials, and by Washington's home, Mount Vernon, on the Potomac, but he liked best of all the Mellon Art Gallery. About his task in the American capital, of course, he said nothing.

His next major stop was San Francisco, whence he flew in a comfortable Clipper, fitted with sleeping bunks, to the headquarters of the United States Pacific Fleet on Honolulu, in mid-ocean. Down across the Pacific he went, slanting south-westwards as he island-hopped to the Marshalls, the Carolines, the Admiralties and New Guinea, passing within a dozen miles of islands still occupied by the Japanese bases, but now treated by the Americans with contempt. So much work lay ahead of him that he signalled in advance for his personal assistant, Second Officer Clare Blanshard, to fly down from Colombo to Melbourne with papers, and meet him there. When he arrived on 22 October he found she had beaten him to it by a few days. She was the first WRNS officer ever seen in Australia, and the WRNAS had given her a marvellous welcome.

Alan was still in Australia when the largest naval battle of the war raged for four days, from 23 to 26 October 1944, near the island of Leyte in the Philippines. For the first time the Japanese used kamikaze (suicide) bombers, whose pilots flew their aircraft straight into ships, and both sides suffered severe losses; but those of the Japanese were far the heavier – twenty-five of their front-line warships were sunk, as opposed to the Americans' six. It was a crushing defeat, and command of the sea effectively passed to the United States' Third Fleet.

By then Alan's ulcer was causing him serious discomfort. As soon as he returned to Colombo he was ordered to bed and told to remain there for a month at least, on a diet of 'milky feeds' ('It sounds oddly indecent,' he told Jean.) The doctors' hope was that, without the irritation caused by hard food, the ulcer would heal over. With his staff officers coming to see him, he could get through a good deal of work, but his doctor told him to move as little as possible. Gradually he progressed from Horlicks every two hours to 'toast and butter and a little fruit and eggs & fish and custard', but he was warned that when he got up he must do things very gradually, and he was told not to ride for six months. At last, after twenty-nine days horizontal, he was allowed to eat some minced chicken, and started going back to the office, much disheartened by the thought that, if he could not ride, he would have to get rid of Timmy. (He did, in the end, sell the horse for 800 rupees to Mr Mehdi Hussain, with the proviso that he could buy the animal back at the same price, should he ever want to.)

In October Admiral Sir Bruce Fraser succeeded Somerville as Commander of the Eastern Fleet, and then in November became Commander-in-Chief of the newly formed British

Pacific Fleet, with his headquarters on shore at Sydney, in Australia. The base there was still being built, and the Fleet Train was gradually assembling (in the end it amounted to 168 vessels). The first warships of the new fleet reached Colombo in December, and on the 17th, in a preliminary strike, Operation ROBSON, a small force of two aircraft carriers, HMS *Indomitable* and HMS *Illustrious*, escorted by three cruisers and five destroyers, sailed out of Trincomalee to attack the big oil refineries at Palembang, in southern Sumatra. This sortie, and a second a fortnight later, this time with three carriers, proved very successful, and provided useful lessons in the use of American tactics, in which many more aircraft (Avengers, Corsairs, Hellcats and Seafires) were deployed than the British had been accustomed to launching.

In a report on ROBSON Alan remarked that 'the "Y" (direction-finding) party in *Illustrious*

> had a successful trip, both reception and working condi-
> tions being good. The lack of reaction by the Japanese
> prevented the information which they secured being of
> tactical advantage to the fleet, but the messages intercepted
> by them consistently enabled them to account for all air
> activity in the vicinity . . . Three fighter formations were
> positively identified and the information passed on to our
> own aircraft.

In Colombo Christmas 1944 was enlivened by the arrival of Ian Fleming, who seemed to have an enviable freedom to fly to any part of the globe that he fancied visiting. On this occa-sion the DNI had sent him to review the intelligence structure which Alan had been setting up – and he did indeed write two reports about it. But his most immediate preoccupation seems to have been with Clare Blanshard, who was 'swept off her feet by this handsome, educated naval officer in his tropical uniform'. She was certainly stirred, and perhaps a bit shaken. 'He's the right shape, size, height, has the right sort of hair, the right sort of laugh, is thirty-six and beautiful,' she told her brother. 'I wish I were more glamorous.' It was she who joked that the initials of Alan's title (Chief of British Naval Intelligence Eastern Theatre) stood for Chief Bloody Nuisance in Eastern Theatre.

In the excitement of a lightning conquest Ian perhaps exaggerated Clare's good looks. One night, in an aeroplane, Alan recorded that she was 'asleep with an even grimmer look than when awake (she's not really grim, but very serious and severe-looking, though first class and invaluable)'. When Ian took her to a Christmas dance in the nightclub of the Galle Face Hotel, she wore a long white silk dress studded with little pieces of silver, so glamorous that he remembered it for years.

After the festivities he took off for Delhi to visit his elder brother Peter, who by then was a lieutenant colonel in the Grenadier Guards, and seconded to command Mountbatten's strategic deception unit, D Division. In his attempts to mislead the Japanese on land Peter was up to every sort of trick – a remit which gave free rein to his irrepressible sense of humour. Many of his ruses were successful, for, as he himself recorded, the enemy's intelligence staff were 'amazingly credulous, and willing to swallow the most outrageous and implausible fabrications'. Knowing this, he encouraged one of his own agents to keep telling a Japanese contact that the ruling family of Japan had short, furry tails, of which they were inordinately proud.

No doubt Peter and Ian exchanged plenty of seasonal jokes. Alan, in contrast, spent Christmas working, and sadly gave his stock of sherry to the servants and orderlies, since his ulcer prevented him from drinking it. But he reported cheerfully to Jean: 'My friend Ian Fleming here on a brief visit . . . He's a help, and what he does for me at home will solve a lot of my problems. It's nice seeing him, because he brings a breath of the big world.'

In January Fleming returned to Colombo, and on the night of 23–24 January 1945 he, Alan and Clare set off together for Australia on what proved a nightmare trip. Their first aircraft, a Catalina flying boat, turned back after two hours with engine trouble, and on returning to base Alan found that the room in which he had spent the first part of the night had been given away. He tried to sleep in another room but was viciously bitten by bed bugs. He then slept for a while on a sofa, but was incensed by further privations: his car was being repaired and unavailable, and his bearer had gone on leave to his village. No wonder he told Jean: 'I felt savage with fate.'

Under way again, the party spent the night of the 26th in an unheated plane at 10,000 feet, wearing flying suits and boots, buried under coats and rugs. They reached Perth on the 27th, after nearly twenty-six hours in the air, and went on to Adelaide, then Melbourne, and finally Sydney, where, in mid-summer, Ian and Clare disported themselves in night-clubs and on Whale Beach, while Alan kept several essential rendezvous.

That journey entitled him to membership of 'the rare and secret order of the double sunrise' and a cheerful certificate, awarded by Qantas Empire Airways to anyone who spent 'more than twenty-four hours continuously in the air on a regular air service'. In Australia he had been made an honorary member of various clubs, and could stay comfortably in them, but he deplored the 'pagan hours' at which members dined – 6.30 or 7 p.m. He had sized up the natives carefully, and told Jean:

The one thing never to do [with Australians] is to let them imagine for an instant that you think you're supe-rior to them. We're not, anyway, and I never would, but they are rather on the lookout for it with English people

. . . They respond immediately to friendliness and good manners. And I genuinely like them.

Fleming left the party at Sydney to continue his global tour, and on 4 February 1945 he sent a heartfelt personal note from the headquarters of the Commander-in-Chief, United States Pacific Fleet, thanking Alan for all he had done:

You could not have been more kind from the moment I stepped ashore in Colombo to the day I left Sydney. I must often have been a pest, but you were patient as an angel. I could not be more grateful or more appreciative.

Then, congratulations from the bottom of my heart on the way you have handled your job. It has been a grand success, and I shall say so forcefully from the housetops. The best evidence is the remarks I heard everywhere from the C-in-C down in Ceylon and from the C-o-S in Sydney – and the devotion of your staff at both centres. If only you could see what you have accomplished, from outside, as I can, you would be very proud, and there would be no depression in your house. You have one of the key appointments in a historical phase of our navy's operations, and a free hand, and hot and cold laid on! You will remember these coming months all your life. Pray see more of the wood and less of the trees.

Please give my best love to the angel Clare. I will write to her from London. She is a jewel, and I miss her protective wing very much.

Well, goodbye again Alan. I will fight your battles in London, and you will be there soon. Look after yourself very well.

Yours ever, Ian.

In London Jean had found herself an unpaid job as a secretary in the Membership Department of the Royal Institute of International Affairs at Chatham House in St James's Square – an organisation (she explained to Alan) which 'collects knowledge of international affairs & does research & works for a better understanding between nations'. She soon decided that she was not cut out to be a secretary ('It isn't me, this role'), but persevered, feeling that she must make herself useful, until she became so bored that she declared: 'It's quite a long time since I felt so rebellious.'

Alan continued to travel prodigiously, believing that only personal contact with his far-flung workforce could achieve the results he was seeking. In 1945 alone Qantas five times awarded him the 'Rare and Elevated Order of the Longest Hop', certifying that he had crossed the Indian Ocean by the Kangaroo air service, on flights taking from sixteen to nineteen hours. Although he wrote thousands of words to Jean, he never made the slightest mention of his secret assignations. Nor did he worry her by describing the hazards of his long-range journeys. On one trip his aircraft started losing height above jungle-clad mountains occupied by the Japanese. The pilot, nursing his sick engines, yelled at his passengers to open the door in the side of the fuselage and throw out all their kit and supplies – which they did, with the result that they lightened the plane just enough for it to skim the ridge ahead and land safely.

As the pressure of Allied attacks built up, intercepted Japanese signals passing through Anderson became increasingly desperate – as in the 8th Base Air Force Orders for 25 March: 'Personnel will be given suicide training. Attack aircraft: Type 1 land-based attack aircraft will be supplied as suicide aircraft. . . Ship-based attack aircraft units, ship-based bomber units and ship-based recce aircraft units will be formed into suicide units'. On 11 April an order went out to all bases to increase the number of operational aircraft 'by carrying out hasty repairs with parts on hand, including those you have thrown aside as scrap.'

Early in April the British Pacific Fleet, by then designated 'Task Force 57', at last had a chance to demonstrate that it could operate as an effective partner alongside the US Navy, when it joined Admiral Raymond Spruance's US 5th Fleet. Compared with the Americans' huge armada, it was still relatively small, consisting of four battleships, eleven cruisers and eighteen aircraft-carriers, reinforced by ships of the Australian and New Zealand navies; but it had one major advantage, in that the steel decks of its carriers were more heavily armoured than those of the Americans, and better able to withstand the impact of kamikaze aircraft. Whereas a crashing Japanese fighter-bomber was liable to penetrate the deck of a US ship, causing disastrous explosions and fires inside the hull, similar planes often bounced off the decks of British carriers or finished in crumpled heaps, which could be washed overboard by the fire hoses. As one American officer put it, 'When a kamikaze hits a U.S. carrier, it means six months of repair at Pearl. When a kamikaze hits a Limey carrier, it's just a case of "Sweepers, man your brooms".'

The Battle of Okinawa – known to the Allies as Operation ICEBERG – began early in April and lasted until the middle of June: eighty-two days of desperate fighting on land and sea. The aim was to clear the Japanese armed forces from the Ryukyu archipelago – the long chain running down from the southernmost point of Japan itself – and to establish a base on the island of Okinawa for a final assault on the mainland. American ground forces fought desperate battles ashore, and the main hazard to the ships were the kamikaze planes, which came not singly but in swarms, making mass attacks known as *kikusui* (one afternoon more than 700 aircraft, including 355 kamikaze, arrived over the US Fleet, and although 300 of them were shot down, they sank six destroyers).

In the course of a lecture on the conflict given after the war, Alan left a vivid description of Japan's latest weapon, the *Baka* (literally 'fool'), a small, single-seat monoplane armed with a 1,000-kg warhead. Carried slung under the fuselage of a medium bomber, it was aimed and launched up to ten miles from its target. The *Baka* had no engine, but rockets accelerated its descent, and it came down at almost 600 mph. Inside was a pilot, 'who had just time enough, at the colossal speed he was travelling, to influence the course a little so perhaps score a hit' – before he and his steed were blown to smithereens.

At Okinawa casualties on both sides were appalling: in the three-month battle the United States lost 12,000 men killed or missing; the US Navy alone lost nearly 5,000 men killed and almost the same number wounded. Twenty-eight Allied ships were sunk, and nearly 400 damaged. But the Japanese suffered far worse: one estimate put their casualties at 95,000 dead, and aircraft losses at 2,300.

In England immense rejoicing greeted VE Day, 8 May 1945 – the end of the war in the West; but in the East hostilities were still in full swing, and on 10 May Alan sent Churchill a substantial report on his activities and impressions, marked 'Top Secret and Personal', not hesitating to offer advice where he thought fit:

> I have been travelling about the whole Eastern Theatre for months now on the organisation and stimulation of Naval Intelligence, and I thought you might like a few observations on the whole battlefield.
>
> S.E.A.C. has at last grown up, by the [recent] capture of Rangoon, and can do almost what it likes now . . . There is a cohesion and a loyalty – and a more realistic point of view – about Admiral Mountbatten's team now which were sometimes lacking before, and he can now move from strength to strength.

The British Pacific Fleet has already established itself by its part in ICEBERG [the battle of Okinawa]. Our fleet carriers, with their armoured flight decks, resist the suicider better than the Americans, and we have borne more of our share of the burden than anyone anticipated . . . Relations with the U.S. Navy are now really cordial after initial suspicion. Sir Bruce Fraser began to break that down, and Operation ICEBERG has completed the process . . .

Australia is in a mood to welcome anything British. We have never had such a chance as we have now, both to consolidate a real feeling of kinship and to enlist Australian participation in the affairs of Empire . . . I feel that you need a Minister of State in the Eastern Theatre. He could watch and advise on all political and diplomatic and economic problems, of which there are going to be legion . . .

Forgive this rather discursive letter and my suggestions, but I feel it is quite likely that some of the things I have mentioned have not been brought to you before.

In July he sent a telegram of congratulation to Rushbrooke on his promotion to vice admiral, and in return received a generous letter of thanks:

I had a most interesting talk with the First Sea Lord [Cunningham] who was charming to me and made it clear that my promotion was a recognition of good naval intelligence in this war. So I am sending round a note to all the chaps to point out that they all, men and women, are entitled to feel satisfaction that their excellent work has been reflected in the promotion of their unworthy boss.

The Allied victory on Okinawa did indeed pave the way for a final assault on the mainland, but this, as it turned out, was never needed: Japan's will to resist further was shattered by the atom bombs on Hiroshima (6 August) and Nagasaki (9 August), which, together with the Russian invasion of Manchuria (also 9 August) precipitated the country's surrender on the 15th.

Alan found no joy in victory. Rather, he realised that managing the peace was going to be very difficult. Units of the former enemy were spread out over a hundred islands and territories; disarming them, taking over government of conquered territories, getting Allied prisoners repatriated from Hong Kong, Shanghai, Formosa, Borneo and Japan itself – all this would be a colossal task. He foresaw that he would soon have to go to London, to sort out 'a thousand bits of the wartime jigsaw'. Besides, he was disturbed by the use of the new weapons. 'I think this atomic business is horrible,' he told Jean, 'and the dangers attendant on it are terrifying. Mankind could have got on very well without it.' Nor was he impressed by the possible peaceful uses of nuclear power.

Surrender day found him once again in Australia. 'The people of Sydney have gone quite mad and have been dancing in the streets ever since,' he reported.

I think I've heard *Auld Lang Syne*, *There's a Long, Long Trail*, *Waltzing Matilda*, *Pack up Your Troubles* and a lot more of that sort, not to mention *Onward Christian Soldiers* and other hymns, at least ten times each. Then they play dance music, and *God Save the King* comes on about once an hour . . . On Saturday and Sunday there were disgraceful scenes and a lot of property was destroyed . . . there were some dangerous fires, some cars were broken up and the cenotaph was desecrated.

Celebrations in London were more decorous, but no less enthusiastic. People found the news of the surrender almost impossible to believe, but when Jean walked home from Chatham House in the afternoon, 'pieces of paper were showering down from windows and people were collecting in Piccadilly'.

Alan assured Jean that he was not 'slackening one instant' in his work, but admitted that he was no longer so actively or intensely interested. His aim, now, was to 'leave a good machine for others', after which his job would be over. Having decided that he must learn French properly – 'It'll be necessary in our new life' – he was reading Gabriel Chevallier's satirical novel *Clochemerle*, about a village convulsed by controversy about a plan to install a public urinal in the square. On his way back to Colombo he stopped at Cocos Island, halfway from Perth to Ceylon, where he was grounded all day by engine trouble. The island had been an important cable station during the war, and the Japanese could easily have taken it at any earlier stage of the conflict, so the British, not wanting to draw attention to it, had refrained from developing it until recently.

Back in his own office, he found that he had been promoted from lieutenant commander to commander on the Retired List for 'distinguished war service'. He also found a letter from Ian Fleming, who told him that Vickers, the arms manufacturers, might be going to invite him to be their representative in Spain and South America – 'an enormous job with a large salary and even larger expense account'. Although pleased by the compliment, he was little tempted by the offer, for he was already considering another idea for peacetime: that he might go into partnership with 'the Old Man' – his colleague in Spanish trickery, Juan March.

He hardly touched down in Colombo before setting off again on a quick visit to Singapore. He was fascinated by his flight down the Strait of Malacca, between Sumatra and Malaya, and then by the sight of two damaged Japanese cruisers anchored off the naval dockyard at Johore. Having looked

down on the whole of Singapore Island from the air, he found
the city 'really rather attractive', and was agreeably surprised
by the shops, which seemed to him to 'make a very good
showing', considering that the British had re-occupied the
place only a month earlier. He bought a thermos and two
pairs of silk pyjamas, both unobtainable anywhere else, and was
taken to dinner with a rich Chinese – 'eighteen courses, four
and a half hours'. He also visited the dockyard, where Japanese
prisoners had been put to work: 'A lot of muddle-headed
monkeys. Of course one can't descend to their level, and they
are made to work, but I don't think we go nearly far enough.
They should be degraded – treated with a constant severity
and beaten for any fault.'

As he expected, he was summoned back to England, and
made the long haul in October – but his stay was painfully
short. He reported to the War Cabinet and the Joint Planning
Staff, and Ian Fleming considered his progress through London
'a triumphal passage', calling him 'a 'useful petard and a good
war-winner'. He also had time to call on his solicitor, whom
he consulted about the formalities of obtaining a divorce, and
then he was gone again, after what he described to Jean as
'about the worst parting of all'.

As soon as he was airborne, he started to write:

Though we have no home, no place to stay in together
and make our own and keep in it the things we have and
will want to have, just now until that time comes all my
heart is your home and belongs only to you, and here
you can be at peace.

The journey turned out one of the most tedious ever. Having
spent a night at RAF Lyneham in a room with six other
officers ('all rather primitive'), he took off in a converted
Stirling bomber at 5 a.m. and stayed for the next night with

Don Gómes-Beare at Gibraltar. Then he went on through
Tripoli, Benina (a Dakota with hard aluminium seats facing
each other), then Cairo (an enforced delay), then Basra, then
Bahrain, then Lydda (two-hour delay for engine repairs), then
Baghdad, then Sharjah (more engine trouble), then Jawani ('a
one-camel settlement on the Persian frontier of Baluchistan),
then Bombay, then Madras – where, the plane having broken
down, he got a small transport aircraft to take him at last to
Colombo.

Three days after reaching Ceylon, he was on the way to
Australia, feeling intensely miserable. 'I love you so much I can
hardly think,' he wrote. 'It's never been as bad as this. Never
mind – this is the last absence.'

Yet again he flew the Indian Ocean to Australia, and late in
October he for once allowed his head to appear above the
parapet, when he and Clare Blanshard featured on the red,
white and black cover of Qantas Empire Airways' monthly
Gazette. The pair were photographed standing side by side in
front of an airliner – he looking thin and drawn in his tropical
uniform, she smartly to attention beside him – and inside a
couple of paragraphs saluted them as star customers:

> The names appearing most frequently on Qantas Kangaroo
> Service passenger lists are those of Captain A. Hillgarth,
> R.N., and Second Officer Blanshard, W.R.N.S., photo-
> graphed on arrival at Guildford Airport, Perth. Both
> officers travel extensively in the course of their duties and
> have made eight crossings of the Indian Ocean, which is
> a record on this service.
>
> Captain Hillgarth has made two crossings by the
> Catalina Flying Boats and six by Liberators, and Second
> Officer Blanshard one by Catalina and seven by Liberators.
> During the past two years Captain Hillgarth has travelled
> more than 200,000 miles by air.

In Sydney at the end of November he found 'heaps of telegrams – problems stacked up waiting for me' – many caused by the fact that the Headquarters was beginning its move to Hong Kong. Once more he headed north, flying up the long chain of the Philippines. As the plane approached Leyte island he told Jean that he could see the 'black and sage green hills of Mindanao a couple of miles on the port side'. Leyte proved a hell-hole: he spent the night in 'a horrid little hut in the jungle – a mosquito-infested den', bathed in sweat and with no chance of a shower. He sought distraction in reading George Borrow's *Wild Wales* – the celebrated account of a journey made on foot through the country from north to south in 1860, in which he perhaps found echoes of his own ancestry and background. It was Borrow's earlier travelogue, *The Bible in Spain* (he told Jean), which had first attracted him to the Victorian author earlier in the war. Next day the aircraft stopped to refuel at Morotai, 'where I had a hurried but important conference with some of my chaps'.

When he reached Hong Kong at the end of the month, the colony had recently emerged from four years of Japanese domination and terrorism. He found the place very sad; and when he drove out to Stanley, where the main internment camp had been, and where the worst atrocities had taken place in the civil prison, black rage descended on him.

In October 1943 about fifty of our people were tried – a farce of a trial – and condemned to death. While awaiting execution they wrote messages to their families – at least, some of them did – on the walls of the cells. Although the Japanese whitewashed these over, they have been uncovered, and I don't think I have ever read anything more moving than some of those messages. I won't try to tell you what they said.

Now, in other blocks of this prison, are hundreds of

Japanese awaiting trial. They include all those we could catch – the majority, I'm glad to say – of those who ordered or perpetrated the crimes against either our own people or the civilian people in Hong Kong. I walked through the prison and looked at these beasts and felt both so murderous and so miserable that it's not possible to describe my state of mind at all.

An important part of his job now was to amass information about the atrocities committed by the Japanese in their prison camps, on battlefields and on ships, and he collected a huge dossier of reports. He found the details nauseating – and a few headings show why: 'Cannibalism. Beheading of Allied Airman. Chopping off toes of Indian prisoners with shovels. Use of Australian solders for bayonet practice. Dissection while alive of two American prisoners of war.' This highly disagreeable work occupied much of his time over the next weeks.

Early in December he returned to Melbourne, and spent a whole day with Commander Long, the DNI Australia, before getting away for a short break in Tasmania. Writing from Hadley's Hotel, Hobart, he told Jean that the weather was 'bracingly cold', with snow on the mountains in the south. He loved the 'deserted country, very barely inhabited', and when he went fishing he caught four black-backed salmon by trawling.

Christmas Eve 1945 found him in Tokyo, 'horribly knocked about . . . with a few small islands of buildings standing out in the devastation'. The British Embassy – a large, walled compound – was isolated in a sea of rubble, but still intact, and after a huge Christmas lunch he was obliged to sit through a show of geisha dancing. On its way from there to China his aircraft circled for twenty minutes over Nagasaki, but there were too many clouds for anyone to get a clear view of the ruins. In Shanghai, although he was busy writing reports, he had time to visit the shops, which he thought were 'incredible

– they're like Paris in pre-war days . . . The silks are a holy miracle.' But then he added one of his less successful prophecies: 'I can't see China as a Great Power for a hundred years to come.'

In Shanghai he had dinner with the legendary General Adrian Carton de Wiart – of whom Peter Fleming once wrote: 'He had only one arm, only one eye, and – rather more surprisingly – only one Victoria Cross.' Alan found the general's views on China '<u>most</u> interesting'. Then he was on his way back to Hong Kong in a Dakota 'which they very kindly sent up to fetch me' – but he did not much care for the 'feverish gaiety' with which the colony celebrated New Year: 'There are so many people wherever we go who seem to think that all we want is parties.' Among the revellers was Clare Blanshard, who surprised him by seeming to have 'lost her heart to an officer . . . and he, I'm told, too . . . Certainly she seems very happy. I'm sending her to Australia from Singapore, via Borneo, partly to do a job but also to avoid the demobilising machinery in Colombo which might claim her for passage home before I've finished.'

On 7 January 1946, from a Sunderland flying boat, en route from Hong Kong to Singapore, he described to Jean 'a quite affecting goodbye lunch' with Admiral Bruce Fraser, who had already been raised to the peerage as Baron Fraser of North Cape. Also present at the meal had been Fraser's Secretary and his Chief of Staff, 'who are two of my best friends – it was hard to part with them'.

On the 8th in Singapore he had dinner with Mountbatten, and a 'most useful private talk' – but before that he had had to endure a two-hour concert given by the Royal Marine Far East Band, mostly of music by Tchaikovsky, including his 5th Symphony and Violin Concerto. For someone as tone deaf as Alan, this must have been torture.

Arriving back in Colombo on 20 January, he was furious to find that he had been robbed. Someone had broken into

his room in the Galle Face Hotel and forced open a despatch
case in which he kept Jean's letters and many of his favourite
possessions, among them diamond and mother-of-pearl cufflinks
and dress waistcoat buttons, a set of five miniature medals
including the CMG and OBE, and an octagonal gold pencil
inscribed on the side 'N.A.Staff, Madrid'.

> The thieves didn't take any of your letters, thank God
> [he told Jean] but they have stolen my wedding present
> to you – a diamond and sapphire bracelet I bought just
> before I went to Sydney two months ago. I didn't mean
> to tell you what it was, but I must. It mayn't sound nice,
> but it was – lovely. It cost £200. I'm absolutely desolate,
> and kicking myself for not putting it in the office safe.

Like Homer's Odysseus, he was pining for *nostimon hamar*
– the day of his return. By the beginning of February he was
in a fever to get home, and he packed a suitcase to go back
to Britain aboard the *Undine*, a destroyer commanded by Cecil
Holmes, who had once served under him. 'It is lucky to find
him here,' he wrote, 'as the problem of getting one's gear home
is formidable.' For once he was able to give Jean a cryptic hint
about his work. A colleague, Air Vice Marshal Pendred – 'a
most likeable companion with no pretensions' – arrived at
Sydney on the 7th and at once the two of them were 'immersed
in all the business of a special mission. We became, and still
remain, a special occasion, accredited to the Australian Chiefs
of Staff, and so invested with a peculiar atmosphere of authority
and consideration.'

Worried by the news of rationing and shortages in England,
he sent off food parcels to his sisters, and arranged for more
to be despatched later. 'I'm going to buy tons of tinned food
to send back by one of our ships,' he told Jean. 'How about
forty-eight tins of jam, for instance?'

In his final days out East he was agitated by a letter from Jocelyn (now sixteen), who had commendably mastered much of his initial hostility but said he still did not want to meet his father. The letter, Alan told Jean, was 'sweet in many ways . . . He is so much like myself . . . I love him all the more for the letter, which must have cost him a lot to write . . . I begin to understand my own father better . . . We were completely unlike in most things, but I recognise now a touch of kindred, a most peculiar, deep-reaching contact. I never had this with my mother.'

In the view of his colleague Commander John Parker, Alan's greatest contribution in the Far East was his success in securing the cooperation of so many varied people, from the US Navy to clandestine organisations in Australia and prickly units like 'the refugees from the Dutch East Indies, and MacArthur's very difficult team in Brisbane and later the Philippines'. Another former colleague reckoned that the quality of intelligence which he helped create went some way to dispelling the hostility towards the Royal Navy at first shown by Washington, and so was an enormous help to Bruce Fraser. It was in part due to Alan's creative diplomacy that the British Pacific Fleet achieved results which otherwise would have been impossible.

In view of these and similar tributes, it seems strange that Alan received no official recognition for his marathon efforts in the Far East; but, soon after he reached England, he did get a small reward in the form of a letter from the DNI:

Dear Alan,
This is an attempt to convey to you more clearly than I did in conversation, my sincere appreciation of all you have done for me and my organisation during the War and since it ended. To my mind you have done a unique

job and I often wonder how I should have got on without
your help.

Naval Intelligence will always be in your debt, and I
personally shall never forget how you eased the burden
of my efforts in sorting out the problems and difficulties
of this complicated machinery . . . You have every reason
to look back with satisfaction on a very fine job of work
which you did during the war and during the last difficult year.

All the very best, Yours very sincerely,
Edmund Rushbrooke.

Illannanagh

Alan returned from the Far East early in 1946. He was officially released from the Navy on 5 July, but he had accumulated more than three months' leave, and was in effect a free man from the date on the release order, 25 March. The document told him that he might wear civilian clothes while on leave, and that he must cease to wear uniform after the date of his release, but that he should keep his uniform intact in case he was recalled for service. His home address was given as the Savile Club in Brook Street, London.

He was forty-six years old, and his domestic life was in tatters. His decision to leave wife, son and stepdaughters continued to cause distress within the family. By the end of 1943 they had all left Spain, and Mary had lived in London for the next three years. With Jocelyn at Eton, she was able to visit him at school and see him in the holidays. She herself worked unpaid for the Soldiers, Sailors, Airmen and Families Association (SSAFA), and at night, while the war lasted, acted as an unpaid air-raid warden.

Meanwhile, Son Torrella had been standing empty, save for caretakers. Oddly enough, Alan does not seem to have been much disturbed by having to abandon the great *finca* into which he had put so much time and effort. Perhaps guilt anaesthetised other emotions. He did go back to Majorca once,

in April 1946, to sort out the books, papers and belongings
he had left there six years before, and to plan the construction
of a *deposito* (reservoir), which collected water from the
Coanegra stream for use in the house and on the farm. As he
told Jean, he found the house 'beautifully in order', and the
land 'wonderfully looked after and improved'. He had long
discussions with Miguel Sans (the *amo*, or farm manager-bailiff),
the carpenter and the stone-mason, and talked to old servants
who had come to see him. His feelings about the place were
mixed: the visit had 'curious and sad moments, but nothing
terrible', and never for a moment did he feel alarmed or
haunted.

Sitting in his old library after midnight, he wrote to tell
Jean that he had never seen Majorca so beautiful:

> Though I love the place and know it as no one else does,
> it has, for a wonder, none of the hold upon me that I
> half felt it might have . . . [I had] no feeling at all that I
> was losing anything. The people are entranced to see me.
> I think they are a little puzzled. [My involvement with
> you] is an accepted fact – except that everyone expected
> that I meant to sell Son Torrella. I have scotched that and
> made it clear that Son Torrella will never be sold but will
> – I hope – be held by my great grandchildren. The rector
> of the village and the mayor came to see me this after-
> noon. They were charming. This is the Big House, and
> whatever I do, I am the Laird. As Jocelyn will be after
> me.

For the time being the cold war between him and Mary
had consolidated into permafrost: they were neither speaking
nor writing to each other. Communication between them was
effected by George Saward, Alan's deputy and then successor
as Consul at Palma – a man of high ability and exceptional

good nature, who represented both parties with equal friend-liness, and was described by Alan as 'one of my loyalest friends'. In retrospect it seems sad that husband and wife were unable to keep in contact, even at a distance, but they were fortunate in having such an equable intermediary. In one typical letter to Mary Saward wrote: 'If there is anything you would like me to write and tell Alan, I will, of course, be pleased to do so if you will let me know particulars.'

Through Saward, Alan gave Mary permission to do whatever she wanted at Son Torrella, and asked him to tell her that he had no wish to interfere or retain any control of the property. Saward it was who supervised the works at the *finca*; particu-larly the construction of the reservoir; it was he who furnished Mary with pesetas whenever she came out, he who made payments to Miguel and Juan Mateo, the contractor, and he who kept Alan abreast of local news. It also fell to him to explain Alan's plans for the future of the house. Both parents wanted Jocelyn to become the eventual owner – and this, in spite of the complexities of Spanish taxation laws, they achieved.

Whenever HMG adopted a disobliging attitude towards Spain, Alan leapt to the defence of the country and its people, usually with a letter to the Editor of *The Times*. One, headed 'The Spanish Outlook' and published on 1 May 1946, drew dozens of expressions of gratitude from Spaniards and British alike – and such was the enthusiasm of the Spanish Embassy that the Press Attaché ordered 5,000 reprints. Hispanophiles were particularly pleased by the timing of the letter, since Sir Samuel Hoare's memoir – *Ambassador on Special Mission*, which was hostile to Spain – was being serialised in the *Sunday Dispatch*, and the extracts, in the view of one critic, were 'further cheap-ening [the book] under banner headlines designed to create an even falser impression than Sir Sam's hurt vanity and personal dislike have prompted him to record'.

Whenever the vexed question of Gibraltar came up – which it frequently did – Alan was quick to put the Spanish point of view. Another letter to *The Times*:

What we need now is a New Look. We might start by respecting Spaniards as Spaniards, which is to say as a nation of thirty million individuals with an outlook in many ways different from our own but none the less sane, reasonable, courageous and sincere. The Spaniard responds immediately to true friendliness. There is perhaps no one more anxious to oblige a friend and no one quicker to resent a slight. While we refuse to understand him, he is at a loss to understand us, and our attitude in many matters, to us sensible but to him incomprehensible, is soon magnified into an injury.

A case in point is Gibraltar. Englishmen who assert that Spaniards do not feel strongly about Gibraltar are doing a disservice to their own country. There are few if any Spaniards who do not feel very strongly on the subject. Certainly they don't think about it all the time, but the feeling is always there, deep-rooted. It is no new feeling. It goes back 250 years and is a question of honour. We can talk about the Treaty of Utrecht and its successors as much as we like, but we shall never make the Spaniard understand our attitude until we begin to understand his.

Freed from the constraints of war service, and free also from ambition, Alan spent much of the summer travelling – but he was not in search of a job. When one of his former intelligence colleagues suggested that he was admirably equipped to become the next head of MI6, he replied, 'No – it would kill me.' At the end of August he flew to Geneva and had lunch with Churchill, who was on a painting holiday in Switzerland. 'It was very family and peaceful and pleasant,' he told Jean. 'I had quite a long yarn with Winston, who was most affectionate, but some of the things he said were rather disturbing. I can't write about that in a letter, naturally.'

Back in London, he began settling into a flat, and bought a newfangled type of pen called a Biro. For a few days he enjoyed using it, but then reverted to pen and ink, which he thought made his writing look more distinguished. Jean, asked about the relative merits of the instruments, retorted: 'I would like it if you wrote with a bit of charred wood, so dearly I love your writing.'

She, meanwhile, had gone to Denmark to stay with Count and Countess Knüth-Winterfeldt, who owned a 2,000-acre farm called Rosendal, near Fakse, some fifty miles south of Copenhagen. Her job was to teach English to the two boys, aged six and three, and she enjoyed being with a family who lived in a lovely place and entertained vigorously at weekends, arranging house parties of ten or twelve couples. On her birthday – 1 September – the company sang a Viking song in her honour, and she reported: 'The Danes have lots of drinking songs which sound very Viking and virile, and Schnapps is always accompanied by song.'

By now Alan was convinced that he and Jean would soon be married – and it was principally the dejected state of England after the war that prompted him to look farther afield for somewhere to live. A Labour government, rationing of food, petrol and clothes, general austerity, high property prices – everything combined to make him seek a home elsewhere. A further factor was his desire to get away from censorious acquaintances, and to take his beautiful young partner into a fresh environment. Before the world war everyone of note in Majorca had known him and Mary, and from 1940 to 1943 they had been pillars of society in Madrid – so that in 1946 it would have been uncomfortable for him to return and live in Spain with a new wife.

In the autumn he was already thinking about settling in Ireland, where many large houses were going cheap, and in September he took the train and ferry to Dublin, to meet Dudley Walsh, a solicitor with whom he became good friends. Walsh was amenable, energetic and efficient, if loquacious: in the middle of one lengthy typed communication he wrote: 'And now to business, as I have been interrupted in the dictation of this letter and I wish to catch the post.'

Alan began by making inquiries about income tax, and how to pay for imported sherry, if he were to live in Ireland; but soon he asked Walsh to help him find a house to rent or buy. The request started a prolonged hunt, which the solicitor conducted with great good nature and acumen. Alan himself collected brochures from estate agents and set off on a tour of distant country houses, but was disappointed to find them all in very poor order. There was one, however, which fascinated him: Lough Veagh House, a substantial property with six acres of land on the shore of Lough Gartan, far to the north in Co. Donegal. 'I've never seen a more beautiful setting in my life,' he told Jean. 'It is on the edge of the lough and in deep forest. It is divine. But the house is horrid and dilapidated.'

In spite of his doubts, he asked Walsh to open negotiations, which he did. But progress was slow. The house was owned, or possibly just occupied – it was hard to tell which – by a Mrs Johnstone, who proved an exceptionally tiresome client, since neither she nor her advisers were given to answering letters.

By then Alan and Jean had become increasingly worried by Mary's unrelenting opposition to the idea of a divorce. She had now taken a religious stance, and wrote to say that for her to grant a divorce would be 'the wrong thing to do *personally*. I think that committing sin oneself is bad but that forcing someone else to do so is even worse – it's like making somebody else blaspheme.'

In desperation Alan imported Don Gómez-Beare, whom
Mary had always liked, in an attempt to persuade her to relent.
At first he failed, and Mary began to demand a Deed of
Separation, which would have frozen the position indefinitely.
The idea appalled Alan, who wrote to Jean in Denmark: 'Please
help me now by telling me – and meaning it without reserva-
tion – that you will stand by me in this last horror, if it has
to be.'

As a final throw Alan consulted a friendly priest, who told
him he must confront Mary himself. He did, and the result
was an acrimonious outburst:

> She said she wouldn't divorce me because of religious
> reasons, because Jocelyn loathes it and is ashamed, because
> I am the most self-centred and egotistical man in the
> world, because I care about nothing except myself. I didn't
> try to argue – I just went on saying that the present situ-
> ation was impossible and that divorce was the only solu-
> tion . . . In the end she said she would think it over and
> let me know in the morning.

Next day at lunchtime she telephoned to say that she had
changed her mind and would go ahead with a divorce. Alan's
relief was inexpressible: he told Jean, 'I feel such a mental and
physical union with you that at times I almost believe I'm not
in this world at all' – and he added that when he went to
Harwich to meet her returning from Copenhagen, he would
be travelling by train 'but really on wings of fire'.

For the time being, however, he was not at all well. The
stomach trouble that had plagued him for years returned, and
in November he had to spend ten days in a nursing home
being treated for amoebic dysentery. Recovered – for the time
being, at any rate – he set off for Madrid on a multi-purpose
trip. One aim was to meet George Saward, who came from

ILLANNANAGH   301

Palma to report on Son Torrella; the second was to see 'the
Old Man', Juan March, who sent a car to collect him at the
airport and put him up at the Ritz, where they discussed
possible business deals, with some success.

The third commitment was to give four one-hour lectures,
on successive days, to the Spanish Naval Staff on 'Some Aspects
of the Japanese War'. He did this not on behalf of the Admiralty,
but on his own initiative, having made a private arrangement
with the Spanish navy; and the talks – before an audience of
about 140, including the entire Senior Spanish Naval Staff, the
Minister of Marine and several leading figures from the army
and air force – made a strong impression. In a report to Sir
Victor Mallet, the British Ambassador in Madrid, Alan's
successor as Naval Attaché wrote:

I should like to stress that they were the very greatest
success. All those present listened most attentively the
whole time to Captain Hillgarth, who of course was
delivering the lectures in fluent Spanish . . . They were,
in my opinion, a masterly summary of the Far Eastern
campaign from Pearl Harbour to the collapse of Japan.

Alan obtained his divorce from Mary on 3 February 1947,
and married Jean in the Sheffield register office three days
later. They then set off on an extended honeymoon, going
down by train through France and Switzerland to Milan, where
Jean was much moved by Leonardo da Vinci's huge mural,
nearly thirty feet wide, *The Last Supper*, which she found 'so
living and so clear in meaning that it would be worth travelling the world to see'. Mary, meanwhile, returned to Son
Torrella – and she spent every winter there until her death in
1982.

In Dublin Walsh had been steadily working to secure the
property in Co. Donegal. Alan and Jean went across to look

at it – and would have taken it had they been able to work out satisfactory terms. 'We should love to have Lough Veagh as our home,' Alan told Mrs Johnstone in a letter, 'but we would be obliged to spend a great deal of money on it, not only for repairs but also for putting in electric light, a complete new water and drainage system, increasing the number of bathrooms, redecorating etc.' He suggested that he should take the house on a twenty-one-year lease, with an option to buy at the end – but nothing came of his proposition.

Walsh turned to the possibility of renting furnished accommodation elsewhere, and on 12 June he sent Alan the particulars of a house called Luska, on the east shore of Lough Derg, in Co. Tipperary, which he thought looked attractive. It was an old-fashioned place, with primitive services, but Alan, reacting swiftly, took a lease and moved in: he and Jean (who was already pregnant with her first child) were disappointed to find the place dirty and run down, but at least they had a base in a beautiful, central part of Ireland from which to continue their search.

Then at last came the chance of a breakthrough. In an advertisement by the Dublin auctioneers Battersby's for 'Sporting and Other Properties' Walsh spotted a 130-acre estate called Gurthalougha, specially recommended for its duck shooting, a few miles up the lake from Luska. Battersby's described the property as a 'Splendid non-basement Residence situate on the shores of Lough Derg', with eight bedrooms, standing on 'a nicely laid-out lawn' and 'well sheltered in the midst of splendid ornamental timber', with a 'walled-in garden well-stocked with fruit trees and two greenhouses'. The vendors might also have said that it was a large, plain but dignified two-storey Victorian house, white, with tall sash windows. What they did say, in capital letters, was, 'IT IS IN PERFECT ORDER AND IS ECONOMICAL TO RUN'. For anyone with low expectations of comfort, the second part of that assertion might have seemed reasonably near the truth, but the first part was a gross exaggeration.

Gurthalougha was certainly in better shape than Lough Veagh, in that it had a generator for electricity and an 'excellent, never-failing supply of water, by gravitation'. But it needed refurbishment from top to bottom, and Walsh strongly advised Alan against paying the £10,000 for which the owners, the Kents, were holding out. Whatever its drawbacks, the house was in a lovely, isolated position, approached by a serpentine, mile-long drive that wound through woodland, and fronting on to Lough Derg – the third largest lake in Ireland, which is in fact a twenty-five-mile stretch of the River Shannon. Outside the front door, around a semi-circle of gravel, an expanse of grass, 100 yards wide and framed on either hand by handsome hardwood trees, sloped down to the water, and in the distance to the west, beyond the far shore, the gentle, grey-green ridge of Slieve Bernagh lay like a low barrier across the horizon, falling almost imperceptibly from left to right. On fine days, with sun glinting off the lake, the outlook from the house was captivating, and Alan came to love the view because it constantly changed with the weather and the seasons.

The house was only five miles from the Hillgarths' temporary base at Luska, so it was easy for them to visit and look around. Was Alan stirred by Yeats's fantasy, 'I will arise and go now, and go to Innisfree/And a small cabin build there, of clay and wattles made'? Gurthalougha was no small cabin, and it was certainly not 'of clay and wattles made', but it did embody something of the poet's haunting vision – lake water lapping on the shore, the sense of peace dropping slow, the promise of escape from the pavements of towns and cities – and Alan was immediately enchanted.

His gallant solicitor in Dublin, wily and patient, was now manoeuvring to outwit Battersby's and the Kents. At the

auction, held in Dublin during September, there were at first
no genuine bids at all: the auctioneer ran the price up to
£6,000, and Walsh then bid that amount on Alan's behalf. His
offer was ignored, so he went to see the vendors and tried to
beat them down from their target of £10,000, but had no
luck:

> I informed them that my clients [the Hillgarths] are rather
> difficult, and have been looking at various houses, and
> that I expected they were looking at another place at the
> present time. However, this in no way moved them . . .
> After the auction in an office downstairs the Vendor said
> he wanted £8,500 . . . I am under the impression that
> when I was unable to pull it off at £6,000 they would
> not sell at that figure for the present. They have, however,
> returned back to their house, and I should imagine in a
> more chastened frame of mind.

Not until 30 October did the vendors cave in. Then at last
they accepted Alan's final offer of £6,500. At once there was
another dispute, because he declined to pay any commission
to Battersby's, on the grounds that the firm had rejected his
bid at the auction and had not handled the sale since. In the
end, however, he did agree to pay 2½ per cent – a mere £162
10s. While Walsh went ahead with the necessary legal arrangements, Alan commissioned an architect's survey, and it was
agreed that he would take possession of the house on 15
December.

Even before the formalities were complete, he decided to
change the house's name. He found 'Gurthalougha' ugly, and
much preferred the romantic-sounding 'Illannanagh', the name
of a small island on Lough Derg which was later subsumed
into the fen and turned into a promontory. So Illannanagh the
house became.

He was still very much on the move, travelling frequently to London and Spain, usually on business. On 6 November 1946 he was elected a member of the Garrick Club in London (the entrance fee was then £26 5s. Od., and the annual subscription £4 4s. Od.). On the 14th he was in Madrid on a business trip when a startling development took place at Luska, vividly described by George Curzon, an old friend who was staying in the house:

2.20 am Jean came to my room and told me that things were worrying her. I sent her straight back to bed and went to her in her room.

2.25 Jean told me that a certain amount of water was coming away and also a little blood.
I dressed immediately, lit a fire, shut the window for the room was cold and told her I would go at once for Dr Courtney in Nenagh. Also called Bridie the maid to make hot water-bottles and covered Jean up to keep her warm.

2.35 Jean asked me instead to go to the Miss Bruces, and as I had not driven the car suggested that I went with Bridie on bicycles. This I did.

2.45 Left Luska.

3.00 Roused the Bruces who dressed at once and got out the car.

3.20 Left the Bruces.

3.30 Arrived Luska with Bridie and one Miss Bruce.

3.35 Started electric light going, lit fires, told Bridie to put on kettles of boiling water, make tea, and left Jean with Miss Bruce. Jean most brave and cheerful. The other Miss Bruce, who dropped us at the gate, went on at once to Nenagh for Dr Louis Courtney. The plan is to bring him back here.

4.20 I am writing this and drinking tea. The doctor should

be here with luck in about fifteen minutes ... Miss
B is still with Jean in her room.
5.20 Miss Bruce arrived back. Dr C. is on the way with
ambulance and nurse.
5.35 Dr C. Arrived. My watch appears to be slow, and I
am told it is 6.00 am.
6.50 Jean left in ambulance.

It was as well that the doctor acted swiftly, for the baby – a
boy, christened Justin – was born six weeks prematurely,
weighing only 4lb., and spent the start of his life in intensive
care in Nenagh hospital. When the local priest thanked God
for his survival, Courtney reacted smartly, saying he thought
gratitude was due also to the medical profession.

Numerous other domestic matters demanded Alan's attention. With Walsh's help he was negotiating to secure a visa and
work permit for his faithful butler-factotum Antonio, so that
he could bring him and his wife Yolanda over from Spain. He
was trying, by remote control, to sell a large Humber car in
London. He was also setting up a company, Illannanagh Estates
Ltd. Insurance on the house had to be arranged, work on the
building supervised, furniture bought. Locals were astonished
to hear that he proposed to install five more bathrooms: the
idea was so extraordinary that the family became known as
'Hillgarths of the Six Bathrooms'. People were even more
amazed when they heard that he was importing the baths,
bidets, basins and lavatories from Spain.

Apart from the plumbing, the house presented certain problems. 'Regarding the sweep brush for the chimney,' Walsh
wrote from Dublin,

This appears to be a very difficult matter, as I have been
unable to get any rods which I understand are not procur-
able in Dublin at the present time. Also they appear to

be a bit shaken by the fact that you wanted the extension to go to thirty-six feet. I may have more news about this tomorrow, but at the present time it looks hopeless.

One small disappointment came in the fact that the right to cut turf (peat) on the bog of Kilfadda, which went with the house, had never been exercised by the previous owner, and so had lapsed. But, as Walsh pointed out, the bog was a tiresome distance from Illannanagh, and in any case it was said to be worked out, so that a better plan would be to buy supplies locally.

As Alan had already discovered from his stay at Luska, he had landed in a primitive rural area. Delicious wafts of peat smoke drifted over the woods and rough grass fields. Country families lived in such poverty that many of the children had no shoes. There was no running water in the cottages. Mains electricity had yet to reach the area. Nenagh (pronounced 'Nina'), the nearest town of any size, sixteen miles away, boasted a cinema, but little else of interest. Only the most basic kinds of food were available: anything more sophisticated like coffee or good cheese had to come from Dublin, 100 miles to the east.

Communication with the outside world was erratic, to say the least. At first Illannanagh had no telephone, but when one was installed, the number was easy to remember: Ballinderry 3. (The Post Office was Ballinderry 1, the Police Station Ballinderry 2.) Making calls, on the other hand, was a matter demanding patience and tenacity. A couple of turns of a crank handle were generally enough to rouse the postmistress on the tiny switchboard in the village, but any request for another number had to be preceded by a discussion of the weather and local affairs:

'Awful weather, is it not?'

'Oh, fierce. What can I do for you, my dear?'

'Will you get me Moneygall five?'

'I will. Hold on now.'

The operator would then crank up her opposite number in the target area – only to be countered, after a further exchange of meteorological and other information, with 'Tis no use calling Five. Five's gone shopping.'

'Nine, then.'

'You'll not get nine, either. Nine's on holiday.'

'Ah, glory!'

The postmistresses knew everything – not only where people were, but even details of what was going on inside their houses. One caller, attempting to speak to Alan, was met with the retort: 'You'll not speak to the Captain. The Captain's in his bath.'

Alan enjoyed being able to alleviate the miseries of rationing in England with the packages of food which he had set up for despatch to outlying members of his family while he was still down under. 'A magnificent parcel of raisins and tinned jam and soup and rabbit and jelly and lots more arrived today from Australia,' wrote his sister Maureen from Peterborough in August 1946. 'When I said I wished people abroad didn't think we were starving I didn't mean I didn't like having things, but only that I didn't like being pitied – which is a bit different, isn't it?'

The parcel was a typical instance of Alan's generosity. He also continued to support and visit his beloved Anne Hamilton throughout her life, and in July 1946 she wrote from her home at Beaconsfield to thank him for sending money to her bank. 'It more than doubles my account,' she told him, 'and takes off my mind a heavy load of anxiety.' She lived to be ninety-two, and towards the end of her days Alan hoped that she would come to lodge with them at Illannanagh: a room was prepared for her, but she died before the plan could be carried through.

Early in March, returning from a trip abroad, he heard that she had been taken into a nursing home. As soon as he could, he hired a car and drove down to Buckinghamshire, only to find that she was dead. He was distraught. He arranged her funeral, and had her old dog put down, but he could not forgive himself for having failed to react more swiftly. He wrote to Jean, who was in Switzerland:

> I could have done nothing to help, but I could at least have seen her, and she would have known me and I could have been with her when she died. I find it difficult to believe she is dead. In a way she never will be for me. She meant more to me than my mother. And she was such a wonderful person. I think she always had a window open on another world. So goes the last link with my childhood.

Another indomitable survivor, supported by Alan, was Aunt Hetty – not a real aunt, but a lifelong friend of the family, who lived in Kent, where she kept hens and ducks and grew vegetables enthusiastically. 'I'm fair,' she told him one spring, when she was eighty-one, 'but more and more limited as to walking owing to the back laying down tools. All my life the back has been a great drawback.' Another year, after Christmas, she wrote:

> I'm snowed up with thank you letters to write, and my old rumattickay hands don't seem able to tackle it at all. The chocolates were a marvel. Every evening sitting over a good fire we had some, two each was the usual ration, three if we felt extravagant and gay, and oh! they were delicious.

Probably the most impoverished member of the family was Alan's youngest sister, Joy, who was married to a parson and had three sons. Alan saw little of them, even though Tom, the eldest boy, was his godson; but when Joy cracked her ribs in a car crash, and wrote with the news that she and her husband were behind with the rates, he sent her £150 (some £4,000 in today's values), saying, 'This isn't the moment for you to be distracted by debts . . . This isn't a loan but a gift. I will help again later on when I can.'

The renovation of Illannanagh went ahead quickly. The roof was renewed, the electrical wiring replaced; internal walls were moved, and handsome fireplaces, rescued from large country houses being demolished, were installed in the dining room, drawing room and library. This last, the largest room on the ground floor, became Alan's headquarters, in which he would sit writing for much of the morning, dealing with correspondence, composing letters to newspapers, or working on his latest novel.

Everything he wrote was phrased with precision and economy: he hated jargon and deplored the general decline in the use of English. It is impossible to tell whether he was the author, or merely an admirer, of a Fourth Leader which appeared in *The Times* in February 1947 entitled 'Anti-Personnel'; but he kept a cutting of it, and the style of the article was very much his, as were its sentiments:

Personnel, though in theory they are men and women, have only to be called personnel to lose their full status as human beings. They do not go, they proceed. They do not have, they are (more often than not) in possession of. They do not ask, they make application for . . . They cannot eat, they can only consume; they perform ablutions; instead of homes they have places of residence, in which, instead of living, they are domiciled. They are not cattle, they are not ciphers, they certainly are not human beings; they are personnel.

The established families of North Tipperary were puzzled by the new arrivals, who seemed to fit into no known category. People recognised that Alan was of higher intellectual calibre than most of the former colonial officers who had settled in the area after the war. They found him slightly intimidating, with his penetrating brown eyes and bushy dark eyebrows, which became ever more pronounced as he grew older. He was never exactly aggressive, but enigmatic and disconcerting all the same. He seemed to run Illannanagh on rigid rules, as if he was still in the Navy. Certainly he *looked* like a former naval officer, for his appearance was important to him, and he was always neatly dressed, his hair slicked back with an expensive brand of oil: even when he no longer had a butler, he would press his own trousers and rub spots out of them with benzene.

Because he rarely talked about his past, most neighbours did not know how long he had lived in Spain, and they had no idea of what he had achieved there. As a result, when they saw him wearing a shallow-crowned, wide-brimmed black hat, or sporting a black cloak lined with scarlet at the hunt ball in Nenagh, they suspected him of posing as a Spanish grandee. They did not realise that he was merely carrying on a habit gained during fourteen years in Majorca and Madrid – and they would have been astounded if they had known that he was in secret, personal communication with Churchill.

With Jean, on the other hand, people felt more at ease. They found her enchanting: always immaculately turned out, but also warm and unfailingly kind, full of generous gestures. With the birth of her second son, Tristan, in 1949, and of her daughter, Nigella, in 1953, she fulfilled Alan's longing for a substantial family. One key member of the establishment was Kate Eames, the children's nanny, who lived with the family throughout their years at Illannanagh.

From time to time old friends on Majorca made contact. One was Robert Graves, who wrote in May 1947 to say that he and his younger family were returning home to Deyá by air taxi, after a long exile. His eldest daughter had been back to the house in February and had 'had a great welcome & found all ship-shape, & no politics'.

If you feel like seeing me again and if you have any private messages you want delivered in Majorca, please look me up at Brown's Hotel, Dover Street, between May 7th and 15th. It would be very nice to see you again . . . I wonder whether you have found time to write another novel; I liked the other very much.

In November Graves wrote again, asking if Alan could help procure a visa for a friend, but also saying how glad he was to be back in Spain. 'It is disappointing that you can't visit the island . . . On Tuesday we kill our pig and make it into *sobresada*; otherwise no news here of importance, except that the oil is very rancid and scarce this year.'

Besides local problems, Alan had more distant worries on his mind. One was Jocelyn, who had done well at Eton and had gone up to Cambridge to read History, but then had taken a deep dive into religious waters and thought he was going to become an Anglican priest. In preparation he went off to Southern Africa for a year, travelling through Nyasaland and Tanganyika to Zanzibar, and when he returned to England he enrolled at Cuddesdon, the theological college near Oxford – only to realise eventually that he lacked the necessary vocation, whereupon he returned to Cambridge in 1952 and took his doctorate in 1957. He then began a distinguished academic career, during which he held senior teaching posts at universities in England, America and Canada, and wrote more than twenty books on Spanish history.

Gradually Alan and Jean transformed Illannanagh into a place of great comfort, beauty and tranquillity. Friends who came to stay were amused to find that Alan seemed to be trying to recreate Son Torrella in another environment: here was another old country house, with big, high rooms, built round a cobbled courtyard, needing extensive refurbishment and protected by its surrounding land, on which he was putting his own stamp. Having the highest standards himself, he sought to replicate the immaculate household which he had maintained in Majorca by importing Spanish staff. First and foremost he had Antonio, a charming factotum, and his rather eccentric wife, who in time were succeeded by Heliodoro and Donina. Jean generally had a Spanish cook and a series of Tipperary girls as maids, most of them lacking even the most basic domestic skills until she trained them (considering that a housemaid's starting wage was £1 a week, this was hardly surprising).

Alan loved wine, and every year would import a barrel of red and a barrel of white *vin de pays* produced by a grower he had met at Valdepeñas, in La Mancha. Each consignment was bottled with great ceremony (and usually some aggravation) in Dublin by a wine merchant called Morgan – except one year, when something went wrong with the import forms, and the whole lot had to be poured into the Liffey. Some vintages were better than others, but Alan never failed to extol their virtues, and even with guests used to drinking French wine he would exclaim, 'Isn't this delicious!' – to which, bracing themselves, they would politely agree. Apart from the wine, he drank little except sherry, preferring a *fino* with the seductive name Real Tesoro – Royal Treasure – which he would enjoy, ice-cold, before dinner.

Because there was no good school within easy reach, he began the boys' education himself, teaching them to read and write. He would also read aloud to them every night before they went to bed, hoping to inculcate the passion for books which he himself had had all his life. When Justin was eight and Tristan six, he engaged a governess, Norah Malone, a Scot in spite of her name, who gave the boys lessons in the School Room, which was properly equipped with little desks and chairs. Her third pupil was Rickard Deasy, son of a neighbouring family and a year younger than Justin, who would bicycle five miles from home every morning – not out of choice, but because during the Suez crisis of 1956 and after it there was practically no petrol to be had. Rickard quickly became used to having lunch with the Hillgarths, to hearing Spanish spoken at meals, and being waited on at table by Spanish servants.

The Deasys were one of the leading local families, Rickard's father, Ricardo, being a prominent farmer who played an important role in rural politics, and from 1961 to 1966 was President of the Irish Farmers' Association, which successfully lobbied the government for a better deal for agriculture.

He and his wife Sheila got on well with the Hillgarths, not least because both families had strong Spanish connections: in the nineteenth century young Rickard's maternal great-grandfather, Lieutenant Colonel James Hickie, while stationed in Gibraltar as an army officer, had eloped with Dona Lucila Larios, of the family later famous for their gin. He brought her to Ireland, where they married, and it was she who commissioned the Roman Catholic church in the village of Terryglass, a short distance from Illannanagh.

The Hillgarth children often went to tea with the Deasys, and once the boys got into a fight with a gang from the village. When they returned to Illannanagh Alan told them, 'It's quite all right to fight your enemies, but you must never fight among yourselves.'

The ground immediately around the house was too rocky to grow anything much except grass and shrubs, but a short distance away was a large kitchen garden about 100 yards square, enclosed by a ten-foot stone wall. There the soil was fine loam, and Alan made the garden highly productive, having new fruit trees planted, pruning the old ones and rebuilding the two glasshouses. The family acquired a few dairy cattle, so that they were able to produce their own milk and butter.

He liked having men about him, and employed several to work in the garden and on the land – at one point there were six outdoor and six indoor staff – and they often won prizes for vegetables at the Nenagh show. He could be quite fierce with them, and sometimes let fly fearful rockets: after one altercation Jean had to walk the head gardener the full length of the drive to soothe him down and prevent him leaving.

Alan himself grew passionately fond of trees, hardwoods especially, and got his forester Martin Dwyer to plant oak, ash and beech saplings by the hundred, also putting in Norway and sitka spruce, European and Japanese larch, and swamp cypress. He was for ever pruning young trees – his form of gardening – and he had every available space planted, including some good farmland, which rather shocked his agricultural neighbours. By no means all his schemes succeeded. An avenue of walnuts was a particular disappointment: perhaps because the saplings were of poor quality, the trees twisted and leaned inwards over the drive, and even now, forty years later, they have not achieved the majestic proportions which their station demands. Later he planted a more successful avenue of limes, and whenever it rained – which it almost always did – he would say cheerfully, 'Well – at least the trees are growing!'

Wet or fine, he went for long walks through the woods and fields, and although never a very enthusiastic rider to hounds, he became Chairman of the North Tipperary Foxhounds. At the same time he was Vice Chairman of the Irish Society for the Prevention of Cruelty to Animals: a combination which some people found baffling, but in which he saw no contradiction. It was from these and other local roles that he soon became known as 'The Captain' – a compliment to his status in the community and to the distinction (however little known) of his naval career. He enormously enjoyed becoming a modest landowner in a backward part of the world.

Some friends were surprised that he should settle in such a place; but it seems that having had so much excitement and seen so much action in earlier years, having survived three wars, and having travelled nearly a quarter of a million miles during the last, he was perfectly content to take life quietly and spend time at home with Jean and his children. It might have been him about whom the sixteenth-century French poet Joachim du Bellay wrote his little hymn on the homecoming of heroes:

> Heureux qui, comme Ulysse, a fait un beau voyage,
> Ou comme cestui-là qu conquit la toison,
> Et puis est retourné, plein d'usage et raison,
> Vivre entre ses parents le reste de son age!

> Happy is he who, like Ulysses, completed a fine voyage,
> Or like him [Jason] who won the golden fleece,
> And then returned, full of experience and wisdom,
> To live among his kinsmen for the remainder of his days.

With Lough Derg at his front door, he developed tremendous enthusiasm for sailing and fishing. Illannanagh had its own jetty in the little round bay below the house, and he always took part in the annual regatta at Dromineer – an important local event. He imported a catamaran called *El Gato* (the Cat), which came over from Southampton – the first ever seen in the area and a fine craft. He and the boys caught large quantities of fish, trolling for perch, which they could land by the hundred in the spawning season, along with big cannibal brown trout. They also shot duck under the expert eye of Jack O'Donoghue, who had lost a leg in the First World War and was known in the family as 'One-Legged Jack'. In spite of his handicap – and of considerable imbibing – he was a deadly marksman, especially at the duck, which he engaged standing up in a boat on his one pin, flailing his arms to keep his balance as he spun round.

At home, when not writing, Alan read a great deal, history in particular: he was keener than ever on his books, and whenever he went to Dublin – perhaps once a month – he would bring back more. Again, as in Majorca, he built up a large collection, which was richly augmented when Anne Hamilton left him her own extensive library. Music, on the other hand, had never meant anything to him: he could not sing a note. But there was great excitement in the family whenever he took the children to the cinema in Nenagh, where Westerns were his favourites. Although he enjoyed good food – Spanish food, especially – he never put on weight, but retained his spare figure, always giving the impression that huge energy was stored inside it.

Safe in Port

As Alan's new family took root in Ireland, Mary was trying to
come to terms with her solitary existence in Majorca. She had
decided to make Son Torrella her home, because she knew
how dearly Jocelyn loved the place, and wanted to preserve it
for him. She worked ceaselessly to embellish her garden, entered
deeply into the life of the countryside round about, wrote
fiction and entertained a stream of visitors. But she was often
lonely and lacked intellectual stimulation; in 1951, when she
was savagely attacked by arthritis and sought a cure in London,
she shocked Jocelyn with the bitterness of a letter she wrote
from her flat:

> You are worried at my being alone and indeed I am very
> lonely but I wonder at you – of all people – imagining
> that I should miss the servants and the material things
> one can have through them. That is the least always. What
> one feels is the unshared life, the lack of a person to laugh
> or weep with, someone who is as amused or as unhappy
> or as indignant as one is oneself. No amount of cooks or
> parlour-maids can supply that, and though I am grateful
> for them when I have them they make practically no
> difference to one's *life*. I thought you would know this,
> but I see you don't and that's why I write of it now.

Jocelyn, for his part, sharply resented the way in which his father had cast them off. For a while, if anyone mentioned Alan in conversation, he would stop talking, and at one stage he vowed he would never see his father again. Quite soon, however, his attitude softened, and he was helped towards reconciliation by the kindness and wisdom of Eduardo Martínez (the doctor at the Madrid embassy), who told him that in all life's crises there comes a time when difficulties fade and a problem which has appeared unsurmountable does not seem to matter any more.

Letters from Eduardo kept Alan aware of his first family's hostility, but the barriers gradually broke down. One morning in London Alan happened to see Jocelyn walking up St James's Street, and, as he told Jean,

> I called his name, and I think he was glad to see me. He was hesitant at first, but began to speak more freely . . . He is about half an inch taller than I am, looks very well but slighter than I am. I don't think he has such broad shoulders. He holds himself well. He was in a grey flannel suit and carrying some books. I was very proud of him, and I think he realised that . . . I'm very glad I've seen him and I believe that casual meeting, which I feel God arranged, will start an improvement in matters between us.

Although Alan had gone to ground in Tipperary, he had by no means lost interest in international affairs. On the contrary, he was still very much enchanted by Spain, went there frequently on business and for holidays, and kept in touch with numerous Spanish friends. In the winter of 1948–9, and again in 1951–2, he and Jean rented a property in the centre of Jerez de la Frontera, taking part of Benavente Alto 6, known as 'the House of Zurita', a grand Moorish property covering several acres, which then belonged to Mercedes Zurita O'Neill, the eccentric widow of an Irishman.

Begun in the thirteenth century and remodelled several times since, the great mansion enclosed two one-acre gardens, a riding school, stables and a spacious *bodega* for storing the produce of the family's vineyards. That it had survived at all seems remarkable, for during the Peninsular War it was occupied by the French, who amused themselves by shooting up the statues in the patio. Luckily their Commanding Officer removed the priceless Gobelin tapestries designed by Rubens, and these are now in the Garde Meubles Nationale in Paris. Jean wrote ecstatically to her parents about the magnificent House of Zurita, with its 'great, imposing, palatial doors', and it was there, during her and Alan's first visit, that their second son, Tristan, was born. When he showed signs of arriving prematurely (as Justin had), the doctor advised Jean to stay put, rather than risk giving birth on the way home.

On the political front, Alan was much alarmed by the attitude of the Soviet Union, and, although he held no official position, he took every opportunity of calling for action to combat what he saw, with exceptional prescience, as a growing threat. He cannot have been encouraged by a letter from Frank Roberts, the British Minister in Moscow, who wrote reminiscing about old times and saying, 'This is an interesting place, but mainly for one's own education. There is little one can do to affect the "monolithic" Communist state.'

Ever since his first experience of Bolshevik Russia in 1920 Alan had hated and feared Communism, and now his apprehension was heightened by events in Europe. In May 1946 the British physicist Alan Nunn May had been convicted of selling nuclear secrets to the Soviet Union and sentenced to ten years' hard labour – the first evidence of nuclear espionage. In May 1948 a Communist government took over in Czechoslovakia, and in June the Russians closed Berlin to road and rail traffic from the west, precipitating an immense Allied airlift, during which American and British aircraft flew thousands of dangerous sorties, taking in food and fuel to keep the city alive.

A Secret Brief dated 24 October 1948, not signed, but apparently emanating from the Directors of Intelligence in London, and addressed to Captain Hillgarth personally, emphasised the dangers of the Cold War which had recently set in. That such a highly classified document should be sent to a retired officer with no official standing was a sign of the influence that Alan still exerted.

One of the Soviet leaders' self-imposed tasks, it said, was 'to hasten the decay of the Capitalist system', and their fundamental aim was 'the establishment of Communism of the Moscow pattern throughout the world'. The Chiefs of Staff feared that the Cold War might be succeeded at any moment by a 'shooting war', and had called for a closer link between themselves and the Foreign Office. The final paragraph of the document was the most telling:

> We feel that there is only one way of averting war with Russia and that is to exploit her weaknesses in the commercial, dynastic, political and cultural spheres and so overthrow the regime. A most powerful body should be set up to see if this is a real possibility, and if so to take immediate and active measures. If it is not considered a possibility, then we must accept the fact that war is inevitable and make preparations now to start it in our own time and not have it thrust on us at the most convenient time for the Soviet.

The document did not allocate Alan any particular task; but, as during the world war, he had no hesitation in communicating his alarm to the most important politician he knew, Winston Churchill. He had been dismayed by the defeat of the Conservative government in the General Election of 1945; yet he still looked up to the wartime Prime Minister as the saviour of the nation. Now Churchill was merely Leader of the Opposition, but still a powerful influence in Whitehall; and in the words of the historian Professor David Stafford, the records show that after the war he sought Alan's advice 'as ardently then as he did between 1939–45'.

'Dear Mr Churchill,' Alan wrote on 20 November 1948 in a letter marked 'Private':

> In your last letter you told me to let you know when I was next in London. It so happens that I have something of very great importance to tell you, and, as I shall be in London on 2nd, 3rd and 4th of December on my way to Spain, I shall be most grateful if you can see me for half an hour.

The result was an invitation to lunch at Chartwell, Churchill's country home in Kent, on Friday 3 December. Evidently the matter of great importance concerned the Soviet Union, in particular the freedom with which Russians were allowed to move around England, and our inability to keep track of them. Next day Alan wrote again, this time from the Army & Navy Club in Pall Mall, marking the letter 'Personal' and confirming matters discussed.

> There are 150 members of the Russian Embassy here, excluding the Trade Delegation and its affiliates. The corresponding figure for our representation in Moscow is eighty-five ... The Russian Trade Delegation here numbers seventy today, but has been up as high as ninety recently . . . Our commercial equivalent in Russia is *one* – the Commercial Counsellor. We have no Trade Delegation.
>
> In addition to the Russian Trade Delegation there are

always a number of Russian representatives with firms, at today's figures numbering nineteen. These also enjoy diplomatic privileges and are considered as attached to the Trade Delegation. Their privileges mean, in effect, unrestricted travel. No one watches persons attached to the Embassy or attached to the Trade Delegation.

All these people are a pest. On the plea of studying our methods they poke their noses into everything. And we have nobody to watch them. As I said, MI5 have no one to spare even to follow the Russian air attaché about England . . . The chief trouble throughout is that there is no one concerned to fight this quiet, cold-blooded war of brains in the background. The facts exist. No one will use them.

In April 1949 Churchill sent a telegram asking for confirmation of the numbers Alan had given him in December: he wanted a comparison between the staff in the Soviet Embassy in London and that of the British Embassy in Moscow. The cable, addressed to the Army & Navy Club, had to be forwarded to Spain, where Alan was staying in Jerez. He replied in a telegram on 4 May: MESSAGE RECEIVED VERY LATE AS WAS TRAVELLING APOLOGIES STOP NUMBERS INCLUDING MINOR PARTS AND ATTACHMENTS IN BOTH CASES ARE NOW TWO HUNDRED AND THIRTY SIX THEIRS AGAINST ONE HUNDRED AND THIRTEEN OURS.

As always, when Alan saw something wrong and considered that action needed to be taken, he said or wrote plainly what he thought. In a series of three annual Top Secret reports for Churchill, beginning in September 1949, he bypassed senior politicians and military commanders, returning again and again to the menace posed by Russia and calling urgently for counter-measures. Fuelled by information from the Chiefs of Staff, who complained vigorously about lack of cooperation from the Foreign Office, he pointed out that Britain and America had no joint plan 'in case of Russian aggression of any kind'. The recent visit to England of the US Chiefs of Staff, he wrote, 'shook everybody up. It showed that there was a very large difference between U.S. and British plans in case of war with Russia.' He predicted that if hostilities broke out, the result would be chaotic. 'The U.S. would drop atom bombs all right but without agreed method, and everything would be pure improvisation.'

The Western governments, he thought, were inhibited to a ridiculous degree by fear of offending the Soviet Union. The feeling in the Services was one of 'being without either lead or backing from the Cabinet, which has no real policy'. The only body concerned with the Cold War was the Russian Committee of the Foreign Office: 'It meets once a fortnight but does nothing, and the [one] Service member can't get it to do anything'.

In his Secret and Personal report of July 1950 he again deplored Britain's reluctance to take firm action 'which might provoke the Russians in any way', and advocated a policy of quietly denying to the Soviet Union key materials which it had to find abroad. He also discussed the problem of 'how to deal with Communism' in Britain:

The Foreign Office is understood to be of the opinion that any action taken about Communism at home might lead to results opposite to those desired, and is uncertain what sort of useful action could be taken unless there is general agreement that the Communist Party should be outlawed. The Chiefs of Staff realise that extreme action of this kind is not possible now, but they hope that something will be done to educate the people of this country on the dangers of Communism, and they share the concern of the Foreign Secretary that the teaching profession and the T.U.C. (to name only two entities) are so deeply penetrated by members of the Communist Party.

He pointed out that British understanding of developments in Russia was 'lamentably weak'. 'Our knowledge of the Russian air forces is out of date. There is no real knowledge of atom bomb progress or of stocks.'

A year later he reported that fear of provoking Russia remained paramount, as did the ban on any form of action. Knowledge of what was happening in Russia was 'still dangerously poor':

We have not broken any important Russian cipher, and it does not look as if we shall, since the Russians are cleverer than the Germans were, and the publicity given to this form of intelligence after the last war has naturally made them very careful. We have penetrated a few minor codes and bought others, but nothing that carries messages of moment.

It had been hoped (he went on) that useful intelligence about Russian weapons might have been garnered from the Korean War, which had broken out in June 1950, but this had proved a disappointing source. Information about the Soviet army was still 'extremely thin', and we had 'virtually no intelligence on her progress with atomic weapons'. The Chiefs of Staff had recently expressed concern about these deficiencies, 'but had not received from the Joint Intelligence Committee any useful guidance about what should be done to improve matters'. Without knowledge of the enemy, Alan concluded, 'no re-armament can be other than wasteful and in spite of lavish expenditure may not be effective. Even a giant is blind in the dark.'

His anxiety was such that on 17 January 1951 he wrote an outspoken letter to *The Times*, which the Editor declined to print, perhaps considering it alarmist:

> The regrettable fact, which is never officially admitted, is that we are already at war, whether we like it or not. We cannot avoid war, for we are already committed to it. Modern warfare is not merely an affair of arms but has many facets. We are under attack by every weapon available to our enemy except direct military force, and even that is in use by proxy. Unless we reply in kind, we shall be defeated.
>
> Russia, under the cloak of Communism, is bent on our destruction. We can only prevent this if we combat Russia with all means open to us. It may be that by doing so we shall escape an actual trial of arms, but it is certain that if we do not, we shall have to resort to arms at a time of Russia's choosing, when we are weakened in other ways to the point that she considers appropriate.

When Churchill was returned to power in the General Election of October 1951, Alan once more offered his services:

> Dear Prime Minister,
> Now that you, thank God, are again in office, I shall be grateful if you will allow me to contribute something, on the lines we have already spoken about, towards making it more difficult for Russia to embark on a shooting war. This need not cost the country anything. I could come to London at any time if you would like to see me.

In reply, Churchill wrote from 10 Downing Street, 'I hope you will continue to keep in touch with me, as you have done in the past, and I look forward to hearing from you . . . P.S.

Let me know when you come to London.' Friendly contact was maintained for some time: in June 1952 Alan thanked Churchill for arranging for him to see 'C' 'to explain to him my idea about the Cold War. I also saw General Strong. They were good enough to say that the idea was a new approach, and since my return from Spain I hear it is to be put into use.' But since Churchill, as Prime Minister, had access to all sources of intelligence, from then on he depended less on freelance assistants.

It would be fascinating to know how Alan obtained his information, which clearly derived from the highest intelligence sources. In one letter to Churchill, in 1951, he alluded cryptically to 'the officers who originally asked me to keep you informed'. Maybe some briefings came in the post – but if they did, only one (the Secret Brief quoted above) has survived. The most likely source was personal contact during his visits to London, which were irregular but fairly frequent, in spite of the tiresome journey involved: a three-hour drive to Dublin, an hour's wait at the airport, an hour and a half in the air and a further hour clearing Heathrow and travelling into the metropolis. During his visits he invariably stayed at Brown's Hotel in Albemarle Street, which Jean had patronised before the war. He was there so often that he became a good friend of the manager, securing a special rate, and other members of the family were always made to feel at home.

Like most of his wartime colleagues in intelligence, Alan deplored the release and exposure of hitherto secret information which might embarrass friendly countries or former colleagues, or still be of use to an enemy. He himself never spoke of his own clandestine machinations – rarely mentioning them even to the family – and in October 1950 he became seriously alarmed when he heard that a novel called *Operation Heartbreak*, by Sir Duff Cooper (formerly Minister of Information

and British Ambassador in Paris), was about to reveal elements
of Operation MINCEMEAT. There was no mention of Spain
in the story, but the action took place in a hot country, and
the central figure was the same as in the real events of 1943:
a body dressed in uniform floated ashore carrying forged documents designed to mislead the enemy about the setting of the
Allies' next major assault. Publication was imminent when, on
21 October, Alan wrote to Sir Roger Makins, then Deputy
Under-Secretary of State at the Foreign Office, in a last-minute
attempt to have the book suppressed:

> As I think you know, one of the most successful Deception
> operations of the last war was called Mincemeat. It was
> brilliantly conceived, and I was lucky enough to have
> some hand in the later stages. Naturally it was Top Secret.
>   I'm writing to you because I have learned – by accident
> – that it is about to be revealed to the world, and I hope
> something can be done to prevent such an act of folly.
> There is far too much of this revelation of war-time secrets
> going on. People seem so anxious to air their own clev-
> erness, or other people's – that they forget all about their
> duty. In this instance revelation would destroy any chance
> of our being able to use such a device again (i.e. a free
> gift to the Russians). It is also, of course, directly against
> the spirit of the Official Secrets Act. Finally, it might (a
> lesser point admittedly) get me into trouble in Spain.

Makins replied that, at the request of the DNI and the
Ministry of Defence, the author had already been asked to
alter the book 'sufficiently to make it unobjectionable (if that
is possible)' – but in fact it was too late, as the novel had already
been printed and was about to appear in America. Alan's friend
Jack Beevor, former head of SOE in Lisbon and now a solicitor, confirmed that there was little chance of having the book

stopped by means of an injunction. He pointed out that the
work included no mention of any naval attaché, and nothing
to identify the country in which the operation occurred: 'There
is a reference to a body being washed up on the shore, but
obviously there are several countries where that might have
occurred.'

When *Operation Heartbreak* came out in November 1950, it
inevitably attracted a good deal of publicity. Joe Baker-Cresswell,
Deputy DNI, wrote from the Admiralty to say that 'I don't
honestly think that any harm has been done' – but he added:
'A lot of people are still hopping mad over the whole thing.'

The matter weighed on Alan's mind, and early in the New
Year he helped his former chief John Godfrey draft a letter to
the Editor of *The Times* questioning the wisdom of premature
exposure:

> Is it prudent to disclose so many of the secrets of the last
> war for the information of a potential enemy or unfriendly
> neutral? While the majority of the memoirs, articles, broad-
> casts and, in some cases, fiction which recount what
> happened are harmless, it is difficult not to feel that, now
> and then, too much has been said, too many lessons, so
> painfully learnt, have been revealed, too many tricks and
> methods evolved from bitter trial have been given away.
> For it is patent that once described they cannot be used
> again . . .
>
> There being no censorship in this country, a duty of
> self-censorship surely devolves on all who write on
> wartime matters of which they have special knowledge,
> and this duty falls also on those who publish what the
> writers write.

Two years later, in February 1953, Alan was again dismayed
by the publication of Ewen Montagu's book *The Man Who*

Never Was, a factual and much more explicit account of
MINCEMEAT, by one of the operation's chief organisers. It
was serialised with explosive prominence in four consecutive
issues of the *Sunday Express*, and Alan's concern was shared by
Rear Admiral Sir Anthony Buzzard, who had become the
youngest ever DNI in 1951. After struggling to suppress parts
of the MINCEMEAT saga, he wrote from the Intelligence
Division of the Admiralty on 9 February:

> We too have been extremely concerned, and the outcome
> is the least damaging solution we were able to achieve
> . . . I hope the result is not too embarrassing to you, or
> our friends in Spain. The whole thing was fought on a
> very high level, so I am afraid there is nothing more
> which you are likely to be able to do about it.

Later, in a letter to Vice Admiral Sir Norman Denning,
Secretary of the Services, Press and Broadcasting Committee,
Alan explained why he was personally worried, disclosing that
during the war he had several times reported to Churchill
about Spaniards who were helping or could help the Allies,
'giving their names and considerable detail'. He feared that if
his reports were published, some of the Spaniards might suffer,
even long after the event. 'Moreover,' he went on,

> on one occasion the PM made me attend a meeting of
> the War Cabinet, with the Chiefs of Staff present, and
> tell them what we were doing, and why. That was fine,
> and it helped to decide our policy over Spain, which
> proved to be right; but disclosure of the minutes of that
> meeting would be disaster for some of the Spaniards
> concerned, not to mention that I might be *persona non
> grata* there.

He hoped (he wrote) that his participation in the meeting had been so secret that no record had been made of it – and he was much relieved to find that this was so: a search of the relevant minutes showed that no mention had been made of his presence.

It was early in 1954 that Alan first met Fr Bernard Basset, a Jesuit priest of superhuman energy, whose humanity and humility were matched by his astonishing literary output. He was forever on the move, teaching, preaching, lecturing, holding retreats – and always writing. He fired off letters in all directions as if from a Catherine wheel, and a stream of popular books poured from his typewriter, many published by Burns & Oates, the firm of which Tom Burns, Alan's friend and former intelligence colleague, was a director.

Basset was forty-five and working on his first book when he made contact with Alan, and in his early letters he addressed him as 'Captain Hillgarth'. When he accepted an invitation to stay at Illannanagh, he sent a cautious letter ahead:

> If I stay with you I would like to be certain that I can say Mass each morning in the Church and if permission from the Bishop is necessary, perhaps the parish priest who is a friend of yours will tell me what I have to do. Tell him that I am fully in union with the Holy See and in every way exemplary and with all my papers in order!!!

His visit was a huge success, and on 24 April he wrote to thank Alan for 'the four wonderful days I had with you. I cannot remember a happier visit in my life, and all the crowd of happy memories have at the centre your great kindness and generosity.' He returned to Illannanagh again and again, and whenever he was away on one of his lecture tours he wrote letters alight with love of the place and its owners – 'I miss you and Alan very much, and even the dogs and that cat qualify for a tear.'

Father Basset travelled widely, to America, New Zealand and India, but one of his pleasures was always to recount minor adventures at home – as when he agreed to go to the little Anglican parish of Corfe Mullin, in Dorset, to encourage the vicar and some parishioners who had started an organisation for Christian Courtesy on the Roads. To his alarm, he found a BBC television crew waiting to cover this sensational event – the first visit of a Jesuit priest to an Anglican church in 400 years.

When Jean suffered a miscarriage in December 1954, the news distressed Basset, who sent Alan a sympathetic letter from London:

> No-one really knows what God does in these cases except that God will not be less sympathetic and courteous than we would be ourselves . . . I desire more than anything to see you and Jean and the children in the One True Church. You believe, I know, and there would be for you all so little to learn. No family could make the great step with so little change. And yet the gain would be infinite.
>
> I say all this from time to time because I am so devoted to you both. Do tell Jean how much I grieve with her and how hard I will pray at Mass for you all.

In 1959, after a gentle but sustained campaign, he succeeded in converting Alan. Having obtained permission from the Archbishop of Westminster to receive him into the Catholic Church, he also had to seek a 'nullity from *ligamen*' from the Bishop of Killaloe, proving that Alan's two earlier marriages were null and void. As Basset cheerfully remarked, 'The first marriage to Mrs Tapper is now clearly finished with as she is dead', and it was the marriage to Mary which might have caused trouble. In the end all went well: Alan was duly received by Basset, and thereafter he regularly observed Mass in the Catholic church at Terryglass. Jean, however, held out against Basset's blandishments: she was prepared to accompany Alan to Mass, and was happy that her children should become Catholics, but she herself remained Protestant. She and Basset maintained a lively correspondence, and he never gave up hope of bringing her over to his shore: 'I become more and more aware of a basic unity,' he wrote. 'We feel so very much the same about God and life and children and prayers; we have the same doubts, the same quest for meaning; and I would shout to high heaven and dance an Irish jig if, before I die, we shared the same faith.'

One autumn found Basset in Houston, Texas, looking forward to visiting Illannanagh, but nervous about the imminent publication of his history of the English Jesuits, on which he had worked for four years: 'The very fact that the book is coming out makes me long to put the Irish Sea between myself and my critics and friends.' By the end of the month he was in Bournemouth, and asking if he might stay for seven days:

> The horizon is golden for me. I need no entertaining beyond you, Jean and the Shannon. One single night near Ballinderry will equal forty-two tablespoons of Parish's Food.
>
> My love to Jean who has no idea how much I love her; for me, two Hillgarths ride like lightships in a very choppy sea.

Basset was by no means the only visitor who found life at Illannanagh congenial. The atmosphere which the Hillgarths created made an indelible impression on guests who came to stay, among them Nigella's godfather Robert Speaight (biographer of Hilaire Belloc) and his second wife, Bridget, who wrote to Jean after a visit:

I am amazed at the beauty of it all, though I have always thought your lake one of the most beautiful in the world. And staying with you is always such a joy. I said to Bobbie as we sat in the train enjoying our Spanish omelette that I wished I could find a chink in the Hillgarth armour: such perfection of everything, children, house, organised life, plans for the future, capable management of everything, serenity and confidence – all this and much more marks you off as a race apart, and I find it rather alarming . . . But bless you, you possess the added and supreme virtue of remaining completely human, which isn't always the case.

Some of the Hillgarths' friends were puzzled (and a little piqued) that they seemed so content at home. 'Do you and Jean ever come to Paris, or anywhere on the continent?' asked Bob Solborg, who had settled in France after acting as the American Military Attaché in Lisbon during the war, and had become another godfather to Nigella. 'You just cannot spend all your time in Ireland, even though you must be very comfortable in your new home, and the surroundings are no doubt beautiful.'

The human inhabitants of Illannanagh were augmented by Nigella's menagerie of animals. She had a Siamese cat, and a donkey called Welkin, patient enough to stand still while she leant a little blue ladder against him so that she could climb on to his back. There was also a succession of black Labradors, and all three children grew up with horses, and hunted keenly with the North Tipperary and Ormond hounds.

Alan sent both boys to St Aubyns, a prep school with an excellent reputation near Brighton, over which the brilliant but eccentric W.H.Gervis (always known as 'Gervy') had presided as headmaster ever since 1940. Until he took over, the name of the establishment had been St Aubyn's, but for some reason he dropped the apostrophe, and it has been absent ever since.

The boys were happy and did well there. When Justin passed his Common Entrance exam, Gervy suggested that he should go to Eton. Alan therefore put him down for the house then run by a mathematics master, Cyril Chamier, who accepted him – but a last-minute change of heart blew the plan away. In the autumn of 1959, instead of sending Justin to Eton, and Tristan back to St Aubyns, Alan decided to take the whole family to Switzerland for three months, so that they could learn to ski and at the same time pick up some French; but when he put the idea to Chamier, the answer was: 'In that case you'll have to take along a tutor of my choosing, so that Justin can keep up with his work.' Alan refused to agree, and his sudden decision changed the direction of the boys' lives. The family all became proficient skiers; both boys went to Ampleforth instead of Eton, and both became Catholics.

Often during the summer holidays Alan took the family to Spain, driving down through France in his big DeSoto station wagon, staying in small hotels and pausing at village markets to buy ham and cheese for picnic lunches. He never missed a chance of advertising his enthusiasm for Spain and the Spanish to the wider world. A perfect occasion presented itself in May 1958, when the arrival of the aircraft carrier HMS *Eagle* on an official visit to Barcelona enabled him to extol the virtues of both the British and Spanish Navies in a letter to the quarterly *Naval Review*. The visit, he reported, was an 'enormous success – so much so that I never heard of any visit to a Spanish port marked by greater cordiality'. Its climax was a day of flying exercises at sea, in which the ship's controllers and pilots demonstrated a high degree of skill. The display impressed the senior Spanish naval officers so much that their comments 'were almost out of this world'.

The Spaniards [Alan went on] are a fine fighting race with
whom we have much in common but with whom we
have not always been allowed to be as friendly as many of
us would have liked. Now that things are changing, it is
to be hoped that we shall respond to the Spaniards' readiness to like us. In this the Navy has a particular advantage,
because the Spanish naval officer is more akin to us than
perhaps we have realised . . . Furthermore, the Spanish naval
officer feels himself intensely European. While admiring
transatlantic might and 'know-how', he feels more at home
with us, and I believe we should cultivate his friendship
and help him forward as much as we can.

Alan also had business interests in Spain, both on his own
account and in association with Juan March, who paid him a
handsome retainer and appointed him a director of Helvetia,
one of his financial companies based in London. Alan also
acted as an adviser on the troubled affairs of the Barcelona
Traction, Light and Power Company, the electricity-producing
giant of which March had acquired control in 1948. An
immensely long and complicated lawsuit over the ownership
of shares rumbled on for years, with March being savagely
criticised for his early financial manoeuvring. Alan stood by
him, and when he died in 1962, aged eighty-two, sought to
modify the murky impression given by an obituary in *The
Times*, drafting a letter (which the paper declined to publish):

In the darkest days of the last war, when it was often
difficult to find a neutral who still believed in us, Señor
March never wavered. I remember hearing him say, to a
despondent but influential personage, that we must win
because we had sea power and that rare quality, the inability
to admit defeat. It was a quality he understood, because
he had it himself.

When Belgian investors appealed to Spanish courts for the release of their bonds in the Barcelona Traction Company, they had no success, so the Belgian government took the case to the International Court of Justice in The Hague. In 1968 Alan signed an affidavit attesting to the late Señor March's integrity, but the proceedings ground on until 1970, when the Belgian claim was at last rejected by fifteen votes to one.

As the Hillgarth children grew older, they came to see that their parents were wonderfully well matched, and they sensed that this was by far their father's happiest marriage. Alan and Jean remained devoted to each other, always at ease together, writing at length if separated for more than a few days, as deeply in love until the ends of their lives as they had been when they first met. Both instilled old-fashioned principles of behaviour into their offspring – honour, truth, fear no man – but within the family Alan was quite different from the rather serious figure he presented to outsiders: always full of jokes, always suggesting projects to the boys, urging them on, always asking what they planned to do that day.

Justin did not enjoy public school, but his time at Ampleforth was relatively short, for at sixteen he left, spent four agreeable months hunting in Ireland, went to Spain to learn the language, and then followed family tradition by going into the Royal Navy at seventeen and winning a scholarship to Dartmouth. After nine months there, and three months as a cadet in the training squadron, he served for a year in the Far East and in home waters. Then, however, his enthusiasm cooled when he found he was faced with another year's training at Dartmouth and further courses beyond it – which meant that it would be two years before he could go back to sea. His father may have been disappointed by his premature retirement from the Navy, but put no pressure on him to stay on.

Tristan left school at eighteen, and at Trinity College, Dublin, read Economics and Politics, leavened by two long summers in Spain, improving his grasp of the language. Then in 1971 he joined Guinness Mahon, a small merchant bank in London, as a trainee in the corporate finance department, before returning to Jerez, where his parents had again rented the House of Zurita. His first full-time job, from 1972 to 1975, was with Arthur Andersen, the international accountants, for whom he spent six months on secondment to the office in Johannesburg.

Nigella was sent to St Mary's Ascot, which she hated. By her own account, she did poorly, and her performance was erratic: one week she would come top of the form, the next bottom. Nobody realised that she was severely dyslexic, and the teachers just thought she was lazy. The result was that after a while she stopped trying to learn. Only after she left school did she realise she had a passion and a natural aptitude for science, little of which had been taught at St Mary's: one of her first jobs was working in the Coto Doñana wildlife reserve in the south-west corner of Spain. After that she lived for several months in London, where she took a secretarial course, then returned home, trying to work out what she wanted to do for a career. Her parents, she feared, must have been thinking, 'My God, what are we going to do with her?', but they supported her nobly, and did not demur when she spent many days hunting with the North Tipp, which she loved.

All his adult life Alan had smoked, and he was so much in the habit that he found his long flights over the Pacific and Indian Oceans, during which smoking was banned, a severe trial. He continued to smoke in Ireland, getting through more than a packet of untipped Chesterfields a day, as well as the occasional cigar. Then in about 1965 he suddenly gave up, and he was aggrieved when, after twelve days, none of the family had noticed – but he never smoked again.

★　★　★

In the twenty-odd years since the Hillgarths arrived, Tipperary had become more sophisticated in many respects, but not in all. One day when Tristan went shopping at a greengrocer's in the nearby town of Borrisokane, he was astonished to see avocado pears among the turnips and potatoes. Avocados! Never before in County Tipp! So he bought three, and as he was leaving the shop, the woman behind the counter said, 'Can I ask you something?'

'You can, of course.'

'How long do you boil them things for?'

Alan was strict with his employees – 'The servants are being very good,' he once wrote to Jean while she was away, 'though I had to tell them off for being late for breakfast this morning' – and he could on occasion become ferocious, bawling out anyone who had performed badly. But his bark was always worse than his bite, and he inspired powerful affection, particularly among the outdoor workmen. This came out in letters from Jack O'Donoghue, One-Legged Jack, who, with his wife Jen (known as 'Dun Dun'), retired to live in north London. When Alan inadvertently blocked a move he was making to acquire a cottage, Jack penned him a sharp complaint; Alan immediately explained how the mistake had occurred, and forgave him his intemperate outburst, whereupon Jack wrote again:

Captain,

To say I was glad to get your letter of 4th would be very very mild. I think I must have been the happiest man in London. Nothing else mattered than the Capt had forgiven me.

Now we wonder how is Madam and yourself Captain also of course the children, never a day passed without some mention of you all and Illannanagh. I feel I could still walk the woods blindfolded and I still see every stone on the shore every low branch and I wonder which way the wind is blowing, to try and outwit the ducks, or to watch for the lights of the car at night and feel very happy and content when you both passed safely in . . .

How is Miss Nigella? We are always drawing pictures of her in our mind whats she doing now how does she look etc. I'm afraid if I was there I'd try to teach her plenty mischief.

Now we hope yourself Madam and family are enjoying very best of health and happiness and will continue to do so.

> Good night, God bless you all, Your very apologetic (but happy) Servants Jack & Dun Dun.

Over the years Alan maintained friendly contact with John Godfrey. In 1948 former members of the NID, including Ian Fleming, had formed a small dining club, the 36 Club, named after 36 Curzon Street, the house in which both Godfrey and his celebrated predecessor Admiral Sir Reginald (Blinker) Hall had lived. Alan accepted the invitation to join, subscribed to the fund for a presentation and offered a supply of sherry; but he avoided the annual reunion dinners, at which Godfrey and his wife Margaret were guests of honour, on the grounds that his home was too far from London – whereupon his former chief tried to lure him with the suggestion of a small party at the Écu de France, Manetta's or the Bon Viveur. 'Personally,' he wrote, 'I like small parties and congenial people rather than larger ones, and have always felt that the ideal number is six at a round table.'

In February 1969 the old admiral, now eighty, sent a glowing tribute, as he recalled the 'resounding years' of the war, with their 'many disappointments and triumphs':

Fate decreed that, as in World War One, DNI should have a finger in the Spanish pie, and what a pie it was. You were in every sense a super-attaché – and one in which we all had implicit confidence – and Don ably assisted you as a sort of Sancho Panza to your Quixote. That you should maintain direct touch with Winston was all in keeping, altho' it might have shocked a more traditional DNI than I. But I trusted you implicitly, knowing that you would instinctively avoid or surmount the pitfalls with which such a liaison was beset.

Two years later, in August 1971, when Godfrey died, Alan sent Margaret a glowing letter of condolence:

For me the Admiral was – and will always be – a very special person. I can't begin to tell you how much I loved and admired him. Few people, even few Naval Officers, have realised how great a man he was and how large a part he played to ensure victory in the last war.

Of course he never blew his own trumpet or schemed to get anything for himself; what's more, he seldom tried to conceal his opinion at critical moments, no matter what the consequences – and that isn't always the way to acquire merit in this silly world. But then he never sought to acquire merit. Only a man like him can really put the cause before himself.

It is an infernal shame he was never given a K, but I'll venture to say that seldom was a K – or a pair of Ks – more truly earned, and some of us, at least, know that. God bless him.

Alan also sprang to defend the admiral's reputation in public, drafting a letter to *The Times*. The paper's obituary, he said, had rightly implied that Godfrey had been one of the architects of victory in the world war; but the notice had pointed out that he was the only naval officer of his seniority and rank to receive no recognition at all:

It is one of the most disturbing examples of ingratitude in recent history. Certainly he had an irascible temper and an inability to suffer mediocrity, but those are no excuse, any more than his energetic treatment of subordinates in the R[oyal] I[ndian] N[avy]. The truth is he was victimised by lesser men.

Another wartime colleague who kept in touch was Don Gómez-Beare. Perennially short of money, but irrepressibly cheerful, Don wrote letter after letter from his home in Gibraltar, reporting family problems, sometimes seeking advice, lamenting business failures and the death of his beloved little dog Trollie, but never asking for financial help. Once when Alan offered to put money into his account in London, he replied: 'I am most appreciative of your kind offer, but I cannot accept. You are my best friend, and that is just the one thing I cannot do.'

For years Alan worked away doggedly at a new novel – *The Valley* – again an adventure story, set in wild landscapes, but more philosophical than any of his earlier works. The book opens with Dan Adams, a banker from New York, setting off on a forty-eight-hour train journey up into the hinterland of some unnamed country. From the sheer size of the place, from its physical features (high, baking sierras, snow-clad peaks) and from its language (Spanish), readers can infer that it is in South America. Dan's objective is the Valley – a fertile area and a community set in the mountains at an immense distance from any other human habitation.

As the train trundles along, he and his companions discuss world problems at paralysing length: the merits and demerits of Communism, Capitalism, Anarchism, Christianity, the dangers and morality of nuclear weapons – all are minutely dissected. Eventually they reach the Valley, to find that a revolution has occurred and the Reds are in control.

At last, after nearly 300 pages, the point of Dan's marathon

journey is revealed. The mayor of the Valley has discovered a
vein of pure mobium, the most valuable metal on earth, the
only one which on its own can contain the products of nuclear
fission. Reactors can be jacketed with it at a fraction of the
conventional cost. The Valley is sitting on unimaginable wealth,
and Dan's bank will handle it.

An earthquake splits the mountain open, creating a chasm
a mile wide and severing access to the mobium deposit. Worse,
the deposit itself is buried under millions of tons of tumbled
rock, lost for ever. The mayor's niece tries to shoot Dan with
a pistol, but misses twice at point-blank range. And then, a
miracle. The quake has opened a stupendous gusher of oil,
from a field whose presence has never been suspected. The
Valley *will* be richer than any Middle East kingdom.

What cripples the novel is its hopelessly uneven pace. Before
any action starts, the travellers talk inconsequentially for a
hundred pages of turgid waffle – and then events accelerate at
a bewildering rate. Had the author cut the first 25,000 words,
he might have found a publisher; as it was, the book failed to
attract a bid. Clearly Alan wanted to air his views on world
affairs, but he could not weave them into his story in a palat-
able way. This was a pity, for the central theme of the novel
– a journey to a strange, remote destination – is an exciting
one, and the book contains fine descriptions of terrain, besides
reflecting episodes of the author's own life: the last stages of
the journey, on horseback along narrow tracks across cliff-faces,
recall the hellish approach to Sacambaya; after the revolution
the whistle of shells passing overhead, and the thunder of their
explosions, are surely distant echoes of Gallipoli.

When not working on his own novel, Alan continued to give
generous help to other writers, pointing out errors and
suggesting improvements in the drafts which they sent him.
Numerous authors – among them his former shipmate Eric

Bush (*Gallipoli*) and Captain Donald Macintyre (a biography of Admiral Somerville) asked him to verify their facts. 'Thank you too for toning down the bit about Franco corruption,' wrote Sefton Delmer, after submitting the text of *The Counterfeit Spy*, his biography of the double agent Juan Pujol García known as Garbo. 'It did read a little bit too much like Michael Foot as it was!' Distinguished naval historians such as Stephen Roskill and the American Arthur Marder approached Alan for advice and information. No author depended more heavily on him than Donald McLachlan, the first Editor of the *Sunday Telegraph* (from 1961 to 1966), whose book *Room 39* revealed some of the secrets of naval intelligence during the war. McLachlan visited Illannanagh several times (usually leaving something behind when he left) and drew heavily on Alan's own unpublished memorandum about his time as Naval Attaché in Madrid, but did not acknowledge help from that quarter – perhaps at Alan's request.

For many years the rift in the Hillgarth family remained open. Then one evening, as Justin was having dinner in the Coffee Room at the Garrick, he said to the wine waiter, 'Please make sure that goes on my bill, not my brother's' – to which the waiter replied, 'But your brother's sitting over there in the corner.' He then went across to Jocelyn and said, 'Do you realise your brother's here?' Looking across, Justin was astonished to see a man with many of his father's features, including the bushy eyebrows, who, he realised, must be Jocelyn. The two had never set eyes on each other before, but now they nodded and smiled at each other, then got up and bowed ceremonially. They immediately hit it off, and when Jocelyn reported the meeting to his wife Nina, she insisted that the family should bury their differences and get together. The result was a joyful reunion at Brown's Hotel, to which Alan invited all his sons for a slap-up lunch.

Many distinguished people still sought his opinion or assistance in affairs concerning Spain, and he was usually able to help them. In July 1975 Ian, 12th Duke of Argyll (the 'little Ian' with whom Jean had played on the floor in Portugal during the war), wrote asking urgently if Alan would 'make discreet enquiries' at libraries and museums in Spain, to find out what (if anything) Robert Stenuit, a Belgian marine archaeologist, had discovered about the Spanish galleon *Florencia*, which was reputed to have sunk in Tobermory harbour on the Island of Mull when the surviving ships of the Armada ran for home in the autumn of 1588. The duke and his forbears had long since claimed ownership of the wreck and its contents – alleged to be worth millions – but all attempts at salvage had failed, and now he was alarmed to learn that Stenuit seemed to be hot on a new scent.

In reply, Alan recommended him to make contact with 'my great friend the Duque de Villahermosa', a retired naval captain – and Ian was delighted with the help he provided. 'I cannot tell you how much I appreciate the considerable trouble you went to in this matter,' he wrote from Inveraray Castle. 'I am immensely impressed by the distinction of your contacts in the Spanish kingdom!' It is no longer clear what results his circuitous searches yielded; but after he himself had gone down in an exploratory dive later in 1975, a disastrous fire broke out in the Castle, the damage being compounded by the efforts of the fire brigade to douse the flames – and the double disaster apparently substantiated a prophecy of the legendary Brahan Seer, that any member of the Campbell family who sought to disturb the wreck of the *Florencia* would be cursed with fire and water.

A heavy blow bludgeoned the Hillgarth family that summer, when Jean fell ill with cancer. Luckily Nigella was living at home, and she was glad to be able to share her mother's last months. Heliodoro came back from Spain with Donina to help

in the house. Alan alerted Father Basset to the fact that Jean
had not long to live, and the old priest, who now described
himself as 'dithering on the brink', sent one last letter heavy
with love and sorrow, but ending with a typical lift: 'Please do
not think of answering this, but one thing you could do if
you do not get better; put in a word for me on the other side.
God will listen to you. Very gratefully in Christ. Bernard Basset
SJ.'

The disease spread with horrible rapidity, and after only
three months Jean died, on 15 August, aged sixty. She was
buried in the churchyard at Terryglass – an exceptional privi-
lege, for the Irish Church did not normally allow a Protestant
to be interred in a Catholic cemetery. Old warrior that he
was, Alan bore up stoically, but his children knew that he was
inwardly devastated: although they did everything they could
to comfort him, it seemed to them that he never fully recovered.

One evening only six weeks later, Justin drove home the
100-odd miles from Dublin airport and cooked some supper,
which he and his father ate. Afterwards they were sitting in
the library over coffee when they saw the lights of a vehicle
go round the side of the house to the front entrance, facing
the lake. Because they hardly ever used the front door, they
kept it locked – and now, since Justin knew that the bell did
not work, he walked through the hall and opened the door,
to be confronted by four men in camouflage smocks and black
hoods, brandishing handguns.

He tried to slam the door shut, but one of the four had his
foot in the opening. A fight broke out, and Justin was hit over
the head. Blood began pouring down his face, and a couple
of shots went off. 'Right,' he thought, 'we'd better stop this',
so he demanded, 'What do you want?'

'We've come for the shorts,' said the leader.

'What do you mean? We haven't got any.'

'Ah, you have. We're acting on information that you have some.'

'Not at all. All we have is some shotguns.'

'We'll take them, then.'

'All right. But will you please respect the fact that my mother died six weeks ago? My father and I are here on our own.'

At that the gunmen calmed down a little, muttering apologies and lowering their weapons. With them following, Justin led the way through the hall. In the library his father was sitting in an armchair reading a newspaper.

'Papa,' said Justin. 'We have visitors. These gentlemen want our guns.'

Alan lowered his paper, instantly took in the situation, and said calmly, 'The first thing you do is point those things at the ground.'

The IRA men did as he suggested. Then he said to Justin, 'Well – you'd better show them where they are.'

Two men stayed with Alan, and the other two followed Justin through to the small playroom, where four shotguns were kept in a mahogany cabinet. The raiders took them all. Back in the study the leader said, 'We need to search the house.'

'Search away,' said Alan. Off two of them went, and when they returned empty-handed, Justin suggested, 'Why don't we all have a drink? I'll forget you've been here, and we'll call it a day.' Declining his offer, the leader said, 'We'll have to tie you up. But don't worry. We'll tell the Gardai we've been, and they'll come and free you.'

Producing a bag of women's tights, they tied their captives to wooden chairs, but Alan managed to sit forward surreptitiously, so as to leave some slack in his bonds. The IRA then left, having cut the telephone line and taken the keys of the car from the garage, but having stolen nothing else except the shotguns. Both prisoners soon managed to free themselves, whereupon each had a very stiff whisky, and Justin put a sign on the back door for the Gardai, saying, 'Don't worry. We've gone to bed. Come back in the morning.'

Next day, of course, he found the sign still in place. Having unearthed some spare keys for the car, he drove the two miles into Ballinderry and rang the Gardai, who reacted with their usual despatch. 'Don't touch anything!' said the sergeant urgently. 'We'll be there.' Two and a half hours later, up he came with reinforcements from the specialist branch in Limerick, and a fingerprint specialist in tow.

A search of the house revealed no clues; but in due course the Gardai concluded that two of the raiders were local amateurs, and that the other two had been imported for the job – both of them murderers recently escaped from gaol. It seemed that the operation may have been based on a misunderstanding, and that the IRA had targeted the wrong house.

The episode evoked much sympathy from the Hillgarths' Irish neighbours, who were shocked that the raid had been carried out in a period of mourning; but it left Justin deeply impressed by the coolness with which his father had reacted. He felt that the intruders, who were nervous anyway, had been almost awe-struck by the steely demeanour of the man who remained sitting in his armchair.

Only a fortnight later, in Barcelona, he slipped and broke his right leg badly, which meant that he had to spend five months in hospital. When he came back to Illannanagh in February 1976, he was (as the Irish put it) pretty shook, so the family converted the dining room into a bedroom, making it easier for Nigella and Nanny Eames to look after him. He made an excellent physical recovery, but then his mind began to wander as he succumbed to some form of dementia, perhaps brought on by hardening of the arteries. Tristan gave up his job in the city to be at home and run the farm, and Justin sent money to help cover expenses.

With his children Alan talked more than ever before about the horrors of the wars he had been through. Nigella got the impression that his experiences at Gallipoli had left him traumatised, and that he had bottled up his fear and disgust throughout his life. Now some of it came out. And yet he maintained that the brutalities he witnessed during the Spanish Civil War surpassed all the dreadful sights he had seen on the shores of the Dardanelles. He talked very little about Majorca, but often about Spain during the world war, happily telling Tristan how he had spied on the Germans, and they on him. Although he would forget something that had happened the day before, he still had a clear memory of the distant past. To the very end he retained his reluctance to make secret information public. When a letter came from Mountbatten asking him for details of HMS Anderson, he looked straight at Tristan and said, 'Tell him I can't remember.'

Alan was bedridden for only the last week of his life: he died on 28 February 1978 and was buried alongside Jean in the churchyard at Terryglass – the only civilian graveyard in Ireland in which all the small, plain headstones are uniform and set out in regular rows, as in a military cemetery.

Heartfelt letters of condolence flooded into Illannanagh. 'Apart from bouts of merciless teasing, he was always amazingly kind and thoughtful,' wrote his niece Denise Fekete from Canada. 'I'm really sorry – partly because I knew and loved him, but also because he was a kind of symbol of goodness and courage and rectitude to many people in many places.' 'I shall always remember your father's brilliance and his kindness, and the lovely twinkle in his eyes, with the greatest affection,' wrote Pam Blunden, who had worked with him in Ceylon. A final word came from his lifelong friend Eric Bush, who was about to set off on yet another return visit to Gallipoli. 'I shall be off Anzac on Sunday 16 April, when I shall be thinking of your dear father and mother,' he told all three children. 'He was a splendid man in every way.'

*   *   *

Later in 1978, when the family put the house on the market, the first potential buyer was an insurance company, which wanted to make the place into a hotel, but was refused permission. Next came a representative of Transcendental Meditation, whose aim was to turn it into an academy; luckily, perhaps, the organisation could not afford the purchase price, and the deal fell through – but not before an unnerving incident had taken place. Eleanor Wilkinson, a member of the TM committee, was looking round the empty house when, in one of the bedrooms, she was surprised to find a man standing beside the fireplace. He told her that her organisation should not buy the place, because it ought to remain a family home. She had never met the Hillgarths, and knew nothing about them, but when she described the man to a friend who *had* known them, the friend had absolutely no doubt that it was Alan whom she had seen. What Eleanor did not know was that the room in which she had the encounter had been his dressing room.

It seemed as if his spirit, or influence, had warded off two undesirable approaches; but then in 1980 the property fell into friendlier hands when Mrs Wilkinson's son Michael, flush with money from the sale of family farmland near Dublin, saw Illannanagh advertised, drove down, fell in love with it and bought it. He found that the Hillgarths had left behind a number of books, many of them about natural history and inscribed with the signature (which meant nothing to him) Dyddgu Hamilton – the last, poignant echo of a lifelong friendship.

Thirty years after the end of the civil war, Alan's reputation was still burning bright in Spain. Tristan heard a rousing echo of it when he went to a huge wedding attended by 800 guests near Tarragona. In the middle of the speeches the father of the bride, the Conde del Asalto, stood up and announced, 'This ceremony would not be taking place, if it hadn't been for the father of one of the people present here today.' He then launched into a long account of how Alan had rescued him from gaol and probable execution.

A still more stirring event occurred in the summer of 2000. There was great excitement – and some astonishment – in Terryglass when a yellow minibus bus full of small, dark Minorcans arrived to pay homage to the man they still venerated as their saviour. Until that moment the people of the village had had no idea that Alan had played such a crucial role during the Spanish Civil War, because he had never spoken about it. Now, twenty-two years after his death, Irish eyes were opened wide when the delegation – the men smartly dressed in dark suits – professed that they owed not only their own lives but the very survival of their island community to Alan.

The visit was entirely unofficial – a spontaneous private tribute paid by three generations of the same family, the oldest man being eighty, and still driving – and the trip had evidently been planned for some time, as the visitors had brought with them a brass plaque, incised in perfect English, commemorating Alan's life-saving work. 'In gratitude and appreciation of Alan Hillgarth, British Consul in Majorca', it read, 'for his humanitarian aid to the people of Minorca at the end of the Spanish Civil War, February 1939. A group of Minorcans, July 2000.'

Representatives of the Hillgarth family assembled from far and wide. Jocelyn, who had organised the event, came from London with Nina, and they put up in the same guest house as the Minorcans at Terryglass. Nigella had flown in that morning from California and stayed in her own cottage close to the main estate. Jetlagged though she was, she found the occasion inspiring. The visitors spoke to Jocelyn in Catalan and to Nina in Spanish, and one or two of them had a little French; but linguistic difficulties could not mask the fact that they were deeply moved to see the place where Alan had lived.

On 21 July a few local people, including Pauline Hickie

and Rickard Deasy's mother Sheila, joined the group for a traditional memorial Mass in the church at Terryglass, and tears were shed as the Minorcans stood in a ring round Alan's head-stone in the graveyard to say prayers for his soul. They also laid flowers on the grave, and on Jean's, next to it. Their organiser, Josep Antoni Pons Roca, had written to Jocelyn two years earlier, saying that he hoped they would sing 'It's a Long Way to Tipperary', but in the event — fortunately perhaps — they desisted.

Nigella took them down the avenue to look at the big white house, which had been stripped for renovation by its latest owner, Gail Getty, first wife of J. Paul Getty II. Standing empty, with its rooms bare, the building looked impressively large, and its sylvan setting, with its view out over the lake to the far mountains of Clare and Galway, struck the visitors as an entirely suitable place of retirement for their saviour. During the speeches at an elaborate dinner in the Annagh guest house, emotions ran high, and Jocelyn and Nigella — the Minorcans' living link with their father — felt an immense warmth of gratitude emanating from their guests. Soon after they had left, the brass plaque was installed on the wall in the church's Spanish side-chapel, and Señor Pons produced a small booklet in Catalan commemorating the event, *Homenatge a Alan Hillgarth*.

In years to come visitors to Terryglass who read the inscription may wonder what it was that Alan Hillgarth did for Minorca. If they go to the island, they will soon find out. If they go to Madrid, mention of his name will quickly evoke glowing reminiscences. And if they inquire after him in Majorca, they will soon be directed to Son Torrella, where the great house, still standing out proud against the mountains, and still belonging to his family, bears witness to his abiding love of Spain.

Appendix:
The role of the naval attaché

Written by Alan Hillgarth, probably in 1946

I. *The importance of the maintenance of a Naval Attaché in Spain may be summarised as follows:*

(1) In time of war or of strained European relations the strategic significance of Spain, whether as friend, foe or neutral, becomes immediately vital and it is essential to have our finger on the Spanish pulse. As in Spain military opinion (in the wide sense of the word military) is the determining factor, no matter what the complexion of the government), foreign service Attachés are nearer to the heart of affairs than they can be in many other countries. Although the Spanish Army has much greater influence than the Spanish Navy or Air Force, the Army does not, traditionally, regard the British Army as the best army in the world, whereas the Navy does so regard the Royal Navy, and this regard persists in spite of the present strength and recent achievements of the United States Navy. The British Naval Attaché, in fact, occupies a position of very considerable strength, which is further enhanced by both the geographical

situation of Spain and the extent of Spanish dependence on maritime trade. His position, indeed, automatically extends his influence beyond purely naval circles.

(2) But it is not only as a contact with opinion and feeling that the British Naval Attaché enjoys influence due to his position. His influence is also positive, in the sense that he can direct opinion, of course only in a limited degree and limited sphere, but still within those limitations very valuably. The reason for this is that the Spaniards are always ready to notice what he says and does, in a way that no other member of the Embassy, except the Ambassador himself, is noticed. This is entirely due to the fact that he is the representative of the Royal Navy. Our prestige is still immense in Spain. As an illustration it is enough to mention that the British Naval Attaché is recognised as a personality of importance by Spanish generals, whereas no Spanish admiral ever worries about the British Military Attaché.

(3) While much of this influence, which, as already explained, is due to position, cannot be permanently impaired by an unsuitable appointment, a great deal of it must be at least temporarily eclipsed if the officer appointed is not the right kind, and his successor is faced with a much harder task, even if none of the lost influence is lost for ever. The sort of officer best fitted for this appointment is described in later paragraphs.

(4) Disadvantages of an equally serious nature must follow if the Naval Attaché is not resident in Spain but only visits it at intervals. From 1923 to 1939 the Naval Attachés accredited to Spain resided in Paris. Although they visited Spain from time to time and made useful reports, they had no knowledge of the place or people and no influence whatever. Spanish naval opinion, moreover, is at once adverse to what may be called

secondary treatment. Although the Naval Attaché was received politely, he was never accorded Spanish confidence.

(5) There exists a view that the presence of a naval command at Gibraltar and the consequent frequent local contacts, combined with visits of H.M. ships (in normal times) compensate adequately for the absence of a resident naval attaché. This view is erroneous. Contacts through Gibraltar are purely local, and naval visits, besides being infrequent, are usually not to the chief naval bases. There is neither intimacy nor continuity.

(6) The view that the appointment of a resident naval attaché can safely be neglected in time of peace, provided one is appointed when war threatens, is not practical because even the best naval attaché imaginable needs time in which to consolidate his position to the degree of strength essential in time of war. Continuity of appointment is therefore vital. While every relief by one naval attaché of another must mean a slight weakening of his position, the right kind of officer will recapture full strength very quickly if his predecessor was good, and within a reasonable period if that predecessor was below the first flight. Such is the inherent strength of the position itself. But if there has been no predecessor, there has been no position, and the newly-appointed Naval Attaché must begin from the very beginning.

(7) In addition to the British Naval Attaché's importance as a source of information on and as a source of influence upon Spanish views and feelings, primarily in the naval sphere but also in wider circles, he has a great importance due to the link between British naval construction and the Spanish Navy. The value of this link to British export is at the moment, for political reasons, dormant, but it represents a potential trade of several million sterling per annum, plus, when trade can again become active, a large lump of capital re-equipment worth not

less than fifty millions. The political obstacle is temporary. If the link is carefully maintained, the link is permanent. An able naval attaché is essential to preserve that link. If it is not preserved, the United States will in due course get the business.

(8) I was appointed Naval Attaché to Spain, to reside in Madrid, in August 1939. A few months earlier Spain had been transferred from the charge of the Naval Attaché in Paris to that of the Naval Attaché in Portugal, to whom I was therefore assistant. He had visited Spain once that summer but was, naturally, too busy to pay another visit once the war started, and during the whole of my time as his assistant I never saw him. This did not matter much, as the important thing was that someone was resident in Spain, although the Spaniards felt even more irritated at being considered subordinate to Portugal than they had when in the same minor position vis-à-vis France, and they were pleased when in January 1940 my appointment was altered to that of Naval Attaché and my subservience to the Naval Attaché in Lisbon came to an end.

(9) The potential strength in Spain of the position of British Naval Attaché had not been fully apparent to me before my appointment, and it surprised me at the time. I do not believe it is sufficiently known, though it should be. At the same time, having had no predecessor for sixteen years, I had to build it up from the bottom. That is, the basis existed, but the edifice had to be constructed. It was only because as Consul at Palma during the Civil War I had fortunately established a certain personal position with the Spanish Navy and with other Spanish Nationalist authorities that I was able to build up the Naval Attaché's position more quickly than would otherwise have been the case. This illustrates the importance, everywhere but particularly so in Spain, of the personal aspect.

II. *Choice of Naval Attaché*

(1) The British Naval Attaché to Spain, in the ordinary course of things, will be – and should be – an officer on the Active List. The appointment should be for not less than three years, in order to enable him to have as long a period of duty at full usefulness as possible.

(2) The first requirement is an intense interest in his job and in Spain. This presupposes a liking for or a readiness to like Spain and the Spaniards, in fact a natural sympathy. I cannot overstress the importance of this requirement. Without it he will be useless, however good he may be in other respects. With it, he has already half the victory. Nor should it ever be difficult to find such an officer. The Service is full of them. Unfortunately it has not always been thought necessary to weigh that characteristic carefully when a naval attaché is chosen, for any post but especially for Spain. There are still some very able officers who believe, though they probably would not actively admit it, that all Dagoes begin at Dover. Anyone who feels this, even mildly, will be bowled out by the Spaniards in five minutes. He will be refused their confidence, and he is ruined.

(3) The second requirement is tact, patience and determination combined. Handling Spaniards is a special technique which, once acquired, yields rich dividends. It is easily learned, in quite a short time, given these three qualities and the natural sympathy mentioned in the last paragraph. One can offend a Spaniard very easily, but it is equally easy to avoid offence if one is careful. By sticking quietly to your objective and contriving whenever possible to make the Spaniard you are dealing with feel that you like him and appreciate his difficulties, you will eventually gain your point. It seldom pays to

quote rules or precedents. Everything in Spain is on a personal basis. One of my best moments in Madrid was when I managed to make the Minister of Marine so sorry for me, because he could not do what I wanted, that in the end he did it, at considerable hazard to himself, just because he felt he was letting a friend down if he didn't.

(4) The third requirement is a generally wide knowledge of one's profession, without too pronounced a leaning in any one direction. I do not mean that a specialist should not be appointed. It is merely that the Naval Attaché must represent the whole execution side of the Service with equal adequacy at all times. He need not be a very brilliant officer, but he should be a sound one, professionally, interested in all new developments and well read in Service matters of current and open discussion. This general professional requirement may be taken to include naval history, including the naval history, however long ago, of the country to which he is accredited. Nearly all Spanish naval officers are intensely interested in naval history. The Naval Attaché to Spain should speedily supply, by study, any deficiencies he may possess in this particular. He need not aim at profundity.

(5) The fourth requirement is diplomatic discretion. Most naval officers possess discretion, but many of them have never been exposed to the necessity for an apparently – and as far as possible genuinely – candid frankness, privately qualified by reservations. It is a habit professional diplomats learn young. Mere uncommunicativeness is no good, though it may be 100 per cent discreet. The ability to talk and to say only what can be said, and none of what cannot be said, without in any way offending others or rousing their curiosity, is important in a naval attaché. The average naval officer can acquire it without great difficulty, if he does not already possess it, but he must be warned.

(6) The fifth requirement is a knowledge of Spanish. The possession of the qualification alone should never influence the selection of a naval attaché for Spain if he does not possess those qualifications already mentioned. Nor should its absence in an otherwise suitable candidate bar his selection. For Spanish is an easy language to learn well enough for simple purposes, and a zealous officer will quickly build up a good, easy, conversational Spanish, in which he can sustain formal or informal conversation all day if necessary. But an appointee without the language must undertake to learn it as hard as he can, for without it he will not be in the first flight.

(7) The sixth requirement is an unquarrelsome disposition. He must get on well with his colleagues in the Embassy. Life in the Embassy is often very irksome because of stupid jealousies. He may find his Air and Military colleagues objectionable.

There have been cases in some posts where service attachés never spoke to one another for months except on service. The Diplomatic and Commercial staffs are also often aggravating. There is a curious suspicion in nearly all diplomats of the service attachés. But perhaps this recruitment may be included in the second requirement. I only mention it separately because of the need for good relations inside the Embassy.

(8) The seventh requirement is common sense. It is hardly necessary to enlarge on this point, since everyone will know what I mean and its importance is obvious.

(9) The eighth requirement is private means. While the absence of a private income should not bar any otherwise suitable officer, it is an extremely useful asset. As an alternative, a more frequent and sympathetic enquiry into the adequacy of the Naval Attaché's consolidated allowance is called for.

(10) There are other minor requirements. While I am assuming that the Naval Attaché will be of sober habits, he will be at a definite disadvantage if he is a teetotaller. A knowledge of French is very useful, not among Spaniards, but among his colleagues of other nations. Without it, he will often be at a loss. A good digestion is important. A presentable wife, who is prepared to learn Spanish and to show the Spaniards that she likes them, is very useful indeed.

(11) The best rank for the British Naval Attaché is that of captain, but the appointment of a commander is perfectly in order. He will not have quite the advantages of a captain, but he will not lose much. The essential thing is not rank but personality.

III. Relations, precedence, collaboration

(1) My first Ambassador, Sir Maurice Peterson, was pleasant, but did not understand the true function of service attachés, especially in time of war. I – and my Military and Air colleagues – had to struggle to get any real knowledge of what was going on. We were treated as skilled technicians who were called in when something in our particular line of business turned up but were kept outside all the rest of the time. It never occurred to the Ambassador or his Counsellor that we were perhaps the best judges of what was in our line of business and that in war or uneasy times almost all subjects have ultimate connection with the trade of the warrior.

Matters changed completely with the arrival of Sir Samuel Hoare. Alive to the inter-relation of problems, he treated his staff as a team. While the Naval Attaché, for instance, had his special province, he was also a member of the Embassy staff as a whole, with his share of the general responsibility. This system worked beautifully. Indeed, it was the only system that could have worked and the only system that ought to be encouraged even in profound peace. In other ways, also, Sir Samuel Hoare was unusual – and unusually successful. He was never too occupied or too bored to listen to any matter that any senior member of his staff thought important and he was always prepared to back his staff up. He encouraged a vigorous policy. He wanted results. That I had occasional differences of opinion with him was inevitable, but they counted as nothing when compared to the successful work of several years.

One cannot, of course, often have such an Ambassador, but there is no doubt that the Naval Attaché must, by tact and persistence, steadily maintain his right – and his obligation – to be in that sort of relationship with his Head of Mission. He must never allow himself to be relegated to a purely technical position. A Mission divided into watertight compartments is a failure, both from the general point of view and from the departmental point of view. The Admiralty suffers from it as much as everyone else.

(2) The Diplomatic Staff, including the Counsellor/Minister, took their tone as a rule from the Ambassador. The tendency, usually only too evident, of professional diplomats to resent – it is not too strong a word – the existence of service attachés was largely absent from the Embassy in Madrid during my service with Sir Samuel Hoare. When, occasionally, it showed itself, we were able, by tact combined with firmness, to suppress it.

Unless the Counsellor or the Head of Chancery is exceptionally difficult, it should not be difficult for the Naval Attaché to make friends with him and become useful to him. I found that by extending my circle of Spanish acquaintances as widely as possible I was from that alone able to help the Diplomatic Staff a great deal, with consequently warmer relations.

Bothersome tasks are also always cropping up, and if the Naval Attaché is ready to discharge them he cannot but improve his standing with his colleagues. It should never be forgotten that the Naval Attaché takes orders from the Head of the Mission alone (from the Chargé d'Affaires, if necessary) and not from anyone else in it. But he must do his very best to avoid a situation in which he has to appeal to that rule. While he must maintain his position, he must not fight the Diplomatic Staff.

I know of one case where the Head of Chancery insisted that the Service Attachés should only see the Ambassador by appointment made through him. The Service Attachés were quite wrong to submit to such a ruling for one minute, and they could have won their point without a show-down. In Madrid the Counsellor tried to make me believe that whenever I had anything to say to the Ambassador I must explain it to him first and get his approval. I declined, but I always let him know what I was doing, so that he never felt I was cooking something behind his back. I often used to go and sit on his desk and ask his advice, and he liked that even when he did not know what to say.

(3) The Military and Air Attachés can be one's most valuable colleagues even if it is difficult to call them one's intimate friends. They have so many things in common with the Naval Attaché, beginning with their rather odd status in the Mission, that it is usually easy to form a close bond with them from the beginning. I found two things very useful. I made a point of asking them to many gatherings which consisted only of 'Spanish naval officers'. I also told them everything – or nearly everything – I found out and I let them see all my reports on maritime matters. They willingly reciprocated. Sometimes they stole items from the reports, but that didn't matter. There are a dozen other ways of getting on with one's service colleagues, and attention to assistant attachés is not the least of them.

APPENDIX 363

(4) The Naval Attaché's relations with the Commercial Staff are extremely important. He will seldom find here any difficulties of jealousy, but a ready wish for collaboration of which he should take full advantage. In Spain, as in many other countries, economic and commercial matters are strongly tied up with maritime affairs. Not only warships and dockyards and naval supplies but also shipyards, both naval and commercial, armament factories, steelworks, mineral resources, shipping lines, fishing vessels, fishing grounds, communications, port facilities and a hundred kindred matters touch both the Naval Attaché and the Commercial Staff.

The Naval Attaché's interest must extend to everything that can concern either the naval war potential of the country to which he is accredited or that country's value to other navies (including his own) in the event of occupation. Only by the closest connection with the Commercial Staff can he begin to understand the problem. He will find them ready to get information he wants – and the Admiralty needs. When there is a Shipping Attaché, matters are somewhat simplified, and the Naval Attaché must cling closely to this gentleman. In Spain the merchant service is in private hands but is largely controlled by a Department of Mercantile Marine. This department, which comes under the Ministry of Industry and Commerce, is directed by an Under Secretary of that Ministry who is a retired rear admiral, and the Department has, in fact, as close a connection with the Minister of Marine as with its own Ministry. Nearly all the senior officials of the Department are retired naval officers or active officers on the non-seagoing list. I got to know most of them well and was able to help the Shipping Attaché a lot, in return for the great help he gave me.

(5) The Naval Attaché in Spain is in the fortunate position of having Gibraltar under his lee. His relations with the flag officer

Gibraltar, with the C.in C. Mediterranean and with the S.O. (I) Gibraltar are obviously important. To begin with, he must visit Gibraltar at not too long intervals. He will find there a general but very innocent attitude that Algeciras and perhaps Cadiz are the most important part of Spain. When people speak of Ferrol or even Cartagena they refer to it as if it were so far off as to be in another country. Of course this doesn't matter, but the Naval Attaché must be prepared to discuss Spain with most – not all – of his brother officers in Gibraltar in a cautious manner. They think they know all about it. Luckily this attitude is more prevalent in the Army than in the Navy, though even there it is by no means uncommon.

(6) The Flag Officer Gibraltar is nearly always very helpful indeed to the Naval Attaché, is delighted to put him up and anxious to discuss every aspect of the Spanish situation and every detail of all outstanding problems. I only had one difficult period with a Flag Officer Gibraltar, and that was because at first he resented the near neighbourhood of a mere captain who was not under his command and whose comings and goings did not require his approval. As soon as I found this out, I did all I could to make him more friendly and eventually succeeded. All the other Flag Officers were helpful and friendly throughout. It is the Naval Attaché's duty to keep the Flag Officer fully informed on Spain and not necessarily in the purely naval side alone. He must find out if other information reaches the Flag Officer Gibraltar by other means, and, if it does not, he must either see that it does or supply it.

(7) The same remarks apply to relations with the C. in C. Mediterranean, who must be kept advised of everything concerning Spain that might conceivably be of interest to him. The Naval Attaché should put himself out to call upon the C. in C. if the flag officer should visit Gibraltar. But the constant

provision of information, both to the C. in C and to the Flag
Officer Gibraltar, is done through the S.O (I) Gibraltar.

(8) Relations with the S.O (I) Gibraltar must be close. Unless
a really high degree of mutual confidence exists, the
Mediterranean Fleet and the Admiralty are not properly served.
It is not enough to expect the dissemination of information
to reach the S.O (I) and the Mediterranean Fleet through the
Admiralty. That it will so reach them is beside the point. Apart
from the provision of urgent intelligence direct, the Naval
Attaché's responsibility for the Mediterranean Command
demands that he should so brief the S.O (I) Gibraltar that that
officer, and through him his superiors, really understand the
Spanish situation all the time. In return the S.O (I) Gibraltar
should keep the Naval Attaché informed of all matters which
could conceivably be of use to him.

(9) The responsibility of the S.O (I) Gibraltar for Naval
Reporting Officers and the way in which the Naval Attaché
should assist him in dealing with them form the subject of a
later paragraph.

(10) Relations with the Spanish Navy should naturally be as
friendly as possible. The best way to achieve this is to get to
know as many officers as possible, at the same time picking
out a few with whom it appears that a greater degree of intimacy would not be difficult. The Naval Attaché need not be
deterred in this by the fact that some of the likeliest officers
are senior to him. Nor should he regard himself as confined
to the officers in the Ministry of Marine with whom he
naturally finds he has most to do.

Most Spanish naval officers come of naval families and have
few connections with other sides of the social picture. It is true
to say that they are instinctively drawn to a foreign naval officer,

and if that officer immediately displays a genuine friendliness, an interest in them and in their profession plus a desire to see more of them, he finds no difficulty in doing so. Even during the worst of the War, when Spanish naval officers were warned to walk with great circumspection where foreign attachés were concerned, I had but little difficulty in maintaining old friendships and making new ones. Intimacy with these Spaniards, incidentally, presents few difficulties over politics. They don't, as a rule, talk politics or worry much about them. If you can show that you, as a brother officer, recognise the tie between you of your profession, you will have little difficulty.

(11) The Spanish admirals should be studied carefully and cultivated. The Minister of Marine is usually nowadays a flag officer (though probably junior in rank to the Chief of Staff). Both he and the Chief of Staff should be visited whenever a useful excuse presents itself. The right attitude is a scrupulous formality on arrival and on departure, plus good stories if you can think of any. Entertaining these flag officers – and their wives – to lunch or dinner is also a very paying thing to do. To some of these functions ask your own Ambassador.

(12) It is important also to get to know Spanish industrialists and shipping men, officials of the Ministries of Industry and Commerce and the Ministry of Foreign Affairs and senior officers of the Army and Air Force. Through the British Council it is also easy to make acquaintances in the liberal professions and in the arts, both useful sources of opinion, and there are some people worth knowing in Society. Most of the people who move regularly in Society and are to be found at all diplomatic functions are, however, of small value to a Naval Attaché or, indeed, to anybody.

(13) Foreign diplomats are always worth knowing, and the Naval Attaché will quickly distinguish between those who are most worth while and those who have little to recommend them. My wartime experience will be of little help in detail, since the Axis representation was then in full strength, and nowadays none of the Russian, Polish, Yugo-Slav, Rumanian, Hungarian or Bulgarian regimes are represented in Madrid. As situations change, however, and regimes alter, it may be useful to mention that our deportment towards the German, Italian and Japanese diplomats, including attachés, was to behave as if they did not exist. If we met at a party, we ignored them. They did exactly the same to us. It was the only way possible in a neutral country.

(14) For the forseeable future a pro-Russian regime in Spain is unlikely. (That is a considered view; the reasons exist but this is not the place for them.) It is probable, therefore, that in the event of a war Spain will be either neutral again or an ally. In the first case there is not much likelihood of enemy diplomatic missions being in Spain, and in the second case there could be none. If, however, the unlikely happened and there were Soviet and/or Bulgarian etc missions in Madrid, the same diplomatic behaviour as we exercised towards the Axis would be essential. For covert action, see a later paragraph.

(15) It is advisable to cultivate foreign naval attachés sedulously. If one can win their confidence, without necessarily yielding any of one's own, so much the better, but it is in any case important to know what sort of men they are, with what abilities, interests and friendships, so as to form some idea of (a) their value as sources to oneself and (b) sources to their own governments. The American Naval Attaché is nearly always ready to cooperate a lot and is often in touch with a number of people the British Naval Attaché does not know. In my

experience, however, of 5 American naval attachés and at least 12 assistant naval attachés, not one really understood the Spanish character, though they all thought they did. There seems to be some curious barrier. Their views, therefore, though never to be ignored, are not always accurate. Of the other naval attachés, the most worthwhile is, I believe, the Italian. He is usually, in a quiet way, in contact with a number of interesting people, and he is pretty sure to respond with gratitude to any show of sympathy and friendship.

(16) The relation between the Naval Attaché and the Admiralty should, presumably, be the same for Madrid as for any other post. The following remarks are, therefore, my own view of what should be general. First, the Naval Attaché is responsible to the Director of Naval Intelligence – and to the Ambassador. There is no clash in this loyalty, and there need never be any trouble if the Naval Attaché uses his common sense. While he must quietly insist on his right of private communication with the DNI, he must never let the Ambassador imagine that he regards himself only or even primarily as the DNI's agent in Spain. He is the DNI's agent, but he is also the Ambassador's adviser on naval – and to some extent all maritime – matters, as well as a senior member of the Mission. Part of his job is to see that the DNI learns, either directly through him or because he calls attention to the channel, everything that could be of interest to the Admiralty in Spain.

Another part of his job is to see that the Ambassador is properly advised. His right of communication with DNI allows him to report anything he thinks of interest but it does not allow him to withhold from the Ambassador – or any appropriate department of the Mission – anything which is not of a purely naval nature, and even such restricted information must be given to the Ambassador if conceivably of interest to him. The reverse of the picture is that he has the right to demand that information of any kind available to the Mission should not be withheld from him, so that he may call the D.N.I's attention to it if he wishes and in any event may use it to supplement his own knowledge of the general picture.

IV. Communications

(1) Communication with the DNI is, on ordinary matters, by reference sheet, aided, where appropriate, by personal letter to the Head of the Section in NID which ordinarily handles his correspondence. He should, however, always feel that he has the right – in which he should be encouraged – to write personally to the DNI on occasion. These letters should deal with major problems or with general views rather than with facts. They may be sometimes a nuisance to the DNI, but it is only by the existence of an occasional personal letter that the personal touch can be kept alive. This personal touch between the DNI and his naval attachés is, in my view, of paramount importance. Without it one never gets the best results. It is important, too, for this very reason, that the DNI should call his naval attachés home now and then, even if there are no desperate questions to discuss.

(2) When communication by signal – by telegram – is necessary, it is advisable, even in peace time, that the Naval Attaché should use his own ciphers. In time of war the reasons for this are obvious, delay alone being sufficient reason if diplomatic ciphers are used, and, since delay is sometimes injurious during peace and has, moreover, a habit of coming quite suddenly, the use of naval ciphers should be accepted at all times. There is, further, the reason that only by naval ciphers can really safe messages be sent to naval authorities elsewhere, such as Gibraltar, unless an extremely elaborate distribution

of non-naval books and pads is made throughout these centres. A final reason is that, although the Ambassador must never be kept in the dark about what the Naval Attaché is doing, it is not always desirable that even he, and much less a number of other members of the staff, should read the exact words which the Naval Attaché either sends or receives. In my own experience I exchanged many signals with the DNI which were certainly not for other eyes, though there was nothing in them that the Ambassador or anyone else should have known and did not know.

(3) Signals from Madrid were usually sent by telegram. There were often many mutilations, but I do not believe that these were ever deliberate. I know that copies of all our telegrams were given to the Germans, but that did not help them much. The worst feature we had to contend with was delays. Sometimes these were undoubtedly deliberate and exasperating and as much as six days between Madrid and London, or vice versa.

One could never count on a signal, even marked with the highest transmission priority, reaching the Admiralty or Gibraltar as soon as it should. Often it did, but more often it did not. The use of our Embassy W/T station, operated by SIS, was resorted to on every special occasion, but it could not be used often because of the volume of SIS traffic and because diplomatic and commercial telegrams were often also so routed. There is no doubt at all that in a country where delays or deliberate mutilation is probable, adequate W/T facilities must be provided, but it is doubted if Spain will again be so tiresome in that way.

(4) The W/T station (there were at one time two, SOE having the other) was certainly known to the Spaniards, but, as nearly everyone else had one, it had become almost an accepted

adjunct of all embassies and legations. The Spaniards adopted it themselves for some of their foreign missions.

(5) Communication by telegram between the consulate and Gibraltar, essential for naval reporting work, was naturally suspected by the Spaniards and often delayed. Telegrams to the Embassy were not often held up, and it soon became our normal practice for all important reporting messages to be sent to the Embassy, preambled in ciphered text for the Naval Attaché, who retransmitted it immediately besides taking any action that appeared appropriate. This was, of course, with the agreement of the SO(I). Similar action might well be advisable in another war, even if delays to Gibraltar were not so likely. At all events, important messages should be repeated to the Naval Attaché, as he must know what is happening.

(6) In an attempt to get rapid intelligence of the sailings of iron ore ships from the northern ports and of movements of enemy submarines forced into Spanish ports by damage or pursuit and not yet definitely interned, W/T transmitters were installed in several consulates, their use being severely restricted. This was done by SIS in collaboration with the Naval Attaché, and it might be necessary again. The extreme reluctance of the Foreign Office was eventually overcome by the Ambassador, on my guarantee that nothing could be known to the Spaniards. Nothing was. This system could be worked again. The operators should be girls, who should work as clerks in the consulates concerned.

V. Relations with SIS and SOE and Covert Intelligence

(1) As SIS (SOE did not then exist) was very weak in Spain at the beginning of the War (because Spain was supposed to be looked after by our French allies), on the collapse of France

a number of extemporised measures had to be taken. I had, in fact, to create a sort of substitute SIS of my own, and when SIS proper was rebuilt I retained what I had created gradually, however relinquishing sections as their usefulness faded. This separate organisation might have led to friction but it did not because (a) my reports went both to DNI and CSS and (b) my relations with SIS in Madrid were first class. In fact, as the work was really theirs, I made my reports available to them and was always careful to see that we were not dealing with the same sources. I did not, in return, ask for their reports (which would, in any case, have been refused, because of the SIS system), but I did get an undertaking that anything I ought to know should at once be passed to me. As far as I am aware, this undertaking was kept. I also asked questions, whenever it was possible that SIS could help in elucidating something, and what information was available was given me. (There was not a great deal). Some arrangement of this kind should undoubtedly exist always, in peace and in war, between the Naval Attaché and the SIS representative in Madrid, at least as long as that individual is covered by diplomatic status. This is not to say that the Naval Attaché should have any knowledge of the organisation or sources of SIS or expect to see reports. But he should be able to ask for help in explaining matters without having to wait for everything to filter through London, and he should feel that he can rely on the SIS representative approaching him direct with anything that may in any way concern him. Of course good personal relations are essential. The extent to which a Naval Attaché should act, as I had to act, in the collection of covert intelligence will be discussed in a later paragraph.

(2). When SOE was formed as a separate entity from SIS, there was inevitably rivalry between them. Though their functions were different, there were unavoidable instances of trespass. You cannot carry out clandestine operations without intelligence to guide you, and you cannot help acquiring intelligence in the course of your proceedings. The natural desire of SOE to operate in the Iberian Peninsula and Spanish Morocco met, however, an even stronger opposition from the Foreign Office and the Ambassadors in Spain and Portugal who were all, very naturally, fearful of some stupid explosion or an ignominious capture of British agents, with consequent harm to our general policy. In this fear they were justified, although my Ambassador recognised that SOE could do important work in preparations against a possible German invasion of the peninsula, provided they were rigidly controlled. A compromise was eventually reached by which SOE were allowed to operate in the peninsula in a precautionary way only, and I was chosen to control them. That is to say, they could initiate nothing without my approval and the progress of what had been approved had to be fully disclosed to me every day. On the whole this worked very well, but it was an unenviable task for the controller. I was continually berated by the Ambassador – and by the Foreign Office whenever I went to London – for allowing anything at all, while the chief of SOE on the other side was continually at me to allow more. Meanwhile the DNI was always fearful that I would slip from controlling into directing and get involved and compromised. So I was under fire from three sides.

(3) I cannot recommend that this system should be adopted again. Yet it is clear that some sort of SOE would be needed in a neutral – even a friendly neutral – Spain. It is in the interest of the Services that there should be one, although it will always be opposed by diplomatic caution, and it is in the interest of both the Services and the Foreign Office that it should be controlled on the spot, to keep it entirely in line with policy, and not directly and independently from London. This applies just as forcibly if SOE is a separate entity as if it

374 MAN OF WAR

is a section of SIS. In the latter case the answer seems to be that the local head of SIS must be a person fully alive to the need for collaboration with the Service Attachés and ready to accept their guidance – even their veto. The Service Attachés could thus protect the Ambassador's interest and that of the Service Departments without quite as direct a contact with SOE personnel as I had. If, however, SOE is independent of SIS, the contact must be with the local SOE head, on the same lines as suggested for the other case. In either case I believe that the three Service Attachés should act jointly. It is too invidious a position for any one of them alone.

(4) The necessity for local control of SOE (whether SOE is separate or part of SIS) does not apply to SIS, because SOE is operational or preparatively operational while SIS is not. But the need for local collaboration with the head of SIS in Spain is, as outlined in paragraph (2) of this section, to my mind, just as important as the local control of SOE.

(5) It is generally laid down that a naval attaché must not engage in covert intelligence. To the extent that he must never personally so engage, this is one of the few rules that I believe should never be broken, but there are circumstances, such as those which arose in 1940 in Spain, which made it imperative for a naval attaché to engage in covert intelligence through others. Even when SIS is active and able to answer most of the questions, there may still be cases where the Naval Attaché has access to sources which are not available to SIS. In a case of this kind, I believe it to be his duty to develop the sources himself – though not personally – always provided that he cannot turn them over to SIS. It is not possible to lay down any definite rule, but illustrations are helpful. It became necessary for one of my Assistant Naval Attachés to be designated principally for developing such

sources, under my guidance. He had, of course, to guard against compromise. While he handled several extensive groups of people, in each group he only saw one man, and this one man was the only man in each group who knew for whom he was working. Furthermore, the rest of each group believed that they were working for Spanish interests. Two instances will show the ease and plausibility of such a system. A senior officer of the Spanish Secret police (who were closely collaborating with the Germans) organised, at our instance, a section of police to report on German agents, ostensibly for the information of the Spanish Ministry of the Interior. Indeed, the reports went to the Minister of the Interior, but they also came to us.

A second case was that of a young Falange intelligence official, who instigated investigations at our request. Of course the individuals dealt with in each and every case were motivated by private dislike of the Germans and of the Spanish Government's policy of collaboration, plus a desire for money, but it was only possible to find them in the first place by patient cultivation of likely and even unlikely people. My Assistant Naval Attaché was exceptionally favoured by character and linguistic attainments to cultivate such people, and in the majority of cases his contacts would not have agreed to deal with anyone else once they had begun to deal with him. I refer to the matter again in a later paragraph.

(6) I found throughout that my standing, and that of my Assistant Naval Attachés, depended absolutely on our being above reproach and in an apparently frank explanation of our position. A Naval Attaché should never try to hide the fact that he is answerable to the Director of Naval Intelligence, in the same way that naval attachés of other nations report to the Head of Section Two in their respective Admiralties. A Naval Attaché has several functions, of representation, etc, of which

intelligence is one. It is his duty to acquire, openly, as much knowledge as he can of the navy and the country to which he is accredited and, in time of war, of the activities of his enemies. He does this by asking questions and by using his eyes and a trained memory. All this is recognised and never regarded as objectionable. To attempt to hide it would be to invite suspicion. On the other hand, he is not a spy and must never do any snooping. His movements must be known and open. If an exceptional emergency arises which makes it unavoidable for him to do something unorthodox or if he has to meet people in secret for their own protection, he must take such careful precautions that he is never even suspected of a departure from his normal, open existence. One cannot be too careful. In Spain no one was watched all the time, but everyone was watched some of the time.

(7) In Spain after the war had been in progress for some time, all Service Attachés were required to acquaint their respective ministries of any projected journey outside the Madrid area. It was not a case of asking permission, as for a visit to a Service establishment or to a naval base, but it was designed to keep a check on our movements. The local authorities were warned to report whether or not we went where we said we were going. In the case of two American Assistant Attachés, they were discovered in an area they had not notified, and their movements were afterwards restricted. I and my assistants found this rule no trouble at all. I used to ring up the Ministry of Marine and say where we were going, roughly, with a margin for deviation if we changed our minds en route. After a little while, when they found that all of us did, roughly, what we said we were going to do, they gave up bothering about us. The Germans, on the other hand, took umbrage at the requirement and were checked on wherever they went.

VI. Security

(1) This falls into two parts: Embassy and Consular Security, and Port Security. The first did not exist, for practical purposes, in 1939. When Sir Samuel Hoare arrived in 1940 I was so alarmed at the absence of security that I represented the matter very strongly to him and he put me in charge of all security both in the Embassy and in the Consulates. Supported by occasional visits by Security Officers from the Foreign Office and always by the Ambassador, I built up a security system which provided against (a) access by unauthorised persons to our premises and documents and (b) careless or deliberate disclosure of information by members of the staff, of whom there were at one time over four hundred in the Embassy alone.

It was almost a full time job and should properly be discharged, in war, by a full time Security Officer, but he must be of at least First Secretary's rank and should not be a career diplomat. In Madrid, with the exception of the SIS representative and the Ambassador himself, there was no one outside the Naval Attaché's office who had any real understanding of what Security meant, and even when satisfactory measures had been introduced it was important to insist, firmly and continuously, that they must be maintained. Because for long periods nothing happened (which was because the methods were efficient) people became careless. Career diplomats were often the most careless of all and most ready to object to the enforcement of security measures. A whole book could be written on the subject of security in embassies, legations and consulates, and there is no need to go into detail here. It is sufficient to say that Madrid was full of spies and secret police, and, although most of them were very amateurish and inefficient, if we had not been very much on the alert and very thorough in our precautions, they must have got something, possibly something serious. As for the personnel aspect, I may mention that one of our security guards, an ex-private in the Black Watch, was got at through a woman in German pay. He was fortunately detected before he had done more than pass on to her the names of all visitors to the Embassy.

(2) In my opinion, if no competent full time Security Officer is appointed in time of war and no adequate part time appointment among the staff is made in peace time, the Admiralty should press for these measures to be taken, even to the extent of offering the services of the Naval Attaché if satisfaction cannot be obtained in any other way. Many of the duties can be delegated, but the responsible officer must be senior enough and energetic enough to see that the necessary measures are devised and consistently enforced.

(3) Port Security is the protection of Allied ships and cargoes against sabotage. It is an elaborate business, necessarily varying greatly in every country and to some extent in every port. In Spain, a Port Security Officer was appointed in each port and a code of security rules laid down in consultation with him. Copies of these rules must still exist in NID files. The usual Port Security Officer was the British Consul or Vice-Consul or one of his staff. As the object of the whole thing was to protect cargoes loaded in Spanish ports and the ships themselves, part of each port's code of rules included a request to the local authorities for official vigilance and protection, and this could not be refused. It was supported by a general directive which the Government was requested to circulate to all centres concerned. Though this official assistance was often grudgingly given and could never be regarded as reliable, it did help. But we did not rely on it. Whatever special measures were possible in each port were put into force, while certain general measures applying to all ports were

invented and instituted. Examples of these last measures were the provision of security guards on board each ship from pools in Gibraltar and the United Kingdom, the provision of special lighting facilities on board, special searches and on occasion investigation of the ship's bottom by divers. This Port Security system (or Ship Security System, as it was sometimes called) was devised and run by the Naval Attaché, in constant touch with the several Port Security Officers and in collaboration with the Security Service in London and Gibraltar. The Naval Attaché is the proper person to handle Port Security.

(4) But even all the measures devised in the last paragraph were not enough. Spain contained a large number of German agents and plenty of Spaniards in German pay. Though they were by no means as inventive or as enterprising as they might have been, they were not inactive and they had some ingenious ideas. We did our best to learn their plans and to some extent succeeded. When information was obtained of a projected attempt in any particular port, not only was the Port Security Service alerted but special agents were sent to the port to contact and persuade the local police, dock watchmen and stevedores to collaborate. This was done through one of my Assistant Naval Attaché's special contacts and appeared to be on behalf of Spanish shipping interests anxious to avoid an incident. Often money had to be distributed but not a great deal considering the importance of the matter. It undoubtedly increased the enemy's difficulties and led to the abandonment of several attempts. In a few cases a bomb was ditched by our agents though reported as successfully placed, and news of a subsequent explosion was disseminated. In spite, however, of all preventive measures, there were several genuine explosions. If every possible measure of prevention which could be devised had not been taken, there would have been many more.

VII. The Naval Attaché and the Consuls

(1) The last section has demonstrated one way in which the Naval Attaché has to have close contact with consular officers. He – I – was acting, naturally, on behalf of the Ambassador as well as on behalf of the Security Service. There was no one better fitted to undertake the responsibility. In the same way, on behalf of the Ambassador, I was responsible for the necessary directives to consuls on the subject of the security of their offices and staffs. That is hardly a naval responsibility, in the same way that the security of shipping is, but besides forming part of my duty as Security Officer, it did help to ensure the Security of Naval Reporting Officers. Practically all consuls in ports are Naval Reporting Officers.

(2) In the section on communications I have already explained how circumstances in Spain made it often necessary for the Naval Attaché to act as a link between Naval Reporting Officers and their SO(I). In other ways, too, it was often unavoidable for the Naval Attaché, on behalf of the SO(I) to give guidance and even instructions to the Naval Reporting Officers. This was contrary to the Instructions to Naval Attachés, but, since it was by agreement and there was no other way to get the desired result, it had to be done, and it would have to be done again. It was not possible for SO(I) Gibraltar to visit his Naval Reporting Officers. (Incidentally, those in the North did not report to him but to the United Kingdom.) The Ambassador was naturally averse to any irregular approach to them, had anything of the kind been possible, and the logical channel, which safeguarded everybody, was the Naval Attaché. In effect, the SO(I) delegated some of his powers to the Naval Attaché and used him as a channel for exercising some of the others. Throughout the Naval Attaché acted in his usual dual personality, as the representative of the

Ambassador and of the SO(I) – and, of course, ultimately, of the DNI and the Admiralty.

(3) In time of peace most of this is unnecessary, but the groundwork for war cannot be neglected. A close acquaintance by the Naval Attaché with the consuls and their problems is most important and must be regarded as part of his job. That he must be on terms of the greatest intimacy with SO(I) Gibraltar I have already said, and they should frequently discuss together and work out exactly what would have to be done in the event of war. The Diplomatic Staff should be made to realise, if necessary at the insistence of the Admiralty, that the Naval Attaché's relation with the consuls are an essential part of his duty and that he will neither interfere with their control by the Embassy nor imperil their status. The Foreign Office has often feared that the use of consuls as Naval Supporting Officers may lead to their compromise, and it should be obvious that the status of consuls and the interest of the Embassy are protected rather than imperilled by the intervention of the Naval Attaché, who belongs both to the Navy and to the Embassy. I can confirm from my own experience, that this is so in practice and that consuls welcome with almost tearful relief the advice and guidance of the Naval Attaché, the only person in the country really competent to guide them.

VIII. Miscellaneous Points

(1) I have no experience of NCSOs in Spain, as it was not possible to appoint any in Spain and the chances are that in a future war, even if Spain were a friendly neutral, the Spanish dislike for all forms of foreign officialdom on her soil, other than normal diplomatic and consular appointments, would make the provision of NCSOs difficult.

(2) The Spanish attitude towards foreign agents, when Spain is a neutral, is always adverse. In the last war, owing to German pressure, Axis agents enjoyed for a long time a lot of privileges and facilities (of course unofficially) but most official Spaniards were delighted when eventually they were able to suppress these Axis advantages. In short, one can safely say that in a neutral Spain unofficial help from official sources will be given chiefly in minor ways, to the side favoured by the regime, but even the side in that privileged position must be extremely careful to convince the Spaniards that all activity is aimed at the enemy and can in no way involve or injure Spain. The Germans – and Italians – were by no means convincing in this respect and lost a great deal thereby. Agents of the side not favoured by the regime obtain, of course, no privileges and are actively persecuted. Agents of both sides can obtain help from private sympathisers, but this is usually less than one would expect and than that often easily obtained in other countries, for the Spaniard is xenophobic and suspicious and wants to keep clear of other people's quarrels. No matter how strongly he may feel about an outside cause, he is usually reluctant to have any truck with it himself.

(3) Rumours, for the purpose of cover plans or for pure propaganda or for any reason, are extremely easy to spread in Spain. The country lives on word of mouth stories, particularly because everyone knows that the Press is quite untrustworthy. A casual word in a club or a café is often enough. The Naval Attaché should select among his acquaintance those who are the most inveterate gossips and, taking into account their connections, use them accordingly. Dozens of other ways suggest themselves all the time. These can often be quite childish yet effective. An attempt, for instance, to buy maps in half a dozen shops will quickly be known in the desired quarter. Naturally, however, if – as is quite possible – there were no enemy

embassies or legations in Spain, the task would not be quite
so easy.

(4) The attitude of the Ambassador to any activities, regular or
irregular, by a Naval Attaché outside his purely naval duties,
must depend on (a) the character of the Ambassador, (b) the
basis on which the Naval Attaché is supported from the beginning by the Admiralty and (c) his success in gaining the confidence of his Ambassador. Consideration of (b) means partly
that the Admiralty must make the Foreign Office agree that
the Naval Attaché is something more than a mere technician
to be confined to a narrow sphere (the general attitude) and
that he is to be trusted, and partly that the Director of Naval
Intelligence should establish good personal relations with all
Heads of Missions which have naval attachés. In short, an
atmosphere of confidence is essential so that the Naval Attaché
is regarded as a valuable and trusted member of the staff, whose
mission is to serve both Ambassador and DNI. In fact, the
interests of DNI and Ambassador are complementary, not
diverse.

(5) The Naval Attaché should be warned that while his relations with the British colony must be friendly (and many of
the British colony can be very useful to him) he must avoid
restricting himself too much to British – or American – circles.
It is easy to fall into this habit because of language difficulties
and national habits but a naval attaché who does not avoid it
cannot be efficient. It is important to remember this from the
beginning.

(6) Foreign newspaper correspondents are useful people to
know, as they hear a great deal and a good journalist can poke
his nose into all sorts of places without arousing any suspicion.
Though he follows many fake trails, he does get on to some

good things (some of which he can't print) and all these are at the Naval Attaché's disposal if a little trouble is taken. One has, of course, to be careful with journalists. Newspapermen of the country are, at least in Spain, of more limited value, since the Press is not free and they are not as a rule men of either principle or brains.

(7) The Naval Attaché to Spain should join at least one good club in Madrid (besides the Golf Club and the Automobile Club) and his Assistant Naval Attachés, if he has any, should join others. These clubs help one to increase the number of one's acquaintance.

(8) The Naval Attaché to Spain should remember that his area includes the Canary Islands and Spanish Morocco. It was not possible for me to visit either during the war, but my successors need not be so deterred.

(9) The accepted rule about visits to naval establishments and requests for information is that these are all on a reciprocal basis. In this respect the instructions are misleading, in time of war. I early established with the Spanish Minister of Marine the principle, which he accepted, that reciprocity was not sense and could not be expected, since Spain was at peace and we were at war. We had, in consequence, a natural right to restrict facilities, whereas Spain had not. As a result I asked for a lot of things – and got a number of them – without any risk of reciprocal facilities being requested.

(10) Spain is intensely interested in Naval Air. In the future presumably all our officers of the Executive Branch will have flown, but that time has not yet come. Yet the Naval Attaché should not be completely ignorant of air matters. He can, of course, rely on the Air Attaché for help, but it is not the same

thing and, in any event, the Air Attaché has probably never had any experience of carriers or catapults. The American Naval Attaché, when alone, had considerable flying experience and an aircraft at his disposal. Later, when there were U.S.N. assistant naval attachés, one of them was always a pilot. One still is. (There is also a U.S. Army Air Attaché, with an aircraft.) I know that for financial reasons it is useless to suggest that an Assistant Naval Attaché with flying experience and complete with aircraft should be appointed to Madrid in peace time, though it would be a very good move if it were possible, but I do recommend that the Naval Air angle should not be lost sight of. If, for instance, there were two officers in line for appointment as Naval Attaché to Spain and there were little to choose between them but one had flying experience, he should undoubtedly be chosen. And certainly in time of war – or when finances allow – one of the Assistant Naval Attachés should be a pilot, with an aircraft. The advantages conferred upon the Naval Attaché by that aircraft are considerable, in spite of flying being restricted to certain routes.

(11) The question of Assistant Naval Attachés generally is most important. In war time, with Spain neutral, the Naval Attaché needs two assistants, in addition to clerical and cipher staff. I found that I could not cope with the work with less than two and could often have used three with advantage. Two, however, are essential for efficiency. They should be Assistant Naval Attachés with diplomatic status, and not Assistants to the Naval Attaché. In the latter case they are accorded neither attention nor respect by the Spanish Navy, and find their comings and goings beset by regulations which do not apply to the officers with diplomatic status. They are also sure to be regarded as spies. It will be assumed that we are trying to disguise their real character. It is folly to appoint anyone other than as an Assistant Naval Attaché. And there is no difficulty in having two.

(12) One of these two, who can be the pilot already referred to, should be a general assistant. He can be R.N. or R.N.V.R. but must be an executive officer, with no colour inside his stripes. The qualities listed for the Naval Attaché apply also to him. If he is R.N.R. or R.N.V.R. he must be professionally competent, so that he will be at once recognised by Spanish Naval Officers as a fellow professional.

(13) The other Assistant Naval Attaché should be a Spanish expert. He could be R.N. or R.N.R. or R.N.V.R. but the suitable officer will almost certainly only be found among the latter; indeed he may well be a civilian when found. He needs no more than a smattering of sea experience and can be R.N.V.R. Special. The great point is that he must know Spanish very well, speaking it as if it were his native tongue, and he must be very intelligent and able to mix and make friends with great facility. I had such an Assistant Naval Attaché, and he was invaluable to me. It was he who handled our special contacts and that was important enough, but it was his popularity with all Spaniards that paid the richest dividend. Spain is the country, par excellence, where the personal touch counts most.

(14) In peacetime the Naval Attaché has no assistant, for financial reasons, and is handicapped thereby. I am reminded of the case of Japan, where for years our naval attachés were helped enormously by a naval attaché's clerk, who was a retired lieutenant-commander. An appointment of that kind in Spain would not be desirable (see the remarks of Assistants to Naval Attachés) and it would in any case cost money. But there is a way in which the Naval Attaché to Spain could be assisted at no cost at all. I refer to the appointment of an Honorary Assistant Naval Attaché. (This appointment existed at one time in Portugal, so there is a precedent.) And a suitable appointee already exists, in the person of my late Assistant Naval Attaché,

Commander (S.B.) S.A.Gómez–Beare, O.B.E., R.N.V.R. The
Director of Naval Intelligence knows all about him, he lives
in Spain, though he is not in business there (an important
point), his loyalty and discretion are unequalled and the
Spaniards, particularly the Spanish Navy, love him. He has
private means and would almost certainly accept the appointment, which would also without doubt be acceptable to the
Foreign Office, and the Embassy, and welcomed by the Naval
Attaché and the Spanish Navy. This is a serious, constructive
recommendation.

Acknowledgements

I am enormously indebted to Alan Hillgarth's children – Jocelyn, Justin, Tristan and Nigella – for entrusting me with the task of writing their father's life, and for giving me such generous help. Their friendly guidance, reinforced by a profusion of family papers, has been invaluable.

Others who have contributed knowledge and advice include: Sir Benjamin Bathurst, Denis Bergin, Mary Cockerill (Southampton University Archives), Rickard Deasy, Gail Getty, Kate Grimond, Thaddeus Holt, John Lewis, David Lyon, Ben Macintyre, Patricia Martinez Alonso, David A. Messenger, Mercedes Morenes, C.J. Sansom, David Stafford, Isabelle Tombs, Roger Welby-Everard (the *Naval Review*), Michael Wilkinson.

I am grateful to the executors of the Ian Fleming Will Trust for permission to publish extracts from the author's letters.

The staff of the Archives Centre at Churchill College, Cambridge, have been outstandingly helpful, as have those of the Cambridge University Library – and for an author living in the country, the London Library is a *sine qua non*.

Notes

Chapter One: Mobilise!

1 **don't let mother worry**: All the letters quoted here are in the Hillgarth family collection.

2 **lyddite**: The first generation of high explosive used in shells, preceding the later HE.

3 **Bitten by Miss Sylvia Pankhurst**: Bush, *Gallipoli*, p. 23.

3 **'restricted to that area'**: Able Seaman Chesterton's diary is in the Royal Naval Museum, Portsmouth.

5 **Eric Bush**: Bush went on to an exceptionally distinguished career in the Navy, winning the DSC for 'his courage and endurance under shell fire' at Gallipoli, and, later, the DSO and two bars. In writing his book *Gallipoli* he received much help from his former shipmate Hugh Evans, later known as Alan Hillgarth.

5 **'A section of the British public'**: Bush, *Gallipoli*, p. 23.

6 **If my son**: Ibid.

6 **It wd. be a vy harsh measure**: Gilbert, *Winston S. Churchill*, vol. 3, p. 171.

6 **prayed that we would not be sent back to the College**: Bush, *Gallipoli*, p. 23.

7 **Vereker's not bad**: Admiral John Jellicoe (1857–1935) was in command of the Grand Fleet 1914–16. Created Viscount Jellicoe of Scapa 1918. Admiral Charles Madden was Chief of Staff to Jellicoe 1914–16. He was knighted in 1916.

7 **Then *Tennant***: Rt. Hon. Harold Tennant was Under-Secretary of State for War 1912–16, and had been Private Secretary to H.H. Asquith (Prime Minister 1908–16).

8 **Gieves**: In 1974 the firm took over its arch-rival Hawkes & Co., which owned the prime freehold of No. 1 Savile Row in London. The combined company became known as Gieves & Hawkes.

Chapter Two: Early Days

11 **a thirty-three-gun fifth rate**: Fifth-rate frigates combined manoeuvrability with firepower and were often used to disrupt enemy shipping lanes.

13 **Far too early for comfort**: Jack Broome family memoir. In 1942 Captain Broome was in command of the First Escort Group assigned to protect Arctic Convoy PQ17 during its voyage to Russia. On 4 July, after attacks by German torpedo-carrying aircraft, the First Sea Lord, Admiral Dudley Pound, fearing that an attack by the German battleship *Tirpitz* was imminent, sent out a Most Immediate signal, 'Convoy is to scatter'. The First Escort Group withdrew, the convoy dispersed, and twenty-four of the thirty-five merchant ships were sunk.

In 1968, when the author David Irving published a book blaming Broome for the disaster, Broome sued him and won £40,000 (worth over £500,000 today) in damages.

14 **'monstrously mechanical . . . '**: King-Hall, *My Naval Life*, p. 109.

15 **the American wife of Hilaire Belloc**: Hilaire Belloc (1870–1963), the prolific Anglo-French writer celebrated for (among many other works) his *Cautionary Tales*. The correspondence between him and Anne is now in the Library of Boston College, Massachusetts.

16 **'I remember when I was a kid . . . '**: When Anne died she left him her books, furniture, porcelain and so on, and all the letters he had written her over the years.

17 **We arrived on board at 6.30**: At 7.35 a.m. on 26 November 1914, *Bulwark* was destroyed by a catastrophic explosion as she lay moored in the River Medway, opposite the town of Sheerness. The blast was thought to have been caused by ammunition overheating, and was so violent that of her complement of 750 no officers and only twelve men survived.

Chapter Three: Gallipoli

22 **but as *Bacchante* steamed**: The relevant logs of *Bacchante* are in ADM 53/34644–54.

25 **the Hon. Aubrey Herbert**: (1880–1923) was the younger brother of the 5th Earl of Carnarvon (who financed the expedition that led to the discovery of the tomb of the pharaoh Tutankhamen). His wanderings in the Middle East were said to have been the inspiration for John Buchan's character Sandy Arbuthnot, and rumour had it that the Albanians wanted him to become their king. He published the outstandingly vivid diary which he kept during the Gallipoli compaign as part of his book *Mons, Anzac and Kut*.

26 **Joppa**: The port now called Jaffa, which has been encompassed by the modern city of Tel Aviv.

27 **Shrapnel shells**: At that date shrapnel was not shell splinters, but lead balls the size of marbles which burst from exploding shells with lethal results.

28 **We loathed the whole thing**: Bush, *Gallipoli*, p. 26.

30 **in the Gallipoli campaign**: General Sir Ian Hamilton (1853–1947) had fought in many conflicts, including the Afghan War, the Boer War, the Nile Expedition, the Burmese Expedition and the Tirah Campaign.

30 **'a young sixty-two'**: Hamilton, *The Happy Warrior*, p. 282.

32 **I'm very glad it wasn't the *Albion***: Willie de Segundo survived Gallipoli, but, along with four more of the Blake term midshipmen, was killed when a spontaneous explosion destroyed the battleship HMS *Vanguard* in Scapa Flow, with the loss of 800 of her crew, on 9 July 1917.

32 **'a finer set of men'**: Bush, *Gallipoli*, p. 75.

33 **The Allied plan**: The poet Rupert Brooke, en route for Gallipoli, died during the afternoon of 23 April from an infected mosquito bite, and was buried on the island of Skyros.

33 **The scent of battle**: Hamilton, *Gallipoli Diary*, vol. 1, p. 122.

33 **'the most wonderful procession'**: Herbert, *Mons, Anzac and Kut*, p. 78.

34 **an uncannily similar scene**: *Aeneid*, Book 2, lines 254ff.

34 **The shore is now about two miles away**: Bush, *Gallipoli*, pp. 99–100.

35 **In the tows of the 11th Battalion**: Ibid., p. 102.

38 **Whether or not**: Ibid., p. 109.

38 **There was no room on the rocks**: Wedgwood, *Essays and Adventures of a Labour M.P.*, p. 190. Josiah C. Wedgwood, MP (1872–1943), a great-great grandson of the celebrated potter, was wounded soon after the landing, and won a DSO.

39 **'The blast of the guns'**: Bush, *Gallipoli*, p. 143.

40 **'clinging like cockroaches'**: Herbert, *Mons, Anzac and Kut*, p. 85.

41 **'had only to fire point-blank'**: Bush, *Gallipoli*, 179.

41 **filled acres of ground**: Herbert, *Mons, Anzac and Kut*, p. 116.

42 **By expert seamanship**: Hersing had skilfully piloted *U-21* the whole way from Wilhelmshaven, its base on the North Sea – a distance of 2,000 miles.

49 **Uncle Charlie**: The family cannot now identify this benefactor. No one remembers who he was, or whether he was the owner of the hotel or merely staying in it as a guest.

50   **Royal Military Academy**: The RMA Woolwich was amalgamated with the RMA Sandhurst in 1947.

50   **'What is your opinion?'**: Horatio Bottomley (1860–1933) was a fanatically anti-German journalist, newspaper proprietor and politician who ran a campaign inciting servicemen to air their complaints. In 1922 he was convicted of fraud and sentenced to seven years' gaol.

50   **he was now five foot eight tall**: He never grew taller than five foot nine', and always gave the impression of being small and slender but full of energy.

51   **News of Hugh's transfer**: 'Glutton' is the colloquial name for the wolverine (*Gulo gulo*), a lithe predator about the size of a large, rangy dog, found in the Arctic regions of Europe and America. Herbert Smart was killed at the very end of the war, and on 16 December 1918 his mother wrote to Hugh: 'You little know how glad I was to get your letter. It helps me in my loneliness more than you may think. Every day I miss our dear Herbert more and more . . . I know full well how much you were to each other . . . Come and see me when you can. I was always told to look to you if anything happened, and it has.'

51   **'The middies are the most splendid boys'**: Herbert, *Mons, Anzac and Kut*, p. 92.

Chapter Four: Around the Med

53   **Hugh described her movements**: The log of *Wolverine* for November and December 1915 is in ADM 53/68912.

56   The fiasco into which the campaign had degenerated forced Churchill to resign from the War Cabinet in November.

56   **some lost their reason**: Bush, *Gallipoli*, p. 300.

57   **gone up in flames**: At Helles, the Allies' other garrison, the evacuation took place early in January. The French troops went first, taken off by their own fleet, and the British followed on the nights of the 7th and 8th. Once again, it had been impossible to embark all the animals and stores: 500 horses and mules had been slaughtered and 1,600 vehicles abandoned, along with colossal amounts of stores.

57   **shrapnel on advancing Turkish line**: ADM 53/68912.

63   **bombarded trenches and houses**: ADM 53/68914.

65   **full of survivors**: ADM 53/46791.

65   **his Christian names**: ADM 53/46792.

67   **half of them are gone already**: Louis Belloc had joined the Royal Air Force, and was shot down over France on 26 August 1918.

68   **the First British Prime Minister**: Sir Robert Walpole (1676–1745),
     1st Earl of Orford, was educated at King's and was Prime Minister
     1721–42.

69   **'the battleship HMS *Barham*'**: On 25 November 1941 HMS *Barham*
     was sunk by three torpedoes from the German submarine *U-331*, with
     the loss of 861 lives. The U-boat commander dived so fast that he did
     not realise he had scored a hit, and the Admiralty kept the loss of the
     battleship secret for two months.

70   **last weeks of the year**: *Ceres'* last surviving log, ADM 53/37503,
     ends on 31 October 1920.

71   **sunk in despair**: Hillgarth, *The Princess and the Perjurer*, pp. 13–14.

74   **poor Peter Belloc**: The younger son of Hilaire Belloc.

Chapter Five: On the Loose, 1922–8

80   **chained to their wrists**: Even before the days of air transport,
     King's Messengers travelled prodigiously. The celebrated Sir Park
     Goff (1871–1939), barrister and Member of Parliament, crossed the
     North Sea thirty times, the Caspian twice, the Black Sea four times,
     the Mediterranean twenty-two times and the Channel 180-odd
     times.

81   *The History of the King's Messengers*: The author, V. Wheeler-Holohan,
     had himself been a King's Messenger.

81   **The methods adopted**: Family collection.

83   **Adventurer was once**: Dedication to Henderson, in *The War Maker*.

83   **interrogates him in gaol**: C.J. Sansom, author of the novel *Winter
     in Madrid* (in which Alan appears as his real self, the British Naval
     Attaché), wondered if the character of the general was based on
     Francisco Franco, later dictator of Spain, who was serving in Morocco
     at the time.

84   **I'm a wanderer**: Hillgarth, *The War Maker*, p. 120.

84   **neck was broken**: Ibid, p. 263. *Bulldog Drummond*, by Sapper (H.C.
     McNeile), was first published in 1920. *The Black Gang* came out in
     1922, and *The Third Round* in 1927.

85   **when she sank**: Family collection.

Chapter Six: Fools' Gold

91   **at today's values**: To translate early twentith-century amounts into
     their modern equivalent, figures need to be multiplied by at least
     thirty.

92   **from the New World**: In July 1773 Pope Clement XIV issued an
      order suppressing the Society of Jesus for all time – but the Order
      soon revived.

93   **a duck or two for a change**: Prodgers, *Adventures in Bolivia*, 2009,
      p. 12.

93   **concentrate of meat**: The beef extract, forerunners of Oxo stock
      cubes, was developed by the German chemist Baron Justus von Liebig
      in 1840.

93   **hurts nobody**: Prodgers, *Adventures in Bolivia*, p. 51.

95   **monastery and other buildings**: Ibid, p. 54.

96   **his original promise to the Señorita**: Prodgers died in 1923. His
      second book, *Adventures in Peru*, was published in 1924.

96   **to keep away snakes**: Prodgers, *Adventures in Bolivia*, pp. 86–7.

96   **The gold was still at Sacambaya, and intact**: The documents
      concerning Sanders's expeditions are in the Hillgarth family
      collection.

97   **the School of Orchard Studies**: the institution became the School
      of Oriental and African Studies in 1936.

99   **the circumstances under which they would have to do it**:
      From the substantial report on the expedition which Alan wrote and
      presented to the Ordinary General Meeting of the company on 23
      April 1929.

103   **repeat this performance several times**: Ibid.

105   **There are also skunks**: Ibid.

107   **'Everybody, Indians and Gringos alike'**: *St Bartholemew's Hospital
      Journal*, January 1929.

109   **match to the gunpowder**: Ibid.

110   **gather their own crops**: Hillgarth's expedition report.

113   **their wish to go to their homes**: Ibid.

113   **abandon operations for this year**: Ibid.

114   **to our disregard of the curse**: *Star*, 15 November 1929.

114   **for a well-known British firm**: Expedition report.

115   **provide the new capital himself**: Ibid.

116   **permanent water level**: Ibid.

120   **Let's have another drink. Edgar**: Hillgarth family collection.

Chapter Seven: Pastures New

123   **the more interesting and cultivated figures of the time**: Hillgarth
      (ed.), *Mary Hillgarth: A Private Life*, p. 24.

123 **become a ballet dancer**: Ibid, p. 21.

123 **a skating instructress**: Ibid.

125 **a couple of good things**: Family collection.

126 **It is a beautiful countryside**: Ibid.

126 **work in Alan's favour**: After a long courtship the two Evelyns got married suddenly without telling either set of parents. Arthur and Kate Waugh received news of the wedding with composure, but Lady Burghclere threw a tantrum and insisted on putting a notice in *The Times* 'to avoid scandal and misconstruction'. Selina Hastings, *Evelyn Waugh*, p. 176.

127 **super-Oppenheim of the next generation**: E. Phillips Oppenheim (1866–1946), the immensely successful English author, wrote some 150 novels of adventure, espionage, suspense and romance, styling himself 'the prince of storytellers'.

130 **chugged the 130 miles to the Island**: Hillgarth (ed.), *Mary Hillgarth*, p. 191.

130 **'excessively honest and friendly'**: Graves, *Majorca Observed*, p. 7.

133 **My monograph, Mary Hillgarth**: Family collection.

134 **nowhere more clearly than in Majorca**: Hillgarth (ed.), *Mary Hillgarth*.

136 **flattered his many influential, Spanish friends**: Delmer, *The Counterfeit Spy*, p. 61.

139 **Yours very sincerely, Robert Graves**: Family collection.

140 **laughing too much**: Ibid.

141 **the boat for Marrakesh**: Local newspaper reports that Churchill stayed at Son Torrella were pure invention.

141 **A library is essential in your house**: Family collection.

142 **'I don't think necessarily improbable'**: Ibid.

143 **Captain Marryat**: Frederick Marryat (1792–1848) published *Mr Midshipman Easy* in 1836, and *The Children of the New Forest* in 1847.

144 **Elinor Glyn**: In the 1920s her audacious novels had given rise to the popular jingle: 'Would you like to sin/With Elinor Glyn/On a tiger skin?/Or would you prefer/To err/With her/On some other fur?'

144 **all I ask for, nowadays**: Family collection.

145 **ample of form**: McHugh (ed.), *Ah, Sweet Dancer*, p. 10.

146 **God bless you all, Swami**: Family collection.

146 **'with exquisite taste'**: Saddlemyer (ed.), *W.B. Yeats and George Yeats: The Letters*, p. 408.

147 **tragic creature with some genius**: Family collection.

Chapter Eight: Saving Lives

150 **countrymen as well**: FO 371/24147.

150 **violence, murder and, finally, war**: Thomas, *The Spanish Civil War*, p. 74.

151 **had taken place around 1450**: Graves, *Majorca Observed*, p. 8.

151 **'with their furniture'**: Elwell, *The Greater Aphrodisiad*, p. 120.

152 **'shed on his departure'**: Ibid, p. 123.

152 **and other vegetation**: FO 371/20533.

152 **'refuse to leave'**: Ibid.

153 **'in return for information'**: FO 371/20537.

153 **'invasion or bombing'**: Ibid.

153 **'left to shoot'**: Ibid.

154 **unguarded comments**: FO 371/20538.

154 **'invincible militiamen'**: Jellinek, *The Civil War in Spain*, p. 405.

155 **with wooden rifles**: FO 371/20541.

155 **what will remain of Spain?**: Family collection. Mercedes Bonsoms lived in part of the fourteenth-century Cartuja (Charterhouse) at Valledemossa, in the mountains north of Palma. She was reputed to be an illegitimate daughter of King Alfonso XII.

156 **'died in the flames'**: Thomas, *The Spanish Civil War*, p. 254.

156 **enter without permission**: FO 371/20531.

157 **when it is all over**: FO 371/20541.

157 **occupied without opposition**: Ibid.

158 **Italy and the United Kingdom**: CAB 24/264.

158 **take sides with them**: FO 371/20551.

160 **disguised as commercial travellers**: One of the pilots who flew SM 79s from Palma was Bruno Mussolini, son of the dictator. Out of 100 aircraft, only four were lost during the entire war.

161 **have bombed Alicante**: FO 371/20546.

161 **'The Mediterranean is ours'**: FO 371/2555.

161 **would certainly be Italy**: FO 371/20551.

161 **'appearance of power'**: Ibid.

162 **'imported are at an end'**: FO 371/20555.

162 **control of the island**: FO 371/21391.

163 **was shot down**: Ibid.

164 **other than by shooting**: Ibid.

164 **would have become intolerable**: Hillgarth (ed.), *Mary Hillgarth*, p. 162.

165 **'Viva Alemania!'**: FO 371/20451.

165 **'will ever be the same again'**: Hillgarth (ed.), *Mary Hillgarth*, p. 162.

165 'is a natural leader': FO 371/21392.

165 'get him to see reason': FO 371/24147.

165 friendliness and respect: FO 371/21391.

166 should not be properly recognised: Family collection.

167 they were almost all blond: FO 371/22678.

167 inclination to revolt: FO 371/21391.

168 last at war with Spain: Ibid.

168 the staidest middle class: Ibid.

168 in any case be resisted: FO 371/22677.

169 with the local authorities: FO 371/21292.

172 has never forgotten: Published in *The Times*, 21 June 1960. On that day, aboard the Spanish cadet training ship *Juan Sebastian de Elcano* which was on a visit to Greenwich, there took place a ceremony which Alan had arranged. Lady McGrigor, Sir Rhoderick's widow, was too ill to attend, but on her behalf Lady Portal received a miniature of the Cross of Naval Merit in recognition of the rescue, presented by the Marquesa de Santa Cruz, wife of the Spanish Ambassador.

173 Mary helped look after her: Massoti Muntaner, *Guerra civil i repressió a Majorca*, pp. 232–57.

174 prevented and does not matter: FO 371/22678.

174 bread thrown overboard: Things moved at a leisurely pace in Port Mahon. When asked what documents two medium-sized cases in his office contained, the acting Vice Consul, Signor Moysi, replied, 'How should I know? I have only been here nine years.'

174 within easy range: FO 371/24146.

175 not prepared to undertake: Ibid.

176 confined to providing transport: Ibid.

176 has been guaranteed: Ibid.

178 such useless bloodshed: Ibid.

179 all proved assassins: Ibid.

180 eight days later: FO 371/24147

181 she is invincible: Ibid.

182 my family would have been here: Family collection.

Chapter Nine: Naval Attaché

183 achievement in practical diplomacy': Churchill Archives, GDFY/ 1/5 p. 295.

184 lesser mental calibre: Beesly, *Very Special Admiral*, p. xix.

184 naval, political and social: Churchill Archives, GDFY 1/11, p. 123.

185 not enough bread: Eccles, *By Safe Hand*, p. 24.

185 **hanging over Spanish life**: Templewood Papers, XIII.

185 **in an indissoluble way'**: United States Department of State publication 2483. Washington, 1946.

186 **no influence whatever**: The remarks about the role of the Naval Attaché are taken from the long memorandum about the job which he wrote at the end of his time in Madrid. The document appears in full in the Appendix.

186 **Needed extensive restoration**: The old Embassy building was demolished in 1966.

186 **'build it up from the bottom'**: Appendix.

186 **in five minutes**: Ibid.

187 **'very useful indeed'**: Ibid.

187 **if he is a teetotaller**: Ibid.

187 **'large and lavish dinners'**: Macintyre, *Operation Mincemeat*, p. 151.

187 **'which had been forged'**: Family collection.

188 **'out of the side of his mouth'**: Burns, *The Use of Memory*, p. 118.

188 **'as their usefulness faded'**: Appendix.

189 **'Spanish Navy love him'**: PRO ADM 223/490.

189 **'or, indeed, to anybody'**: Appendix.

190 **'anything openly himself'**: ADM 223/490.

191 **inimical to capital**: Ibid.

192 **knew nothing about it till afterwards**: Ibid.

192 **sacrifice everything for Franco**: Ibid.

193 **to the world in general**: Family collection.

193 **well, it wasn't**: Ibid.

194 **'in touch with agents ashore'**: ADM 223/490.

194 **'courage and ingenuity were invaluable'**: Family collection.

195 **'the man behind them'**: Delmer, *The Counterfeit Spy*, p. 48.

195 **'Peculiarity: shifty eyes'**: PRO KV2/102.

197 **'actually existed'**: Howard and Hinsley, *British Intelligence in the Second World War*, vol. 5, p. 233.

197 **must have liked her funeral**: Family collection.

198 **'My dearest love to you'**: Ibid.

199 **'the horrors of another war'**: Stafford, *Roosevelt and Churchill*, p. 92.

199 **Pierre Laval**: After Mussolini's army had invaded Abyssinia, the aim of the Hoare–Laval pact was to end the war by partitioning the country and making it into an Italian colony; but news of the plan leaked prematurely, and both politicians were forced to resign.

199 **'want him out of the country'**: Cadogan, *Cadogan Diaries*, p. 282.

199 **'good chance of S.H. being murdered'**: Ibid. p. 287.

200 **might well be kidnapped**: Hoare, *Ambassador on Special Mission*, pp. 122–3.

200 **almost complete isolation**: Ibid, pp. 31–5.

201 **not available at all**: Templewood Papers, XIII.

201 **'quickly and closely together'**: Ibid.

201 **'due to him'**: Ibid.

201 **in a book of 300 pages**: Hoare, *Ambassador on Special Mission*. pp 132–3.

202 **I shall not get out of it**: PRO PREM 4/21/2.

202 **'any diplomat I know could do'**: Ibid.

203 **work of several years**: Family collection.

203 **on the table in a restaurant**: Family collection. Later in the war, Fleming regaled Mary with stories of how he escorted Prince Bernhard of the Netherlands to various nightclubs in London. One night people were dancing away when a huge explosion shook the building. No one paid any attention until a window was thrown open and the helmeted head of a fireman appeared in the gap. 'Don't you realise there are no floors left beneath you?' he yelled through the music – and he carried the scantily clad girls one by one down his extending ladder.

203 **at a cost of £110**: ADM 223/490.

204 **winning the war**: Family collection.

205 **as the best solution**: CAB 66/12/12.

205 **would not be enough**: Ibid.

206 **had to fight Germany**: Ibid.

206 **Chiefs of Staff were present**: Family collection. Alan's presence at the meeting was omitted from the minutes.

207 **to tell me about Operation MENACE**: CAB 66/12/12.

207 **'unique knowledge of the political situation'**: ADM 223/490.

208 **'our activities in Spain'**: PREM 4/21/2.

208 **'though not my direction'**: PRO HS6/962.

209 **detail on these projects**: ADM 223/490.

209 **under fire from three sides**: Appendix.

210 **be useful elsewhere**: ADM 223/490.

210 **in that sort of thing**: Family collection.

211 **the officer in charge was Alan**: Forty years later Alan appeared as a character in C.J. Sansom's novel *A Winter in Madrid*, which painted an evocative picture of the city during the war. The author had become fascinated by references to Alan in historical accounts, and, although he had never met him, presented him as an imperturbable prop to Sir Samuel Hoare, the nervous, brittle Ambassador. If the fictional Hillgarth is more brusque and clipped than the real man, the portrait bears quite some resemblance to his true self. 'Captain Hillgarth seems pretty fearless,' says one character after the attack on the Embassy, and

another replies, 'Yes – and I think he enjoys danger.' And then – another echo of reality – 'It's what the captain thinks that counts with Churchill.'

212 **like Spain, and we left**: ADM 223/490.

212 **at the expense of so few**: Family collection.

213 **half throttled with paper**: ADM 223/490.

213 **'Germany probably will'**: Ibid. Churchill's faith in March lasted through the war. In July 1946, when Alan offered to bring the financier to meet him, Churchill replied that, although he could not find the time, 'It would give me much pleasure to meet Mr March . . . Perhaps you would be so kind as to give Mr March my regards and express my regret that I am unable to see him on this occasion.' (Family collection)

213 **released to buy the ships**: Lycett, *Ian Fleming*, p. 110.

214 **to the breaking of them**: PREM 4/21/2.

214 **was being well spent**: PREM 4/32/7.

214 **'speed is important'**: Ibid.

214 **Hillgarth is pretty good**: Ibid.

215 **had married David Muirhead**: David Babington Smith later became a clergyman and developed an ungovernable fascination with ghosts, which he saw at every turn.

215 **'country on their behalf'**: PRO HS9/61.

218 **remained lifelong friends**: HS9/25.

219 **'their chance has come'**: PREM 4/21/1.

219 **'rather a charlatan'**: Cadogan, Cadogan Diaries, 25.4.41.

219 **'dirty little dog'**: Ibid. p. 286.

219 **'illusions of grandeur'**: Philby, *My Silent War*, p. 39.

220 **'gets the best results'**: Appendix.

220 **silenced him for ever**: Jeffery, *MI6*. pp. 404–5.

220 **'a sort of merry-eyed potato'**: Holt, *The Deceivers*, p. 12.

221 **dress and shoes fitted him**: Jeffery, *MI6*. pp. 406–7.

221 **'you might like to see them too'**: Churchill CHAR 20/25/ 47–52.

Chapter Ten: Enter Jean

223 **'a University education'**: Family collection.

223 **unusually refreshing**: Ibid.

224 **Mrs Ian Campbell**: Ian Campbell succeeded his cousin as 11th Duke of Argyll in 1949, and Louise became the Duchess.

231 **a complete radar installation**: McLachlan, *Room 39*, pp. 205–6.

231 **launched from below the waterline**: Two riders sat on each torpedo,

facing forwards, and when they reached their target, planted their detachable warhead on it as a limpet mine.

232 **cut open its secret**: McLachlan, *Room 39*, pp. 197–8. It was this episode that gave Ian Fleming the idea of the underwater trapdoor in Emilio Largo's yacht in his novel *Thunderball*, first published in 1961.

233 **the SS *Empire Tern***: ADM 223/794.

233 **'abandonment of several attempts'**: Appendix.

234 **'came under Somerville's command'**: Howard, *British Intelligence in the Second World War*, vol. 5, p. 205.

236 **we have had to endure hitherto**: ADM 223/490.

237 **can do things in this country**: Ibid.

237 **'will not sink in the harbour'**: Ibid.

238 **'anything going wrong'**: Ibid.

Chapter Eleven: Making Mincemeat

240 **'made available to the Germans'**: CAB 154/67.

241 **'washed up on his beat'**: Ibid.

241 **'Request onward route'**: ADM 223/794.

241 **'No details yet'**: Ibid.

242 **arranged for funeral today**: Ibid.

242 **'funeral Sunday noon'**: Ibid.

243 **'what has happened to them'**: Ibid.

243 **'maintain normal appearances'**: Ibid.

244 **'what was taking place'**: Sometime in 1943 Andros became a useful double agent, when, having been approached by a German intelligence officer, he continued to work for the British and began to feed Berlin scraps of disinformation given him by Alan.

244 **'if it comes ashore later'**: PRO WO 106/5921.

245 **'which is already aroused'**: Ibid.

245 **to open the letters**: Pardo's identity was revealed only in 1945, when British naval commandos captured the German Admiralty archives at Schloss Tambach, near Coburg in Bavaria.

245 **'out through the hole'**: Macintyre, *Operation Mincemeat*, p. 127.

246 **to recover case intact**: CAB 154/67.

247 **anything further that I can do?**: Ibid.

248 **'no suspicion should be aroused'**: Ibid.

248 **'being taken to ensure this'**: Ibid.

248 **'Might be a serious matter'**: Ibid.

249 **'in Huelva and Cadiz'**: Ibid.

249 **'friendship is most sincere'**: Ibid.

250 **no one in Spain had read them**: Ibid.

250 **Pro patria mori**: Ibid.

250 **'From Father and Pam'**: Ibid.

251 **I am, Sir, your obedient servant**: IWM 97/45– 1.

252 **photograph of the grave**: Ibid.

252 **a very valuable source**: CAB 154/67.

254 **compliment to him personally**: Ibid.

255 **'as well as the bombs'**: PREM 4/21/2.

255 **you will not mind one more**: Ibid.

256 **'a complaisant line towards Franco'**: Wigg, *Churchill and Spain*, p. 189.

256 **if you think it would help**: PREM 4/21/2.

256 **'on their demolition'**: Ibid.

257 **regret at my leaving**: Family collection.

257 **'great initiative and determination'**: Ibid.

Chapter Twelve: Far East

263 **never equalled in naval history**: The number of ships of all types in the US Navy went up from 1,899 in June 1941 to 5,612 in June 1942, to 18,493 in June 1943, to 46,032 in June 1944 and to 67,952 in June 1945. Roskill, *The War at Sea*, vol. III, pt II, p. 191.

263 **'thousands of miles of sea'**: Family collection.

266 **condemned to work on the coast**: Ziegler, *Mountbatten: The Official Biography*, p. 279.

266 **'I can find no records'**: Family collection.

268 **W/T equipment remained**: Marder, Jacobsen and Horsfield, *Old Friends, New Enemies*, vol. 2, pp. 458–9.

268 **flying-boat squadron**: PRO HW 4/1.

269 **alterations in January**: HW 4/2.

269 **operational patrols**: HW 4/4.

270 **just before leaving'**: Family collection.

270 **in the limelight**: Ibid.

271 **'will be good experience'**: Ibid.

271 **charge of the organisation**: Ibid.

274 **anything else in this world**: Ibid.

276 **to our own aircraft**: HW 4/5.

277 **'I wish I were more glamorous'**: Lycett, *Ian Fleming*, p. 155.

277 **deception unit, D Division**: Peter had gone out to the Far East to serve under Field Marshal Sir Archibald Wavell, but came under

Mountbatten's command when Wavell was made Viceroy of India in the summer of 1943.

277 **inordinately proud**: Hart-Davis, *Peter Fleming*, p. 283.

279 **Look after yourself very well**: Family collection.

281 **'thrown aside as scrap'**: HW 4/8.

281 **'Sweepers, man your brooms'**: *National Defense University Joint Force Press Quarterly*, Issue 40, 1st quarter 2006.

282 **blown to smithereens**: Family collection.

283 **brought to you before**: Ibid.

283 **their unworthy boss**: Ibid.

286 **'a good war-winner'**: Lycett, *Ian Fleming*, p. 158.

288 **domination and terrorism**: The Japanese had invaded Hong Kong on 8 December 1941, a few hours after they bombed Pearl Harbor, and the colony surrendered on Christmas Day. British control was restored after the Japanese surrender on 15 August 1945.

293 **All the very best**: Family collection.

Chapter Thirteen: Illannanagh

297 **We begin to understand his**: Article 10 of the Treaty of Utrecht, signed in July 1713, ceded Gibraltar to Great Britain in perpetuity.

312 **I liked the other very much**: Family collection.

312 **twenty books on Spanish history**: Jocelyn taught for many years at Harvard University, Boston College and the University of Toronto. He is a fellow of the British Academy, and his books on Spanish history include *The Mirror of Spain, 1500–1700: The Formation of a Myth* and *Spain and the Mediterranean in the Later Middle Ages*. In 1966 he met Nina Foster, an administrator at Harvard, and they were married in March that year. He has been out to Son Torrella every year except 1966, and later made the estate over to his half-sister Elspeth.

Chapter Fourteen: Safe in Port

318 **Why I write of it now**: Hillgarth (ed.), *Mary Hillgarth*, p. 75.

320 **'monolithic Communist state**: Sir Frank Roberts (1907–98) was later British Ambassador in Moscow. The first time he met Stalin, in 1945, the Soviet leader said, 'I know you. You are our enemy. And what's more, you are a member of the British Intelligence Service.'

321 **most convenient time for the Soviet**: Family collection.

322 **'as ardently then as he did'**: Ibid.

322 **see me for half an hour**: CHUR 2/36.

323 **no one will use them**: Ibid., 2/39.

323 **One hundred and thirteen ours**: Family collection.

324 **'can't get it to do anything'**: Ibid.

325 **members of the Communist Party**: Ibid.

325 **carries messages of moment**: Ibid.

326 **She considers appropriate**: Ibid.

326 **if you would like to see me**: Ibid.

327 **Freelance assistants**: Ibid. After Churchill's death in 1965 Alan wrote a note of condolence to Lady Churchill, saying, 'It is now several years since I last saw him, but his kindness to me and his friendship are always present in my mind.'

328 **get me into trouble in Spain**: Family collection.

329 **'that might have occurred'**: Ibid.

329 **'hopping mad'**: Ibid. Family collection. Baker-Cresswell was in command of the destroyer HMS *Bulldog* in the Atlantic on 9 May 1941, when he sent a party to strip the disabled U-boat *U-110*, and so captured the submarine's Enigma cipher machine in what King George VI told him was 'the most important single event in the whole war at sea'.

329 **what the writers write**: *The Times*, 24 January 1951.

330 **the youngest ever DNI**: In 1945, as captain of the aircraft carrier HMS *Glory*, Buzzard took possession of the Japanese commander's sword after Japanese forces had formally surrendered at Rabaul, on Papua New Guinea. He retained the trophy until his death in 1972, whereupon it was presented to Churchill College, Cambridge.

330 **able to do about it**: Family collection.

330 *persona non grata* **there**: Ibid.

331 **with all my papers in order**: Ibid.

332 **at Mass for you all**: Ibid.

333 **Catholic church at Terryglass**: Jocelyn and his mother had been received (separately) into the Catholic Church in the 1950s.

333 **in a very choppy sea**: Family collection.

334 **isn't always the case**: Ibid. Robert Speaight always sent Nigella books on her birthday, and so gave her a great love of literature, poetry above all.

336 **forward as much as we can**: *Naval Review*, Issue no. 1, 1959, p. 127.

336 **because he had it himself**: Family collection.

337 **fifteen votes to one**: John Godfrey agreed with this estimate of March, recording that when he and Alan met him at the Ritz Hotel in 1952, 'everything turned out as he had advocated in 1939'. Churchill College Archive, GDFY 1/6.

340 **Jack & Dun Dun**: Family collection.

340 **Sir Reginald Hall**: (1870–1943), nick-named 'Blinker' because of a facial twitch, was the first Director of Naval Intelligence, appointed in 1914, and was instrumental in bringing the United States into the First World War.

341 **such a liaison was beset**: Family Collection.

341 **God bless him**: Ibid.

342 **victimised by lesser men**: Ibid.

346 **he never fully recovered**: Alan's first wife Mary outlived both Jean and him, dying in 1982 at the age of eighty-six.

349 **'a splendid man in every way'**: Family collection.

350 **had been his dressing room**: Another curious incident occurred in that same room. Again, the big house was empty, but on the morning after Mrs Wilkinson's husband died, the housekeeper found the prints of bare feet leading from the next-door bathroom to the side of the bed.

Sources

Beesly, Patrick, *Very Special Admiral*. Hamish Hamilton, London, 1980.

Beevor, J. G., *SOE: Recollections and Reflections, 1940–1945*. Bodley Head, London, 1981.

Boyle, Andrew, *The Climate of Treason*. Hutchinson, London, 1979.

Burns, Jimmy, *Papa Spy*. Bloomsbury, London, 2009.

Burns, Tom, *The Use of Memory*. Sheed & Ward, London, 1993.

Bush, Eric Wheler, *Gallipoli*. Allen & Unwin, London, 1975.

Cadogan, Sir Alexander, *Diaries 1938–1945*. Edited by David Dilks. Cassell, London, 1971.

Cooper, Duff, *Operation Heartbreak*. Rupert Hart-Davis, London, 1952.

Delmer, Sefton, *The Counterfeit Spy*. Hutchinson, London, 1973.

Eccles, Sybil and David, *By Safe Hand: Letters 1939–42*. Bodley Head, London, 1983.

Elwell, Charles J. L., *The Greater Aphrodisiad*. Ferrington, London, 1995.

Gilbert, Martin, *Winston S. Churchill*, vol. 3. Heinemann, London, 1971.

Graves, Robert, *Majorca Observed*. Cassell, London, 1965.

Hamilton, General Sir Ian, *Gallipoli Diary*, 2 vols. Edward Arnold, London, 1920.

Hamilton, Ian B. M., *The Happy Warrior: A Life of General Sir Ian Hamilton*. Cassell, London, 1966.

Harris, Tomás, *Garbo – the Spy Who Saved D-Day*. Public Record Office, 2000.

Harrold, Dr Jane, and Porter, Dr Richard, *Britannia Royal Naval College, 1905–2005*. Richard Webb, Dartmouth, 2005.

Hart-Davis, Duff, *Peter Fleming*. Jonathan Cape, London, 1974.

Hastings, Selina, *Evelyn Waugh: A Biography*. Sinclair-Stevenson, 1994.

Herbert, Aubrey, *Mons, Anzac and Kut*, by 'An M.P.' [Aubrey Herbert]. Hutchinson, London, 1919.

Hillgarth, Alan, *The Princess and the Perjurer*. Chapman & Dodd, London, 1924.

——*The Passionate Trail*. Hutchinson, London, 1925.

——*The War Maker*. Thomas Nelson & Sons, London, 1926.

——*What Price Paradise?* . Houghton Mifflin, Cambridge, Mass. 1929.

——*The Black Mountain*. Ivor Nicholson & Watson, London, 1933.

——*Davy Jones*. Ivor Nicholson & Watson, London, 1936.

Hillgarth, Jocelyn (ed.), *Mary Hillgarth: A Private Life*. Privately published, 1984.

Hoare, Sir Samuel (Viscount Templewood), *Ambassador on Special Mission*. Collins, London, 1946.

Holt, Thaddeus, *The Deceivers*. Scribner, New York, 2004.

Howard, Michael, and Hinsley, F. H., *British Intelligence in the Second World War*, vol. 5: *Strategic Deception*. Stationery Office Books, London, 1990.

Jeffery, Keith, *MI6: The History of the Secret Intelligence Service, 1909–1949*. Bloomsbury, London, paperback, 2011.

Jellinek, Frank, *The Civil War in Spain*. Gollancz, London, 1938.

King-Hall, Stephen, *My Naval Life*. Faber & Faber, London, 1952.

Lewis, John, *Gurthalougha: A History*. Privately published, 2011.

Lycett, Andrew, *Ian Fleming*. Weidenfeld & Nicolson, 1995.

Macintyre, Ben, *Operation Mincemeat*. Bloomsbury, London, 2010.

Macintyre, Captain Donald, *Fighting Admiral*. Evans Brothers, London, 1961.

Marder, Arthur J., Jacobsen, Mark, and Horsfield, John,

Old Friends, New Enemies, vol. 2: *The Pacific War, 1942–45.* Clarendon Press, Oxford, 1992.

Martínez de Vicente, Patricia, *La Clave Embassy*. La Esferade Los Libros, Madrid, 2010.

Massot i Muntaner, Josep, *El Cònsol Alan Hillgarth i les Illes Balears (1936–1939)*. Abadía de Montserrat, 1995.

——*Guerra civil i repressión a Mallorca*. Abadía de Montserrat, 1997.

Masterman, J. C., *The Double-Cross System*. Yale University Press, 1972.

McHugh, Roger (ed.), *Ah, Sweet Dancer: W. B. Yeats and Margot Ruddock*. Gill & Macmillan, London, 1970.

McLachlan, Donald, *Room 39*. Weidenfeld & Nicolson, London, 1968.

Messenger, David A., *Against the Grain: SOE in Spain*. University of Wyoming, Laramie, 2005.

Montagu, Ewen, *The Man Who Never Was*. Evans Brothers, London, 1953.

Philby, Kim, *My Silent War*. MacGibbon & Kee, London, 1968.

Pons Roca, Josep Antoni, *Homenatge a Alan Hillgarth*. Petit Format, Minorca, 2001.

Pujol García, Juan, and West, Nigel, *Operation Garbo*. Biteback, London, 2011.

Prodgers, Cecil H., *Adventures in Bolivia*. J. Lane, London, 1922. New edition: General Books LLC, 2009.

Rankin, Nicholas, *Ian Fleming's Commandos*. Faber & Faber, London, 2011.

Roskill, Stephen, *The War at Sea, 1939–1945*, vol. III, pt II: *The Offensive*. HMSO, London, 1961.

Saddlemyer, Ann (ed.), *W.B. Yeats and George Yeats: The Letters*. Oxford University Press, Oxford, 2011.

Sansom, C. J., *Winter in Madrid*. Macmillan, London, 2006.

Smyth, Denis, *Diplomacy and Strategy of Survival*. Cambridge University Press, Cambridge, 1986.

Speaight, Robert, *The Life of Hilaire Belloc*. Hollis & Carter, London, 1975.

Stafford, David, *Churchill and Secret Service*. John Murray, London, 1997.

Stafford, David, *Roosevelt and Churchill: Men of Secrets*. Little Brown, London, 1999.

Thomas, Hugh, *The Spanish Civil War*. Eyre Spottiswoode, London, 1961.

Wedgwood, Josiah, *Essays and Adventures of a Labour M.P.* Allen & Unwin, London, 1924.

Wheeler-Holohan, V., *The History of the King's Messengers*. Grayson & Grayson, 1935.

Wigg, Richard, *Churchill and Spain*. Routledge, London, 2005.

Ziegler, Philip, *Mountbatten: The Official Biography*. Collins, London, 1985.

Unpublished Sources

National Archives in the Public Record Office (PRO) at Kew.

Churchill papers in the Churchill Archives Centre, Cambridge (CHUR, CHAR).

Templewood Papers in the Cambridge University Library.

Montagu Papers in the Imperial War Museum, London (IWM).

Hillgarth family collection.

Index